KT-369-875

The Centenary History of the Blackheath Harriers

F.H. REED

1869 1969

Perfer et Obdura

The Centenary History of the Blackheath Harriers

D. K. Saunders
A. J. Weeks-Pearson

Published by the Honorary Secretary of the Blackheath Harriers

under the authority of the Committee.

© BLACKHEATH HARRIERS 1971/1989

PRINTED BY RIVINGTON LITHO PRINTING LTD., AT SYDENHAM, LONDON, S.E.26.

2nd EDITION PRINTED IN HONG KONG

"Gentlemen, we know - we don't want to talk about these things we know"

(Tom Crafter of Blackheath Harriers)

To the Members
of the Blackheath Harriers
Past and Present

FOREWORD

Blackheath itself in light and shadow
is the real hero of the story
D.K. Saunders

There are certain landmarks in the lives of individuals and organisations when one pauses to look back over the way one has come and to realise the significanèe of incidents and acquaintanceships that, though seemingly trivial at the time, prove on retrospect to have been turning points in the personal or corporate saga. Such an occasion is provided by the Club's Centenary and in commending this fascinating study of our history to all members and indeed to all friends of the Club I should like to make a few comments on how it came to be written and to express on behalf of the Club our gratitude to the authors for bringing the 'hero of the story' to the attention of us all.

The Club has been extremely fortunate first in possessing records going back almost to its foundation and secondly in having in its membership men quick to perceive the value of this heritage. Foremost amongst these was D.K. Saunders who many years ago went through the various journals, minute books, scrap books of early newspaper cuttings and the like and with the skilled historian's approach set about further researches to fill in the tantalising gaps which even these extensive records left in our knowledge of the earliest days of the Club. The fruits of these investigations were first seen in a series of articles in the Gazette in 1961-63, which attracted widespread interest. But Saunders was not only a researcher into the beginnings. Having joined the Club in 1920 he knew many of those who had been with the Club in the heroic days of expansion from a small group at Peckham to a thriving enterprise at Blackheath and he took a leading part in what almost amounted to the re-creation of the Club under the dynamic leadership of H.J. Dyball after the devastation of the first world war. He is therefore uniquely qualified by study and by personal knowledge to interpret the character and tradition of the Club to the present generation of athletes.

It is indeed a happy arrangement (which owes much to an inspired initiative by L.E. Hammill) that he has been joined in the preparation of.the book by one of that generation, who has been in the forefront of the Club's activities in the period since the war. Tony Weeks-Pearson joined the Club in April 1949 and rapidly developed into an outstanding athlete. He captained Oxford University's Cross Country Team in 1954/55 and was first home in the match against Cambridge. Later that season he was placed 11th in the English Cross Country Championships, the first one of four occasions on which he has led the Club contingent home in this event. And in 1957, a season which saw victories in international competition in France and Belgium, he became the first member to win all three of the Club's cross country championships in one season. He has given the same energy and determination to the writing of the book as has characterised his running and, with it, that imaginative outlook to which the apposite and witty chapter headings testify.

I have no doubt that for many years to come successive generations of Blackheath Harriers will be grateful for the time, thought, study and effort that D.K. Saunders and A.J. Weeks-Pearson have put into this book and the Club is deeply in their debt.

Sydney Wooderson

CONTENTS

Page

Prologue   1

Part One 1869-1878   5
   " 'Law' for the Hares"
   The beginnings at Peckham

Part Two 1878-1919   31
   "Gone Away"
   Blackheath & "The Green Man"
   The Edwardian Era
   The Great War

Part Three 1919-1939   103
   "Fresh Trails"
   The Moves to West Wickham and Hayes
   The Nineteen Thirties

Part Four 1939-1969   147
   "View Halloo"
   The Second World War
   The Post War Period

Part Five   191
   "Full Cry"
   Today
   The Members and Character of
     Blackheath Harriers
   For the Future

Epilogue   201

Part Six   203
   Centenary Year
   The Next Twenty Years

Notes to the main text   225

Appendix One   229
   The origins of Peckham Hare and Hounds with
   some general notes on the background and
   sources consulted

Notes to Appendix One   240

Appendix Two   242
   Blackheath Harriers List of Officers 1869-1969

Appendix Three   247
   Blackheath Harriers Trophies

Appendix Four   248
   Blackheath Performances in Southern and
   National Cross country Championships

Appendix Five
   Blackheath Harriers All-time Best Performances   252
      (Track and Field)

Appendix Six
   Blackheath Harriers AAA Champions   254

Appendix Seven   255
   Names of Club Groups

Appendix Eight   258
   List of Archive material

Index   259

LIST OF ILLUSTRATIONS

F.H. Reed	Frontis-piece
Nunhead Cemetery	facing P.1.
Hare & Hounds, Cartoon	5
One Tree Hill	6
A page of the 1870 Peckham Journal	8
Peckham A.A.C. Rule Book 1877	9
Hare & Hounds and Donkey - Cartoon	10
Peckham A.A.C.: report of a run	15
The Rosemary Branch today	17
The path beside Nunhead Cemetery	25
The Rye Hotel	26
Brockley Bridge today	28
Beside Brockley Bridge	28
The original Green Man, a drawing	31
The Green Man, Blackheath, 1969	34
Kidbrooke Lane	39
W.S. Smith	40
Trail Layers, 1904	41
J.H. Reay	43
A programme of the 1890's	45
W.G. George by 'APE'	48
W.G. George and Sydney Wooderson	49
Trevor Davis	50
C.G. Wood	51
Club Group 1881	54
Club Group 1887	55
Club Group 1893	56
Fixture List 1888-89	57
The Private Banks Ground	61
'Blackheath Day', by S.T. Dadd	62
Annual Rowing Match	64
A Blackheath Crew, 1960	65
A Group of Blackheath Officials	72
AAA Medley Relay Champions 1911	73
AAA Medley Relay Champions 1966	74
Letter from Reed to Ponsford	75
Ernest Neville	77
T.E. Hammond	78
Fifty Miles Walk, 1904	79
Cross Country by S.T. Dadd	80
"Horses for Courses": Tommy Hammond	81
Club Walking Race by S.T. Dadd	82
Club Group 1908-1909	85
Competitor's ticket, 1905	86
William Parrish	87
Water Polo team 1896	90
Opening run, Blackheath 1900	91
Opening run, Hayes 1955	91
Tom Crafter	92
Crafter, Gale and Grant	95
The Club Territory	100-101
Club Group 1919-20	102
Bourne Way, Hayes	103
The Bottom of Fox Hill by L. Norris	106
Clay Thomas - Cartoon	107
AAA Championship – competitors 1930	109
Club Group at Hayes, winter 1930	109
H.J. Dyball	111
R.A. Lindsay	113
Club Figures by John Scott	114
Club Group 1924-25	115
Club Dinner, 1923	116
Match against Oxford, 1929	118
The Clubhouse as it was	119
A group at Hayes, 1966	120
The Club room at Hayes	121
Punch Bowl Night, 1969	122
A nostalgic handbill	125
A group of notables	127
A sprint relay team of the 1930s	130
Group at White City, 1935	133
Sprint relay team 1937 - cartoon	133
S.C. Wooderson AAA 3 miles champion 1946	136
S.C. Wooderson, Inter Counties Mile champion, 1939	137
S.C. Wooderson: world mile record holder 1937	138
S.C. Wooderson: European 5000 metres champion 1946	140
A group on Hayes Common 1946	145
Wartime cartoon by Gittings	147
Club Group 1938	148
Letter from Thwaites to Saunders	150
Winter at Hayes	153
Roll of Honour	156

Layhams, 1946	158	G.L. Hamlyn	182
Club open meeting 1946	159	J.E. Day	182
Arthur Wint	160	R.J. Harker	183
Cross country team 1947-48	161	The Top of Fox Hill by L. Norris	186
London to Brighton Relay 1951 -		Club Mile Championship, 1966	190
Scotting, Brent and Fletcher	162	Sydney Wooderson, a drawing by	
D.E. Reynolds and L.E. Piper 1951	165	L. Norris	191
Road running team, 1950-51	166	The pylon field by L. Norris	192
J. Braughton	169	Club Tour - Switzerland 1958	194
Club Group 1951	171	Club Group 1967	195
N.W. Page	173	R. Richardson	197
Group of members at White City	173	Centenary Goblet	198
Grenville Trophy 1953	175	"The other Reed" by C. Pollard	202
AAA Junior Relay 1956	175	Club Group, October 1988	204
AAA Junior Sprint Relay Team, 1957	177	Centenary Dinner Sketches – J.M. Scott	207
B.M. Shapcott	178	George Brooks	208
Southern Sprint Relay Team, 1962	180	R. Coles and W. O'Donnell – Club '5'	216
J.B. Herring: Southern 3 miles		Blackheath Geriatrics 1983	222
champion 1962	181	Young Athletes Team 1989	224
J. Watts	181		

PREFACE

Writing in "The Gazette" some quarter of a century ago, that notable Blackheath Harrier, Arthur Thwaites, expressed the doubt that a history of the Club would ever be written. For better or worse this is now achieved. How it came into being is another story, though one scarcely less intriguing than the saga of Blackheath itself. It is only relevant here to remark that with its completion there is, as well as a feeling of doubt and relief, a sense of privilege in recording the history of what is by any standard a remarkable institution. Together with this is our profound gratitude to the many people, both within and outside the Club, who have sustained us with their active assistance and encouragement.

We have, ambitiously no doubt, attempted a history and not — as so often has been the case — a simple record of events and performances. The exception to this is the account of recent years which we have given largely without attempting to interpret that period historically. At the same time, at the risk of offending those who may feel they have been unjustly omitted or neglected, we felt it desirable in a centenary book to carry the story up to the present for the sake of completeness. We hope that it will be of interest not only to members but to a wider public who may see in our small affairs a vital fragment of social history.

Any degree of failure in our enterprise is largely to be attributed to the ambition to do justice to Blackheath Harriers. We may therefore adapt the words of the Elizabethan, Michael Drayton, in a foreword to his "Poly-olbion", to our own situation: If we have not done her right, the want is in our ability, not in our love.

D.K.S.
A.J.W—P.
December,1968.

PREFACE TO THE SECOND EDITION

A history of the History might be told, better suited to sober a Punchbowl Night than to adorn these pages. The First Edition overcame certain difficulties of production to burst upon a fairly un-astonished world in 1972: the Gazette uttered a back-page review of some dozen lines. Despite these modest beginnings it has long since sold out to connoisseurs. Hence this new Edition.

The main body of the original Centenary text is re-printed here, with a number of corrections but otherwise un-revised. However, the Appendices have been brought up to date as far as possible by P.P. Peter Baigent. A Supplement covering the past twenty years is daringly included, which may be of use to a future historian as well as of interest to members who have joined since the Centenary. Remembering how hard it was then to track down sources of information, there is now a select bibliography of some key items of the Club archive.

Once again, thanks are owed to members without whom the work would not have been completed in the short time available. Especially, therefore, as twenty-five years ago, to P.P. Harold Thompson for various advice, help and scrutiny; P.P. Peter Baigent, who has not only laboured hugely among the lists but supported the author in all manner of ways; P.P. Colin Brand for his technical expertise; past and present Editors of the Gazette; Barry Shapcott and P.P. M.A. Walker for help with new photographs.

A debt also to the following – for information or for reading the text of the Supplement: Gary Botley, Bill Clapham, David Dunn, Andy Frankish, Mike Peel, John Powell, Les Roberts, Brian Saxton, and P.P.'s Alan Brent, Ian Smith, Brian Stone. And, of course, to Ken Johnson, who gave attention to all this fiddle in the thick of an already over-busy Presidential year.

None of these will fail to understand when I say that the one missed most from this enterprise has been my Centenary co-author, P.P. D.K. Saunders, who died in 1975. In his first days, as Dyball's right hand, he was "the young man who always turns up". Now that he is no longer here he is vividly remembered as one of the few of whom we can genuinely say it was "an education to know him". The Appendix on the Peckham origins written by him alone gives those who did not know him a good flavour of his humour and his scholarship, the greater part of the latter grounded in original research. Without him the recorded history of this Club would have been different, inferior – absent, even. These influences are still to be traced in his Gazette articles and this History: what we miss are the penetrating insights and comments of the man – his dry humour, the toughness and stoicism he retained through the illness of his last days. The Trophy in his memory is appropriate: for the winner of the Closing '5' Handicap. The innovation, in 1988, of a Club Committee Chairman for continuity and to aid the Presidency was originally his idea. I have kept all his letters.

TONY WEEKS-PEARSON
October, 1989.

ACKNOWLEDGEMENTS

We wish to thank the very many people who have helped us in producing this book: the Editor of "Punch" for permission to reproduce their cartoons; J.H. Page and the Amateur Rowing Association for information about the Hope Rowing Club; Thames Rowing Club, The Worshipful Company of Saddlers, C.A. Wiard for information about the Reed family; L.A.G. Higdon and B. Willis of the Amateur Athletic Association who made their files of newspaper cuttings available to us; P. Heyworth of Messrs. Geo. Harrap and Co. Ltd., for advice; L.F. Moore for inspiration; L.R. Conisbee who showed that the history of small institutions can furnish as much interest as that of large concerns; A.V. Hayday and B.G. Stone who made the copyright arrangements for the illustrations; D.G. Child for most welcome general assistance; D.J. Tingey for information about the Inter-Schools Races; J. Sims, R.H. Thompson, K.N. Wilcockson for advice on and reading the manuscript; Mrs Denbigh Hilton, J.R. Allen, E. Short of Belgrave Harriers, R.E. Taylor, G.R. Last, P.J.G. Baigent for advice on and reading parts of the manuscript; A.D. Forshaw and H. Lee of Orion Harriers for their generous advice and help in reproducing some of the older photographs; M.A. Walker, R.H. Thompson, J.R.D. Cockburn, J. Sims for the use of photographs or scrapbooks; A.A. Oldfield, L. Pendered, C.W. Starnes, J.R.D. Cockburn, J. Sims for help in identifying members in Club photographs; most numerously, those many members who talked, answered questionnaires and wrote letters about their reminiscences.

A major debt to the following: the Editors of "The Blackheath Harriers' Gazette and Club Record", past and present; P.G. Stenning for his long and patient researches into the files of local newspapers; P.J.G. Baigent for compiling the list of best Club Track and Field performances; G.R. Last for compiling the list of Club Southern and National Championship performances; J. Sims and R.H. Thompson, not only for various particular acts of assistance such as providing details of the story of the Club Headquarters at Hayes, but for generally easing the authors' work in so many ways; L. Norris for his drawings; B.M. Shapcott for taking photographs and reproducing others; Mrs. Carolyn Last also for reproducing photographs; C.M. Brand for his expert lay-out advice, work and patience; Mrs. G. Demar for her work in producing the book. Most of all, our gratitude is due to G. Demar among the most accommodating members of his craft, without whose goodwill this book would never have appeared in its present form. Lastly, to Mrs. D.G. Child and Mrs. A.J. Weeks-Pearson, to whose assiduous typing of all too often obscure manuscript we are indebted, our most sincere thanks for the performance of a tedious task and, to the last-named, in addition to much reading of manuscript, advice, indexing and correcting of proofs, for her encouragement and for putting up with it all!

We are grateful to Ed Lacey for permission to use the photographs on page 180 and 181 (left) and to J.H. Hammond, F.R.P.S. for assistance in reproducing various illustrations.

In addition to those acknowledged in the text, the photographs on pages 1 (facing), 6, 17, 25, 26, 28, 34, 122, 181 (right), 182, 197 and 198 are by B.M. Shapcott, and that on page 175 by Sport and General.

Every effort has been made to trace the owners of copyright photographs included in the book but we ask the indulgence of any whose photographs have inadvertently been included without acknowledgement.

"Here's to those sportsmen, good and true,
That made our Club; give them their due -
Long may they still among us shine,
Who laid the trail in '69!"

"SONG OF THE BLACKHEATH HARRIERS"

(probably by F.D. Carr.)

PROLOGUE

Normally he wouldn't have let himself be caught, but the out-thrust cap of the man whose other hand turned the handle of the street-organ conjuring Sousa from its interior took the young man unawares as he hesitated at the entrance of Blackheath Hill Station (London, Chatham and Dover Railway Company) wondering which way to go and he stumped up. Not a thing he was anxious to do, for though not mean he was only just starting work and this particular Saturday afternoon might, he thought, be more expensive than he wished. So that he was in no less disturbed state of mind as he set off up the hill. In fact, he was downright nervous, though he wouldn't have admitted it to anybody. Perhaps he even regretted the acquaintance struck up with the fellow at the desk opposite his in the City which, after one or two brief lunch hour airings together, had led to today's outing to the headquarters of the Blackheath Harriers. His ignorance of the existence of this organization when the subject was broached by his business house companion with some considerable air of importance mingled with mystery had been greeted by that worthy with what he told himself was a somewhat unnecessarily extravagant whistle of amazement. Still, here he was, but in his pre-occupied state coming close to being run-down by the homeward-hastening stream of business men's broughams and landaus. Since it was Saturday they were finishing early — it was only just after three — and their small sombre carriages nipped in and out among the many-coloured buses; really, this traffic was getting worse all the time — especially these mad-cap hansom cab drivers.

He wasn't much given to reflection but London was certainly a lot brisker than his Norfolk home which he had only left fourteen months before. You could feel a certain comfortable assurance in the air - not in the back streets, of course, but one didn't see much of them though he'd heard his superiors at work grumbling about the unrest down in the docks. For the rest, though, it seemed a pretty settled, easy-going world with big events like the death of General Gordon last year taking place at a comfortable distance. Still, Queen Victoria's Jubilee next year was going to be close enough and by all accounts something to write home about into the bargain. Different anyway, from what he was bent on this afternoon. It struck even him as rather peculiar to be travelling somewhere in order to take exercise - and doing it in a Club! ("But there's more to it than that, old chap - you'll see!") Of course, he was quite used to physical exercise - had he not strolled well over twenty miles this time last autumn over the North Downs? And he thought nothing of walking the seven miles from town to his lodgings. He had heard of clubs of course, but not thought of joining till his friend had insisted on putting his name up on the "Club Board" a few weeks ago. There was little enough variety in the pleasures even of London to a more sophisticated eye than his. The pleasure gardens of Vauxhall and Cremorne had closed ten or twenty years ago and now there was really only Crystal Palace - leaving aside the hundreds of theatres and music-halls that seemed to flourish on almost every corner.

By the time he had finished wondering whether to turn back he had arrived at the edge of the Heath and soon after that found himself standing before 'The Green Man' eyed only by a few cows being led past, on their way to supply their "fresh glass of milk from the cow" — a habit which had caught on as being especially healthful — to the businessmen's children. These latter were certainly not among the less respectable ones he saw by the nearby post office playing one of the recently popular "street games" - "Foot It", "Gully" or "Golden Puddings". Then he turned in through the main entrance of the public house, which a year or two ago would have represented an adventure in itself.

"Black'eath, are you, sir? Up the stairs there on your right". And after climbing he was standing then in the doorway of a large, comfortable-looking room with a big centre table, lounge seats and many smaller tables and seats. He would have gone on to note a large and roaring coal fire had it not been obstructed by an even larger body mass planted in front of it and doing its best to embellish the effect of conflagration by puffing at a bull-dog pipe. This figure cut short his notice of other details of the room for not only was he a giant of height and chest but the boom of the ebullient greeting he now expelled made the prospective member feel like running away. Who was he, the prospective member? The giant was informed and returned his own name. "I'm Crafter! No misters in Blackheath! - Call me Tom!" Stroking mutton chop whiskers he turned to look at - no, quiz - the proposal forms of all such Prospective Members, the particular present specimen of which he then proclaimed, turning and eyeing him once more, must be elected at once so that he could compete that very day for a receptacle he called the "Novices' Pewter".

The prospective Member soon ceased to curse his luck at not being the first to arrive, for it was strange how friendly this large man was, and, really, his size had prevented the P.M. from realizing that the other was of much the same age as himself, while, looking closer, one saw that he had fine eyes and a warm, humorous mouth beneath the waxing moustaches. And anyway, as Crafter said, he had to be early on the scene. "For the Trail, you know".

Very soon others began to arrive and laying bowlers, top hats and frock coats carefully to one side, for they too had come straight from work, began to change to a quite alarming accompaniment of loud leg-pulling and chatter which was not at all subdued even when older, bearded members — some of them very nearly as distinguished-looking as young Crafter — began to arrive. He was introduced to one of them — a light, active and well-knit man who was kindly enough though he said little to him, and whose name was Reed. There was a tone of respect in the voice of the person who told him that this was the man who had more or less started the whole Club going ages ago — more than ten years in fact — over in Peckham, he thought — though he couldn't be sure.

Today was special because of the Club photographic group which had become quite a custom. They all lined up but took care not to look too formal, with some facing in different directions and some not looking towards the camera at all. And all this took simply ages so that his friend who had luckily turned up at last could pass the minutes pointing out some pretty important people who were about — no, not the Champion Miler W.G. George, nor, he was afraid, their patron the Earl of Dartmouth, but there were quite a few champions present he could be quite certain . . . er . . . yes . . . Jack Reay — *great* hurdler *and* a swimmer and a dabhand at whist and cribbage — and wait till you hear him sing "Phil the Fluter" tonight. Oh yes, we're good all round in Blackheath. And . . . Yes! Birkett the half-miler; he'd beaten George to win the A.A.A. title. And there were plenty coming along very strongly: Monk, look, over there — 10th in the Southern Championship last year, we're expecting great things of him this time, and Nehan and Nash.

Then just as the photographer had it right, up puffed a jolly, round-looking man with a small terrier and they had to wait for him, though no one seemed to mind. Indeed, they all appeared to think that the group wouldn't be complete without him, for was not Walter Rowland one of the grand 'old men' from the Peckham days? Since then they had come a long way with fellows now ribbing others in the group at not having yet paid their visit to Pile's, (more jokes) the athletic outfitters in Fenchurch Street, to get the all-black outfit which was now evidently de rigueur, together with — was it Reed's brainwave?-the badge with entwined squares.

By the time this was all done with, the New Member, now duly elected, had forgotten all about the nerve-racking run to follow as well as his fears lest they should leave him far behind. As they set off about ten minutes after Crafter and two other "Trail-layers" who had been each laden with a long sausage-bag he was surprised to find himself not only having no difficulty in keeping up with the rest but actually conversing easily as he ran with a senior-looking gentleman who, if he had met him at the office he would have called 'sir' but who looked as if such a courtesy would be the only thing that might possibly offend him, so friendly he seemed in his willingness to have the New Member tell everything he could about himself. Many of the others appeared to be concentrating on their running rather more than he, taking great pains to run in what they evidently understood to be a proper fashion with toes pointed towards the ground and a very special kind of arm carriage which, together with black vest and white pullovers, made an exaggeratedly impressive picture of style.

As a result he was not at all anxious to pull into line when the leader announced that they would start from that point to race a mile home for the Novice 'Run-in'. But he had little time to worry for they were off: past the pond just by the Paragon near Christopher Wren's Morden College, past men exercising horses, past children with hoops, and dangerous young men on "bone-shakers", past an extraordinary number of spectators all, he noted with a feeling of exhilaration, standing still as he himself winged back across the broad and open levels of the Heath on easy ground with some of these onlookers cheering them on though he seemed to feel alone in front like this so that he thought they must surely be encouraging him and not the others. Small lads not of the best families yelled other kinds of encouragement at him: "Now we shan't be Long!" or "Chase Me!" and "Oi! Does yer Mother know yer out?" — but he scarcely heard any of this as he crossed the line flanked with Club faces smiling and congratulating while he, turning to glance behind, saw that a small wiry figure had dogged him home and that far from being alone on his run-in he had only won by a few yards.

Still, now it was all good: the relief he felt, the patting on the back, the busy talking to his fellow novices whom he suddenly felt he knew very well: the entry into the warm interior, the luxurious hip-baths in the basement dressing room, though he was half-scalded by a ladleful pitched in straight from the coal-fired copper; and, after really a very fine high tea even to enjoy — well, in a way — not only having to get up in front of everyone assembled — about fifty of them by now, — but even the sudden shock that came of being asked by Reed, backed vociferously by Crafter and the others, to make them a little speech and tell them something of himself — he might postpone singing a song till next week, they generously conceded. Which he was very grateful for as he sank back to listen to others do just that later that evening, and do it very well, especially when it came to "Phil the Fluter" which even had a very individual dance to go with it.

So, long before they went their several ways later still with reminders to him not to miss the evening run round the Heath the following Wednesday to get up an appetite for the chops and steaks to come after, he sat there amid the jocularity feeling that not only they but he too had been there a reassuringly long time — that it was a Club that "belonged". And if he had been morbidly curious about the past instead of the typical Blackheath member that he now was with his mind fixed on the proper matter of life as it is at the present moment with its runs, steaks, songs, friends, jokes and ale, he might have gone on to wonder about the distant origins of this seventeen year-old and hence venerable and ancient Club which had survived down to 1886 like the old Queen herself and certainly showed no signs of giving up. Hardly anyone among its dozens and dozens of members seemed to know much about those origins — except, of course, for those old boys like Reed, Rowland and Bennett . . . . They knew — but as Crafter was later — rightly — to say: "Gentlemen, we know — we don't want to talk about those things we know . . . . . "

PART ONE 1860's - 1878

" 'Law' For The Hares"

The Beginnings at Peckham

HARE AND HOUNDS—AND MAY THEIR SHADOWS NEVER GROW LESS.

Mrs. Miniver. "HOW EXHAUSTED THEY LOOK, POOR FELLOWS! FANCY DOING THAT SORT OF THING FOR *MERE* PLEASURE!"

Little Timpkins (his bosom swelling with national pride). "AH, BUT IT'S ALL THROUGH DOING THAT SORT OF THING FOR *MERE PLEASURE*, MIND YOU, THAT WE ENGLISH ARE—*WHAT WE ARE!*"   [*Bully for little Timpkins!*

(by courtesy of "Punch").

"......... Thought I should've died -
-Knocked 'em in the Old Kent Road!"

(Victorian Music Hall Song)

"Say not, the struggle naught availeth,
The labour and the wounds are vain ...."

(Arthur Hugh Clough 1819 - 1861)

VIEW FROM ONE TREE HILL

BEGINNINGS

. . . Crafter knew, and all his colleagues too. Even if they didn't say so in as many words they agreed with him. Just so do we today . . . 'know'. We are conscious of our superiority in looking back at the past; after all, we are alive — they are dead — and that constitutes a superiority in the eyes of the living. So we stand today: the Hayes Headquarters of the Club in this Centenary Year reassures us: the dressing room below, the Clubroom upstairs are full — the car-park even more so; there is the loud talk, the confident laughter — everything that communicates a re-assuring sense of life and its essential rightness in being . . . . thus.

The depiction of the Club in the prologue above is of that body some seventeen years after its formation — a thing remarkable enough itself at a time when organized sport was very much at a formative stage. But it is so presented more with the future it implies in mind than for its antiquarian curiosity. Blackheath Harriers will readily understand what is meant by this — and most readers of this history will in the nature of things be Members. These will readily have apprehended from the prologue how the essential nature of the Club was formed already at that early time. In this sense it is impossible to go forward from here: Members can recognize its main features and character already moulded long before the century was over and can welcome it as familiar and known to them.

All this we know.

But go back not only past our own day, but past Crafter's day, beyond "The Green Man", to a time seventeen years before this picture of the mid-Eighties and there is a quite different image — a tableau of an institution whose beginnings are far removed from the settled confidence of this Club Centenary or its allied days of Victorian patronage of earls, baronets and knights, a time when there was as yet nothing achieved and all to play for . . .

Early morning. Mists. A chill and silence in the air. Nothing stirs in Southwark Park at this hour of six except a figure solitarily setting out small flags. With them he marks a rough course around the large open space of grass. He waits then. In a little while another arrives and they stand talking for a few minutes — quietly because of the quiet hour. Then they walk a mile race — two laps of the field — plodding around together till, with two hundred yards left, they struggle for the lead and one has to give up with stitch leaving his companion to carry on to the post alone. An early hour for violent exercise: still, there's a virtuous glow comes out of it as they make for home and, after, the day's work . . . . .

Thus the beginning of Peckham A.A.C., with a handful of friends competing weekly in a single event which varies from jumping and steeple-chasing to hurdling and swimming, the choice made by the loser or the last man in the previous week's competition. A year and a half before this several of them had formed a club by the name of Peckham Hare and Hounds, its first official run being reported in the sporting paper, "Bell's Life in London" on Wednesday, October 27th, 1869:

"THE PECKHAM HOUNDS"

The first meet of this Club took place on Saturday, the 23rd inst., at the King's Arms, Peckham Rye, when the following gentlemen were present, viz.: Messrs. C. Black, Cornell, A. Johnson, W.H. Williamson, S. Collins, A. Darnell (Trafalgar C.C.), J. Dryden (Hope R.C.),

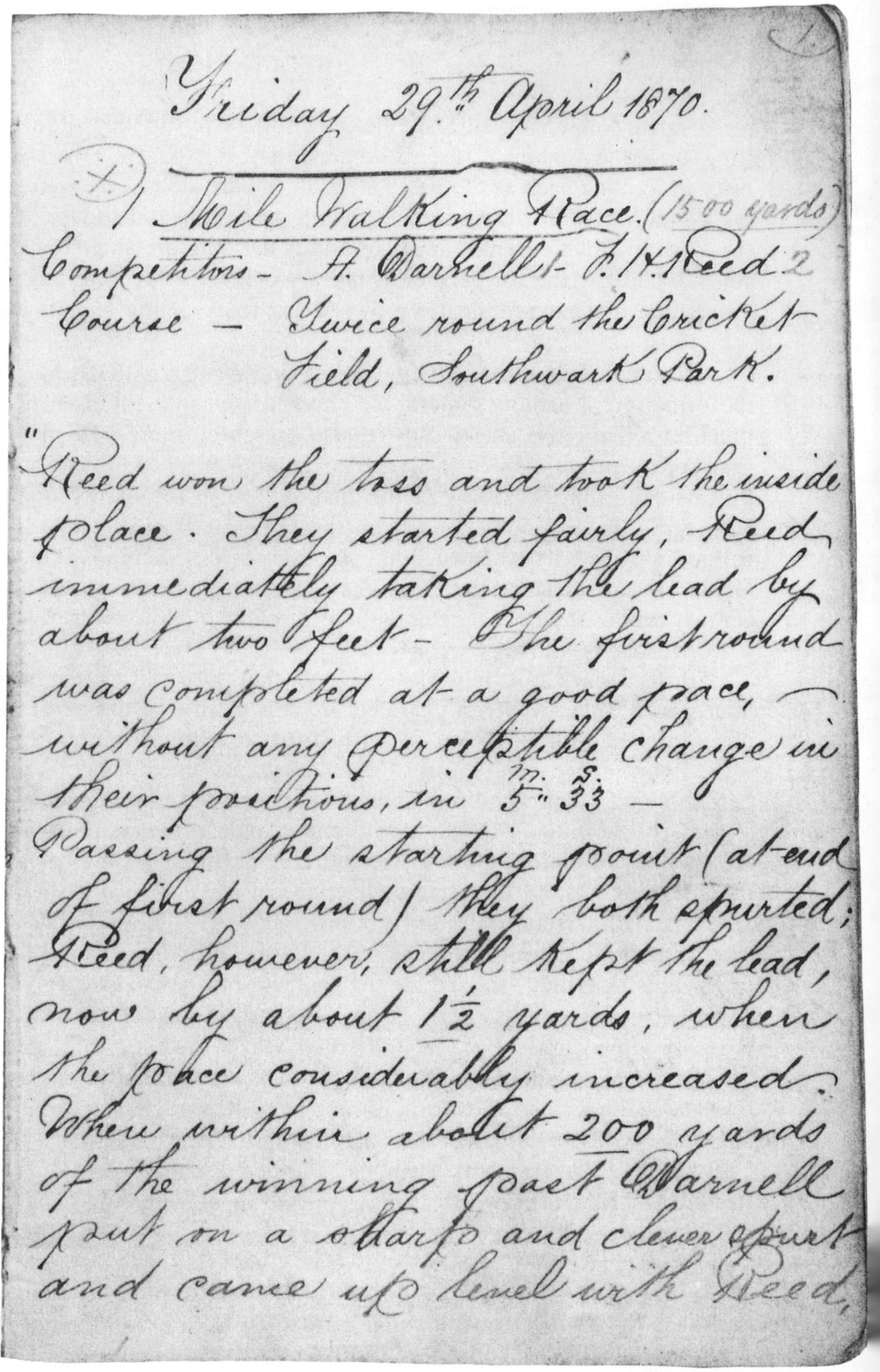

Friday 29th April 1870.

⊕) 1 Mile Walking Race. (1500 yards)

Competitors - A. Darnell 1. F. H. Reed 2

Course — Twice round the Cricket
Field, Southwark Park.

" Reed won the toss and took the inside
place. They started fairly, Reed
immediately taking the lead by
about two feet — The first round
was completed at a good pace,
without any perceptible change in
their positions, in 5 m. 33 s. —
Passing the starting point (at end
of first round) they both spurted;
Reed, however, still kept the lead,
now by about 1½ yards, when
the pace considerably increased.
When within about 200 yards
of the winning post Darnell
put on a sharp and clever spurt
and came up level with Reed,

A PAGE OF THE 1870
PECKHAM JOURNAL
WRITTEN BY
FREDERICK REED

J.H. Easthie (Argyle C.C.), W.H. Hawke (German G.S.), W. Henman, (Croydon A.C.), and F.H. Reed (Thames R.C.). The hares (Messrs. Black and Easthie) were sent off at four o'clock, and led the 'run' through Goose Green, Denmark Hill, Lordship Lane, Dulwich, Sydenham, Forest Hill, and back to the Rye, making a run from nine to ten miles. Time of running, 97 minutes".

As oarsmen, cricketers, gymnasts and general sportsmen, they, in company with others of their time, appear to have taken up paper-chasing — at Peckham and elsewhere usually once a fortnight — as a means of keeping fit and for recreation rather than for serious competition. Although the sport was not yet widely practised in London there is no doubt an explanation as to why a group of sportsmen in a comparative backwater of London engaged in such activity but it is no longer apparent to us today and the paradox remains unresolved. The answer may be found in the fact of early members like F.H. Reed belonging to Thames Rowing Club who had launched attempts at this sport. Almost certainly this group, or some members of it, had engaged in informal runs prior to the irrefutable testimony of this date in "Bell's Life" — indeed, W.H. Blanch's standard history of the area, "Ye Parish of Camberwell" published in 1887, refers to Peckham A.A.C. as having formed in 1867, as well as giving the names of Samuel Bevington as its President and F.H. Reed as Secretary. It was this latter, although possibly not a founding member of Peckham Hare and Hounds, who in May, 1872, wrote the following letter to the "Camberwell and Peckham Times".

"Sir,

I beg to state that in October, 1869, a Hare and Hounds Club was started under the title of 'The Peckham Hare and Hounds' (the rendezvous being at the 'King's Arms') by the gentlemen who were the originators of the present Peckham Athletic Club.

"In addition to the above, I should mention that the South London Harriers were started during the past winter by some former members of Peckham Amateur Athletic Club.

(Sgd) Frederick Reed".

PECKHAM A.A.C. RULE BOOK 1877.

The conversion from "Hare and Hounds" to "Athletic Club" was no empty form of words as we might think today, but marked a real distinction of activities. The change of name therefore denoted an extension of the Club's pursuits into what we today understand as track and field events. Whatever may have been the truth about the origins of the oldest athletic clubs — and it is most unlikely that, given the circumstance of so many clubs springing up in so short a space at this period, there was a single proprietary source of organized club athletics — Peckham does seem to be the earliest instance of a Club deliberately incorporating both track and cross-country in the basic purposes of its existence. Even today this distinction between two different kinds of athletic club is by no means a

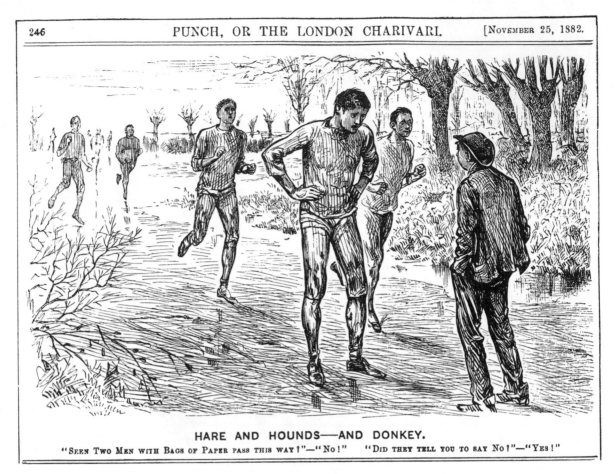

HARE AND HOUNDS—AND DONKEY.
"SEEN TWO MEN WITH BAGS OF PAPER PASS THIS WAY?"—"NO!"   "DID THEY TELL YOU TO SAY NO?"—"YES!"

(by courtesy of "Punch").

dead letter: London Athletic Club, for example, has never entered a team for a cross-country event, while Thames Hare and Hounds tends to confine its activities to cross-country.

The diversity of its activities at this early stage would, however, be a source of strength then as now and one major factor in the Club's survival, given the measure of luck required to see all such ventures over the teething stage. It is not at all unlikely too that the very modesty and privacy of its beginnings by shielding the infant organization from demands beyond its resources contributed not a little to ensure its achieved longevity.

Gladstone's description of the time as having been an age of emancipation was just. Though it was in 1868 that the last man was publicly hanged, still, Darwin's "Origin of Species" had appeared nine full years before that, nor was it an isolated phenomenon in this era of invention and discovery which was fraught with an optimism backed by what seemed an unshakeable permanence. [1] The concentration of the population into towns and the accompanying rise of the middle classes had also produced its effect, characterized for the latter chiefly by the extolled virtue of industry but an adherence to a respectable sedentarism where all other activities of life were concerned. The notion of leisure as being inseparable from vice was long in breaking down, but the reaction against it was inevit-

(1) See notes at back of book for references.

able. Even so, Saturday remained a working day with only slightly shorter hours than the others and hence late starts of 4 p.m. were the rule for the athletes of the time. There are frequent mentions of the difficulty of following trails and running across country in the dark. In passing, many will recall Blackheath runs starting at 3.30 p.m. as recently as 1921.

For the people of London, half of whom had been born in the provinces or the country and who had behind them an ancestry of vigorous and robust yeoman stock, sedentarism could have no lasting appeal: their energies were left unsatisfied and must find some outlet. Besides sports of direct rural origin like the paper-chase which itself derived very possibly as much from the old country boys' pastime "Hunt the Fox" as from the public schools' popularizing influence of its more systematized form, there were moves towards organized sport of all kinds. By 1873 already the Football Association had been founded, as had the Rugby Union; the County Cricket Championship was under way, while the Queensberry Rules had been introduced, aided by the revulsion which the bloody slaughter of the contest between Tom Sayers and "Bernicia Boy" impelled. More specifically, by the time of Peckham's founding there were a number of established sports meetings. The Erith and Belvedere and the Richmond Cricket Club Meetings had started in 1866, the South Norwood Club's Fete two years earlier, while there were very old sports indeed associated with the Army particularly, inaugurated by the Royal Military Academy, Woolwich, in 1849 and by the Royal Military College, Sandhurst, about 1812. Significantly too, a book on Athletics written by H. Hewitt Griffin in 1891 tells us that the West London Rowing Club had held some sports "by gaslight" in the Ashburnham Hall, West Brompton, in November 1863. Moreover, the same writer describes "the ball of reform" as having been set rolling by this club also starting, as an "off-season novelty" a few running events in the winter of 1861-1862.

By 1868 there were a number of well established athletic clubs besides those already in the text. The Civil Service Sports Club and the Amateur Athletic Club — the latter founded exclusively for former Oxford and Cambridge athletes — were in existence in 1866, and outside London provincial city clubs such as Liverpool Athletic Club and Birmingham Athletic Club had been formed by 1867. Northampton Cricket and Athletic Club was also well established by about 1868. Besides these specialist organizations, there were a number of others of a possibly less permanent constitution which appear to have their origin in the annual fetes held by the larger cricket clubs: instances are the South Norwood Athletic Club already mentioned, the Blackheath Athletic Club several times referred to in early records, the Croydon Athletic Club, to which our original member Henman belonged, and others. A curiosity is the existence before 1870 at least and possibly some years earlier of two annual athletic meetings in the Peckham district, the one promoted by the local volunteer unit and the other by the Peckham Social Club, a literary and cultural society: but these seem to have been simply promoting bodies and did not organize themselves specifically as athletic clubs for the purpose of holding the meetings, as the cricket clubs seem to have done. Just why the cricket clubs adopted the practice of creating a derivative athletic organization is far from clear and is one of the many minor challenges to research thrown up by the early records.

The situation at this point is therefore best seen as one in which there was a fairly thorough familiarity with the types and nature of formal competition — the different events and distances, for example, were well-known, together with terms to describe them that we retain today, such as "heats" and "finals" — but without any specialized organization for their permanent and continuing practice. This is the portion of athletic history which flows parallel with our present study; the institutionalizing and framing of athletic activities into that form in which we have received them today.

The occasional ventures instanced above and the influence of the army seem to have been the most important ones. Montague Shearman in his "Badminton Library" volume on Athletics and Football[2] suggested that this latter influence had been exaggerated by the preceding generation but though it is quite certain that this military factor was part of the much larger and more complex trend already referred to of reaction against suppression of energies as well as exploitation of an atmosphere more favourable to amateur sport, nevertheless it is one not lightly to be disregarded. The "volunteer" or as we might term it now, the "Territorial" phenomenon was an important feature from the middle of the century until well after the 1914-1918 War. Other more intangible influences apart, it arose out of anxieties over such real or imagined threats of inferiority to the nation as the Crimean War, the Indian Mutiny, and the friction with Napoleon III. The shocks that these administered gave an impetus to a flourishing and virile national activity whose scale we are likely to underestimate today. In illustration there is the instance of "The Times" reporting a field day above Brighton in 1863 involving 20,000 men. By the mid-Nineties the Volunteers numbered over 200,000.

The possible stimulus to athletics afforded by this movement is likely enough if we remember the part traditionally played in military training by muscular education. It is most probable that regimental interest in athletics and gymnastics passed on to the civilian population via the volunteer army between 1852 and 1861 was nearly as great in extent as that via the schools and universities, and, so far as the common man was concerned, may have been greater. Certainly the army, especially the light infantry formations — and most of the volunteer units were rifle regiments — had to perform many of their movements at the double and under quite strenuous conditions. The native English energies were engaged in such pursuits in a sociable manner and these in turn were morally backed by patriotic sensations of doing one's duty. Blackheath as a Club always had pleasant connections with territorial units right up to the Second World War but it is not widely realized that these extend to the earliest Peckham days where not only did the bands of volunteer groups play at the Club's athletic meetings but some at least of our membership — such as the useful sprinter, J.H. Wrenn — derived in particular from the 1st Surrey (Foot) Artillery, later the 1st Surrey Rifles.

This unit is a useful as well as a peculiarly pertinent example of the kind of parallel development discussed above, for it was founded in 1849 as a society for the encouragement of outdoor exercises acquiring its military bent when its secretary, a Mr. Boucher, formed a rifle club which in turn developed into a volunteer unit with, among other side lines, athletic sports in the summer.[3] When the Crown recognized it in 1859 it gained its official name. The same was true of other units like the Hanover Park Rifles in Peckham for they also had athletic meetings, no doubt in the now-disappeared park off Rye Lane where, however, there still stands the Hanover Arms. With Sergeant Major Wrenn probably as the chief medium Peckham's closest link was with the 1st Surreys. They participated in one another's runs, for the volunteers also had their headquarters at Brixton. A word about this pastime which so engaged their attentions should follow now before we examine further the individual Peckham history.

"It would be safe to say that there is not a single pack (not even excepting the oldest club) that knows how to hunt in the systematic way of nearly twenty years ago".

(Walter Rye in the Badminton Library volume, "Athletics and Football" - 1888).

"Care must be taken not to cast scent on any common over which the London County Council has control, or more will be heard about it". (H.H. Griffin - "Athletics" - 1891).

There were still nearly twenty years to go before London was to come under one governing body. By that time the art and skill of Paper-chasing as a quite sophisticated pursuit had been largely forgotten, so that it is little wonder that an explanation of it should be required in speaking of it today. It was no rudimentary pastime but one with a highly developed code, or rather, codes, for different traditions grew up in various quarters. Practised in the public schools, for example, were the Marlborough code and the Rugby system — to mention only two — the name of the latter being popularized by Thomas Hughes' description in "Tom Brown's Schooldays". Rugby was said to be the first school to take up the sport as a formal exercise with rules. Its precise origins generally speaking are dubious however. There are all kinds of alternative , but at this distance of time, unascertainable versions, [4] as for example, in the same area of Rugby, that the football club organized Hare and Hounds runs also in the early Sixties, with the Rugby Railway staff doing so earlier still in imitation of the school-boys — though once again, there is the problem of the chicken and egg variety.

Such controversy, together with its appearance of often being a sideline, should not obscure the fact that the sport was anything but casual. It had a definite and developed technique capable of exciting its own absorbing interest. The art of the game, it is worth pointing out to modern athletic competitors, lay in the element of tracking as much as in the speed of pursuit, and — like a modern equivalent, orienteering, which satisfies many of the same recreational demands — called for mental activity and ingenuity on the part of both Hares and Hounds. The hares necessarily going more slowly had to preserve their distance by making skilful use of cover like dead ground, hedges and woodland and by laying false trails intelligently, using, for example, "doubles" — trails laid away from the true line in the opposite direction by one hare while the other continued the proper scent till overtaken by his colleague. One hare was usually a good deal faster than the other so that he could make a considerable detour in laying a false trail and rejoin the other further on, using the cover of high ground and the like to conceal his later movements.

They were, of course, given an initial start, the "law", as it was called, after which the hounds set off under a limit man who set the pace necessary to make the eventual "kill" and who was thus in some sort the ancestor of the modern leader of a training pack whose pace it was a breach of etiquette to exceed. The practice varied but generally on sighting the hares this man's control was "thrown off" and any trail or scent disregarded; the "view halloo" was given and direct pursuit ensued — though in the case of an early sighting pack control might be retained. The essence of this was that a "view" released the pack from following "scent" or paper trail till sight was lost again. From this stage possibly the

13

true cross-country race in part emerged and certainly the practice of loosing the pack to race the last mile or so home whether or not the hares had been sighted by that time. With this in turn the custom of the Novices "Run-in" was associated, together with its traditional award of a pewter. Victory did not solely depend upon the hares being run down, but more often upon their initial time allowance being cut by the end of the run, the whole practice occupying well over the hour normally. Since adult clubs were less apt than boys to force the pace their runs would frequently be extended to beyond ten and once at least covered twenty-three miles.

Just as this activity derived from imitation of the incidents of the hunting field, so too did the other cross-country form, the steeplechase, from which as much as from hare and hounds derives the modern cross-country race. This event was the pedestrian equivalent of the point to point race, still in some cases having a trail, but one which was laid wholly to assist and not in any wise mislead. Peckham A.A.C. had their first recorded one in the January of 1873 and this was significantly from an outlying point, " The Green Man ", Southend Village, into their headquarters at "The Rye House", Peckham Rye. ₅

It is temptingly tidy to conclude that since such clubs as Peckham came to steeple-chasing by way of paper-chase that this is how they developed chronologically. Both these activities obviously emerged as imitation of equestrian exercises which had of course long been established and the order in which the pedestrian variants appeared would seem to have been determined very largely by the internal history of athletics itself. The whole matter is somewhat obscure and it is not helped by the fact that the foot steeplechase developed two parallel forms, to neither of which can priority be assigned with any great assurance. On the one hand there is the "artificial" steeplechase modelled on horse racing "over the sticks" with made-up obstacles on a levelled lap course; and on the other the "natural" steeplechase imitated from point-to-point riding, i.e., a circuit of open country with such obstacles as naturally occur in the form of fenced enclosures, streams and so on. Without going into the background of practice at the public schools at an earlier period it would seem correct to say that the sophisticated steeplechase of the kind included in the first Oxford-Cambridge Sports of 1864 was the earlier to emerge, precisely because organized competitive running on the flat anticipated winter running across country by some years. To what extent paper trail was used in the earliest winter steeplechases is rather an open question. Some at least seem to have been based on the principle that the competitor was free to "take his own line", i.e., select the easiest approach between the obstacles he was required to negotiate in order to complete the course, and umpires were stationed at the obstacles to ensure that this condition was observed; but whether paper trail was used to assist the runner at all is by no means clear. At Peckham it would seem that a paper trail was always laid, not only by our own club which was not the first in the area to promote this type of event; but whether this was imposed by local conditions or by general practice cannot be stated with any certainty. South London Harriers were before us in introducing steeplechasing to the Peckham area, but at least one of our members, John Metcalf, took part in an Open Track Steeplechase of four miles in 1873.

The two variants of the steeplechase in effect existed side by side and developed concurrently, but the relationship of the winter variant to paper-chasing in generating the modern cross-country race is somewhat obscure. There seems to have been some cross-

14

fertilisation at a very early stage for Thames Rowing Club, the parents of Thames Hare and Hounds, are on record as awarding pewters for a kind of hybrid paperchase and steeplechase in 1868. It may be somewhere near the truth to say the *idea* of the modern cross-country race derives from the steeplechase but much of its special character evolved from paper-chasing.

> *"A committee, by the way, is quite unnecessary for a paper-chase club".*
> (Walter Rye).

These are dry historical matters. They will remain thus if we do not see beyond them to the people for whom they were affairs of actual life. This humanity is the justification for such historical and general discussion. For these reasons we pursue them. Who were the men who brought a club into the way of an existence which was to endure for a hundred years? What were they like? Of what stuff were they made and why did they take such courses as must have made their parents and onlookers wonder to behold, just as we do at contemplating them even after such an interval of time? To them attaches the glamour and mystery of remote times which characterizes that comparatively recent phenomenon of historical, as distinct from purely personal, curiosity about our forebears.

PECKHAM AMATEUR ATHLETIC CLUB.

THE members of this club met on Saturday last, the 23rd inst., for their usual fortnightly run across country, Mr C. J. Naylor representing the hare, and leaving the Rye House punctually at four o'clock he commenced the trail at the Newlands. Turning to the left he made for Nunhead Cemetery, and past the lower end of Brown's ground, over the London, Chatham, and Dover Railway, and a series of meadows to the Brighton line. Across the line and through the adjoining brickfield, from which he made straight for Brockley Cemetery, down Ivy-lane to Lady-well-bridge. Running through the churchyard of St. Mary's, Lewisham (a spot well-known to the club), the hare laid the trail out into the Lewisham High-road, and then up the lane leading through the market gardens opposite. Getting into the road he turned to the right, and after planning a strong false to the left over the fields worked his way along the road for some considerable distance, as though bent on reaching Bromley. Finding the paper run short, however, he turned off to the right, and, after traversing the cross-road for some two hundred yards, finished the scent, and made for home across the fields by way of Catford and Brockley. The pack, eight in number, consisted of Messrs S. A. Bennett, S. Lake, A. H. Peniston, Fred. H. Reed, W. Rowland (P.A.A.C.), A. Bultitude, A. A. Holmes, and H. C. Larette (South London Harriers). A severe check was received directly the "throw off" was reached, owing to several old tracks being visible, and the pack had therefore to hunt somewhat cautiously throughout the run, as the wind, which was blowing very hard, would not let the paper settle at all, especially on the hills. Lake had a series of lucky "finds," by which he obtained some capitally long leads, but the others were always soon after him. In the false in the road after Lewisham was passed, Peniston and Reed suffered sadly, being left totally in the rear, and were not able to reach the main pack until the latter were baulked over the finish of the trail. All being together again here, it was decided to return by road in preference to the fields, and the whole set accordingly made for home by exactly the same route as they had gone, Bultitude, Bennett, Lake, and Larette immediately taking the lead, then Peniston, the other three straggling. Warming to their work the leaders gradually increased the pace, Larette eventually winning on the Rye, Bultitude running in second, closely attended by Bennett. The times of the starts and arrivals were as under:—Hare: Naylor started at 4h, arrived at 5h 11m. Hounds started at 4h 15m; arrived—Larette, 5h 25m 20s; Bultitude, 5h 25m 25s; Bennett, 5h 25m 27s; Lake, 5h 25m 45s; Peniston, 5h 26m 45s; the remaining three coming in at long intervals in the following order :—Rowland, Holmes, and Reed.

The next run of this club takes place from the Rye House, Peckham Rye, on Saturday, December 7, at four precisely.

PECKHAM A.A.C.

A report of a run November, 1872.

Although we have in our possession a unique archive of Club records almost from the earliest days of the Club and in detail from 1870 in the nature of writings, journals, minutes and cuttings, these all have in common the maddening feature for the historian of having been written for the time and people they concern and not for posterity. A considerable process of deduction is therefore involved in arriving at almost any background or general conclusion about the men and their affairs.

We can see from the first report of Peckham Hare and Hounds in "Bell's Life" of October, 1869, that the list*is divided into two categories one of which surely comprises members, the other what we may inaccurately term visitors. The former are four in number, being those who come first and have no credentials attaching to their name. This suggests that they are the original nucleus and very possibly survivors of the informal chase or chases of the previous season which Reed in 1908 told Haslegrave, the then secretary, had begun the previous October. Among them he himself, though later the dominant figure in the Club, had possibly not figured, since he appears in the "Bell's Life" cutting as a "visitor" and a member of Thames Rowing Club. The latter organization at about the same time was fostering the sport on Wimbledon Common under the vigorous tutelage of Walter Rye, also a member of Thames Rowing Club. However they were concerned in the events of 1868 these four — Black, Cornell, Johnson and Williamson — were presumably the moving spirits in es-

*See page 7

15

tablishing the Club formally. Though others from the list were to re-appear on later occasions they were to do so only intermittently or even, as in the case of such as Hawke and Henman, uniquely. It was the trio of Williamson, Darnell and Reed who were at the centre of things initially, but at the end of 1871 the first two of these disappear leaving Reed only of the originators. The possibility of Reed's not being in at the very beginnings of the Club may incidentally explain why on the rare occasions in later years when he referred to the origins he did so in a manner suggesting second-hand rather than direct knowledge. Moreover in the written record there is nothing anywhere suggesting that Reed ever did claim to have personally established the pilot Club. This, together with a sort of reticence to move to public utterance in the way of controversy which characterized this enigma of a man, very likely explains his continual reluctance to enter into public wrangling of the kind Walter Rye engaged in in urging the claims to superiority of his club Thames Hare and Hounds, aided as he was by the convenience of his newspaper column in "The Sporting Gazette" in which he wrote with such petulant liveliness under the pseudonym of "Easterling". The common background of the two men in their membership of Thames Rowing Club together with their separate ways so doggedly pursued and the quite exceptional virulence of Rye's attacks upon Reed's Club — pursued on and off for over thirty years — provoke intense curiosity today as to the underlying reasons — not necessarily personal ones — which must however remain matters for speculation only by now. At the time, however, it was Rye who was the dominant figure. His word, emitted as it was with a matching Mosaic authority, tended to be taken as gospel, while the rest — of whatever club identity, for his targets were many — usually suffered in silence except when especially stung to retort as in 1874 after he questioned the origins of Peckham Amateur Athletic Club. On this occasion, though, he made what he called, "the amende honourable" in admitting error — "I had no idea the time had gone by so rapidly . . . . "

Research into contemporary directories and other sources discloses little about the individuals like Williamson, though he was presumably the chief instigator or senior, being the first Captain and Chairman.

But almost certainly he, as we have learned of the others, was one of the local Camberwell and Bermondsey people who came the mile or so down into Peckham for their activities. More particularly they centred on Grange Road where Reed lived, with his father, Hayter Thornton Reed, a corn and coal merchant and importer with premises in Mill Street, Dock Head, S.E., Bermondsey Wall and the New Corn Exchange, Mark Lane, E.C.

In the same road and trade was John Eastty — a name which seems to have been misspelled in the original "Bell's Life" notice — of Edwards, Eastty and Company, merchants on the Baltic Exchange, while round the corner in Upper Grange Road, besides Hayter Reed, who is presumably grandfather, elder brother or uncle of Frederick Henry, there is William Darnell Esq., Jun., of W. Darnell and Son, Granary Keepers, with, in addition, S. Collins living at "Fort House" in the same road. As for the Croydon member of the original list it is significant, taken with the fact that Reed became an architect, that the only Henman listed in Warren's Directory of Croydon is of that calling.

Whatever the cause of their coming together it is clear that the form of association from which the Club sprang was among a group of young men living on the northern fringe of Peckham or just over the parish boundary in Bermondsey in the general direction of the Old Kent Road, with middle class business people as the pool from which the original membership was drawn. But it was the indefatigable threesome of Williamson, Darnell and Reed who provided the nucleus and energizing focus. Probably conscious intention played little or no part in all this — our earliest members were busy doing something they liked and that was all. Still, they took it very seriously with Williamson as Chairman signing Secretary Reed's minutes — as meticulous as the scrapbooks he kept — and Reed combining with these duties what would nowadays be the responsibility of an Honorary Treasurer, just as in 1875 the Captaincy and chairmanship became one.

These men not only ensured the long survival of the Club but set the stamp of character upon it of a family institution which it long retained. A larger unit might well have broken up but the small enterprise of Peckham A.A.C. could carry on in a modest way unaffected by larger storms or troubles, though one or two sufficiently worrying were to come their way within the first two or three years.

"In diving off Darnell had slightly the advantage but stopped on reaching the water".
(Peckham Journal 27th May, 1870).

To start with, however, all is peaceful enough and modest in pretensions. Of momentous policy decisions and their backgrounds there is no record but, in these scrupulous early journals cum minute books, from the first entry of 29th April, 1870, there is an abundance of closely detailed descriptions of runs and other events. Early on Friday mornings they hold a competition at a different event each week

"THE ROSEMARY BRANCH" AS IT IS TODAY
The public house which gave its name to the recreation ground, formerly a cricket ground, (left of picture) where many of the early morning events were held 1870-71.

with Reed turning up by 6.30 a.m. to mark out a track, on the first two occasions in Southwark Park and subsequently on the Rosemary Branch ground in Southampton Street.

The trio turns up for everything and sometimes they are all who do turn up. They fine the rest one shilling for not joining them in the weekly meetings to decide the single event, however bad the weather, and they make the last lazy bounder to arrive forgo the privilege of matutinal and violent exercise by creating him judge, or "umpire" as they call him, for that morning. The Club run hare and hounds or track events all the year round to suit their current tastes and see nothing incongruous in struggling to decide a hundred yards contest in clogging snow. Reed conscientiously and gravely condemns himself for "lifting" in a walking race, while the second week of the season again sees only Reed and Darnell there, long-jumping half-heartedly perhaps, "neither being up to much the jumping was bad." When the three unite for a 500 yard Steeplechase including "two broad ditches"

17

the results once more seem disappointing, with Darnell dropping out at the first ditch, Williamson falling at the second and Reed left alone to win, "trotting quietly in," but at least by now they have three companions as starter and judges. They themselves do not consider these early competitions wildly successful; nevertheless they stick at them till December 13th, 1872 — "a most disgusting morning". Even then it is as a result of a reasoned decision and not because of the weather that they discard them in favour of more ambitious Saturday Athletic meetings.

Between June 1870 and October 1871, the period covered by the first journal, they held some fourteen races over 440 yards, twelve walking races of various distances, seven short sprints, three races of two miles, six high jump contests, five races of one mile, four hurdle races and some twenty other competitions in addition. The record suggests a pleasingly human mixture of strength and weakness: they were no supermen and did not pretend to be. Some would turn up but not always compete — "None of the others daring to strip in consequence of the intense cold, snow lying on the ground" — and if they felt like it while actually competing they would drop out, conveniently at the "dressing shed" to which, incidentally, each committee member had a key. They were not casual, but the description of a Club 100 yards race in 1872 typifies the general atmosphere of the period — as it will also serve to do for many a more recent race of our streamlined age: . . . . . "Time — Doubtful".

We may well find something more sympathetic about these early morning gatherings with the uncertainties which attend the beginnings of all enterprises than in the greater achievements that came later — records, vast Nicholls Cup fields and all.

There is about these first months a quality of innocence which is Eden-like. But something of the serpent was to disturb the tranquillity of this "Rosemary Branch" paradise, though later after his departure from Peckham A.A.C. the chief protagonist was to find some element of redemption in founding South London Harriers. In October, 1871, a new tone of competitive urgency starts to enter with the advent of a "Handicapper's Challenge Cup" given for the quarter mile distance by the new holder of that office, one Ernest Smith, followed shortly by another gift from the same quarter of a "Challenge Belt" for a mile steeplechase. He seems to have been a man of somewhat strongly developed ego, for the Committee found themselves embarrassed by having to turn down such requests of his as that the results of races for his Cup should be reported in the newspapers and that the Trophy itself be re-christened "Mr. Smith's". Between December, 1871 and January, 1872 several members broke away — not all at once for the secession seems to have developed by stages — to form South London Harriers. Although this had doubtless been building up for some time it was precipitated by "unpleasant remarks" passed in the early hours of a Friday morning by and concerning a Club Handicapper who was thought to have his own competitive ambitions closer to his heart than the just handicaps of others. Though at a subsequent business meeting the Chairman might request the members to "let all unpleasantness end on that evening", it is clear that ill-feeling within such a small and tightly knit circle would not easily suffer such a state of affairs particularly since the greater number of events were handicaps. The same month Smith departed, F.T. Pridmore taking his place as Handicapper. Some five others left subsequently also — a grave loss for a small Club which at the time probably did not number more than twenty in all.

18

The truth of the matter is probably that Smith was quite innocent of corrupt intentions of using his office to gain victories for himself. He was simply insensitive about such matters, a demonstration of which came when he offended against the unwritten law of the "Gentleman Amateur" by communicating — quite jocularly no doubt — with a fellow handicapper about his own mark as a performer at a forthcoming meeting. His bewildered anger alone in subsequent newspaper correspondence suggests an innocence of intention voicing itself in what we take to be typically Victorian expression in letters which do not begin but commence: *"Sir, Let it not be imagined that the effusion of 'One of the Opposition' has escaped my notice . . . . . "* When, as a member of South London Harriers, he actually objected to his allotted handicap in a Surrey Volunteer Artillery Athletic Club Meeting there was a great storm and he resigned that club too, founding a new one, Albert A.C., until forced out of that also. Since the latter was formed in 1874 at Nunhead closely adjacent to Peckham and South London Harriers were established on the immediate west edge of the Rye itself the combination must have constituted a grave threat to Peckham's survival, not only taking members away but making recruiting more difficult with local competitors thus in the field. There are aspects of what at the time was undoubtedly an unpleasant affair which it is impossible not to find amusing, but our admiration if not our affection must attach to certain of Smith's qualities for it is clear that he was possessed of many good ones. He obviously enjoyed enterprise; he was a dynamic personality with plenty of drive that stirred Peckham A.A.C. out of what could have become by all the signs a dangerous and inbred complacency through which they could have remained content to drift along self-approving in a back water. He stimulated them to take their early morning contests more seriously — the trophies were clearly presented with this in view — and after he left they continued to extend something of this boldness to more ambitious and public enterprise. Among other things he seems to have been personally responsible for the inauguration of "Sealed Handicaps". But undoubtedly his greatest service to athletics was the founding of South London Harriers the achievement of which club has been so outstanding at all levels that it is little exaggeration to describe it as the most important happening in the athletic world in the first half of the 1870's.

Had Smith remained with South London it is likely that the two Peckham clubs — the connection, inescapable on both sides, was recognized — would have remained unreconciled. Largely due to the good sense of the South London Harriers' authorities the breach was very early healed however, and, later, the impressive paradox arose of the great sporting event held in annual competition and now known as the Nicholls Cup Race. But already by the autumn of 1872 S.L.H. members were quite regularly joining Peckham's fortnightly hare and hounds runs at the weekends. This alternate pattern remained for many years, and allowed members to go elsewhere to experience fresh pastures — one of their chief pleasures in country running. This was a general custom and where two clubs shared the same country they might thus stagger their outings to avoid clashes. Runners would, as with S.L.H. and Peckham, belong to two or more clubs to be able to enjoy this advantage of access to various country. Dual membership in these early days produced confusion, of course. Objections such as those made before the 1884 "National Championship" by Northern clubs to the mixed membership of Blackheath and S.L.H., probably provide origins of the present "second claim" system. Although Blackheath does not seem to have objected to second claim members in the first years therefore, they did by the early 1900's.

December, 1873, saw the first amalgamated and official run with S.L.H., and though this was long before the competitions began in real earnest it is interesting that the spirit was already there as "The Sportsman" pointed out:

"Although it was understood that these runs should not be considered as matches between the two clubs, but only friendly unions, still, as the time drew near, the representatives of each pack seemed somewhat anxious that the honour of first place should fall to one of their own men, the leading runners of each club being pretty equal in pace." And the resemblance of that day to the present does not end there for afterwards, "A large number of members and friends from both clubs sat down to tea, after which some capital songs were sung, all present seeming thoroughly to enjoy themselves."

The winter of 1872-73 saw an understandable failure of enthusiasm for the Friday morning events and more stress upon hare and hounds. Generally, there were signs of development: orders were given to printers; rules were formulated and regularly revised; a club uniform was established. The colours were dark blue and white, with white jersey and knickerbockers and there was also a dark blue cap carrying a monogram badge. By now there was an "Anniversary Dinner" and progress reached even to refinements such as the proposition that each member should have a handicap flag with his personal choice of colour.

Altogether there are considerable signs of re-organization, most of all in the abandonment of the early morning events. With their increasing number of members coming from further afield they could not all reach the "Rosemary Branch" grounds at that hour. Accompanying this decision was the replacement of those gatherings by half-yearly members' athletic meetings. The first of these was duly held in May, 1873, with an Open Mile Flat Handicap — open, that is, to "members of organized clubs and gentlemen amateurs introduced by members". With half a dozen members' events this was an ambitious step forward with the President's wife presenting the prizes and silver and bronze crosses first mentioned here in Club records. There were L.A.C. Officials imported especially for the occasion, 250 people present, 38 entries for the Open Mile of whom 25 ran, and the Police Band of 'P' Division playing away — all on Bennett's Field, Queen's Road, Peckham. A great success, they thought, and though the financial side was not so rosy they decided to repeat the venture the following autumn, this time adding an Open 100 yards Handicap and engaging the band of the 10th Surrey Rifles.

The same autumn saw the change of Club journals to purely business uses — again, a significant alteration — newspaper reports substituting for the old manuscript records of events. All told, the general feeling we get is of a move towards greater vigour and efficiency coupled with a desire to see everything done well and tidily down to the last detail, as typified by the 1872 amendment to Rule 7, "That the least successful competitor be he who passes the winning post last". They had also acquired three eminent figures as Vice-Presidents in the persons of Frederick Leighton, the painter and future President of the Royal Academy, Emanuel Boutcher, F.R.G.S. and Jonah Oastler, J.P.

The most important confirmation of their changing nature and status, however, came in the increasing success of the athletic meetings and the Open Steeplechases they were now promoting. Even the money side was now no worry, a small profit even being made like the

£3 14s 2d from the Spring Meeting of 1874. But of course, like all good committees they did worry, since printing costs had gone up accordingly, what with extras like the bills they put up in trams and buses. By 1875 they were booking the Kennington Oval and securing entries of 62 for the 100 Yards, 59 for the 440 and 69 for the Mile. They made a pretty sight for the spectators with each competitor wearing not team or club colours but individual ones like jockeys and every bit as colourful so that the judges and other watchers could pick them out easily. They had also started to acquire runners who could lay claim to such big prizes as their own five guinea values for each Open event: sprinters like Metcalf, Hornidge and Oliver, and in longer distances, H.D. Thomas, the man from Hereford whom J.E. Fowler-Dixon called "one of our best and prettiest milers in the early "Eighties". He, like Metcalf, was to remain a staunch member for many years, and at this time could contend with the best, winning the Two Miles at the large L.A.C. Autumn Meeting while in races like the Thames Hare and Hounds Ten Mile promotion he was virtual scratch. Of course, there was the notorious weather too, but things would still go ahead — "the numerous spectators dismal and defiant". More often, though, there would be, as in 1876, "a numerous and fashionable company assembled" at the Oval. What was more to the point Rowland — "thrown in", as the newspaper said, at 290 yards in the Members' Two Miles Handicap — Rowland won a race.

One hears much of the Smiths and the Reeds in the Peckham era. We must not forget that there were all the time a good number of other participants in this venture. Of these none is more worth our notice than the same Walter Rowland, one of the earliest to combine with the original trio, and a constantly interested member down to his death in 1922. Characteristically he first appears as "umpire" of an early morning mile race in July, 1870, and in his record of continuous service to the Club he typifies those hundreds of often unrecognized members whose contribution is sometimes intangible but no less vital for that. It was said of him in 1918 that he never missed an annual general meeting and rarely any Club dance or other social function, while he inaugurated the "Bohemian Concerts" that were popular for so long. When others failed to turn up in the early days he was usually there beside Reed. Then or later when delicate or unpleasant matters had to be handled he was often asked to chair the meeting. Indeed, he himself was twice to be embarrassed in the first ten years of the next century by having a rival candidate for the Presidency proposed against him, only the generous and dignified way in which he conducted himself on these occasions retrieving the situation. From his youth he could hardly have been of ideal athletic build and in the competitions he was often left behind, though his persistence sometimes won him unexpected success. He was certainly a "sticker" and twenty miles was not too much for him. Once when a visiting runner, Child, came down "a regular lump on his side" in trying to scale a high fence on a hare and hounds run, it was Rowland, together with another Peckham official, Felix Pridmore, who helped him home. And when the Committee decided in 1874 that it was time that a Club of their stature possessed a bath for the convenience of members and visitors, the cost not to exceed ten shillings and sixpence, it was Rowland who subsequently lent them one. It is difficult to demonstrate in words the importance of a key but unobtrusive member like Rowland — it must suffice to say that for nearly half of this history he must be thought of as present, supporting and guiding through all the crucial years. Perhaps the best memorial to the man is the Cup he presented for the Club's longest championship distance across country.

There were of course many others — the number of nineteen active and thirty-six Honorary members of 1874 had increased to twenty-five and fifty-four respectively by the following year. Already a signal advance had been made from the earlier handful. Besides Bennett, who had been one of the so-called original men, and S.A. Peniston, who had succeeded Williamson as Captain and Chairman, there were the new men — and ladies too. Three of these males claim our attention, both as good performers and as members who had some lasting influence on the Club. For Peckham there were two Olivers for a Rowland in the brothers Ernest and Alfred, who were members of the Norwood Club and joined Peckham in 1872. Their lasting fame in Blackheath was that they were — or to be more accurate and surprising — their sister, Charlotte, [11] was responsible for introducing the great Blackheath Harriers family of Metcalf into the Club: a father, John, in the Peckham days, and two sons, John and Adrian, from the marriage in 1876 with Charlotte which is the romantic sequel to this recruiting story. The Club is thus in the debt of John and "Toppy" as she was familiarly known, for their sons gave yeoman service to Blackheath athletically and officially. The close connection with the Private Banks Cricket and Athletic Club which was an important aspect of the Club's existence for so long was Adrian's doing in particular, while his father was proposer of the adoption of the Club's entwined squares insignia in 1878.

"A man was not a gentleman-amateur whose occupation had a tendency to develop his muscle. It was a difficult task, however to say what was a gentleman"

(Preston County Court Case —
Sutcliffe v. Vanstone 1875).

"The Committee will be pleased to see any gentleman in the pack"

(Newspaper announcement of Peckham A.A.C. Run, 1878).

Already in this narrative there have occurred a number of hints that the age under discussion differed from our own in respect of social class. We have seen how Ernest Smith offended unwritten "gentlemen's" laws, how one club could frown upon another's status and how one man might well reject another's society because of difference in the way of earning a living. It requires an effort of modern imagination to recognize, let alone accept, the attitudes of a time when, it must also be remembered, there was no female vote and forty per cent of men were still voteless. It was the age of the middle class and it was they who provided the impetus for the contemporary development of sport of which the rise of Blackheath Harriers was an expression. Prior to this, sport had been an aristocratic preserve as far as control of it was concerned and even to a large extent, participation also. The upper class patronage of sport with its accompaniments of professionalism and corruption from betting meant that the aristocrats and their proteges had brought sport under a cloud of disapproval which the adoptive middle class interest had to disperse if it was to become socially acceptable.[12] It was undoubtedly a very considerable difficulty that amateur sport had to contend with in its early days and we do well not to dismiss their scruples and their heated controversy on such matters without a proper understanding of the problem. There was of course more to it than that: no doubt something of the revival of puritanism which marked middle-class values entered into their thinking, while another ingredient might equally have been the need to elevate athletic philosophy to a level sufficiently high to defeat sedentarism as an idea. Whatever the explanation there was certainly a real need to make sport for adults acceptable in the climate of opinion which prevailed in the mid-Victorian era. It cannot simply be termed what we today call snobbery.

"The only hope for sport," wrote H.H. Griffin in 1891,[13] "was to adopt a high basis to start with, and accordingly the gentleman-amateur came into vogue". There had to be an impassable gulf between themselves and the professional. We get some hint of contemporary professional corruption from such newspaper records as that of the destruction of the famous Lillie Bridge grounds in 1887 "by riot, ravage, and fire owing to a pedestrian fiasco". The conception of the gentleman-amateur originated in the rowing world where the Henley rule distinguished between this category and that of the amateur pure and simple. In Peckham A.A.C., as in other similar organizations, the term amateur was held not to include "a mechanic, artizan or labourer," and although again it sounds snobbish, it was in fact very unlikely that at this time any artizan would be an amateur: it had not been many years previous that one regatta in the Pool of London had an entry from a crew whose qualification was that every member should have done a stretch in Newgate Prison. When in 1874 some Peckham members competed in the open events of an annual Warehousemen's sports known as the Bow Churchyard A.C. Sports they afterwards earned not only the rebuke of Walter Rye but an injunction by their own Club authorities to avoid such participation in future.

Peckham was actually far more tolerantly democratic than this might suggest, though they would carefully reject a certain number of entries for their own Open events, and this scrupulousness in what was generally a liberal body is a convincing demonstration of the problem's reach. The law suits brought by aggrieved competitors whose entries had been rejected or who had been denied prizes after winning them, rare though the legal expense made them, are proof too of the seriousness with which the long controversy was taken. Such trials were often Gilbertian in their absurdity, usually when witnesses attempted to satisfy judicial minds as to the definition and general detectability of a gentleman. But though these cases, together with such expressions as the oft-quoted tag of the later member C. Val Hunter, "the purity of sport", may afford us some amusement today in the last thirty years of the century during the emergence of amateur athletics they had real meaning. For those who might suffer from the rigidity of rejection in this interim period before the rules admitted them, they constituted a genuine grievance. It was a state fraught with contradictions, as this extract from an 1875 letter to "Bell's Life" shows:

"The proprietor of any large retail firm, moving in the first society, and perhaps never doing aught but signing a cheque, should he or his son enter for a competition, would be liable to an objection from his own counting-house clerk".

The passing of time brought its solution in the end, but in this, as we shall see again, the history of the Club is the history of the sport. Blackheath were to be instrumental in the further development of the organization of athletics which led to the Amateur Athletic Association in 1880 throwing the sport open to all who had neither competed nor taught for money.

". . . Colson and Thomas meanwhile taking matters coolly and immersing themselves in a pond . . . "

(Report of Peckham run in "Bell's Life" - 1875).

We have seen how Peckham were establishing themselves with growing assurance generally but not least with the wider-reaching and more public enterprise of the Athletic Meetings. This enterprise extended also to their cross-country interest where a growing enthusiasm for racing in the form of steeplechases now began to parallel that for hare and hounds. These started with an experimental one for members only in the January of 1872. For this Reed and Rowland laid the trail before competing themselves and C.H. Larette acted as Umpire. They extended the next to visitors that spring, seven turning up to make a total field of two dozen and by 1874 these had become quite important events. Jonah C. Oastler, a friend of the Reeds and now the Peckham President, had offered a five guinea Cup; they had accepted fifty entries and were adding to their growing reputation for organizing efficiency by well-marked courses with smart blue and white flags, a blue and red trail to show up on the snow and a supplementary force of boys engaged for the occasion to act as markers. The course was nearly five miles with only three quarters of a mile on the road, the rest being grass and ploughed land, by way of Goose Green, East Dulwich Grove, the Grove Tavern, "better known as Mother Bussey's," Lordship Lane, right of Honor Oak Station, the Newlands and down Rye Lane to finish at the Rye House Inn.

Life had by no means become an affair of earnest competition however, and the enjoyable routine of running across their country continued in the same relaxed spirit of old. Sometimes, usually because of the weather, they would abandon the planned programme to adjourn to Brown's Ground and enjoy "a game of football", or else, instead of a two miles race, "a pleasant game of snowballing" at "The Rosemary Branch". Enjoyment did not mean an absence of rigour though, and their pleasures often came hard: now and again, a policeman doubtless unfamiliar with their pursuits would attempt to arrest their flight on suspicion, on one occasion at least without success. At other times the Law could prove more co-operative, as when one of the force came to the aid of the party by telling them that the hares were just ahead getting a lift on the tail of a cart. There were drawbacks enough: tripping over signal wires in crossing one of their several railway lines; baulked by the scent having been scattered by the wind; experiencing "severe trial of their powers" in the shape of ploughed fields; or, the day after they had sprinted a hundred yards race "though snow lay thick upon the ground", going out when it lay five or six inches "deep across the fields". They had little need of coloured trail paper then, the hare's steps "being plainly marked in the snow", but it told upon them all heavily, "especially Rowland". And if it wasn't the snow it was getting a "thorough ducking" in the Ravensbourne. But though there were all these hardships recognized by cross-country runners down to today, together with less familiar ones such as the embarrassments caused through trespass, or the hare under pressure not always able to choose his route but forced to scale garden walls and take unexpected turns, like today also discomfort was fleeting and pleasure the lasting impression. Their "feed" as they called it, was a great delight to them and for us further reinforces the feeling we get of a resemblance of this close-knit group to that of "Three Men in a Boat": .... After the run was over, the whole pack, together with a number of friends sat down to tea, and it was a late hour before they left "The King's Arms", all being very pleased with one another and with the day's run."

"England will shortly be London, London England."

(James 1.)

"A barren, dreary expanse of uncertain grass."

(Peckham Rye — Walter Besant - 'South London').

24

Go today to the top of One Tree Hill and looking northwards the impression from that height with its fresh breezes is still one of a pleasing rusticity, even though St. Paul's and the sky-pointing pencils of the new buildings are less than four miles off. Trees are a dominant feature still and even in winter there is an abundance of green, with the Rye stretching out beneath girdled by the hill on which stands the Nunhead Cemetery where Reed and Rowland now lie. Alongside it you can see the very path cresting the side of that eminence by which they penetrated to their country to the south-east. It is surprisingly easy to picture the immediate vicinity, if no further afield, as a starting point for cross-country. The hill on which you stand forms part of a very steep range through which there was only limited access for hares wishing to disappear rapidly from the sight of those watching a mile away below. Moreover, in the 1860's these hills had a water defence in front of them, a complex of water courses so deep and intricate that only one pack is recorded as succeeding in getting across them. From these the Rye gets its name no doubt. It was still possible to lose oneself on One Tree Hill, as a pack in fact did in the 'Seventies, among the gorse bushes, vestiges of which remain there to this day. The Rye itself then probably resembled the Mitcham Common of today as a piece of heathy ground with a thin wiry grass, rather infrequent clumps of gorse and, in autumn, the fain-

THE PATH BESIDE NUNHEAD CEMETERY
which led the runners out from Peckham South-East to the Brockley Jack and open country.

25

test sprinkling of harebells. Before urbanization the area, like so much more of South London, was a region of scattered homesteads and market gardens, cottages of plank timber dotted among garden ground and fields with high hedgerows. Names like Honor Oak and "The Rosemary Branch" are redolent of a less crowded environment and a more leisurely world in which hare and hounds could take place on terrain where today the hares would be run literally and finally to ground by motorcars and prosecuted posthumously for spreading litter.

THE RYE HOTEL
formerly the Rye House, at the northern apex of Peckham Rye.

The built-up area was concentrated north of the Rye with a long finger of development, little more than a single line of buildings, running down Rye Lane and continuing along Peckham Rye Road, both sides of the way as far as the Rye and only one side as far as "The King's Arms". So that Peckham A.A.C. in this public house had as their headquarters the last building in the developed area of that period with open country west of it and south. The other premises they used, the Rye House, today the Rye Hotel, was not so well situated for a break-out from its position a little further north at the apex of the Rye.

The difficulty for running packs was firstly to pass the screen of steep hills with the formidable quag at their foot, and after, to reach genuine country and the farmlands on the far side of the hills, out into Perry Vale and the Ravensbourne basin. They could go westward through the lanes to Goose Green and Dulwich flanking the hills to achieve a less abrupt climb from that direction. They might also, though they seldom did, go out through the neck or pass between One Tree Hill and Honor Oak, by which route they more often returned; or go via Lordship Lane leading easily to Perry Vale over the low saddle between Sydenham Hill and the ridge of One Tree Hill. As a final and most frequent alternative, they would go out by the Newlands estate and Nunhead making for the Ravensbourne direction and turning the east flank of One Tree Hill. This latter choice was confirmed by the formation of S.L.H. at their headquarters on the west side of the Rye and the probably tacit agreement that they should exploit the country to the south-west, while Peckham confined itself to the south-east, a necessary division with two clubs likely to confuse each other's paper trails. [14] There were other clubs like Albert A.C. and several informal packs to worsen an already crowding situation.

This of itself was sufficient to cast their eyes firmly and habitually towards the east, but it was strengthened by a very real and physical manifestation of Victorian progress, though one that the Victorians found themselves witnessing with feelings of helplessness rather than of pride, as voiced by the following contemporary account: "Every succeeding year we see some waste ground in the suburbs covered with dwellings, some little village or hamlet in the suburbs united by a continuous street to the great metropolis." By 1869 Peckham was fast becoming a commuters' suburb with only vestiges of its old character in odd nooks and corners. The Rye itself had only been preserved by the inhabitants banding together to prevent the erection of buildings there, following this, as Walford tells us, with the vestry of the parish purchasing the manorial rights in 1868. They were more fortunate than their Sydenham neighbours whose acres of commonland had been enclosed early in the century and who learned in 1868 that they were being incorporated in Greater London. The harassment was general and extensive for South London had little in the way of vested economic interests to oppose to the headlong spread of urbanization. Writing in the 1870's Blanch says that by 1871 landowners and gentry were being driven to move to Dulwich, their place being taken by an army of clerks who rented their houses in increasing numbers. The population of London had started to explode and in Peckham alone had gone from 28,135 in 1861 to 42,160 ten years later by which time it was close to the minimum size of a modern county borough. Another decade still and with the constitution of the London County Council the whole vast area of London had become an entity.

So it was that at the very time our packs began to operate there not only the country immediately at the door of their headquarters but the more ample facilities beyond it were directly threatened by the developing urban sprawl pushed tirelessly on by the expanding bridgehead and the demon of rustic destruction bred at the southern foot of London Bridge. The growth of Greater London is the hidden presence on all critical occasions in the Club's history, and this was never more true than of the earliest phase of all.

Meanwhile, back at "The Rye House", such threats apart, the Committee and members were contented enough with the progress of the past eight years. Numbers had climbed steadily towards the fifty mark and we find the first signs of a modern graded pack system [15]

BROCKLEY BRIDGE TODAY
one of the limited number of escape routes across the railway from
Peckham for the hares of the early seventies.

BESIDE BROCKLEY BRIDGE
the old canal lock-keeper's cottage, no more than four miles from
St. Paul's.

in a mention of the Club having two divisions for hare and hounds by the autumn of 1878. The summer runs too had become very popular as they were to remain for many years. These had led them out as far as Chislehurst and its Windmill Inn, an excursion which finds Reed in rare rhapsodic mood: "A prettier piece of country — interspersed as it is with hills, woods and common — the latter covered with furze — could hardly have been chosen for a run." Afterwards they adjourned to Samuel Bevington's house there where the President regaled them "with a sumptuous dessert", and no doubt other entertainments — for surely the madeira was good that evening as the June sunset barred the fading sky with pink and green and dove grey, and the trees of Chislehurst Common were limned forth black and brooding at the fall of light? Among other places they visited thus were Streatham Common and "The Pied Bull Inn", "The Royal Hotel", Eltham, together with members of Ulysses A.C. and one, Dicker, from a club called Blackheath Hare and Hounds, "The Imperial Arms", Chislehurst, which was to become well known to members as the starting point for the Club Walking Race, and once they went from their favoured "Robin Hood", Penge, as far as West Wickham and its woods.

It is through one of these summer outings that we first hear the name of Blackheath as a place for their runs in a May committee meeting of 1878. After this is repeated in the first week of July we are prepared for the surprise — if, as good Blackheath men we do not already "know" — of learning that six days later at a Special General Meeting on July 12th, 1878, it was resolved not only to move to "The Green Man" at Blackheath, but also to act on the proposal of 18th June when, the minutes state, "the general opinion was in favour of Blackheath Harriers but nothing definite was decided". All this with a minimum of discussion and fuss and without mention of any alternatives as though it were merely the putting-through of a decision long since meditated and by now resolutely determined.

Even so, they could hardly have anticipated the impetus and drastic change this move was to impart to their fortunes — and with no delay but within the next four years. So great an alteration was to come about through this expansion that the Club was soon to be peopled largely with men who knew nothing of the Peckham days and whose appearance on the scene must have blurred the recollection of those who did know, so different were the contrasting new circumstances they then found themselves in. It was surely a transformation which must at times have almost bewildered Reed or Rowland who could recollect the origins at once so far away and yet so short a time before. It is well therefore before embarking upon "modern" history briefly to assess the achievement of the Club up to the move in 1878.

In 1873 Walter Rye typically but with a certain refreshing accuracy described Peckham as "This Club, which has for some time been generally considered as a sort of hybrid between the exclusive and radical athletic societies . . . " For once Reed and the others may very well have been flattered by such a description. Certainly the steering of a middle course between the extremes to which all too many clubs flew at this period and which likewise caused many to succumb was one of the chief virtues of Peckham and no doubt an ingredient in her success — for in contemplating its modest scope we should not doubt that it was successful. Most important of all and no joke as a matter for congratulation was the bare fact of survival. At this distance we are apt to dismiss their difficulties as minor ones. They were not. Wastage, problems of recruitment with all the accompanying limitations of the time, enthusiasm fading after the first novelty, the smallness of their numbers and the differences such as split their ranks in the winter of 1871-72 — all these they combatted. Yet too they continued to expand the scope of their activities: from paper-chasing only to running "on the path" as well, pursuing both these activities all the year round and then progressing from these to the quite daring enterprise of Open Athletic meetings and monthly steeplechases. Leavening all this was an influence that was all the more pervasive and subtle because unexpressed and even unconscious. It is perhaps best though inadequately to be described as the principle of cohesion — a determination, possibly, on the part of Reed and his friends that the Club should be an association of friends with like interests rather than a factory for athletic careers. The principle has been decisive. It possibly remains the chief characteristic of the Club, giving it, moreover, a flexibility which renders it a protection against the chances of fortune. It was this, so early established in our history, which surely ensured a long future for their brave new enterprise.

At the heart of all this was Reed who was present from the stage when it had something of the flavour in its casual beginnings of a party of boys making up sides for a game through to the time of the move when, though the Club was yet rather insecure financially, it was undeniably firmly set up, though not of the first rank. Reed was to remain at the centre of things for another thirty years but already the debt to him was great. Had it not been for his perseverance the Club might easily have been extinguished, while to him was directly owing the peculiar quality of the family relationship which, especially in the days of "The Green Man", was Blackheath Harriers' outstanding quality and charm. He was one about whom even intimate friends knew only a limited amount and to those who knew him not at all, a riddle. There are certain definite facts such as his Presidency of 22 years and nine months — from 1882 to 1905, during eighteen years of which he was Treasurer — from 1885 to 1903. More intangible are personal memories like those of C.W. Bache who remembered the man as when he first saw him in 1883: "When I joined, his running days were over . . . but he still had the figure of a racer — light, active, and well-knit." In the photographs of the same period surrounded by the mounting numbers of the Club at whose centre he sits he has the air of a reticent and youthful, possibly shy man whose beard changes in style but does not conceal the suggestion that this is one who does not feel aged enough to suit the father-figure role that circumstance has thrust upon him. Whatever he himself may have felt one cannot deny that he was an exceptional man whose persistence was witnessed many times both in action and in vision from those first days when, as the journal tells us, "Reed collapsed with stitch in Lewisham churchyard", to the latest date of his connection and his moving farewell. One time Warden of the Saddlers' Company, architect of the Hotel Cecil where the Club held many meetings, President of Blackheath Harriers — Frederick Henry Reed, though he may not literally have been the founder of his Club, yet was essentially so. His portrait occupies its position in the Clubroom by natural right, as do these words concerning him which fittingly conclude the account of the first crucial years.

PART TWO 1878 - 1919
"Gone Away!"

.DRAWING OF THE ORIGINAL 'GREEN MAN', BLACKHEATH

Blackheath and "The Green Man"
The Edwardian Era
The Great War

"Underlying much of the heath are the Blackheath Pebble Beds of Eocene Age consisting of remarkably well rounded and graded pebbles of flint, jet black in colour. The scanty soil is podsolized, with a black surface layer."

('The Commonlands of England and Wales'
- W.G. Hoskins and L. Dudley Stamp.)

"Clubs ought, therefore, in their own and the wider and greater interests of the sport, to fix on some outlying hotel, where they can not only obtain suitable headquarters with abundant ablutionary resources, but a place which is close — the nearer the better — to a common or open land where they can get, with a minimum of road-running, genuine cross-country work. There may be a difficulty in finding such a place, but it is worth searching for."

(H.W. Griffin - 'Athletics' - 1891.)

"Wot! Only two on yer? I thought the whole Bloomin' Force was after me!"

(Charlie Peace, captured at Blackheath
October, 1878).

Blackheath, where the re-christened Club opened its official activities on October, 5th, 1878, "with a strong muster of cross-country athletes" and "every prospect of the season being a success", was by no means an historical or athletic backwater like Peckham. From its golfing association with James the First it derived its standing as the oldest golf club and in addition it was the home of the senior Rugby, Lacrosse and Hockey clubs of the country. Its long record ranges from the Viking army camping there in the eleventh century, to royal meetings and official welcomes involving such as Henry the Fifth, Henry the Eighth and Anne of Cleves, Charles the Second — together with sundries like the Cornish Rebels against Henry the Seventh and 'the "filth and scum of Kent" led by Jack Cade. From the repetitions of such perils and the destruction of its nature by gravel-digging the Heath had been rescued in 1866 by the Metropolitan Commons Act which, as Walford said, "secured Blackheath to the public as a place of healthful recreation". Although, as he said, the place was "much infested with donkeys", it became in the 1870's a fitting resort for the Victorian public, with the suppression of its "hog and pleasure fair" in 1872, the Metropolitan Board of Works having assumed management of the Heath in 1871.

The whole process of improvement continued at least until it received the presumable setback of becoming the home of Blackheath Harriers. At any rate no such lavish reception as that accorded Manuel Palaeologus, 'Emperor of the East', by Henry the Fourth awaited the Club on its arrival at the famous site, but landlady Mrs. Orchard made them welcome enough at their new home, "The Green Man" to feel that the change had been for the better.

This hostelry partook of the historical fame of its 270-acre surroundings, for it too enjoyed a certain renown beyond that of its popularity with Victorian holiday-makers. Evelyn had observed long before in his diary that there "appeared nothing but an innumerable assembly of drinking people from London", yet "The Green Man" had changed little by the nineteenth century as Richard Best remarked severely in a letter of March, 1810: "On the Bowling Green there I have seen them drinking and singing hymns etc., till they have rolled about on the grass." After military reviews on the Heath the officers used to dine there, while it is recorded that on the Trafalgar Anniversary of 1811 a hundred sat down to dinner. "The memory of the late Lord Nelson" was drunk in silence and an ode recited. R.H. Barham, author of "The Ingoldsby Legends", went there and sober purposes were

THE GREEN MAN, BLACKHEATH.
(B.M. Shapcott)

executed by the old bench of magistrates which sat at "The Green Man" before the Police Court was established. Among these Justices was Sir Thomas Maryon-Wilson whose family presented the Club with its Swimming Cup. 1833 probably saw the last appearance outside London of Madame Tussaud's famous Exhibition of Waxworks which was on view there, "admittance to the Chamber of Horrors, 6d". Reverence to the shades of Blackheath Harriers on the same premises forbids drawing of a parallel with "the ghastly line" of Marat's features murdered in his bath, though baths, "a crowd, steam and a smell of embrocation" remain dominant impressions in the minds of more than one "Green Man" generation of Blackheath Harriers, just as they were the first to strike A.C. Telfer when he arrived there.

Beyond the superior and comfortable accommodation of which they were now posessed there was the acquisition of a new security and dynamic which they inherited in this removal. It was without question the most important single event in the Club's history. The distance they had moved was slight — a matter of not much more than three miles — but for the Club it was a decision of moment. The Peckham achievement assessed at the conclusion of the previous section was considerable, yet it should not conceal the fact that there was not at that early stage much to preserve it from the fate that extinguished so many other clubs of that time after only a few years of life. Without the move to Blackheath it is more than probable that the Club would not have survived. In passing, there is a hint of the importance of this event to the Club in the fact that though the name was changed then no one has ever again suggested an alteration of title despite more than one removal of headquarters since leaving the geographical area from which that name was taken. It was a name that had appeared previously in the athletic world, as has been mentioned above, through the club "Blackheath Hare and Hounds", and though one or two of its members and, in particular, H. Van Putten, were frequent visitors to our own Club there was no direct connection and its doings remain something of a mystery.[16]There was apparently no more than a handful of competing runners in that institution and even these seem to have disappeared from the scene round about the time of Peckham's removal to the Heath. About the only thing certain about them is that several were footballers, Van Putten, a member of Queen's House and Grapnels Football Clubs and C.H. Dicker, who ran with Thames Hare and Hounds as well as with Blackheath, belonging to Selborne Football Club. At the same period of the mid-seventies there also appears a member, A.J. Law of "Blackheath Athletic Club".[17]Of these two clubs — if in any effective sense they were ever so — there is little other trace.

The Club was known for some time after 1878 as "Blackheath Harriers, late Peckham A.A.C." and appears thus in the press notices of the time, stressing the fact no doubt of its continuous existence. With little more visible upheaval than that change of heading indicates the great step was taken. If there was more to it we today are left unaware. Our ancestors were usually strictly practical and the Peckham members were no exception: it was a matter of necessity that they should find other ground and they took steps accordingly. It was a question of finding suitable country and also, to reduce it to crude simplicity, a pub. to take them in. In this they were only executing a further stage in that aspect of the Club's history which can irreverently be regarded as a "pub. crawl".

It is no doubt a shocking thing to modern minds, but nonetheless the truth, that the early Peckham and Blackheath men were little interested in business for its own sake. At times committee members could grow quite heated at the unpunctuality of their fellows and this would be "severely commented upon" but annual general meetings, for example, were a very different matter from today's profusion of affairs and their ordering. A report of Reed's handling of one of them says: "Our President so engineered matters that the business was put through in record time, thus enabling the Smoking Concert to have a look-in." Such attitudes on the part of his subject are very pertinent to the would-be historian who is left at this juncture without records of any substantial kind relating to the inner workings of the Club, especially as shortly after this the Committee decided, with an extreme disregard for posterity and strangely forgetful of the future Centenary, to cease the practice of keeping minutes of meetings and moreover obstinately persevered in this course through the early 'Eighties.

This was a strange paradox at a time when the Club entered upon great prosperity with, moreover, amazing suddenness. The previous January they had been calling ten runners including some S.L.H. men "a capital muster". And, though the Annual Dinner at the Lombard Restaurant had an attendance of between thirty and forty, the accompanying A.G.M. — for it was the practice, as hinted above, thus to combine business and pleasure on the same evening — revealed a deficit in the balance sheet of four guineas. This, though made up by the Vice-President and Honorary Member, Henry Ecroyd, lent substance to the reference by "Senior member of the Committee", Reed, to "difficulties".

Yet, from a membership in 1875 of about forty and, in 1878 at the time of the move, thirty-one, but certainly far less as an active force, Blackheath were[18] now to soar within four years to close on two hundred and by 1883 to exceed that number. This vast increase within so short a spell was formerly supposed to have occupied the entire space of the next decade but researches have shown the situation to have been as it is sketched above. It would have been remarkable enough within ten years but is much more so, occupying as it does four short years. In fact, the expansion was even speedier than this suggests, for although there were new members proposed at almost every committee meeting after the move to Blackheath they were no more than a satisfactory trickle in 1879 and 1880. It was from 1881 onwards that the acceleration took place, nearly four dozen new members being elected between March, 1881 and the end of that year. The process continued so that some eighty joined in a twelve-month period from 1881-1882. From that time the future was assured until the existence of the Club was threatened by the First World War.

It was a dramatic advance which led it to be described by 1884 as being, with S.L.H., one of the "two Principal cross-country Clubs in the metropolitan district."

Naturally one is curious as to the reasons for this increase and it may fairly be supposed that Blackheath's merits as a catchment area from at least three sides played a part in this. One is tempted to assume also that its social superiority to the late home of Peckham A.A.C., was a contributing factor. After all, though Walford about this time said, "In former times, apparently, Blackheath was not considered an aristocratic neighbourhood", nevertheless it is clear that it now offered, as those Victorians would have said, "a better class of people". In fact, the greater part by far of the membership did not derive from the immediate vicinity of Blackheath and we must look further for a satisfactory explanation. Whereas before members from outside Peckham and Bermondsey districts were the exception, now they came from a widespread area of London. Most, as expected, came from south of the river but these were supplemented by a good quantity from such places as Finchley, Brentwood, Upton Park, Kensington and Central London. It seems likely that the name of Blackheath becoming generally known attracted these men together with some very vigorous work on the part of several active workers like C. Cattlin, H.D. Thomas and J.C. Milligan and an important name, D.T. Mayson. These had wide connections with the whole field of athletics in London and beyond, being themselves athletes of no mean ability and reputation.

Other clubs than Peckham were struggling for existence and it is not surprising that from now on the growth of Blackheath should have attracted a quantity from such organizations as found it impossible to continue an independent existence. This was the source of some two dozen new members joining more or less en bloc in 1882 from the South London Athletic and Bicycling Club. It was in fact considered so far complete as to be termed an amalgamation. They took the decision at the same "Rye House" Inn headquarters of Peckham A.A.C., and D.T. Mayson promised to obtain their election so that they were elected without a ballot and with a guarantee of two representatives on the Blackheath Committee. Thus a Members' Bicycle Handicap appeared on the programme of the next Club Athletic Meeting and thus did T. Crafter of later fame enter the ranks of Blackheath Harriers.

Altogether, the reports and activities we have from the first years at "The Green Man" strongly suggest a new lease of life which represents an extension even of the more hopeful later days at Peckham; there is the feeling of a confidence not sensed in the earlier accounts — an absence of tentativeness and the presence of an atmosphere of belonging and establishment. In the autumn of 1878 at the Opening Run a new man, D.T. Mayson, joined from Spartan Harriers, which club up to then had been among the best; he went out as hare with Rowland who doubtless brought back a favourable report of his colleague for Mayson was a more than useful runner as well as a walker. At this time he was the coming "organization man" in the new world of modern athletics which was rapidly establishing itself and more was to be heard of him, other bodies than Blackheath benefitting from his vigour and enterprise. The following month there was a Members' Steeplechase with the 1875 Peckham member, W.W. Davis, hitting fine form and in subsequent months going on to confirm it. In the evening there was what became an institution in itself — though they had always enjoyed a few songs at the old Rye House — "songs and glees by the Blackheath Glee Club", and almost certainly among the performers would have been Walter Rowland and H.D. Thomas. At the end of November there was the first Amalgamated Run at Blackheath with S.L.H., but now the latter were greatly outnumbered, Blackheath having twice their number, and, since this was apparently a race, or at any rate turned into one, they had the first two home and tied for third place. By the following year the "Blackheath names" like C. Cattlin and J.C. Milligan were starting to appear, while that summer H.D. Thomas continued his victorious way on the track. He did not turn out in August, though, for what was apparently the first of the 2¼ Mile "Round the Heath" Road Handicaps which were to become the principal Blackheath competitions for a great band of mid-week runners. The fixtures listed for that winter with such clubs as Thurlow Park Harriers and Hampton Court Hare and Hounds remind us yet again of these and so many others that have disappeared.

For a year now there had been two "divisions" or packs going out because of the increase of numbers. Walter Rye was to say in his article on paper-chasing in the Badminton volume which appeared in 1888, "They have now . . . come to be known as the Blackheath Harriers, and have a pretty country". For once these gentlemen could agree with his sentiments: not only did they have the grassy space of the Heath but, beyond Morden College through whose grounds they passed on their way, the unconfined expanse of Kidbrooke, Eltham, Shooter's Hill Wood and the many others besides — Shepherdsleas, Oxleas, Castle, West, and Clothworkers Woods — a good stretch lying to the south-east and extending round to Lee and Mottingham.

"Some evil-disposed persons not only took up the trail but took the trouble to re-lay it in exactly the contrary direction . . . . . . "

("Bell's Life" – October 23rd, 1880).

The pattern of cross-country continued to change. By the 1880's paper-chasing in the form of hare and hounds as the basic routine of cross-country runners was beginning to be superseded by cross-country running of the modern type. In 1898 there is mention of only one paper-chase in "The Gazette", while in 1904, a Club correspondent refers to "an old-fashioned paper-chase" being held — as it has been since in Blackheath once a year on Boxing Day until the recent law against litter compelled the substitution of a "treasure hunt". The emphasis, and one that extended in this decade to all branches of the rapidly organizing sport, was upon competition, and that meant racing. The paper still formed a trail to be laid with skill and so followed, but this was no longer the main point. However, it was never formally dropped but gradually and as it were involuntarily disappeared as fields became larger and lap courses were introduced for the coming cross-country championships out of convenience and necessity. But clubs, as distinct from national and district organizations, continued to exact skill in following trails up to World War Two. In the Club photographs from 1885 onwards — and 1881 is the earliest we have — the foreground is occupied by the holders of a new office — though it is really ex officio — that of Trail Layer. These went out, as they do today, a good leisurely time before the main body of runners to lay out the course to be followed that afternoon. This responsibility is a permanent one of theirs and not as in former days with the hares, a job that was swapped about.

From Tom Crafter, joining in 1882, onwards through the generations the trail had been as the early ones, Crafter, Gale, Culver and the other used to dogmatize, "Well And Truly Laid", and all the rest have maintained it as a tradition: W.S. Smith, N.H. Prior, S.D. Taylor, W.R.J. Clarke down to K.N. Wilcockson today with his fellows. Some of the greatest among these are less than patient with lesser mortals who cannot follow their trails, but they have always had their human side to appeal to ordinary members who seek irreverently to suggest that such a Royal Academy painting as that executed in 1952 by the present-day artist-trail layer, Laurie Norris, is inspired by the hindward views he has obtained of his companions in action, bearing as it does the title "Twilight of The Gods". Assuredly there is a Valhalla somewhere for these doyens of the trail with their accompanying "Fiends-in-knickers" as some reward for our debt to them all through the years. It is a worthy line including such as the giant Crafter and "Bill" Smith, leader of novice packs, oarsman, great lover of the countryside and its people, and, as H.K. Grant has said, a kindly character who did much good behind the scenes in smoothing over troubles. Latest in a numerous line is Keith Wilcockson, a Past-President, yet, "always take my orders from the Captain". Many of the latter have sometimes found it difficult to take him at his word, not realizing at first

KIDBROOK LANE AS IT WAS
when it formed part of the club courses.

that here is nothing more forbidding than a successor to the Crafter tradition. Diffused though their contribution is throughout some ninety years of the Club's history, here where it commenced it seems fitting to digress to celebrate their self-denial, their planning, early attendance and late return — their patient waiting.

In the same way as the function of the "hare" is thus seen to have altered within a short space of time. so too had that of the erstwhile pursuers. They no longer, in short, pursued a hare; if anything, they made after the man in front, for, as intimated above, a sort of "team handicap" system had replaced the old method of running together. The pack system which evolved at this time is not today clearly understood. By allowing the slowest to start first and so upward through packs graded by ability and starting at intervals, its function was to enable the medium runners to work through the slows and the fast ones through both. In this way men who had under-estimated their powers could join up with a faster pack and those who had over-estimated them could drop into a slower one. This was what evolved during the 1880's with the appearance of a considerable number of runners and their organization into "divisions".

There were far more dramatic changes afoot than these, however. The enthusiasm which had arisen for all kinds of sporting activity in the 1860's and 1870's is somewhat comparable to the recent diversification of leisure interests in the western world and the addition of large numbers of alternative sports to the few traditional ones which have dominated the scene up to the last fifteen years. Since the Victorian interest persisted it was obvious that, especially with the serious thoroughness of our forefathers, formal organization would have to follow in order to regulate, channel and establish.

1881 saw the first "National" Cross-country Championship — first in the sense of being in any way truly open to entries from the country as a whole. There had been a number of

W.S. SMITH
Trail Layer and Countryman.

races under the aegis of Thames Hare and Hounds which had been termed "The Cross-Country Championship", but until 1880 these had been confined to a small number of London clubs. The first had been a triangular match at Buckhurst Hill but the trail was lost, and since "some emerged face to face, the race was declared void." These continued for the next few years, the 1879 report in one paper being written by "a well-known athlete who followed the race on horseback". The distance was usually about 11¾ miles and with the runners still following a trail again in 1878 they missed it, cutting off 1½ miles in error. In this race Thames Hare and Hounds were beaten by Spartan Harriers with S.L.H. coming in third. The last of this series in 1880 included the first "outsiders", Moseley Harriers, who won with Birchfield Harriers second, while Blackheath had G.M. Nehan and H.D. Thomas in 5th and 9th places respectively.

When the race became a true championship in 1881 Moseley repeated their victory and continued a run of success for three more years, while after them clubs like Liverpool Harriers, Birchfield, Salford and Manchester Harriers ensured that the Midlands and North dominated it for the rest of the century. In these races and increasingly appeared a new hard spirit of competition and it naturally brought with it new conditions, as evidenced in the changes in courses mentioned above. Not everyone liked it, of course. In "Bell's Life" a letter signed "Exon" voiced what many must have felt at the time in protesting about

THE BLACKHEATH AND SOUTH LONDON HARRIERS TRAIL LAYERS
outside The Swan, West Wickham, 1904. T. Crafter on the left

the course chosen for the first Southern Cross-Country Championship held at the Welsh Harp in 1884 — and indeed that voice is by no means unheard at the present day:

"If steeplechasing is to be only a test of the *running* capabilities of men, it is time that these so-called chasers advertise a gate-money, road-toddling championship; but if they will take on a good steeplechase course, across fair hunting country, and select a dozen from those who scrambled over last Saturday's fences, there could be found, say, half a dozen who would show them a lead, and then will not call themselves champions".

In this same race Blackheath were third behind S.L.H. and Highgate Harriers with yet another of the brilliant constellation of early distance athletes in F.W. Monk who took third individual place. But their chief pride in this was to have supplied the stimulus for the creation of its official organizing body, the Southern Counties Cross-country Association. This had been formed the year before in 1883 with D.T. Mayson as first Secretary to the new Association as well as its moving spirit. When the next year the National Association came into being also, Mayson was the proposer of that motion and again he became the first Secretary. In this meeting at Anderton's Hotel, Fleet Street, where too the first General Committee meeting of the A.A.A. was held in 1880, Mayson was supported by fellow Blackheath members, Reed, J.C. Milligan, A.H. Davies and C. Val Hunter. His motion was opposed by Thames Hare and Hounds and S.L.H., possibly through their antagonism to the suggestion of enclosed courses to obtain gate-money from these championship races. [19]

Mayson had earlier been a member of South London as well as Spartan Harriers before he settled with Blackheath in 1878. Elected in June — at the very meeting which first considered the move to Blackheath — he was made a committee member the following month and proposed the motion that the new Headquarters be "The Green Man". Clearly he made an instantly favourable impression on the Club for by January 1879 he was its Honorary Secretary, an office he held till 1882 when he resigned presumably under the pressure, at first of his new official positions in the new Associations, and subsequently of ill-health.

If we seek an explanation for the Club's dynamic at this period it would seem almost sufficient to find it in this man alone of whom the bare facts bespeak a person of originality and vigour. The debt of the Club, not to mention other bodies, is very great indeed though by now it is next to impossible to rescue his name from the shadows. It is more difficult since, although he continued in influence up to about 1885, he had died by 1891 still quite young. Given more knowledge of the part he played it might very well emerge that he was one of the handful of absolutely outstanding creative administrators the Club has possessed. His contemporaries evidently perceived his quality for they presented him with a 30 guinea diamond ring when he retired from office.

Nor did he supply the only initiative Blackheath gave to the new movement. In the next ten years there were Blackheath Presidents of the S.C.C.A. in Charles Val Hunter, J.E. Fowler-Dixon and C.T.W. Hickman. Fowler-Dixon was the best known of all these to the world at large, for he had been one of the early amateur runners of great distances in this country, holding the 40 and 50 miles records at a time when such doings were entirely exotic and mysterious to the general public, including an aunt of his who asked why it was necessary for him to run so far. A small but genial figure he founded Dixon's Sporting Agency and was Life President of the "Centurions", a member of Thames Hare and Hounds, Honorary Secretary of the original North of the Thames Cross-country Union from 1880 to 1884 and a President of the National Cross-country Union. When he died in 1943 at the age of 93, he was the sole survivor of the original sportsmen who had formed the Amateur Athletic Association at Oxford in 1880 and discussed the amateur definition which led to the prohibition on "mechanic, artisan or labourer" being removed.

Such public participation by the Club at this time is almost too extensive to detail; there were many others, some of whom, like H.J. Barclay, who joined in 1884, attained the highest office. It was their work which was instrumental in establishing the settled climate of modern amateur athletics in this country. Again we have to make a mental effort to visualize the contemporary conditions upon which the governing body succeeded, as the A.A.A. did in 1883, in imposing an authority which ensured that amateurs might only enter competitions approved by that body. It was a gradual and painstaking business like all creation. They had to eradicate all kinds of abuse that persisted from the bad old days. It was yet another Club man, J.H.A. Reay, who detected the incorrect entry form which led to the first suspension effected by the A.A.A. in 1882 and showed that they meant business in suppressing the falsification that was rife in the days when handicap competitions were the norm.

J.H. REAY

The club of Reay's active track years was, as for so many athletes who ran for it as summer members only, London Athletic Club. He joined Blackheath in 1882 together with several of his number, partly because of its winter training and social facilities but also possibly because of London Athletic Club's crisis about this time. He had been A.A.A. High Hurdles Champion in 1877[20] though by all accounts he would not have drawn the approval of modern hurdlers, apparently, from what we can tell, striding rather than hurdling over the obstacles, trailing his leg behind him and so jumping higher over the hurdle. He was an all-rounder to satisfy the most demanding, however, and drank life in full-blooded Irish fashion to the lees. We find him throwing the hammer, winning tricycle races at Brentwood and the Ilex Club Plunge two years in succession, with a best of 54ft. 7 , winning the long jump in the Civil Service Championships, and, presumably by way of recreation, serving as Secretary of the British Anglers' Society. When members were characterized by various Shakespeare quotations in a "Gazette" article later, his was from "Two Gentlemen of Verona": "A fine volley of words, gentlemen, and quickly shot off", which gives us a splendid impression of an upholder of the Irish reputation for articulateness, even if we lacked Crafter's testimony: "One of the best after-dinner speakers we ever had". His lasting reputation, though, rested on yet other qualities as an anonymous versifier has commemorated: *"He dances and sings with a merry air, With an Irish accent so perfectly rare, And voice so splendidly mellow".*

He deserved a Club medal for the number of times incalculable that he sang "Phil The Fluter's Ball" during his Blackheath career and this is how they always remembered him:

"The Gazette" said once that a member travelled eighty miles on the off-chance of hearing him do it. Four of his sons ran in the Boys' Race on different 'Blackheath Days'; he himself ran cross-country with the[21] Club up to 1897; though many members dared at this formal Victorian period to hold pipes while the Club Photo was being taken, only he had the admirable Irish cheek to actually be snapped for that ceremony smoking a cigarette; he signed his notes "Ever Thine". Hadn't he the Gaiety! What a man!

Reay was but one of the more scintillating stars of Club entertainment in what must have seemed a veritable galaxy of talent to a member joining the company in the Blackheath Concert Hall or the warm Club Room at "The Green Man", after a post-race settler of gin and ginger such as was introduced to A.C. Telfer ("We have only known one abstainer who was anywhere in the first flight of cross-country runners", quoth Walter Rye). The theatre was the main entertainment for London and well before the end of the century there was a theatre or music-hall within easy reach of every part of the metropolis. Like all good Londoners, Blackheath Harriers needed no introduction to the delights of popular song nor, like all good Victorians, to the virtues of self-help in providing one's own entertainment. It was during the flourishing years of "The Green Man" that many of the nation's most celebrated figures were "on the Halls": Dan Leno, Vesta Tilley, Marie Lloyd, Albert Chevalier, Florrie Ford, Little Tich and Harry Tate — and while the Club's performers would laugh at being bracketed with such troupers, nevertheless they could put on such a show as did not disgrace them. "Bell's Life" described their social evenings as "enlivened by the excellent music and singing for which this Club is so justly famous". From the first months at "The Green Man", through the early eighties, from 1883 onwards, with crowds a hundred strong, with County and Borough Members' patronage for the Smoking Concerts and even original compositions dedicated to the Club like the "Harriers' Gallop" composed and played by H.V. Lewis (R.A.M.) the Blackheath entertainments were among the Club's most attractive features. So popular did they become that the Concert Room was crowded out and over-heated with the press of folk so that arrangements were made to use a larger room on the ground floor in the Gay 'Nineties.

Everything spoke of expansion and an expansive way of life. With Viscount Lewisham and Baron de Worms among the Vice-Presidents, 200 members on the books by 1883, the balance sheet "in a most prosperous condition" and Reed as President following the death of Oastler[22] Blackheath was set fair and grew from its former character of a private family party to a great public sporting institution yet without losing the best of its inheritance.

"Look, my boys! Take my advice, stick to athletics, and KEEP OUT OF THE WOODS!"

(C. Val Hunter to a party of Blackheath Harriers).[23]

In 1882 the demon Spofforth took 14 wickets for 90 runs and "The Sporting Times" reported ironically, "The body of England was cremated and the Ashes taken to Australia". The most perceptive no doubt failed to see that these were also the ashes of the old amateurism with all its pristine innocence, the significance of whose loss we are only realizing today when amateur sport in the international field is a hotbed of controversy and the ancient Greek Olympic festival as a truce to conflict is mocked. Spofforth was only one of the new rising aristocracy of expertise which developed into modern professionalism and whose sheer efficiency and skill were to set an almost unbridgeable divide between them and the amateur. The 1880's saw the start of this process which is still growing today and

SMOKING CONCERT,

In Large Hall, at 7.45 p.m.

Chairman - - - - Mr. J. H. A. REAY.
Vice-Chairman - - - Mr. A. J. FOWDEN.
Musical Directors - - Messrs. WALTER & PONSFORD.

PROGRAMME.

Mr. E. W. Edwards will sing .. { "Tommy Atkins." / "Two Grenadiers." }

Mr. Hal. Godwin will sing .. { "Tableaux Vivants." / "P'raps, P'raps Not." }

Mr. Hunter will sing .. .. { "The Romany Lass." }

Messrs. Edwards & Morris will sing { "Excelsior." }

Messrs. Hunter & Rushforth will sing { "Army and Navy." }

Mr. James Ponsford will sing .. { "The British Lion." }

Mr. F. H. Norman (*Violin Solo*) .. { "Tarantella." }

Mr. J. F. Ponsford will sing .. { "The Sons of the Sword." }

Mr. Edmund Roche will sing { "Time is Money." / "Winkle's Wedding." }

Mr. W. J. Rushforth will sing { "The Deathless Army." }

Mr. Horace Sims will sing .. { "I didn't till afterwards." / "The long and the short of it." }

Mr. C. Spencer West (*Flute Solo*) .. { Selection from / "An Artist's Model." }

Mr. Arthur Cranch will sing.. .. { "The Gallants of England." / "The Buccaneer." }

Accompanist - - Mr. RUSHTON O'DELL.

COMING EVENTS.

January. "The Rowland Cup." 10 Miles Yacht Handicap.
,, 28. Annual Dance at St. Martin's Town Hall.
September 5. Annual Athletic Meeting at Catford.

Blackheath Harriers.

7 Miles Inter-Club Handicap

WITH THE

SOUTH LONDON HARRIERS,

Saturday, 11th January, 1896

Officials.

Starter and Timekeeper—C. VAL. HUNTER, B.H.

Judges.

GORDON C. INNES, S.L.H., A. J. FOWDEN, S.L.H., R. B. BALDRY, B.H., and G. HAMAR JACKSON, B.H.

Referee—J. H. A. REAY, B.H.

Handicapper—ARTHUR COOK, B.H.

HANDICAP.

		min.	sec.				min.	sec.
1	E. Gavin, S.L.H.		Scratch	19	E. C. Pulbrook, S.L.H.		3	20
2	C. E. Haydon, S.L.H.		55	20	B. H. Willis, S.L.H.		3	20
3	A. E. Magill, S.L.H.	1	0	21	S. Lanyon, S.L.H.		3	30
4	B. Lawford, S.L.H.	1	5	22	E. F. Vowles, B.H.		3	45
5	S. H. Yoxall, S.L.H.	1	20	23	W. Yeo, S.L.H.		3	45
6	F. L. Rowles, S.L.H.	1	25	24	S. T. Pugh, B.H.		3	45
7	P. Titley, S.L.H.	1	45	25	P. Mouchot, B.H.		3	50
8	H. C. Burrows, B.H.	2	0	26	H. T. Haydon, S.L.H.		4	25
9	J. P. Arkell, S.L.H.	2	10	27	M. Z. Kuttner, S.L.H.		4	30
10	F. H. Godwin, B.H.	2	15	28	E. Knott, S.L.H.		4	35
11	H. W. E. Sercombe, B.H.	2	35	29	W. C. A. Landon, S.L.H.		4	35
12	T. C. Davis, B.H.	2	45	30	F. W. Crimp, S.L.H.		4	45
13	E. F. Moates, S.L.H.	2	45	31	F. G. Shortland, S.L.H.		5	0
14	F. Stephens, B.H.	2	50	32	A. V. Morris, B.H.		5	15
15	H. Simpson, B.H.	2	55	33	H. Baillie, B.H.		5	25
16	J. W. Palmer, B.H.	3	0	34	W. T. Colter, B.H.		5	45
17	S. A. Musson, S.L.H.	3	15	35	C. F. Warren, B.H.		5	45
18	E. F. Nicholls, B.H.	3	20	36	G. T. Burch, S.L.H.		7	20

1st 2nd 3rd. 4th.
Time mins. secs.

45

these early years showed an increasing number of outstanding performers who, as John Arlott in his essay on Sport in "Edwardian England" has said, "represented the transition from lighthearted to expert play". Of these it was Blackheath's good fortune to possess several who assisted in making the Club's name known more and more widely in the ensuing decade though it may be questioned whether their influence was not more daunting than encouraging upon the ordinary Club member.

In this respect the early history of the oldest Club Trophy extant, the Club Five Miles Challenge Cup, is an illustration both of the class distance runners they possessed at the time and of the essential differences there seemed to be between them and their fellow Blackheath mortals. The Cup competitions date from 1880 and for many years they differed materially from those held since. The term "Challenge", whose significance today is largely ignored, is a reminder of the original nature of the competition when, at shorter intervals than that of a year, the holder of the Cup could be challenged to defend it by a member; thus names appeared on it then more frequently than today. What is not generally realized is that any one race today outnumbers several of the fields of that time put together − not because modern numbers are so much greater but simply because the majority of Blackheath runners did not enter them. The entire field indeed did not exceed half a dozen for several years. In the first race held, of the five entries only three started; in 1884 the winner had a walkover; in 1888 there were only five running. The others simply did not bother, being certain not to win. They competed, of course, but in other races; in other words, it was in a real sense a challenge cup.

The ordinary Club runner took part in the cross-country handicaps of which there was more than an ample profusion, including the Club's own continued with even more signal success without break from the Peckham days. They called this a steeplechase and its distance was a standard one of four and three quarter miles. It remained a fixture run over the same course until − shadow of the future falling − the encroachment of railway and builder compelled them to abandon it after the 1895-96 season, since when the distance has been five miles. At about this same time it merged with the Challenge Cup race and was held, as today, once a year only because of the increasing number of team races. This latter fact is a reminder of the individual nature of contests in these early years, team races as we recognize them only starting to appear regularly in the mid-eighties. Prominent among those early ventures were the Club's races against Oxford and Cambridge Universities, the latter often said to be the oldest inter-club fixture sustained anywhere and still continuing.[24] This was first run in 1884 and was apparently one of the last occasions when Reed took the field, the fixture being fostered by the then Cambridge Captain, R.R. Conway, who later joined Blackheath and subsequently encouraged P.H. Francis in his running development. Crafter, now a seasoned member first encouraged by newspaper reports in the early eighties that he "showed good form for a novice", was the prime mover in the 1886 Oxford fixture − literally so, for, as he later recalled, "I had some difficulty in getting together a team to leave their offices early enough to go so far". The Club won in this novel venture by 23 points to 32, the weighty Crafter, more at home in the water than on land, excelling himself by coming 10th, and the teams dining in hall at Merton.

At Blackheath the Open Steeplechases regularly attracted entries of well over a hundred − in 1884 a hundred and thirty-two, of whom only nineteen failed to start. In these races the Club sometimes formed as much as a third of the field, and there were handsome prizes paid for from the handsome receipts of entries.

The entry fee for the Challenge Cup at the time may well have been a strong deterrent to all but the most ambitious or most likely, standing as it did at the fairly massive Victorian sum of half a crown. The Open Handicaps on the other hand continued to draw fields that twice beat the record for the number of entrants and starters for this type of race, while in January, 1884, the first Ten Miles Steeplechase was held, forerunner of the Rowland Cup Competition. But the Challenge Cup remained the preserve of Blackheath's athletic "aristocracy" — for four years a trio composed of C. Cattlin, G.M. Nehan and the famous W.G. George. S. Golder, though, together with J.C. Milligan, who was a prominent Club official until he departed for the British Consulate in Zurich, took part in races held before 1884 in which year the monopoly of the three was ended.

These three were all obviously fine runners by the standards of any age. Cattlin, the first name on the Challenge Cup, though never winning the same public recognition as the other two, nonetheless won this trophy five times between 1880 and 1886, more than Nehan and George who were national champions. Even though we may add one or two pounds in allowance for the muscular standards no doubt informing Crafter's description of Cattlin as of "somewhat frail physique", he must have impressed them in his day. But with such tough opposition he could not succeed in obtaining the gold medal which was awarded instead of the customary silver for three successive wins.

A press reference early in the 1880's described G.M. Nehan as "the greatest cross-country runner in the London area". Besides setting up an unbeaten record for the classic two and a quarter mile circuit of the Heath of 11 minutes 6 seconds, he is remembered outside the Club too for his A.A.A. Four Miles Championship won in 1881 with a time of 20 minutes and 26 seconds. Crafter, writing in 1928, thought him possibly the best distance runner the Club had ever had.

To C.G. Wood, however, this title belonged to W.G. George whom he called simply "the Great One". Certainly it is this man who has come down to us as a legend. The record shows that he bestrode the by no means petty world of his athletic rivals like a Colossus: ten A.A.A. Championships and in addition two won in 1879 before the A.A.A. was formed, with four second places; twice in these winning the 880, mile and four miles on the Saturday afternoon and the ten miles race on the Monday; a setter of British records at 1000 yards, one, two, four and sixteen miles; winner of two National Cross-country Championships; reliably recorded as running a mile at Surbiton on a track six yards over the distance in 4 minutes 10 seconds — this in 1885; and withal no athletic automaton but a very human person and a considerable humorist. No doubt the song on the occasion of the Complimentary Dinner given him in 1883 after his success in America was of a different kind from the anthems he intoned as a treble chorister at Worcester Cathedral when a boy. When he finished 13th in a Blackheath 4¾ miles steeplechase that year the press remarked that he was "in anything but condition consequent upon the way his friends have persisted in feting him lately". After the A.A.A. reluctantly refused his application to run as an amateur against the best man of the time, the professional Cummings — an important case, by the way, at this juncture — he renounced his status in order to beat his opponent over one and ten miles, winning both at Lillie Bridge in 1886 — the former in a world's record of 4 minutes

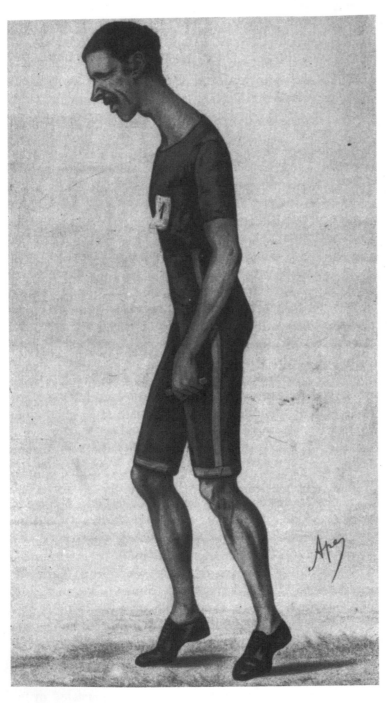

W.G. GEORGE as seen by the celebrated caricaturist **'APE'**.

12¾ seconds.[25] He had then to resign from the Club, to which he had been introduced by Cattlin in 1882, but he always maintained his connection with Blackheath up to the 1930's without rancour and with affection. There was more than the link of the mile record between his approach and that of the modern world represented by Sydney Wooderson whom he congratulated at Motspur Park in 1937, for there was in George's training the modern champion's seriousness and application. He has told how, training in 1882, he would walk twice a week from Shepherd's Bush to Wimbledon where he would run eleven miles then walk back again, a round trip of 25 miles — though at Wimbledon before returning there was alleviation afforded by warm, spiced port, a chop or steak and a tankard of beer. Tall, lean, and, as Shearman tells us, with "a prodigious stride", he was a practiser of the training system of running at varying speeds which we today know as "Fartlek".

In a letter written years later to "The Morning Post" George recalled the thoroughness as well as the originality with which he approached his training: ". . . When I first became prominent in the athletic world, I was soon convinced that most of the existing records were beatable, and in consequence I made a complete

48

list of those I considered the easiest to lower, and the best way to attempt it. There were very few books then to help one, and no trainers, coaches, or anyone else to rely on for advice etc. When at last I had absolutely convinced myself, I made known my list and plans to my friends and associates. I was more or less ridiculed, and my ideas were pronounced impossible".

Not only was he ahead of his contemporaries in his training philosophy but, as something of a "card" he was, we suspect, not above employing what is today familiarly known as "gamesmanship" upon his opponents. As Conway later recalled of that first Blackheath match against Cambridge University, George, after changing in a cab on the way from the station, apparently toyed with his opposition. After vainly trying to run him off his feet and tearing along at his side "teeth clenched and corks gripped" they were finally shattered in morale by his calm comment of "Jolly day, isn't it?" followed by appreciative observations concerning the countryside through which they were passing.

W.G. GEORGE AND SYDNEY WOODERSON
world mile record, 1937   (Sport and General)

It was possibly through George that the Club enjoyed a connection at this time with the now defunct Moseley Harriers [26] whose victory in the 1883 National Cross-country was honoured by a dinner given by Blackheath. This was after a race in which the first man home for the Club was A.H. Davies who had suffered at George's hands previously in finishing second to him in the 1880 A.A.A. Four Miles and was to endure the same fate again the following year as had H.D. Thomas in finishing 3rd to George in the 1881 A.A.A. Mile.

49

By now the growing popularity of the Cross-country Championship was reflected in the complaints about the thousands on the course, including horsemen, hampering the judges at the finish.

Over the country in the 1880's the man who probably best deserves remembrance today is J.B. Nash. "Found" by Tom Crafter at a Wednesday evening run of Lennox Rugby Football Club at Dulwich he was drawn to "The Green Man" and started to make his presence felt in 1886 by winning the Challenge Cup. Having failed to finish in the scoring six in the Southern the previous year, he did not fail to do so again in completing a remarkable series of ten Southerns in succession for Blackheath. A comparable feat was accomplished by G.M. Harris in winning the Challenge Cup eleven times between 1890 and 1896. Whatever the quality of his opposition it was remarkable enough as a demonstration of consistency, though not to match the career of T.C. Davis, who, joining in 1887, was to continue running effectively indeed for the next forty years.

At the time Trevor Davis started, J.F. Ponsford had received the mantle of George and Co., for not only was he three times winner of the Challenge Cup but he was the Blackheath "scratch" man on the track during the 'eighties. Ponsford was one of the great foundation laid in this period of members who were to give a life-time of service to the Club. Described as possessing "illimitable pluck" and as being one of the

A racing career of 40 years.
TREVOR DAVIS in his seventies

Club's best Cross-country Captains he carried his ability successively into such offices as Secretary, his chairmanship of the new-formed Entertainments Committee set up in 1920, and, ultimately, the Presidency where he impressed L. Pendered as not only genial but "looking a presidential figure", after forty years of membership. He was also a member of the Ibis Club, another with whom Blackheath had a long and fruitful connection.

The alteration undergone by cross-country in this period by changing radically from the paper-chasing routine to the discipline of training by packs and regular competition over standard distances marked by a paper trail together with the more serious attitude adopted towards competition and training by some of those described above was paralleled not surprisingly by a similar development in track athletics generally. Whereas in the 1870's the Club had produced only one first rank runner in H.D. Thomas, in the eighties there was a number and the decade saw an increasing and successful participation in first class track athletics. The track and cross-country success of the 1880's provide the readiest signs of the Club's development. In addition to those already mentioned there was an abundance of talent of the second order as for example, F.H. Denman, 3rd in the A.A.A. Steeplechase, a track event, in 1886, and, in the same year, C.A. Morgan, 3rd in the Four Miles, but obtaining greater subsequent credit in thirty years of official work for the Club. It was said that he did not once fail to attend an annual general meeting from 1884 to 1930, and to-day he is remembered as the donor of the Club Two Miles Championship Cup. In the old days he was more often celebrated in his nickname of "Play Light", which he earned by admonishing the most raucous members when things became more than usually obstreperous with the words, "Play Light, Lads"

Of the more notable performers J.M. Cowie, a Scottish Champion, was the best sprinter, his ability extending to the quarter mile. After twice being runner-up in the A.A.A. 100 Yards he won both it and the 440 Yards in two successive years, 1883 and 1884, winning the hundred again the following year and coming second in the 440.

"To Cowie and Wood," wrote their contemporary Shearman, "the·quarter is really a sprint and nothing else". The medium-sized Cowie was to be supplanted by his Blackheath fellow, Wood, "the fastest farmer in history", winner of the gold watch made from two coins by the King of the Belgians and presented with it by that monarch for an international victory. More to the serious point, he was the first Englishman to beat fifty seconds for a quarter mile, which he did in 1886, having been runner-up to Cowie in both 100 and 440 yards two years before. His performance of 49 4/5 seconds was achieved luckily

C.G. WOOD - 'The Flying Farmer'
First man to beat 22 secs. For 220 yards
First man to beat 50 secs. For 440 yards

for Wood in a straight final for he had already run two rounds of the 100 yards to finish second in that event, and he repeated both of these feats in 1887. With best times of 31.5 seconds for 300 yards and 21.8 for the 220 — a time which stood a long while before Wood himself was first on to the track to congratulate the fine sprinter, Willie Applegarth, on beating it in 1913 — the Norfolk man with the "bright blue eyes" was Blackheath President in 1911-12 and a life-long supporter.

Field events suffered even more neglect then than present-day practitioners complain of. [27] E.H. Horwood might win the A.A.A. Long Jump with 21 feet 9 inches — but greater acclaim was reserved for such as W. Birkett when defeating W.G. George in the Championship 880 yards, H.D. Thomas having persuaded the former to try this event. A brother of the one-time Secretary, G.H. Birkett, he himself joined in 1882 and is a notable example of the multitude of members who hold to the Club long after their active days, which Birkett did until his death in 1947. With such talent available from which to form a team it was small wonder that in an early and rare inter-club track match as that held at Birmingham against the formidable champions, Moseley Harriers, in 1883, and repeated the following year also,

Blackheath should run them to within six points.

The modest private undertaking at Peckham had indeed long before the eighties ended advanced to become a national sporting institution, and as the Club was by about 1885 so it would essentially remain cast in the same mould well into the period of recovery from the 1914-18 War.

In the series of photographs surviving from the period we can trace the emergence of the Club in aspects recognizably akin even to those of today. Then they were evidently taken twice yearly; Crafter boasted of being the only one to appear in each photo from 1883 to 1920 — "And in uniform too!" In 1881, "the Photographic Group", as it was known, is best characterized by the words of "An Ancient Heathen", probably Crafter again, who wrote in 1918, "In the old days the Club was one great family with one father in the person of the late Fred. H. Reed, and all the rest just brothers — some older and some younger, but just brothers of varying ages". This certainly suggests itself very strongly in the 1881 picture[28] with its effect of haphazard informality, most of them cheerfully relaxed with no great sense of its being an official act or ritual in spite of one or two who are determined to make it an occasion. The only uniform feature of those in running kit is the home-made badge, which in any case not all are wearing and whose size on the chests of those who do carry it varies from a few inches to a foot wide.

By 1883 Reed is seated formally and officially at the centre — he was President by now, of course — of a larger and more tidily clad and disposed group. It has the look for the first time of a real Club as distinct from a crowd, while in the picture of 1887 this sense is even more strongly reinforced. They are symmetrically placed in tiers and rows with one line on chairs; all present full-face to the camera and, in short, they are arranged. Furthermore with but three exceptions they wear the same size of badge of entwined squares and the same number are all dressed in the Club's black uniform.[29]

The 1893 photograph has the appearance of long establishment and, as might be expected, has the greatest resemblance to those of modern times for by then, as now, the Club had had time for men to grow old with it and there are thus more men of middle and greater age and the whole range therefore of living generations. We know almost all of their names — as we do of so many of their predecessors, but with a few exceptions like Reed — tucked self-effacingly away on the left, yet with some of the most responsible-looking members surrounding him — we cannot attach these names to the faces. It is a lesson we now and future Blackheath men should learn from.

The process of change here is partly suggested by the increasing incidence of uniformity of dress, and merely from what has been said of these photographs something can be inferred of the history of the badge and the all-black running kit that became the mark of Blackheath. The badge was adopted in 1878 no doubt to signalize the move and to give them a sense of identity in their new surroundings. Variously said to have been suggested by H.D. Thomas and F.H. Reed its origin or symbolism, if there is any — it may have been selected purely as a design — is unknown. Numerous suggestions have been made citing precedents ranging from China to Rome, while an interesting coincidence was pointed out in "The Gazette" of a Roman tessellated pavement excavated in Bucklersbury in 1869 which embodied the entwined squares — not be it noted, one superimposed upon another. Some have gone so far as to assert that Reed, taking natural interest in such matters as an architect, saw and adopted it, but there is no substantiation of this. The reason for a new badge was the nature of the old one which, it will be recalled, was in the form of a monogram inapplicable after the change of name. Certainly the facts that Reed was both an architect and a freemason would make his acquaintance probable with a symbol that is by no means uncommon and it is possible that he was concerned in its choice. Whatever the original significance it symbolizes sufficiently to us the Club's continuity and unity despite the transference of ground.

The black uniform came more gradually, as indeed did the principle of team or club colours generally to all clubs. Probably the greater number of individual competitors and, even more, the appearance of team contests over the country were the first impetus for their adoption, for we have seen how the emphasis on individual competition was accompanied by each athlete wearing colours that were anything but uniform. Certainly the first team races as a regular kind of fixture commence in the early eighties and run parallel in their increase with that of the number of Club uniforms worn by members. On the track at this period black very commonly is a constituent in Blackheath attire until by 1888 for members the former technicoloured appearance has disappeared, so that in the Club meeting that year only six in an entry of thirty-nine in the Members' 880 Handicap are not dressed in Club uniform, and even they are pusillanimously in white apart from the odd maroon rebel.

The blue and white ingredient in the Club colours is, by the way, a commemoration of the Peckham uniform but early on the agreed shade was lightened to a royal blue, presumably to show distinctly against its black background. Thus after about ten years of the new translation had elapsed, members could purchase running drawers of cashmere for four shillings and sixpence or be lavish in Italian cloth for three pence extra; the badge was of blue and white silk for one and sixpence and there was a cricket cap with badge, a specimen of which is visible in an 1887 photo of the Club, "optional and intended more for men when up river etc".

The position for the badge was evidently likewise a matter for personal taste, the centre of the chest being originally favoured, but though today it now seems to have settled there have been moments of doubt quite recently as to the rule governing its disposition, as one Lloyd's member was anxious to celebrate in a letter to "The Gazette":

"Allow me to compliment the Committee on the unique position they have selected for the Club badge on the uniform — the left breast of the knickerbockers (vide Rule 15 in the new Book of Rules). Strikes me as being a really original idea . . . . . ."

CLUB GROUP - 1881

CLUB GROUP - 1887

CLUB GROUP - 1893

BLACKHEATH HARRIERS

Head Quarters: "GREEN MAN" HOTEL, BLACKHEATH HILL.

CROSS-COUNTRY FIXTURES, 1888-9
TWENTIETH SEASON.

1888.

* Oct. 6. Opening Run (Blackheath).

„ 20. 2¼ MILES MEMBERS' HANDICAP and Ordinary Run (Blackheath).

* Nov. 3. Ordinary Run (Blackheath).

„ 10. Inter-Club Run with Ranelagh Harriers at Putney.

„ 17. 4¾ MILES MEMBERS' STEEPLECHASE HANDICAP (Blackheath).

* Dec. 1. CHALLENGE CUP RACE and Ordinary Run (Blackheath)

„ 8. (Tower R. & A.C. Open Steeplechase).

* „ 15. Ordinary Run (Blackheath).

* „ 29. Ordinary Run (Blackheath).

1889.

Jan. 12. 7 MILES MEMBERS' STEEPLECHASE HANDICAP (Blackheath).

„ 26. Inter-Club Run with Ranelagh Harriers (Blackheath).

(Finchley Harriers' Open Steeplechase).

Feb. 2. (Lewisham H. and H. Open Steeplechase).

„ 9. 4¾ MILES MEMBERS' STEEPLECHASE HANDICAP (Blackheath).

(Highgate Harriers' Open Steeplechase).

„ 16. SOUTHERN COUNTIES' CHAMPIONSHIP.

* „ 23. Ordinary Run (Blackheath).

Mar. 9. 1 MILE MEMBERS' HANDICAP and Ordinary Run (Blackheath).

* „ 23 CHALLENGE CUP RACE and Ordinary Run (Blackheath)

FIXTURE LIST 1888 - 89

"We rely upon a well-balanced combination of active members and old fossils".
(Fred. H. Reed at the Annual Dinner - 1902.)

"We can, however, speak from an experience now covering nearly twenty years, and we can positively say that we know of no man of the hundreds with whom we have been acquainted who has been injured by distance running, and the rate of mortality among running men is singularly small".
(Walter Rye in "Athletics and Foot Ball" - The Badminton Library - 1888).

"Our merry Harriers will be found careering across the famous heath and the ploughed and green fields".
("The Club Gazette and Club Record" - 1904).

It is about now that we get the sense of something going wrong — at any rate by contrast with the possibilities of the eighties and the rich future they promised and certainly as regards the cross-country of the Club which did not pick up proportionately but remained in an indifferent state almost up to the First World War. It may be to apply modern attitudes inappropriately but it seems to us at this distance that the signs which had been so strong of outward-looking virility and enterprise were missing in the 1890's, together with the competitive participation in the great developments they themselves had such a hand in launching. They were content to continue as they were, even priding themselves on their lack of susceptibility to change, ignoring as they did Gibbon's truth that all that is human is retrograde if it does not advance. Possibly those who handled the Club's affairs were less realistic than their fore-runners; also, one senses that their rivals in competition were nearer in attitude to modern times, not to mention the likes of W.G. George, in their willingness to sweat a little over training. Already it was not as easy as in the past to achieve good results by a weekly run supplemented by some walking. This inward-looking and rather parochial attitude persisted for many years: one has a strong sense in surveying their words and activities that they seldom seemed to think they had anything to learn from the outside, and while a loyal Blackheath Harrier can agree with as well as be amused by the words of a Blackheath Crafter — "We of the Blackheath Harriers *KNOW* about these things" — he can also recognize the dangers implicit in them. Still, it may be that the above view of the 1890's is a falsely simplified one: after all, the field of competition was widening at this time so that perhaps any decline in Blackheath standards was relative rather than absolute, certainly in respect of track participation. In any case, possibly we today judge too competitively by standards of public success whereas these are clearly not the aim of members at this stage of the Club's history. Their criteria and aims were different, "domestic bliss' - of "The Green Man" variety — rather than any dynamic policy described their values, and together with it something of the complacency that comes with settled and established habits such as they now enjoyed. Then too the forceful initiators had by then receded — both athletes of the calibre of Cattlin, Nehan and Thomas, all still members nonetheless, and administrators like Mayson and Milligan. In analysing this elusive period at the end of the century it is best to confess that one simply cannot be sure of explanations. We have less contemporary material from which to draw conclusions and too, no doubt, as is usually the case, a complexity of factors forms the truth. Among these are the possibilities that Blackheath was now getting more sportsmen of generalized interests and purely social inclinations than formerly, but fewer dedicated running specialists and that the efficiency of other contemporary clubs was increasing while others were emerging, thus vitiating the near monopoly of London talent Blackheath had established for a short time.

Once again also, it is unwise to judge without reference to historical context. What we have said of Blackheath professional historians have said of the age. There had been struggles for both Club and society as a whole up to this time; now both of these had largely faded, certainly in respect of the struggle against extinction that could have been the lot of the little Peckham Club just as the burning ethical battles of the Victorian era had died, even if much still remained to be desired and done. There were signs of the social groupings becoming less inflexible in two different forms — the movement of organized labour to secure better working conditions and the resentment of an emerging lower middle class against the privileged advantages of the governing class and the associated mercantile middle class. Yet though a new and undreamt-of world was stirring, a faint suspicion of disquiet could infect only the more percipient at the appearance of Ford's first car in 1893 or the signal Locomotive Highways Act of 1896 abolishing the hated red flag and raising the speed limit to 14 m.p.h.[30]

As for the ordinary amateur sportsmen of Blackheath who had grown up in the unselfconscious pleasure of engaging in their pastime without cloying trace of any modern neurosis of standards, they had perhaps lost that early innocence by seeing themselves weighed in the balances of competition with class athletes drawn from far wider areas than they had ever thought of contending with in the pre-historic Peckham past. The business of measurement had started and the notion of inferiority had been thus implanted. Still, sport for sport's sake was everywhere the watchword of amateur sportsmen and Blackheath members could very well find their satisfactions elsewhere, in the important part played by individual members in the administration of the sport, for example, for this was something that did not weaken. The tradition was continued by such as Arthur Cook who, after five years as Secretary of the Southern C.C.A., commenced in 1893, was President of that Association at the turn of the century. Just so have modern times found the tradition of public service maintained in the contemporaneous Presidencies of Northern and Southern Cross-country Associations held respectively by C.W. Starnes and A.D. Thwaites.

There was in any case for the men of the nineties a sense of satisfaction in the reflected glory of the achievements of the previous decade which by the new century was to take on the semblance of a golden age whose memory was jealously cherished. Even when present feats demanded due credit as in the period leading up to the Great War, to their annoyance several athletes — cross-country rather than track men — could find themselves undervalued by certain sections of the Club harking back to an age before the gods had died.

One undoubted glory continued in even greater splendour than before in the shape of the "Blackheath Day". If one were vouchsafed glimpses of the Club's past one spectacle worth beholding would be that institution, as it had become by the late eighties, the foundations of which had been soundly laid in the Peckham days. They could rightly be proud of those colourful gatherings which had continued as part of the new life and which were held at Stamford Bridge with its lines of trees, clipped turf and clockwise track, and even more memorably at the Private Banks Ground at Catford Bridge, "verdant and peaceful in its summer setting", as one 'Gazette' correspondent described it. The Press called these meetings, "The Ascot and Goodwood of athletics", and there, in addition to nearly every contemporary athlete of any note in the Open races, would be a "brilliant galaxy" of spectators, the ladies' dresses and the multi-coloured garb of the runners combining to create a splendid kaleidoscope of colour in what was all too often a drab age.

In those perfect summers of dusty calm there would be the white and cream straw hats with Club hatbands, the latter considered most important. Occasionally a bowler hat would be worn by a competitor, as H.F. Pash related, but this was not considered good form with running clothes. Some would wear a short coat for the safe-keeping of their valuables, or else a light overcoat so as not to betray immodest legs to Victorian eyes. Pash remembered being driven out "with withering words" by Gordon Innes of S.L.H. when he strayed across the bounds of etiquette and the reserved enclosure in running clothes. Not so grim a fate as met the Americans who by now were coming to compete at Stamford Bridge and, appearing all on the track in gaily coloured dressing gowns for the hot day, caused the Cockney crowd to become "almost incapacitated with laughter".

A number of the small neat, light grey or blue programmes have survived and they suggest the same crisp organization for which the Club had always been praised. There is a large and varied body of officials listed, reinforced at times with a professional time-keeper as was the custom often, and these, while adding colour to the scene with their rosettes, would clearly, one feels, have run a meeting of today with ease and efficiency. The programme of music to be played during the afternoon by the band of the 2nd Middlesex Rifles under Mr. H. Lambert or by the Coldstream Guards is published there with the popular Arthur Sullivan's selections well to the fore and backing from Verdi, "Carmen", Waldteufel and such exotica as "Electric Post", "Mynheer Van Dunck" and Lumbye's "Krolls Ball Klange". As the cornet solo sent the strains of "The Lost Chord" across the clipped and immaculate turf a dozen heats in one sprint event or else a field of close on five score spread around the track in the Open Mile Handicap would wing their oblivious and single-minded way. Often there would be an international flavour rare in those days as when a party of Americans from New York competed, and, in 1892, when New Zealanders competed in the sprints and hurdles.

The men of the nineties would certainly have looked askance at any criticism of their doings — most of all of their vitality. It was in many ways a thriving time when, besides the "Rowland Cup" of 1896, there were numerous track trophies presented by members, all still competed for today. The "Barclay-Esson" for the Club Half Mile Championship, dating from 1890, is the oldest of the set and commemorates two Honorary Secretaries of the time. The "Rampley" 100 Yards Challenge Cup came from a donor who up to his death in his 90th year never omitted to send a message to the winner, the first of whom, H.G. Brockman, was himself to be a celebrated modern "Trophy name" — while Rampley's own finely bearded Victorian face appeared in several photos long after the end of his career as Surgery Beadle at the London Hospital. The "Walter" Steeplechase Cup was first competed for in 1896, and was won for the next two years by another future A.A.A. Secretary, H.F. Pash whom the Committee invited to join them in 1896, "feeling that some young and active members were required", as the minutes said. And indeed, whatever we may think of the nineties, the last years of the century saw the advent of brisker men who would not leave the club to rest in any doldrums: Nicholls, Pash, Rat-

THE PRIVATE BANKS GROUND, CATFORD BRIDGE
A club evening meeting

cliff and a man, H.W.G. Haslegrave, to whom the Club owed a considerable debt for something more than simply the best efficiency but who appears at this distance to have been treated by them with something less than his due in the controversy which led to his partial severance from the Club.

The loyalty of a very intense and sometimes blind nature to Blackheath which manifested itself long before the end of the century in men's reference to it as "The Old Club" has had its adverse side where the conduct of executive business is in question, as the circumstances of Haslegrave's retirement from official work, not in itself an isolated instance, make all too plain. It has tended to be a very hard master to its officers just because it puts the Club interest before any consideration of the individual's circumstances or private needs. There have been occasions when despite extenuating circumstances and high service in the past such individuals have found themselves unjustly treated. This is to underline somewhat starkly an unfavourable aspect of the Club's most distinguishing characteristic. It is not to say that in the larger view Blackheath would have been better without it, for it has existed and maintained itself by virtue of an emotive loyalty which, at once uncritical and intolerant, is nevertheless a very remarkable achievement in its own right and without which — granted the aid of ever so much cool administrative and businesslike planning — there is every reason to doubt if the Club could maintain itself for very long. It is such considerations

61

'BLACKHEATH DAY'. one of the celebrated club meetings as seen by S.T. DADD

62

which make one reluctant to level unqualified adverse criticism at a stage of Blackheath's story like the 1890's when there emerged this intense tradition of allegiance to the Club which is perhaps Blackheath's greatest and most characteristic achievement.

In cross-country on the other hand there was a real and a steady decline which again is difficult to account for save by the absence of the stars of the previous decade. There was plenty for the pessimist then and the morbid modern now to frown upon: the winning of "wooden spoons" in the Southerns of the time; the compelled rejection of an invitation to compete in France from the Stade Francais because a strong enough team could not be raised at that date — but an unusual enough invitation, for it would have been the first time an English cross-country side had visited the Continent; the poor attendances at some of the committee meetings; the depressing debate over whether the Club should withdraw from the Southern Championships, though this was not out of despair but was a protest at suspected malpractices by other teams of the time. Even reports of the Club matches they enjoyed more than any of the Championship races were at times fearfully glum, as at Cambridge in 1892 with a South Polar air: Sercombe lost in a blizzard "and all the men terribly done up". So that taking it all round there seems to be a wry irony attaching to the 1897 decision of the committee to mix confetti with trail paper as a distinguishing mark.

And yet. And yet — so much to be pleased about. They could not at the time claim as their own the success in 1895 in the A.A.A. Four Miles of the giant future member and President with the George-like stride, H.A. Munro, nor of Harold Wade winning the Mile in 1892 in a time of 4 minutes 19.2 that only George had beaten in the Championships, but they could do so with the runner-up position of L'Argent O. Keer in the 1891 Steeplechase. Then there was the pleasant summer training at the Private Banks Ground. Steamers were hired with S.L.H. to follow the Boat Race. E.F. Nicholls proposed the re-establishment of H.E.J. Barclay's old Northern Division of the Club for mid-week running. There was encouragement for members in the regular award of a gold medal for the Blackheathen scoring most points in Open events during the season.

Most notable of all, linked with the enjoyable trips to the neutral ground of West Wickham to meet S.L.H. and climb the ancient "Stocks" Tree which was their starting point outside "The Swan", was the presentation of an impressive new trophy for that match by Nicholls, which they pleased themselves vastly by winning on that first occasion, making all sorts of boasts about how often they would repeat the dose. The West Wickham ground was "neutral" in standing between South London's Croydon area and that of Blackheath. Walter Rye would have construed the term of neutrality in its military sense: in his Badminton Library essay he wrote of the clubs, "Between the two a ceaseless feud has always existed". So deathly has been the struggle that only twice — in 1899 because of fog and in 1907 because of a dispute over the terms of the contest has the race failed to take place, apart, that is, from the war years. With the consent of the[31] donor they abolished the neutral course condition, converting it to the alternate "home and away" fixture of the present day and in 1923 it was held at Coulsdon for the first time. Each side has enjoyed long successions of wins to the discouragement of their opponents but the present score of Blackheath's thirty to South London's twenty-nine wins bears witness both to the long-term balance and the satisfying keenness of this competition. In its early years at "The Swan" the runners would change in crowded outhouses or stable buildings in the yard and, in the

ANNUAL ROWING MATCH   weary rivals help to land our boat

late autumn when this race takes place, their only lights after it was over would be lanterns. There would be hip-baths in the shed if they were lucky. or in the stable yard if they were not

The tie between the two Clubs was now closer than before, aided by this formal kind of deed-agreement as to its conditions drawn up by the two parties, although there was still something stronger than rivalry and less insipid than mere friendship between them. The association was helped even more by the prominent South London official, A.J. Fowden, who had joined Blackheath also in 1891, by which time they were running regular seven mile steeplechases against each other.

Besides incidental contests between the two almost as old as the foot-races such as football, there were the rowing matches between S.L.H. and Blackheath which had become established in the 1880's. The race was sometimes rowed at Henley, the two Clubs again sharing a London Bridge steamer for the day. The St. John Mathews Cup donated by the Club's stroke and Captain $_{32}$ in 1902 when his crew were beaten by a bare yard has been competed for every year since. This competition has remained between the two Clubs but Ranelagh joined in in 1929 for the Frankeiss Cup race which is nominally open to any London athletic club. Since 1934 the two races have been rowed concurrently. At times too, oarsmen of distinction like that great influence, H. Blackstaff of S.L.H., have taken part.

Uncomfortable though the hardships of cross-country running may be at times, they seldom rise to the level of those endured by Club oarsmen. These have been portrayed in "The Gazette" with a vividness and atmosphere which would seem to match the conclusion of "Great Expectations" rather than a sporting contest, with the frail competing shells weaving their precarious way in and amongst the tugs and barges going up on the flood.

In 1910: "A start was not effected until 6.30. At that hour rain was falling in torrents — the night had closed with an inky blackness, and apart from the few lamp-lights on Putney Bridge, nothing could be seen of either crew or of Mr. C. Mc Arthur, Captain of tne Vesta R.C., who kindly acted as starter".

Throughout the history of these races which still persist despite such temporary lapses as that just before the turn of the century the crews and clubs have been indebted to a number of hosts: Thames R.C., the Curlew Club with whom Blackheath have had an association very nearly as old as that

A BLACKHEATH CREW 1960

with Reed's old Club; Vesta, National Provincial and most recently of all Cygnet, the Civil Service Rowing Club.

A connection with another Club proved less fruitful during this decade. An amalgamation like that with the South London Athletic and Bicyeling Club in 1882 was proposed in 1897 by Lewisham Hare and Hounds who were more demanding in their terms than Crafter & Co. had been. Their insistence seems to have centred in the person of T.H. Warland who was a member of both clubs, for he was the rock upon which this venture foundered. Apart from its curiosity interest the proposal is relevant to this history in demonstrating the firm foundations that the Club had established by this time. This was evidenced in their unequivocal rejection of Lewisham's demand that the name of Blackheath Harriers should be altered, although they agreed that the Lewisham men should continue to wear their own colours as long as they wished. Lewisham eventually accepted this and amalgamation got as far as the drawing-up of quite elaborate terms, but the Blackheath men could not stomach that which demanded the election of Mr. Warland as handicapper for all Club events for the following three years and that was the end of that.

More than anything else it was life at "The Green Man" that gave most pleasure and was their raison d'etre. This was the great centre for sportsmen of all kinds for though cross-country was at the heart of the Club it was an association for every imaginable sport and pastime, supplying an echo of the old Peckham days when those worthies could find themselves walking a race one week and swimming one in Lambeth Baths the next. This latter sport was indeed of parallel importance at the least to athletics in Blackheath during the nineties. Through the identification with Lewisham S.C., not only did they become the first Harriers' club to win a County Water-Polo Championship but in 1893 were presented with a trophy for a swimming race which is still competed for. This continues to surprise those new members who have excessively rigid notions as to what constitutes the proper limited activity of an athletic club. Charlton House had long been in the possession of the family who were lords of the manor in respect of lands which formed part of the ground contingent to Blackheath. The generosity of the donor, Sir Spencer Maryon-Wilson, provided an odd adjustment to the irony of the situation created by his predecessor, Sir Thomas, who was something of the reverse of a patron saint for those who, like Blackheath, had an interest in preserving open space whereon to disport themselves and who had suffered in the past from its lack. He had attained to a rare notoriety in a saga of resistance to his long campaign to do as he liked with Hampstead Heath to which rights he succeeded in 1818 and stubbornly fought to monopolize for the next fifty years. It was his successor Sir Spencer who settled the issue so that among other things there can be national cross-country championships there today. He it was also who made handsome and benevolent amends for his predecessor's reputation, expressed his wish for the Club to encourage swimming, presented the Maryon-Wilson Trophy and himself became a vice-president. Besides the first holder of 1893, E.R. Harvey, there was for many years an abundance of these Crafter-like amphibians in Blackheath Harriers. Where our own race was concerned there were Boning and S.T. Pugh dominating the rest of the 1890's, the former winning four times in succession. But they represented only a fraction of the total interest. Numbers of others had not only helped found the Lewisham Swimming Club as they had done a few miles away on dry land with the Peckham venture but so close was the identification that Blackheath membership, it was remarked at one time, was apparently a stepping stone to the Lewisham Presidency — as the names of T.K. Grant, E.W. Stafford W.S. Smith and A. Anderson amply certified. [33]

The fact of the place, Blackheath, as a traditional centre and focal point of a number of common sporting interests within such a limited space was mutually invigorating for them and undoubtedly it was an important formative influence in the growing character of the Club itself in the twenty years and more following the move to "The Green Man". The Harriers consciously prided themselves on their catholic and all-round participation:

"We can turn out teams at running, cricket, rugby, swimming, rowing, whist, boxing, billiards, wrestling, draughts, chess, spillikins, hunt the thimble and tip-it, and we get excellent fun, winning or losing". And it was no exaggeration either. Members like C.W. Starnes and Herbert King have remarked on the recreational aspect of running and socializing at the Headquarters as being "the great feature of Club life". True, at times, life might present a stern aspect for the novices with Crafter, himself keeping fit for water-polo, taking them out sometimes over twelve miles before setting them to "run in" for the Novices Pewter, though after the ordeal the new holder then graduated to a regular pack. The award was a custom prompted by a member, R. Beveridge, who, going abroad in 1883 presented half a dozen pewters as a leaving present to the Club [34] This increased Rye's conviction as to the essentially corrupt nature of Blackheath and news reports like that appearing in "The Sportsman" could hardly have served to improve his opinion: "The mile race resulted in a very exciting finish barely a foot separating first and second men, Scott falling over a dog level with the tape, and securing the Club's Pewter, Crafter being second", while prior to this drama a horse had bolted "over a hedge with a cart full of milk cans".

Yet for most members Blackheath life was more hedonistic and the Club Dance, begun in the mid-nineties, the Wednesday evening and Saturday runs with their joints and chops and steaks to follow, together with cards, billiards and a quantity of beer were what justified the Club in their eyes. Most often the racing was considered the extra spice of running and not the object: there was still something in the nature of that generation which made for an essential difference between them and the modern athlete who is typically a townsman. If we are to find something more than condescending amusement from their attitude we have to look beyond the joke afforded by the following which expresses the general feeling of the time:

"It is impossible to name a more pleasurable way of exercising one's muscles and lungs than slow cross-country running. I do not mean racing, because that sort of exercise is decidedly bad if indulged in too frequently; but a steady jog-trot across country, properly clothed on a bright afternoon, will be found not only exhilarating and pleasureable but particularly beneficial and healthful to the ordinary healthy individual".

If their memories did not seem to go back beyond the Blackheath beginnings, that was natural enough for men who were practical rather than contemplative, just as it was for them to be satisfied in retrospect with the Homeric age of the eighties rather than go back further to seek after the secret of that success. The Peckham days were truly remote in a changing world and went unregarded save as an antediluvian time of reverent myth almost entirely expressed in the figures of Reed and Rowland. So thoroughly had the membership identified itself with its Blackheath environment and become domesticated in it. In twenty years the Club had passed from a struggling small scale undertaking to a powerful and highly organized entity which by then had lost sight of the nature of its origins, but not of their pride in the historical fact: in 1899 they were congratulating themselves on being "the oldest combined cross-country and athletic club in the United Kingdom, or, for that matter, the whole civilized world".

THE
Blackheath Harriers' Gazette
AND
Club Record.

No. 1. Vol. I.   EDITED BY H. R. HOPPER.   SEPTEMBER, 1898.
Registered at Stationers' Hall.

For Private Circulation amongst Members only.
Published by E. F. NICHOLLS, 63, *Crouch Hall Road, Crouch End, London, N.*

"Briefly, our desire is that the contents of The Gazette should be interesting and 'up-to-date' but not unduly personal. 'Peace, harmony and goodwill' is our motto".

(Editorial - "THE GAZETTE", 1902).

". . . Seems to have deteriorated rapidly during the last few months".

(Letter to the Editor - "THE GAZETTE", - 1911).

One need make no apology for what seems an arbitrary date to begin this section any more than for the event which warrants its choice, namely, the appearance in 1898, the year following Queen Victoria's Diamond Jubilee, of a new ingredient in Club life, "The Blackheath Harriers' Gazette and Club Record". Started in monthly issues which served the purpose also of a fixture list, with H.R. Hopper as its first Editor, "The Gazette" is surely one of the most remarkable features of the Club.₃₅ It is no exaggeration to claim that in its nature and its continuity unbroken down to today it has been a major factor in holding the Club together — and not alone in times of war — as well as in moulding and maintaining the Blackheath personality.

From the first it established an individual format and general character which have remained substantially the same since that far-off year, yet without any offensive sense of entrenched refusal to change with the passing of time. It was and is essentially a family journal read eagerly by so many members young and old, not only up and down this country, but, as a 1965 issue observed, in over twenty other lands as well. There is no need to inform a Blackheath Harrier of its importance.

What is significant to the historian besides recording the part it has played in creating and sustaining the Club we know is that in the very first issue of September, 1898, is to be seen so little that is foreign to a member of today and so much that is still actively preserved and flourishingly alive. In discussing it therefore we find ourselves engaged in a kind of summary of the essence of Blackheath directing our gaze Janus-like to the past and future both. In its pages already are not only the format it still possesses — its lay-out, size, print, its small snippets of information and paragraphing together with longer reports — but also its style, familiar, chatty, facetious -- all expressing exactly the disposition of the body of which it is a limb — a mingling of jocularity, disappointment, congratulation and cajolerie which has remained a curiously constant feature from its inception to the present day.

There, too, is registered the catholic nature of its members' activities, as true now despite this age of specialization as it was then: a tandem record, the all-important swimming, the regular cricket match with South London Harriers as well as a tug-of-war. In 1898 too there are the same social occasions of Punchbowl Night, Smoking Concerts and Musical Evenings. Recognizable also are the lists of officials and their addresses, greetings on births, mentions of the same trophies — the "Rowland", the "Walter" Steeplechase Cup, the "Barclay-Esson", the Five Miles Challenge Cup and, of course, the "Nicholls" — though the race was still at this date a representative, not a large team-scoring fixture.[36] Besides these, we find the Opening Run of the winter season a settled tradition, nearly as long-standing as separate matches with Oxford and Cambridge.

Naturally, there are features which have disappeared, perhaps regrettably, like the "Married versus Single" race — or "Bachelors versus Benedicts" as it was colloquially known — but overall there is little difference. The same wry smiles were as surely provoked then as now whether by congratulations on the Club moving up from twelfth to seventh in the County Championships, by the endemic querulousness of Treasurers or by their praise of members' munificence. Holders of Club office are always fair game but the shots are harmless bullets which bounce off, like this sample in characteristic tone directed against "that popular Blackheath official" who after the Southern Supper hung his bowler on a lighted gas jet and "is now able to talk more than ever through his hat".

With further issues appearing and "The Gazette" establishing itself, we find in the news of that still wickedly innocent Edwardian age the same Blackheath gossip of today, however times have changed. We hear of Haslegrave's team at Le Touquet and French member Maurice Bandeville's discussions with his fellow club-men leading to France's first entry in to the International Cross-country Championships; or, on a different level, the rowing President, R. St. John Mathews, taking a Blackheath Bowls team to his Bowling Club at Pembury; A.G. Fentiman, his race-cycling days over, winning international races at Cowes with his motorboat, "Javelin" — the subject of a rare photo in "The Gazette"; news of our quite numerous contingent of South African settlers, best known of which was A.B. Godbold, so prominent a figure in the early formative days of athletics in England; Frank Denman, second in the Christmas Morning Handicap in the Serpentine and "swimming like a true Blackheath Harrier"; while, once again on a more august level, congratulations are offered to local M.P. and Club patron, Major E.D.C. Coates on his baronetcy.

News came then as still from all quarters and enables those long parted to keep up a connection which became heartfelt during the wars ahead, whether it was of "our popular German member H. Kleeblatt", writing from Bolivia or C.W. Starnes from wherever he happened to be — Tokyo, South America, Bangkok or U.S.A. Many of the messages were cryptic but encouraging: "Dewsnap IS still alive!" or else, quietly desperate: "Found in Farrell's bag a pair of running drawers, with the name Benetfink".[37] And at home always there was the old life going on: Summer Runs ending with bicycling members shinning up lamp posts to obtain a light for their machines; at the concerts, Nirvana rendered by our gymnastic expert, J.H. Williams, or E.H.C. Hitchings' splendid rendering of Gunga Din , and on one occasion at least, Tom Crafter running on a Wednesday evening round the Heath accompanied by four of his sons, the fifth unfortunately detained in the City.

It is an immeasurable debt that is owed to the dozens of Editors and their assistants through the years for the unbroken continuity of their work and the good it has done. Not the least notable among these in its long history was H.A. Wilkinson who served "The Gazette" from 1922 until 1946, his family's printing firm together with his own dedication always ensuring a fine standard of production. In more recent years still an editor with a strong sense of both the Club's and its journal's tradition has been the equally quiet and sincere R.H. Thompson since he has not only administered the publication efficiently but has done much valuable work in reviving and sustaining many old members' connection with the Club. It is thanks to the efforts of such men and "The Gazette" that we can, years later, catch some flavour of the Club's life in the past — not principally perhaps the eye-catching events, but those unimportant and trivial ones that nonetheless give life its texture and much of its significance.

As well, then, as recording the birth of what was to become a remarkable journal, these words serve as a commentary on a stage when the Club both was and clearly felt itself to be thoroughly and comfortably established. A shaking war was to come within less than two years and twelve years after that one far more devastating, not to mention two other domestic crises serious for Blackheath in little over twenty years. All the more notable therefore that so much of what is particular about that institution should not only have been so at this period but should have remained so till now, at its centenary, with no sign of remitting. The degree of this continuity is probably unique among comparable institutions.

No. 573. Vol. 71.   December 1968–March 1969

THE

Blackheath Harriers' Gazette

AND

Club Record

"Perfer et Obdura"

"Something tells me I am needed
At the front to fight the foe. . . . . . .

"Goodbye Dolly" – Song of the Boer War .

For once, the arrival of a new century was something more than an arbitrary date and while there was much to remind one of the past, ranging from W.G. Grace's 126th century to muffin men, lamplighters and hansom cabs, there was undoubtedly enough to convey the sense of a changing world where motor-buses were now mingling with horse-buses on the roads. But in these years sovereigns were sounding their last golden ring upon shop counters, and before long that world was to be changed utterly by an unprecedented catastrophe that would shake Europe to the core. Already now there was a taste of what was to come in the disturbing experience of the Boer War, though it was too remote for the lesson to take hold and the terrible disillusionment was postponed till 1914 when the full destructive power of modern weapons became apparent. 1900, however, saw the first hint of the rush to the colours which was to mark August, 1914. Some ten per cent of Blackheath's active list volunteered; the City Imperial Volunteers went from Nine Elms — every man created a Freeman of London, with every Blackheath volunteer declared a Life member of the Club — and the London Scottish with whom the Club has had such close connection sent a hundred picked men. Swimmers and runners of the Club all flocked off to this new adventure: Lorimer, Eames, Pugh, Dale, Kipling, Sturgeon and the rest:

> "Our athletes now are turned and wheeled
> . . . As ever glad for fun or fame
> To play this other stranger game. . ."

Jokes were made about the possibilities of our water-polo team playing the rest of England in the Tugela River, but a hint of the reality came with the first death — that of M.W. Holland, of the Club's Northern Division — and can be discerned in the letter which conveyed the news:

"I regret to inform you that Private M.W. Holland died yesterday, about half-an-hour after receiving six wounds, the effect of a shrapnel shell bursting on him. We were attacking a kopje in extended order when we received six shells in the middle of our section. He was buried by the Clergyman of the 15th Brigade after the action, about quarter of a mile in rear of the place where the Boer shells exploded, about seven miles east of Brandfort. We did all we could for him at the time, and there was no better man in my section. We all deeply regret the loss of him and Sergeant Kingsford, they were both splendid Volunteers who never flinched at anything".

That it was no game was soon confirmed in even more grim earnest by the additional toll of disease adding to their hardships and by such letters as S.T. Pugh sent to his brother. An extract from one of these, written on June 11th, 1900 at Vredfort Road, bears tersely eloquent witness to the dawning of this realization:

"We were out scouting nearly every day with some regular Mounted Infantry; these had three killed and four wounded. Three days after we left Rodeval the line was being blown up and the station burnt. Our company has been reduced, by sickness and loss of horses, down to about seventy men. Our section alone having gone from about thirty to nine men". At the start of this War "The Gazette" printed the inscription ". . . blessed are those among nations who dare to be strong for the rest". It expressed a proud mood which as time passed it became increasingly hard to sustain.

For the Club too it was a time of change after the doldrums of the nineties. Something of a new dynamic began to operate at this time not readily apparent to the superior gaze of our modern hustling age, but it was there, and some members at least were conscious of a difference. At the Annual Dinner of 1908 at the Trocadero Jack Reay said Blackheath had done as much as any Club in existence to bridge over that period "between the halcyon days of athletics and the present revival". Conscious effort was made to encourage younger members with the formation of a junior division at half the normal subscription in 1899. In that year too, they started to confine their athletic meetings to members and in 1907 dropped the cycling events from the programme, while a serious attempt was made by the Club to form a Kent County Athletic Association in 1899, though it was not till 1920 that the existing Association was established. Still, Blackheath ran what were virtually Kent Championships for years. Generally, the Club was to the fore in all branches of athletic counsels and its members attained high office, chief among them H.J. Barclay who saw the growth of the A.A.A. into its modern stature and for his service as its Honorary Secretary was knighted in 1930, and H.F. Pash, who also held this position. Both of them were Presidents of the Club, the latter perhaps somewhat austere but, as numerous teams could testify from the five-course dinners they enjoyed from him, most generous and hospitable, while Barclay received the accolade from Crafter: "Quite a good plunger".

A RELAXED GROUP OF BLACKHEATH OFFICIALS
early this century: T. Crafter, J.H. Reay, R. St. John Mathews, A.D. Metcalf J. Rampley.

Though our old 220 record holder, C.G. Wood, could object in "The Gazette" to the new-fangled "crouch start" — and correctly too, probably — "In my opinion it is an un-natural position for a biped," there were signs of a motion towards the modern state of athletics in this first decade, helped in England by the effect of the 1908 Olympic Games held in London. Correspondents to the "Daily Mail" might object to "pot-hunters" and the general selfishness of track athletics with no reputable meetings or respectable clubs for young men to join, but the movement of the times was against such reactionaries.

In Blackheath there were distinct signs of a track renaissance prior to the 1914-18 War, with B.J. Blunden, the Clapton Orient football player, the first to emerge as A.A.A. 880 Champion in 1903 but rivalled by M.P.S. White, the Surrey 880 and Mile Champion on several occasions between 1903 and 1908. There were good sprinters like J.P. Wardle, quarter milers like C. McLachlan, and a class hurdler in A.H. Healey who won the 1908 A.A.A. 120 Hurdles title, while the past glories of Cowie in the eighties were now revived by J. McLean winning the Scottish 100 and 220 titles in 1901. These were to lead on to crowning triumphs before the war came.

The A.A.A. Mile Medley Championship win of 1911 in a world record time came from a formidable combination in W.D. Lancefield, C.N. Seedhouse, J.T. Soutter and F.T. Browne running for the first time together. Seedhouse won the A.A.A. 440 yards title in both 1912 and 1914, but it was Soutter's 1.56.4 880 leg in a strong wind which clinched the relay, "passing the flag", as it was then, to win by some fifteen yards. Soutter was 2nd in the 1912 A.A.A. half-mile to the German, Braun and the advent at the Championships of such continentals and of Americans in larger quantities than when they first started coming in the 1880's was another sign of development in the sport. Both Seedhouse and Soutter ran in the 1912 Stockholm Olympics in the Mile Medley team which gained 3rd place. Browne too was selected but unable to go through injury. "Really", said "The Gazette" of it all, "this is quite exhilarating!" Nor were they alone: there was one R.A. Lindsay, in 1914 Club Champion for 100, 220 and 440 yards who had to wait till the twenties for his A.A.A. title and international team colours, and generally too Blackheath athletics was thriving: twenty-six first places in open events in distances from 100 to 880 yards during 1911, and in its own meetings, habitual fields of four dozen for two mile running and walking handicaps.[38]

Membership continued to climb steadily without any of the methods being employed that were causing controversy in the contemporary world and had led some Blackheath members to advocate withdrawal from the Southern Cross-country Championship. But the Club joined the newly formed and progressively minded London Athletic League formed by the six leading metropolitan clubs to encourage relay racing which had started to claim notice with such events as the first "Flying Squadron" race staged at Ranelagh Harriers' meeting

A.A.A. ONE MILE MEDLEY RELAY CHAMPIONS 1911
W.D. Lancefield, C.N. Seedhouse, J.T. Soutter, F.T. Browne, Sir Harry Barclay

A.A.A. ONE MILE MEDLEY RELAY CHAMPIONS 1966

D.N. Wright, R.M. Porter, B.E. Shurmer, M.W. McFarnell

at Stamford Bridge in 1895 in which the Blackheath team finished 5th.

Everything did not go swimmingly though. The older members were conscious of a threat to the very existence of the Club in 1904-05 when they were forced by circumstances to break with the long-standing habit of relying on Reed's paternalism as the result of a crisis arising out of his personal and in those times casual handling of bills which he had always in the past paid himself but now, beset by personal financial losses, found himself unable to do. It was a sign of how the Club had grown far beyond its former scale that the

74

old informal method would no longer do. Out of this handling of a severe difficulty by several members as opposed to one largely arose the modern constitutional practice in Club government.

In 1909 Reed died. To us today he is the most enigmatic of all Blackheath's figures, but so he seems to have been very largely even to his oldest friends during the later stages of his life when indeed, he seems to have preserved a certain mystery about himself. He was to most members a rather remote father figure with only a few intimates of an older time. At no time, apparently, was he very communicative, and such a disposition could well have contributed towards his tribulations where one more forthcoming might have stimulated active assistance from those surrounding him. His farewell was the more strongly tinged with pathos therefore when, in replying to the presentation made to him at the Annual Dinner in 1905, he said that the Blackheath Harriers were his only child and he could not therefore forget it.

PART OF A LETTER WRITTEN BY F.H. REED TO J.F. PONSFORD

In the same speech he also gave his blessing to the arrangement now to operate of an annual president — a principle only departed from since in times of war. With Reed's withdrawal from the scene various developments took place in the constitution of which the most important is the convention by which selection for the Club Presidency is regulated. The years of 1905 and 1906 saw two embarrassing double propositions for the Presidency with an alternative proposition coming from the floor of the meeting, both involving Rowland who withdrew. Possibly this was the last evident expression of a sense of difference between the old "Peckham" and the more recent "Blackheath" tradition — but this is speculation. Certainly the contention appears to have arisen out of claims in terms of seniority as opposed to the more general criteria on which the then Committee had based their selections. From the time of the Special General Meetings of 1907 the practice was adopted of making the outgoing President responsible for the choice of his successor, the formality of election at the A.G.M. being discharged by "acclaim" without the embarrassment of alternative proposals from the floor of the Meeting. This procedure is not unknown in other organizations and has the object of safeguarding the dignity of the office and of freeing it as far as possible from the risk of becoming involved in the controversies of faction, and it may fairly be added that this is a conception which has served the Club well since it was introduced. What is important is that thus was built in the now-traditional safeguard of the appointment being made by the previous President. It can therefore be seen that it is not, as is often thought, a matter of prestige, and that though it may be a peculiarly English compromise with whatever accompanying disadvantage, it has led to the greater advantage and larger principle of preventing domination by any faction. Together with this development there were complementary changes which led to greater responsibility by the Committee.

Two members of this body, the Secretary, H.W.G. Haslegrave, and the Honorary Treasurer, A.D. Metcalf, had performed an enormous task in extricating the Club from the financial difficulties mentioned above. Adrian was one of the sons of John Metcalf — himself one of the great originals, though his wife Charlotte Oliver had actually been a member of Peckham A.A.C. before him — and was known chiefly for his perfectionist organization of social activities in the early years of the century. Haslegrave had already by 1908 established a record number of years of Club secretarial service. Yet another fine all-rounder — at rugby, running still as a veteran to finish 8th Blackheath man in the Southern, and as a cricketer topping the Sydenham Cricket Club averages — he was a man who yet found time to fulfil a number of official responsibilities from his secretaryship of Norwood Rugby Football club to acting as Club representative on the A.A.A. Committee for many years. With so much administrative energy at his disposal he was likely to cross some who were more leisurely disposed. No doubt his pince-nez glittered at the A.A.A. meeting when the Chairman, the then Lord Chief Justice, Lord Alverstone, having suffered, as it seemed to him, too many contributions to the proceedings by Haslegrave and interpreting a certain nervous physical movement by that gentleman as signalling yet another such intention informed him severely that if he, Lord Alverstone, saw him, H.W.G. Haslegrave, on his feet once again, he the Lord Chief Justice, would send him down for a stretch of five years' penal servitude without remission. Then — after a pause while the meeting digested this and His Lordship reflected deeply — "What's more, you'll richly deserve it!" Nonetheless Haslegrave was not the sort of man that any club could afford to lose. He stands out even after the lapse of time as one of the best of many able administrators whose services the Club has enjoyed in its history. Like Mayson, he played a prominent part in the public life of the sport and its still continuing development during the early years of this century. He was instrumental in securing a greater measure of representation by many Clubs in the Amateur Athletic Association at a time when dozens of clubs were faced with the unsatisfactory privilege of being qualified to call a meeting of the organization but of being unable to vote at it. His influence extended to the international field and he helped to build up the International Cross-country Race by being directly concerned with the entry of France into that competition, as well as acting as Timekeeper in the races, rubbing shoulders with such historical figures as the modern Olympian, Baron de Coubertin and being created a Membre d'Honneur by the French Amateur Athletic Association, the U.S.F.A. In 1908 he was President of Surrey Walking Club, and, too, he was the prime mover in leading the secretaries of athletic clubs to meet in periodic conference so as to avoid clashes of the dates of sports meetings. As for his long service to Blackheath as their Secretary, his years of office saw the membership

ERNEST NEVILLE WITH MEGAPHONE

A.A.A. Championships. Stamford Bridge, London.

rise from 169 to 400. Once again we find a sad irony in trivia in contemplating the title of the song he sang at concerts: "It's a Great Big Shame". Whatever the truth of the grievances which brought about his withdrawal from the scene and the justice of which we today cannot determine it was surely a serious loss to the club.

"HOW LONG DID THE FIRST HOUR TAKE?"

(Question put to J.E. Fowler-Dixon timekeeping at Blackheath 24 Hours Walk).

Generally, Rowland was being quite objectively accurate when he said in his Presidential message of 1908, "There was never such a time in the existence of the Club in all my forty years' experience of it when the prospects were brighter than at present". One of the justifications for this optimism was the signal success of the Club's long-distance walkers and the important record-breaking promotions by Blackheath which brought the Club into the public gaze.

These were held in conjunction with Surrey Walking Club which had formed with a large percentage of Blackheath men just before the end of the century. The first impulse for them was the 1904 performance of the Suffolk man, T.E. Hammond, on the Brighton road in a race against Ranelagh. Ideally built for such tasks — six foot in height and weighing 10½ stone — in his late twenties he became a Blackheath hero of the time by a

77

series of wonderful exploits. The best of these came in 1907 when — aided by comforts produced by the methylated spirits stove on his accompanying car — he set up a record of 18 hours 13 minutes 37 seconds from London to Brighton and back — taking over 2¼ hours off the previous best and incidentally bettering the American Running Record of the day. He regained his London to Brighton[39] record in 1909 with a time of 8 hours 18 minutes, 18 seconds, having floored a man en route and found the Crawley railway crossing closed, a hazard well known to later long-distance men and road relay runners. He also set new bests for 24 hours, covering 131 miles 580 yards, and for the London to Oxford course. In describing such feats as his 1907 Brighton return trip "The Gazette" waxed lyrical, bringing a past to life that seems more vivid than the present while we read, "Lamps were lighted as a few spots of rain came down. The moon was practically covered by a mist. Brown went past in the darkness".

A fine stylist, Tommy Hammond was a name to conjure with and he is still impressively remembered by friends and admirers today such as Norman Beyfus who wrote at Hammond's death in 1945:

"He loved the simple things of life, for much he did not care. Achieving for achievements sake, he shunned the limelight's glare. Firm friend, great walker, sportsman true, his cheerful smiling face Will be remembered by the friends he passed in life's great race".

A performer to rival Hammond was S.C.A. Schofield, one not only good enough to remove two minutes from Hammond's Johnson Bowl Record in 1910 but holder of the 15 Miles and twelve hour British records set in 1911. Together with

" .....FIRM FRIEND, GREAT WALKER, SPORTSMAN TRUE" -T.E. Hammond

these was E. Neville[40] not only walking in races — he was the first Blackheath "Centurion"[41] — but already at this time starting over half a century of organizing them.

Descriptions of the grand promotions at the Crystal Palace and "that vast and unlovely wilderness", the Stadium, as the White City was then called, are almost as impressive as their performance must have been. We are told of large invited fields of fifty with elaborate arrangements meticulously carried out from months beforehand by Haslegrave but reinforced by the services of the "Oxo" Company, the Official Caterers, supplying "Oxo Athletes' Flasks" supplemented by Oxo with Champagne, rice pudding, bananas, raisins, soda and milk, brandy, whisky and champagne, all of which lent meaning to the official note: "Competitors will receive every attention". And modern sufferers from transistor radios will understand the competitors' ordeal reflected in the "Gazette" correspondent's complaint about the "series of excruciatingly painful discords" experienced during the night from Messrs. Pathé Frères' Majestic Grand Concert Parlophone.

BEFORE THE START OF 50 MILES WALK PROMOTED BY BLACKHEATH & SURREY W.C., OCTOBER, 1904

T.E. Hammond in centre background; E Neville (No. 3); F.H. Reed in flat cap with H.W.G. Haslegrave by post on right; T. Crafter in city dress 4th from left. The winner was No. 20, F.B. Thompson of Ranelagh Harriers; J.H.A. Reay is next to him smoking pipe. Note the starting pistols.

CROSS COUNTRY by S.T.Dadd.

80

"HORSES FOR COURSES":
Tommy Hammond & Water Trough on the Brighton Road

THE FINISH
HARDING DEFEATS
HAMMOND.

S.T.DADD.

'CROSS COUNTRY: THE BLACKHEATH HARRIERS' EIGHT MILES WALK FROM CHISLEHURST
TO BLACKHEATH.

THE CLUB WALKING RACE, CHISLEHURST TO BLACKHEATH
drawn by S.T. Dadd

In addition to these joint ventures with Surrey W.C. there were the regular and pleasant "strolls" in their company and, in 1894, with another of their future President and Blackheath member, Arthur Cook's "brainwaves" — as was the race with S.L.H. — the inception of a "short walking race", in ordinary clothes, from the "Imperial Arms", Chislehurst, to "The Green Man". They might have to walk on the sidewalks because of the muddy roads, but the fields were large — forty-eight in 1898 — and anyone who felt impelled to drop out could always ride in the brake carrying the clothes. In 1902, H.G. Johnson, secretary of that Blackheath splinter, the Northern Division [42] — known to some as "our nocturnal division" — presented the Johnson Bowl for this race, won first by one of his own "Green Man", Muswell Hill crowd, A.E. Culver. It was always popular with athletes who had largely given up active participation and today still enjoys a pleasantly relaxed atmosphere injected with a little tension by the participation of Surrey members. After a lapse between the wars it had recovered something of its old popularity, with sons of Hammond's Brighton road successor and 1912 Centurion, Harold Rhodes, as well as runner turned walker, H.N. Nunns, sharing honours with F.D. Holt after the good walker, N.L. Burt had dominated the race for some years in the early thirties.

Though we find mention of it as far back as 1896, it is just after the turn of the century that Punchbowl Night seems to have struck root as a tradition which "has the effect of making one love and respect even one's own brother", as the correspondent said in 1930. The basic pattern has remained untampered with: "the talk frequently grows quite intimate", there is punch piping hot brewed from an obscure receipt and provided by the Vice-Presidents, always a rich cake as well as the main meal, and such incidentals as candles, "a Stilton cheese apparently self-propelled", and churchwarden pipes together with, above all, "the unearthing of many orators". In fact, at one time, all present had to speak, whereas nowadays a few are excused. An "Invention" of Toasts is proposed, with equal exchange of formal respect and informal insult, for there is no inbred back-scratching or complimenting. To those who have attended, the reticence of correspondents reporting on it in "The Gazette", and even, in other years, a failure to report at all, comes as no surprise. The important image always retained is of the sound of talk, the shining faces of old members, the white napery and the sight and scent of the punch going round.

On the night of a "private subscription Cinderella dance" at "The Green Man" in 1898 there had been an infiltration by some of the ladies on a conducted tour into the Clubroom which they much admired — "The very best, bar none, in the kingdom". This may well have assisted in promoting the first Bohemian Concert in 1900 as the result of a decision that "something should be done to enable ladies to participate more fully in the doings of the Club". Two hundred attended: Walter Rowland was in charge — "here there and everywhere" and, as Val Hunter would say, "Compelling thankful hearts". Already by 1904 such evenings were being described as "another triumph for Walter Rowland", with backing from "Herr Fischer's Orchestra" which would "render a choice and up-to-date selection of dance music". Among the latter appeared a strange new manoeuvre more than once calling forth comment, the "Tango". Assisted by such as Madame Michaelis and "How Do I Know That Spring Has Come", "When Bright Eyes Glance" gallantly rendered by Mr. Purdy of the Anerley Bicycling Club, mandolin solos and "When The Boys Come Home" given by Mr. Edgar Edwards — its success was to be repeated on many subsequent occasions and become a favourite institution for the next half-century. Though some of the talent for such special occasions might be imported the Club was, as ever, more than capable of holding its end up. At Club Smokers two dozen individual turns were nothing uncommon in an evening, whether they were E.G. Lymbery on his banjo, Ramsay Moir's fine baritone, Gillie Reay's "I Know Of Two Bright Eyes" bidding fair to match his Surrey cricketing prowess, or W. Robinson with his "Blackheath Hymn," which at times in its usefulness in admitting additional verses was not as religious as its title suggests.

Apart from such innovations life at "The Green Man" was much the same as it had always been, with Saturday runs still late at 3.30 p.m. and Wednesday evenings providing exercise with the regular 2¼ Mile Runs round the Heath for the dozens unable to run on Saturdays through playing other games; these started opposite the Gibbet. With a steak for 1s. 3d. with cheese and half a pint of beer for measure, still leaving a penny for a tip, there was good value to be got from one's annual subscription, not the least of which was the social side and the pleasure of meeting unexpected outsiders introduced to the Heath circuit, like

C. Aubrey Smith, the cricketer later to achieve higher renown by playing Ruritanian Colonels in Hollywood. Of connections with other sporting clubs there were plenty, from J.H. Williams' St. James's Athletic Club with their Gymnastic displays at Rye Lane, Peckham, to the brothers G.L. and O.J. Hopkins setting up tandem records for Anerley B.C. as well as running for Blackheath. In addition to the long identification with Lewisham Swimming Club there were links with Park House Rugby Football Club, the Blackheath Lacrosse Club, and Curlew Rowing Club, with county representatives from most of these in their respective sports. And when members went abroad, as they did too frequently, there would be strange new links created with such exotica as "Shanghai Harriers". Among all these was a constant admixture of older members, for it was always a Club that one came back to, as did G.M. Nehan after a quarter of a century in 1908, H.A. Munro, and, even if he was kept by his consular position in Zurich, J.C. Milligan, who had been one of the most useful officials in the eighties. Cattlin and D. Basan were still competing about the place, though fifty years old, while F.W. Monk, the old Southern star, as late as June, 1898, had undertaken to run, ride a horse, cycle, row and swim a quarter of a mile within 25 minutes at Kingston-on-Thames and succeeded with nearly ten minutes to spare. Though, of course, the activities of H.R. Hopper winning Manual Fire Engine Drill Competitions with the Merryweather Volunteer Fire Brigade, and of Dr. R. Newby-Smith, President of the brother-club, Lewisham Swimming Club, up in his balloon made their own modest appeal to appetites not yet cloyed by Northcliffe's new sensation-seeking age.

". . . . the other Blackheath men encroached upon the track and shouted at the top of their voices until a policeman requested them not to make so much noise".

(Report of Sports Meeting at Hitchin –
"The Gazette" - 1899).

'Do We Only Go Round Once?"
(New Member - 1904).

They could still go out for ten mile runs over ploughed fields round Sidcup and Eltham, for there was still access through the Morden College grounds to Eltham Church and over the fields round Sidcup and Grove Park – though a Ranelagh visitor said the initial "B" in the name was now superfluous with so much road in the course. Then too, as late as 1899 the old Challenge Cup principle still held with only Ratcliff and G.H. Bull taking issue, and correspondents to "The Gazette" could urge it as a grave error that teams were being over-trained in turning out two evenings a week after Christmas as though they had the "constitution of a horse". There was not the same movement forward among the cross-country men as there was with the track section. T.C. Davis, returned from police service in South Africa and now turned vegetarian, found that even at 36 years of age he could have the beating of almost all his Blackheath rivals, winning all the Club Championships and while he was good, he was too often left untroubled by any challenge. Nor was he challenged in the histrionic field as a result of his vividly performed accounts in the Club room of ridding himself of worms or triumphing over the hangover bequeathed by a clubbing from a Zulu knobkerrie.

Much of the time the Club would lose but by 1910 things were starting to look up and with increased competition over the previous years with such as Malden and Roath Harriers, with a Closing Five Miles Handicap initiated as well as a Five Miles Novices' Race, not to

CLUB GROUP, 1908-1909

CRYSTAL PALACE.

Blackheath Harriers Annual Sports,
Saturday, MAY 13th, 1905.

TRAINS to PALACE from LUDGATE HILL	...	...	1.53	2.20
,, ,, ,, VICTORIA (Chatham Line)	...		1.50	—
,, ,, ,, VICTORIA (Brighton Line)	...		2.12	2.22
,, ,, ,, LONDON BRIDGE ,,	...		2.8	2.28

Sports commence at 3.15 sharp.

COMPETITOR.
THIS TICKET ADMITS TO DRESSING ROOM.

No. **284**

[SEE OVER.]

J. H. COZENS,
General Manager & Secretary

This portion to be retained.

---

mention Veterans' Races against S.L.H. there was something to show by the 1914 Southern Championship when they had risen out of the slough to eighth place. The scoring six packed into the first eighty-five with H.C. Cooper, C.A. Glaeser, B.H. Lymbery, W.A.W.B. ('Henery the Eighth') Purchase and A. Preedy all led home by the new find from King's School, A.C. Telfer,[43] though Lymbery too at 19 years of age gave hope for the next year. It made a change from self-congratulation on finishing all their twelve men which had often in the past been the only source of gratification in this event they prized so much. The attitude they valued was epitomized by E.R. Small who, approached by a prospective punter before competing in an Open Handicap and asked by that gentleman if he was trying, replied indignantly, "Of course I'm trying!" which satisfied not only the aforesaid gentleman who walked away calling to his companions, "It's all right, Small is trying!" but "The Gazette" also, which cited it approvingly.

Together with a few others, he also "tried" by no means ineffectually at long-distance running with the stimulus of the 1908 Olympic Games upon them. In April, with Small finishing first of five they ran a twenty -four miles trial with the added handicap of a severe thunderstorm. The newspaper report remarked upon a consolation, strange to our modern ears: "the rain softened the roads which was a welcome relief to the runners, who were beginning to feel the effects of the hard surface". Undeterred, they attempted the Olympic Trial Race of twenty-two miles at the end of the same month which inflicted even worse weather condition on them with hail, snow and mud. "The

WILLIAM PARRISH

Sporting Life" reported roads "ankle deep in cold slush" and "the coldest of cold winds". Even so, four of the five Club competitors finished ⸺ E. Wade, E.V. Norman, F.D. Carr and E.R. Small — between 23rd and 36th positions.

Often there would appear hopeful signs but too often they would be blighted by bright young professional men ambitiously emigrating so that the team would never really consolidate. Such was the case with the brilliant runner H.E.J. Southwell who, having won both Five and Ten Miles Championships three times in succession as well as other matches and working up to 19th place in the Southern, then was seen off by Club members from London Bridge on his way to Canada. It was all the more shock to them when they heard within weeks of his death. Only E.F. Judson was superior to him and he tended to be an exception in going out after other demanding competition like the A.A.A. Ten Miles Championship. This was entirely typical of the man for, quiet and with little to say, Judson was given to actions without words; even his wife was unaware of his having won the Military Medal in the 1914-18 War until, when he died years later, she found it in a drawer together with the citation.

Summer training at Crystal Palace which became a Blackheath centre; moving back to the Private Banks Ground by the end of the decade for the Annual Club Open Meeting and Banks Meetings with their garden party atmosphere of lawns and strawberries and cream; the banked roses and Japanese umbrella tents at the Bishop of Colchester's grounds at the Chelmsford Meeting; lady bicyclists performing "musical rides" like the "fascinating team" of Miss Hilda Hemsley's; the Crystal Palace Military Band "in attendance" — all these summer activities found their complement in the easy-going mood typical of winter cross-country engagements.

No grim and unrelieved struggles were these matches, hard-fought though they might be on occasion. Special saloons would be attached to the train, the journey down to Oxford, Cambridge or whatever would pass away quickly under the "fascinating influence of solo whist", and after a race in which the result was largely incidental, they would return, "the wild drive on the roof of a railway bus and subsequent proceedings having no bearing on athletics in general". Suffield would nearly get left behind and have to be dragged through the window of the train, there would be "Jameson-like raids on the refreshment room" and "Shrimp" West would declare that he had never laughed so much as on this outing — while the result sheet would even show the unimportance of being earnest with Ratcliff beating a runner from St. John's with the Wildean name of Bunbury.

One match they did start to take very seriously was that mentioned above, which was suggested by Arthur Cook between themselves and South London Harriers in 1894 and for which E.F. Nicholls, the Honorary Secretary and later President had presented his Cup. They would turn out well for this and shared honours evenly with S.L.H. until the war, winning seven times from 1900 to 1913. It was during this period that the now traditional relations with S.L.H., Ranelagh and Orion as a whole took firm hold. A pleasant kind of fixture was the inter-club run as distinct from a match. These were often held in some outlying situation to yield the pleasure of the trip down as well as that of the run. Eastbourne and Brighton were visited in this way as well as clubs like Orion and Ranelagh. The former were met for the first time in 1913, J.H. Williams having had an active hand in founding their club and the races started after the war; signally it was run in appalling conditions of mud and sleet, a foretaste of those that often confront Blackheath when they visit Epping Forest for this fixture today, unpleasant immersions being frequent among the more stunted members of their spearhead. The Ranelagh Match was remarkable in being the first to be run under "all to score" conditions, [44] the competition with South London Harriers always having been for the first ten to finish, though a large number would always turn out for each side. When the 1907 Nicholls Cup Race fell through Blackheath invited Ranelagh Harriers to run at "The Green Man" — "under novel conditions" — the number to score being that of the club with the smaller numerical strength. "I doubt", wrote "The Sporting Life" correspondent, "whether the novelty will catch on".

The field for the 1909 race from "The Green Man" was said to be the biggest muster ever from there, with fifty Blackheath to twenty Ranelagh runners. This number and the race, which the Club won but Judson lost to Lintott of Ranelagh through the handicap of wearing spikes on the finishing stretch of road, were not the only noteworthy features of that February day. 169 Blackheath men all told were said to be present, while 125 members and friends sat down that evening to the dinner furnished forth by Mr. Smith, the new proprietor, and presided over by Walter Rowland. Haslegrave, they declared, "worked like a Trojan", arranging the race, selling the dinner tickets and directing the concert. It was a foretaste of the even greater number of the twenties and thirties. E.H. Pelling, the fine Ranelagh sprinter, joined Blackheath also in 1905 and from this fruitful connection came not only the race but, in collaboration with the successor to Nicholls in the Blackheath secretaryship, the Pelling-Ratcliff Cup for it in 1922.

After too long a break the Club resumed active connection also with Thames Hare and Hounds in an interclub run [45] though there was no match until 1927, and, too, Oxford University paid Blackheath the compliment, under their secretary and later writer and broadcaster, S.P.B. Mais, of leaving home ground for their fixture with the Club, an unusual occurrence at this time. By 1910, as yet another sign of resuscitation in cross-country as well as track, we were beating both them and Cambridge and after 1905 business was increasing generally so as to necessitate the alteration of Rule 1X to allow two Club handicappers, one for country and one for the flat.

These outlying and inter-club runs were among the favourites of most, together with others such as Lea Harriers or United Hospitals Hare and Hounds with whom we had run many times, the latter using the club's "Green Man" premises on Wednesday afternoons. Or perhaps better still was the long-standing custom of the summer runs at West Wickham where in the long evenings they would jog out up hills "like Spion Kop without the Boers", then down along by the side of yellow cornfields, through forest glades with visions of the setting sun at their far ends. Then, especially if the temperature was up in the Edwardian eighties, when the lakes of Keston broke into view "with a whoop of delight" the Pack would suddenly disappear in three or four feet of water and swim to the far side. Arriving back at "The Swan" again they would find many others waiting for them — Reay, Rapley, H.D. Thomas, Frank Baldry and the rest — "in various graceful poses on the lawn", on which after an excellent repast, they would hold a concert alfresco, Jack Reay presiding and the whole concluding with the National Anthem and with grumbles at South Eastern's lack of consideration at starting their last train back at 10.10 p.m. This formed the routine, unless of course, something exceptional came up, as after Crafter had heard and been impressed by the Pennsylvania men's college cry at the A.A.A. Championships so that he announced the first rehearsal of one for Blackheath after the August Summer Run. With the result that, even though they were far from being in the mood after their run and swim — "Shrimp" after conversing with two dairymaids upon the difference between toadstools and mushrooms — they were compelled by Crafter to rehearse it fifteen times before he gave in and allowed organist Ratcliff to approve the arrangement of "the little nursery rhyme followed by the big war cry".

And they brought the summer of 1900 to an end with that and with a rather ungrateful goodbye song from West — "There is a Tavern in the Town". But as they got into the train at West Wickham they heard Thomas, Rushforth and Rapley rehearsing still as they rode their bicycles along the country lanes and from the carriage windows re-echoed the strange cry of the wild men of West Wickham:-
"Black — lack, lack, lack Black — lack, lack, lack Black — HEATH! '
By 1909 with further rehearsal they had brought it such a state of Caruso-like perfection that it would shatter a gas-globe at "The Green Man ' when they welcomed the Cambridge Second team there.

Perhaps these were the last halcyon days. For all, life seemed destined to go on for ever in this Edwardian serenity: for Blackheath Harriers — the run, the bath, the rub-down from the excellent and perennial Parrish, the tea — bread, butter and jam, a piece of cake and a pot of tea all for sixpence — and a penny for George the waiter. Yet with Reed's death there was the end of an era, historically, and, ere long, geographically also, while in 1911, with the impact of another death upon him, that of King Edward V11 and as though he was already conscious of impending Armageddon, Elgar gave expression in his Second Symphony to the elegiac celebration of that long summer age.

BLACKHEATH HARRIERS WATER POLO TEAM
S.T. Pugh, E. Boning, H. Sulley, W. Boning, E.R. Harvey,
R.J. Wilson, Tom Crafter (Captain)
KENT WATER POLO CHAMPIONS 1896

OPENING RUN OCTOBER 6th 1900
THE MEDIUM PACK SETTING OUT FROM THE GREEN MAN

OPENING RUN OCTOBER 1st, 1955
THE FAST PACK SETTING OUT FROM HAYES

The seven in front are, left to right, G.R. Last, R.A. Morley, A.J. Brent, D.H. Hopgood, A. Wood, R. Webb, J. Withers, Behind them are A.A. Oldfield, A. Ball, A.J. Woodrow, W. Lake, A. Brill, D.A. Pinkard, D. French, G. Geere, G. Ness. G. E. Monshall & G. Scotting are to left and right at rear of group. (photo Kentish Times)

Reed, buried, as Walter Rowland was to be, in Nunhead Cemetery, their graves looking out over the country they had known together and had rejoiced in the strength of their youth, was to be followed by Val Hunter in 1914 whose own passing seemed to reinforce this sense of a fast-vanishing world. That "Apostle of Purity in Sport", as "The Sporting Life" called him, would assuredly have found the new ethos increasingly alien to his spirit.

". . . . The bright day is done and we are for the dark".

TOM CRAFTER PRESIDENT 1914 - 1920

THE GREAT WAR 1914-18

"I see them in foul dug-outs, gnawed by rats,
And in the ruined trenches, lashed with rain,
Dreaming of things they did with balls and bats,
And mocked by hopeless longing to regain
Bank-holidays, and picture-shows, and spats,
And going to the office in the rain".

(Siegfried Sassoon - "Dreamers" - 1917).

". . . So he opened the door . . . and when
they had looked, they were conscious of all
the evils they had ever sustained, and of all
the friends and companions they had lost and
of all the misery that had befallen them, as if
all had happened in that very spot; . . . and
because of their perturbation they could
not rest".

(from "The Mabinogion").

For more than most there is for the historian who is personally engaged with his subject matter the difficulty of contemplating, much less writing about a disaster which decimated the Blackheath membership and in this, moreover, the greater number of its active athletes — a war which has continued in its repercussions for this nation to the present day. If the hundred years of Blackheath's elapsed history are the history of athletics, so just as surely is its record sunk into and merged with the cataclysm of those four terrible years. "The Gazette", normally devoted to fitting trivia and facetiousness, becomes at this time a tragic vehicle for facts which are all the more painful for being bare.

The bulk of the Club's active membership - some two hundred and fifty — joined up and forty-four of these names were to be inscribed in the Club's Roll of Honour. The October "Gazette" told of the first to fall — A.J.N. Williamson of the Seaforth Highlanders, who had been Public Schools Half Mile Champion as recently as 1907 — and already by then a hundred had enlisted. Coming after a longer period of peace than any known in the recorded history of Europe, as A.J.P. Taylor has observed, it may well be that they, in common with thousands of others, were unconsciously weary of peace and security. Whatever the cause, they were all volunteers — none was conscripted; whatever the case, grievously were they to pay for it. Throughout the long years sorrow came in a steady stream of news which never dulled with familiarity the sensibilities of those who had to hear it. H.C. Cooper, the Cross-country Captain, went in the appalling fighting in Flanders, E.G. Glass in Gallipoli where R.W. Davis and Cyril Jarrett were "underground like rabbits"; S.J. Marshall, the pre-war Summer Captain and one of the Club's best sprinters died on the Somme, with A.D. Morton, the Cross-country Vice-Captain; Nicholls was to lose the son whose christening, only yesterday it seemed, had been referred to in the first volume of the "Gazette"; leading a bombing attack H.W. Gifford lost the light; Cecil Baxter, fifth in the A.A.A. Four Miles Championship the year before the War, was gone by 1917 when E.R. Small became the first Club Veteran to die. Harold Alexander, who became a Field Marshal in the Second World War, was matched in the first by his great friend E.B. Greer; Both Irishmen, both Guardsmen, they went up step by step in rank and honour together until their David and Jonathan friendship was parted by Greer's death in action in 1917. And in 1916 one of the famous trio of Lewisham Swimming Club forwards, G.F.N.

93

Wilkinson, was mourned by his friend also: "No more in the height of a match shall we hear Soll say, 'Now, Wilkie — Ralph!'"

There was a different kind of horror for those who preserved their lives through the ordeal. To "The Gazette" J.A. Allen wrote eloquent pieces which conveyed something of this to people at home who could have no real idea of what was meant by life in the front line, even in what passed for a hospital where his wounds had landed him: "The ground vibrates incessantly, casting showers of loose earth from the ceiling, the guns roar, men shout, groan, swear, die . . . " For others like L.J.L. Gaul, "our cox", there was "that most dastardly system of fighting", gas; for S.D. Taylor and M.C.C. Harrison there was the limbo of prisoner of war camp, the latter escaping after many attempts, the former to be buoyed up through four years of dreary confinement by his famous cheerfulness: "Am a prisoner here, but quite fit except for a couple of bullet holes". They were to return after an interval. Not so with many of the all-rounders of whom the Club was so proud: Frank Benton of the King's Royal Rifles, who had excelled at rugby and cricket, having been a regular member of W.G. Grace's London County Team, as well as an athlete; E.H. and S.G. Dadd, two of a famous trio of brothers recorded out together running on the Heath in 1910 — Julian, Edmund and Gabriel — the latter, like his great-uncle and his father both, a fine artist. One of his last works before the war came, though an animal sculpture bore the ominous motto of "True foes once met are joined till death". Their father, S.T., had been like them a swimmer and a champion plunger and the few surviving drawings we have of Blackheath Athletic Meetings from "The Illustrated Sporting and Dramatic News" show him to have been a considerable craftsman, as in his different field of caricature did the sketches of John Scott in the "Gazettes" of the twenties and thirties, times undreamt of in the midst of this holocaust where the immediate dread occupied all the mind, as Allen found:

"Saw moving, moving masses of kilted men,
Saw Boche Machine-guns firing hard,
Saw dead and dying every yard . . . ."

With this mass exodus from the Heath and the Club it would have been an easy and even an obvious step to close down the Club, but though it soon became evident that there was to be no quick victory as at first hoped the Committee persevered in a strong determination to sustain the Club. At the 1914 Annual General Meeting "the hope was expressed that those members unable to volunteer would do their best to keep the Club going" Fixtures would have to be cancelled — there were no men to run in them. It should also be clearly understood today that as the massive slaughter gathered momentum it became increasingly possible that there would be no men to run in them when the War was ended either: it is in the light of such knowledge that we should assess the nature of the older ones' stubborn refusal to allow the Club to dissolve — an absence of which in Blackheath would have seen our most assured overthrow. A considerable effort of imagination on the part of the reader is required to grasp what this must have entailed.

There were no fixtures or Club life in the old thriving, social sense but from the outset it was decided to maintain publication of "The Gazette" and in fact this never went out of print, thanks to the co-operative efforts of a number of men, but principally E.J. Denney, G.D. Gray and, once more, its first Editor, Harry Hopper. As was described after the War, it was sent to each man at the front month by month, "and many a member has told how the treasured record has crumbled to pieces in his tunic pocket before he has disposed of it".

Though the Heath became hedged about by soldiers' camps and allotments and though there were complaints about the fallen standards of "Green Man" suppers — "Fish", complained H.E. King in 1918 — every Saturday the trail was laid for any serviceman who might be able to turn up — and at least one did on every occasion but three. This was faithfully carried out by A.E. Culver, T.M. Gale, T.K. Grant and one who was the guiding spirit and a veritable beacon and symbol of this Blackheath resolution — Tom Crafter.

Norman Beyfus recollects that it was Crafter's kindly personal interest that decided him to join. He recalls going down one Saturday afternoon in October, 1907, to Blackheath: "At the top of the hill we saw the trail going out headed by Tom Crafter. He hailed us cheerily and I was struck by his white hair". Crafter was a prominent figure from the first when he joined in 1882 — eighteen stone of genial humanity was bound to be, given his fine personality, general bearing and generous sentiments. He is still remembered by members for his great laugh and his ability to make the younger ones feel at home in the circle of the Club. For years, when they thought of Blackheath Harriers they thought of Tom Crafter as "pre-eminent in expressing", again in Norman Beyfus' words, "those qualities of good fellowship and good sportsmanship to all that knew the joy of his cheery personality".

If he was not a legendary figure by 1914 he certainly was so by dint of his efforts and what he stood for during this War. Each and every week he was at "The Green Man", waiting for any serving man to turn up. Sometimes he ate a solitary meal in the evening

TOM CRAFTER, T.GALE and T.K.GRANT at the Green Man, 1913

there on a Wednesday or a Saturday rather than risk disappointing an unexpected member. None of these absent men were required to pay their subscriptions for the duration and it was Crafter who organized the compensating War Emergency Fund which realized £97 and ensured that, whatever other handicaps the Club would labour under after the war, there would be no financial ones.

The portrait contained in the Prologue to this History characterizes Crafter as so many knew him — a man of decided opinions and never afraid to express them loudly and dauntingly, yet possessed of the capacity to inspire affection and ease in young members. He was always known as Tom, even in a period when surnames were more used by intimates, except by those like R.W. Pattison, who committed the error of addressing him as "Mr. Crafter" — "There are no misters in this Club. Call me Tom!" H.K. Grant recalls that he would send a Club tie to each new member on his first Christmas after joining. He knew every member personally; the story deserves commemoration of how, later, at "The Swan", word was brought to him that an old Club member was outside, in greeting whom Crafter said, "I don't know you. You must be W.W. Davis". It is a story that was to have a warming parallel when in 1944, Arthur Thwaites, the man who then was performing the office of a Crafter in another war, welcomed a large man with a Canadian accent who walked into Hayes Headquarters saying that he hadn't been there before and was afraid they wouldn't know him, with the retort — "Yes, I do — You're Bob Crafter".

Besides his epic Presidency lasting from 1914 till 1920 he is remembered as Chief Trail Layer; this is how he is always pictured, besides the daunting image of him in the water playing water-polo "Six goals in rapid succession from my own goal line!" It was said that no competitor failed to follow a trail he had laid, or dared to do so. The first Chairman and a founder of the Kent A.A.A., a founder-member of Kent Krawlers, a Vice-President of Surrey Walking Club and of Lewisham Swimming Club, a rugby football player, an Assistant Secretary, Honorary Secretary, Handicapper, "Gazette" Editor, self-styled Club Whist Coach and general Presiding Genius, he was a man of unquenchable energies during forty years of the Club's history. Was it not he who shamed F.R.A. Glanville's father into abandoning his horsedrawn phaeton and walking back to Bromley from Sevenoaks where they had met the middle-aged Tom out strolling with a Club party — though Glanville pére did have to take a cab from that point and remain in bed for two weeks?

Even if on a Club concert platform he couldn't remember more than the first line of "The Fairy Queen" he was the progenitor of many forceful expressions of conviction which retain their bullet force even after half a century:

"There's nothing like cross-country running to keep a man fit!."

"We of the Blackheath Harriers know about these things!"

"Spikes, must have spikes; Edwards — lookatim — he wears spikes. No man can RUN unless he wears spikes! No. I don't wear spikes. I'd bend em!"

The jokes came less easily at this time of his greatest honour. With all six of his children serving — one daughter, a nurse, and five sons with fighting units in France — all of whom their father had had the great joy of seeing in one race at a Club meeting in 1906 — he suffered the blow of first the eldest, his namesake, then the next, Jim, taken from him, both killed in action. Only those like I.W. Nicholson, who recalls one evening at Blackheath at this time when he and Crafter were the only ones out in heavy snow and a biting wind could by any means guess at the feelings he must have experienced. And it was Cratter who, more advanced in years, saw further than most into the hearts of the young who were age-ing almost overnight in the crucible of war: "It is the boy in these days who knows every-thing. It is the boy who has become accustomed to look death in the face as a matter of daily routine". In this article written near the end of the war we get a rare but moving in-sight of a man who was not afraid to wear his heart on his sleeve. He hopes, he says, that he does not appear to the young as older men have to him in the past: "Do I, I wonder, look so dignified? Do I look aggressively respectable? I hope not". And it was character-istic that with these personal reflections he fused his great love and concern for the Club: "We know men whose hearts are evergreen; who see things through young eyes: who think the thoughts of youngsters, and understand their son's hopes, aspirations and pleasures as though they themselves were still in their boyhood. And, what is more, we don't have to go further than "The Green Man" to look for them".

It was to there that men's thoughts reached out repeatedly: "I want nothing better than when the war is over to meet all my old friends at that magnetic haunt, 'The Green Man'", wrote Allen, and spoke for more than himself. Crafter stood for all that and they loved and revered him for it. Though there was not a single race, though no turn-out numbered, as many as twenty excepting the inter-club run with Ranelagh in the first year of the war — "a season without precedent in the annals of the Club" — nonetheless for its mem-bers the Club was a live thing and "The Gazette" a means of communicating that life.

Another was lauded side by side with Crafter when the war ended. This was E.J.D. Ratcliff who, originally proposed by the efficient Nicholls, followed him as Honorary Secretary and is likely in the story of the Club to be overlooked in contemplating the pic-turesque figure of Crafter. Secretary and Cross-country Captain from 1900-1902, he assumed the former office again in 1910 and remained in it through the war for a total per-iod of ten successive years, after which he became President. He was an outstanding runner good enough not only to win the Club Five Miles Challenge Cup but to take the third place in the A.A.A. Four Miles Championship in 1899. When these active days were over this chain-smoking, coughing, Guinness drinker was still recognized as a characterful identity with a fondness for practical joking — he once brought an Italian organ-grinder's donkey into the bar of "The Swan" for a pint. Yet, although as A.C. Telfer recalls, he was the life and soul of the place, this was true in a more practical sense also, for his inconsequential nonchalance concealed a hard worker of distinguished executive ability. Above all, in this time of war he was something more than a complementary force to Crafter.

In one way and another there was still a good deal of athletics going on, but it was militarily organized and sponsored, and there was the paradox of sport stimulated by the war with, for example, a field of 864 runners in a single relay at Aldershot. In Flanders the Reverend W. Telfer organized a paper-chase for four hundred behind Arras — though he sus-pected they were tempted as much by the free tea as by the exercise. At home, members like Clay Thomas of the Artists' Rifles and D. Basan were helping to run athletic meetings, and at "The Green Man" there were occasional contingents like the hundred and twenty of the Honourable Artillery Company in 1915 to enliven the normally vacant scene. But an old and peppery colonel seeing them out on the five mile run in their civilian appearance was "most irate at seeing so many able-bodied young men frivolling away their time instead of joining the army and serving their King and Country".

For Blackheath, though, there was, as Ratcliff said in his 1915 Report, "little to which he had to refer . . . . Until the War was successfully concluded Blackheath Harriers would have but little interest in anything else". And hostile onslaught impinged even upon "The Green Man", its windows blasted by zeppelins. There was better or more cheerful news to lighten their mood from time to time, though: J.A. Allen had his pleasant memories of the war as well as grim ones of wounds and coast patrols — like his balloon trip extending from Hendon nearly to Oxford where he had lunch with some officers of the Indian Army he had "dropped in on". Tommy Hammond was patrolling on push-bike and getting his leg pulled for his pains before departing for Mesopotamia; Schofield was going in the same direction to Baghdad, W.R.J. Clarke to a less romantic-sounding destination as a wireless operator on a whaler. There were M.C.'s for others than Telfer, S.G. Beer and F.R.A. Glanville, and reflected glory from the V.C. for the brother of E.F. Judson after his single-handed attack on a machine-gun post. Seedhouse got public acclaim for manoeuvring his plane back to base though shot in the back in setting two Fokkers to flight.

But long before 1918, in France among the men who fought and by then even in the comparative oblivion of England, all were weary of a war that seemed interminable and were near the end of their tether: "The Club is divided into those who are young and unfit, and those who are old and unfit", wrote Crafter in 1918. Being the man he was he could not see that as leading to a conclusion, but the fruition of his hopes was to take longer than he imagined when he confidently proclaimed: "When the new world . . . . shall arise from the embers of the old one we used to know, there will certainly survive one institution, which will emerge stronger in body and spirit than ever before". And indeed, before the end of the year, the silver lining did at last seem to be visible, even if it was to be detected in the fact that A.R. Pearson's pessimism concerned the peace-time instead of the War in sending "some rather doleful notes" to "The Gazette" commenting on the growing scarcity of country for the next season, for, since the last run he had described for that organ, fields through which they had run were being built on. With the sad wisdom of the born treasurer he was right, even though the Editor blithely and obliviously commented, "We can't leave the old "Green Man" even if we have to run over the house-tops". Since the Well Hall estate growth to the South-east was now completing the encirclement of Blackheath that form of exercise seemed the only choice left open to them if they were to remain in the old home.

Still, for the time being, the cessation of hostilities by the autumn offered more than sufficient reason for thankfulness, and already by the Opening Run the numbers were up to thirty-two with fifteen at the Committee meeting and Trevor Davis afterwards biking 14 miles for the 2 a.m. start to his City Police duties. Though by no means sedate in its celebration in London generally there was not the hysteria of a Mafeking Night but more a tired relief. Then too the protracted peace negotiations and the accompanying slowness in demobilization meant that even the potential resources were not available for the Club to carry out a programme even in the following summer of 1919, though the winter after saw fixtures arranged again and something of a return to normal.

But for the time being it was enough that the nightmare was over. Some rejoicing there might be, but others like Julian Dadd's war-companion, Robert Graves, the peace found feverishly walking the hills, "cursing and sobbing and thinking of the dead".

As Crafter had prophetically written over a year before with the full weight of the horror upon him:

"Are these notes too serious? Will it be, think you, all noise and gaiety when the boys come home? Will it be all rejoicing? . . . .
Look on these pages; look at the slowly increasing list of departed Blackheathens, and say, if you can, whether you will greet our dear boys with laughter or with tears?"

The wounds would, gradually, heal. Meantime, even before Neville was once more laying on mid-summer strolls to Brighton, before summer runs were being re-started from "The Swan" — the new hostess there "quite an acquisition" — before Pearson was again turning out minus the old cap but with the jersey still holding together "they were glad to see", they had "Punchbowl Night" as the first Post-War Club function. Again too, by the following March they were enjoying "a cut from an excellent sirloin, chopped off by Tom Crafter, who carves in no fairy-like fashion", with Jack Reay at the other end, "busy with a leg of mutton". And the Club Cry was heard for the first time since March, 1914, while despite the fact that they would have to wait until April, 1920, for a full Reunion Dinner, at least those present now could drink the long-awaited toast to Crafter.

". . . . Tom it is who sits enshrined
Within the hearts of all our kind,
True champion of the squares entwined".

Both here and at later meetings like the 1919 Annual General Meeting when Crafter was re-elected "with great acclamation", not only he and Ratcliff, "those two pillars of the Club", but others from Hopper to Tommy Gale who had not missed more than a couple of Saturdays in the last thirty years, let alone laying the trail in the last four — all were rapturously toasted and gratefully thanked. Judicious preparations were made for the days ahead by providing for a new water boiler and by laying in a store of new towels, sponges, two dozen packs of playing cards, "at a nominal price" by courtesy of Adrian Metcalf, and . . . . a dozen Novices' Pewters.

Some surer provision against the future was to be necessary though. By comparison with other sporting clubs they were fortunate: the Blackheath Hockey Club found itself with a possible four returned of its pre-war representation of four teams and was forced to disband. Even so there were lean times ahead. Few who went through the war with minds fixed on "The Green Man" could have dreamt that when the Memorial to the fallen was unveiled by Walter Rowland as oldest member it would be at West Wickham and consecrated by the Rector of that parish, the Reverend H.B. Roberts, in a new clubroom some few miles and a whole world away from "The Green Man" whose passing they were signalizing together with that of so many of the Blackheath members who had whiled away so many hours there in an age that, unknown to most, had already gone.

"You shall know a man by his deeds and by the friends who shall mourn him".

99

THE CLUB GROUND – PECKHAM BLACKHEATH WEST WICKHAM, HAYES

Reproduced from the Ordnance Survey map of 1927 with the sanction of the Controller of H.M. Stationery Office, Crown Copyright reserved.

1919-1920

PART THREE 1919 - 1939
"FRESH TRAILS"
THE MOVES TO WEST WICKHAM AND HAYES
THE NINETEEN THIRTIES

     .... quassa tamen nostra est, non mersa nec obruta navis, utque caret portu, sic tamen extat aquis...."

 (....Yet my bark was but shattered, not submerged and overwhelmed, and though it is deprived of a harbour, yet even so it floats upon the waters....)

Ovid-Tristia X ì

"How long will it be before we are compelled to seek new cross-country Headquarters? Or, to put it more crudely, how long can we maintain our strength as a cross-country club unless we migrate to sweeter courses? One need not fear for the social side of the Club, or the flat-racing section. They are probably more brilliant today than they have ever been but of course, the present question does not affect them at all. What we must bear in mind is that the Blackheath Harriers were formed to encourage cross-country running, and sooner or later we shall have to face the question, unless we copy the ostrich and bury our heads in the sand".

("The Gazette", October 1911).

The effects of the War were not the only adversity the Club had to contend with. The continuing menace of London's growth could not be ignored, even by the most die-hard adherent of the beloved "Green Man". Indeed, Tom Crafter himself, going out with T.K. Grant in March, 1921, to find a course for the first Kent Cross-country Championships in the area, was forced to concede that the ground was not as open as it had been and "The Gazette" correspondent reporting their reconnaissence ventured diffidently: "It is rumoured that the mushroom growth of alleged houses which is menacing the important points of our country did not altogether escape their notice". The 1911 writer quoted above had asked his question "in lively anticipation of caustic remarks by some of our vice-presidents and other older members", and certainly there was a reluctance among many of these to send down new roots which was never completely overcome. For all it was at best unpleasantness to be faced rather than greeted: H. Bellman, who joined in 1913, wrote recently, "I 'endured' the change from "The Green Man" to West Wickham". Nor was this simply a matter of sentiment; the Blackheath home had become a riverside and North Kent institution. It was easily accessible from all parts of London and served as a general social centre both in the week and on Saturdays: people were always "dropping in". The move to West Wickham meant a sacrifice of this central situation which was an advantage we are apt to forget in these days of easy movement. At that time the suburban fringe ended at Elmers End. The Hayes Branch was a genuine rural railway service and Eden Park was in the country. In fact, it was not to be until well after the Club had moved from West Wickham to Hayes that, as a result of the electrification of the railway, the greater number of the houses in the area were built. But in 1921 West Wickham was a village of about nine hundred inhabitants, ringed in by fields and woods. Therefore to reach West Wickham you had to make a special journey so that anyone from North London, for example, had to watch the clock, and no one used it mid-week. In short, it was at this time a place for special gatherings associated with the winter programme and not a handy centre where people could meet casually at any time, so, all in all, not so different in function from its former use as an outlying place they visited. Naturally this loosened ties somewhat: people who were no longer actively concerned tended to limit their visits to special occasions, and, where their journeys were difficult, to lose touch, though not usually allegiance, once they retired from active participation. The vast growth of Greater London continued to accentuate this tendency, though it was eventually to be offset by increasing recruitment from the areas immediately accessible from our Headquarters, as might be expected.

But at the time it was a melancholy event and no occasion for self-congratulatory rejoicing. For a little while some flicker of life continued at "The Green Man", but the heart had gone out of its habitues and in the autumn "Gazette" of 1922 appeared baldly the notice, "Training runs and Club evenings will no longer take place at "The Green Man" as hitherto"

In its place for mid-week activities was the Private Banks ground at Catford Bridge which already held place in Blackheath affections and now would do so again for more than one generation. Later in the same issue came the quietus: "To most of us the final severance of the Club from its old and familiar surroundings . . . . will come as a decided wrench. But one has to admit that the ancient glories of our old headquarters have long since departed, and naught but sentiment could have kept us there in more recent years among its gloomy and dilapidated surroundings and the general air of neglect which pervaded its precincts . . . . It was, therefore, regretfully decided at the eleventh hour, and certainly not before such adverse conditions had had their effect upon the Club, no longer to shut our eyes to them and live in the past, but to look into the future".

In the new physical surroundings of the weekend runs though, there was a beauty and atmosphere in addition to there being open ground for running over which for long retained its subtle influence. The whole country of West Wickham and Hayes until the 1930's was more genuinely rural and unsophisticated than anything that had been regularly experienced by the Club for a long time. Except for some larch plantations and a few iron rail fences the wedge of country about the County Boundary might have come straight out of the eighteenth century with lonely landscapes belonging to an older world. A ploughboy driving his team at West Wickham where now are hundreds of houses told some of our members in 1922 that he had never been to Croydon and had no wish to go beyond West Wickham and its fields, and the beautiful country there proved him no fool. There were the autumn and winter sunsets over the fields and wolds that seemed timeless, the great stretches of purple ploughland that ran down from the fields above Addington, while in spring and summer there was an abundance of wildflowers, among them rare ones like scarlet pimpernel: all a reminder of the old, old England that nearly everyone has lost now. They really were for a time a country club and this tended to cut the winter men off from the mainstream of cross-country running which then as now tended mainly to be concentrated in the half-suburbanized fringe of the big centres of population. Our courses were special and they were difficult, calling for endurance rather than speed — and not least for endurance under the severe weather conditions of more exposed places in these courses. Quite naturally it tended to make our men sluggish in a six-months' season and they were apt to be out of their element on the faster courses which even then were the peculiar choice of the organizers of the big championships. The Club chose difficult country out of preference and on the right day in really rough weather their teams could show a staying power that shook visitors, as in the violent blizzard which overtook the Kent Cross-country Championship race held at Hayes in 1930. Parochial such an attitude might have been — the Southern was the important race for the Club, not the National which we only entered when it was held in the south — but it was certainly the product of circumstances and their history and not, as some today may be willing to think, mere perversity.

While our country was not the best preparation for the essentially competitive and specialized championship racing that was then developing it nevertheless gave much pleasure to those privileged to use it, not only as a challenge but aesthetically also. There are today many who hold in grateful memory impressions not only of breathlessness but enjoyable ones evoked even after many years by names like Coney Hall, Boundary, or, to give it its old name, Rowdown Wood, Bourne Valley, Dog Farm and Bunker's Nob later built over in the New Addington expansion but holding a special place in Club lore and providing a standby for any "Gazette" contributor whose inspiration flagged. The same nostalgia was later to apply equally to the courses which generally fell further to the west after the move to Hayes and whose ways still intermingle with those of yesterday so that their followers too entertain similar feelings regarding the names of Fox Hill, "The Gully" and Leafy Grove,

BOTTOM OF FOX HILL   by L. Norris

Blackness, Rouse and Layhams Farms, Midden, Nash, High Gate, Well Wood and Pylon Field. Known as Nicholls Hill to one Blackheath generation and Layhams Hill to the next nevertheless the same ambivalence is felt by both towards its steep and muddy slopes. Many changes were to come to this untouched area, but for now only the lights from a few distant cottages on high ground at Keston reassured the tardy runner that he was in the twentieth century and not among Saxon wolds as he picked his way along flinty tracks topped by great briar hedges and overshadowing woods, spurring his way towards the comforts of "The Railway Hotel".

These latter to be sure were not great; the clubroom on the first floor was not as large as we had been used to, though there was "a large adjunct to the main building" which could be used for the big matches, but there again the boiler wasn't large enough for the hot water needs of such great numbers, while the walls, floorboards, seating and lino were among the priorities for renewal. Still, with "The Swan" not available it did very well and though the location had changed other things could continue unaltered. The Blackheath attitude remained inwardlooking, even self-congratulatory, always sociable. It was now that

106

the Entertainments Committee was set up, under the chairmanship of J.F. Ponsford — and just as we have seen that F.H. Reed had always dispatched Club business with the minimum delay to the ensuing "smoker", so in these early twenties social events seemed more important than competitive or organizational matters. [46]

The annual Town Dances were a popular feature of the social round of this period. The same host, hundreds strong, that attended the Bohemian concerts rolled up to such events as the Fancy Dress Carnival, the ladies attracting especial attention in their various guises: "Snow maidens", "belles of the South Seas" and "Ultra-modern flappers". In "The Gazette" the report of Punchbowl Night commonly exceeded that of the A.G.M. in length by more than ten times, while the same relaxed attitudes obtained on the competitive track where in provincial meetings one might unremarkably find iron gates for hurdles, rolled newspapers for relay batons and, as in the previous century, a man might collide with a sheep on a grass track and not consider it as more than an amusing incident "in passing". The atmosphere of the Club up to this time can be caught in reports of almost any event, as witness that of the team en route to meet Cambridge Hare and Hounds: "After discussing steaks at Smith's the party of nine left Liverpool Street in two carriages thoughtfully reserved by Ratty", while the characteristic remark — of and by — Blackheathens was that heard as our tail closed in one year in the Southern: "They may be a long way behind, but they are sportsmen".

UNCOMMON CLAY

Post-war recovery was indeed painful for them — far more than, for example, S.L.H., though in fact from 1919 elections nearly every week swelled our numbers. The need to revise their settled attitudes and policy to match the altered conditions of the post-war world was strong and it was unfortunate that it should coincide with the very time we were forced to break the forty years-old tie with the place that gave the Club its distinguishing name. Still, there was the consolation of the highest membership to date — 482 in 1920 — and, too, there were other signs of progress: the old standard mile "run-in", [47] for novices disappeared and the pewter was awarded to the first unplaced novice in the Club Championships and the three big matches. The valuable Points Handicap Competition was instituted soon after; Open 6and 7 Mile Handicaps were held; subscriptions and "The Gazette" were targets in economy drives, while perhaps the most moving instance of valediction to a fast-vanishing past was the decision in 1921 that towels should no longer be provided free of cost in the winter season. Most noteworthy perhaps was the continuing prominence of Blackheath officials in the larger athletic world, with H.J. Barclay still A.A.A. Hon. Secretary and a crowd of Blackheath officials assisting at the A.A.A. Championships: H.F. Pash, F.L. Gilbert, the then Blackheath Secretary and, in 1928-29, President of Southern and National C.C. Associations, H.A. Butler, D. Basan and well-remembered names like J.E. Fowler-Dixon, Ernest Neville and Clay Thomas — on the megaphone. They represented a tradition members pride themselves upon.

Tradition also was evident in the rare phenomenon of an historical review in a "Gazette" of 1921, an article which is significant not so much for what it tells us of the past as for what we learn of contemporary attitudes. We notice that, except for the long-gone individual achievements of the 1880's and 90's and the isolated glories of men like Hammond and Lindsay subsequently, the writer boasts of little in the way of athletic feats. It shows us what Blackheath men were proud of: their long tradition, their past champions, the virtue of participating rather than winning, and their relish of other sports — rugby, lacrosse, swimming, not to mention ping-pong — allusions to which occupy nearly as much space in the article as athletics. It is a matter of fact that with notable exceptions like the Club's A.A.A. Mile Medley Relay win in 1911 the exploits of our water-polo players represented the best in Blackheath team achievement to this date — and that had been in 1896. It notes with satisfaction as well it might, the Club's longevity and persistence in holding regular Wednesday and Saturday runs from 1878 to 1921 apart from the war years. That was the full tally to date as far as they were concerned: enough to satisfy many but in the light of the difficulties facing them hardly encouraging for the long term.

One of the facts mentioned in the article is that there remained at the time two original members, Walter Rowland and S.A. Bennett. The former had stood for the best in the competitive and social spirit of "the old Club" and when he died the following year both the Peckham and "Green Man" eras could be said to have disappeared finally with him, though the symbol that was Tom Crafter was to survive for many more years. With Rowland's passing there seemed much else, if not moribund then static, in the Club he had helped give us. Once more we are faced with a living demonstration of the principle that an organism that does not continue to evolve and develop is in the long run headed for extinction. At this stage — the years immediately following the war — the potentialities for further growth and development were nearly exhausted and something amounting to a transfusion of life was necessary if it was to have a new lease. Our great good fortune was that there had appeared a man who could make such a constructive contribution to our destinies.

As had been said, the numbers of the Club and therefore the weight of business had been increasing continuously since the War on a scale which would have alarmed our predecessors who could conduct the small necessities of business in relaxed, familiar fashion. The onus as always was on the Secretary whose duties had proliferated in extent and in degree so that at the A.G.M. of 1922 F.L. Gilbert resigned, apparently because of this increasing pressure, even though they passed an amendment to Rule 3 to increase the Hon. Secretary's assistance in effect to four men. No one could be found to replace him, however, and the Committee was left to appoint, Gilbert persevering till someone was found.

CLUB GROUP, SUMMER 1930

CLUB GROUP, WINTER 1930

109

" He was a big-hitting batsman with a long reach". In the case of H.J. Dyball this description of his cricketing ability can be extended to the dynamic of his life in general, a fact which he himself now demonstrated in five brief, crammed years of service to Blackheath as its Secretary which he became the following January. A capable sprinter but not a cross-country runner, he had been Hon. Secretary to Dorking Town F.C. and, once again suggestive, a centre-half prior to his joining Blackheath in 1912 and holding office as a popular Track Captain, and after as Assistant Hon. Secretary and Club Handicapper which office he combined with his secretaryship till 1927. By that date, when he was forced to give up because of the demands of his work in the Treasurer's Department of the Southern Railway, the membership had almost doubled, largely through his efforts.

For it was he who was the leader of the Blackheath renaissance, the second in its history, which now followed and ensured the centenary we are occupied with as a Club at this time of writing. Recruiting was an unusual word in Blackheath before his day but it was firmly in Dyball's mind as the chief means of maintaining the Club's virility, and that by a constant stream of new members, and he lost no opportunity of pressing it home in his speeches at meetings and dinners. The record membership of 523 in 1923 included a strong contingent of young men between the ages of eighteen and twenty-three, Dyball himself introducing nearly a hundred before the end of the same year. Many of these, the banks as a source of recruitment being largely closed to us, came from the insurance companies, though indeed they came from everywhere and "easily", as he himself replied to those enquiries how he succeeded. Perhaps the unknown lady was close to the truth who remarked of him, "He spoke so nicely to the younger men". A natural diplomat, he had a remarkable gift for establishing relations with outside bodies, for interesting school games masters and secretaries of business house sports clubs and inducing them to send along new members. Many fixtures he introduced with this primary aim. The decade saw the inception of inter-schools races as distinct from those against single schools, together with the encouragement of local schools especially; the introduction of novices' races into each Club Evening Meeting, with fields of dozens in middle distance races as well as over the country. He knew everyone and never missed an opportunity of talking to an individual member and making him feel he belonged and had a personal stake in the Club. No new member was ever missed by him on his first appearance or neglected afterwards; nor did he reserve notice to the talented only — he stimulated them all, the gifted, the not so good and the down-right rabbits. In fact, he was a focus of energy and personal magnetism pouring life and energy into the Club all the time against a background at first of adversity and at times shattering reverses — for this is no straight or sentimental success story. Even such a man could not encompass all, given never so monumental will-power, and there must have been moments where he felt the weight of things utterly against him, not least because such spade-work does not yield its best results for many years, as was to become apparent. It was unfortunate for him that it is mainly since his day that we have reaped the full benefit of his dedicated genius.

To all intents and purposes a young man still in his late thirties he was vigorous in mind and constitution alike. He was one of the tallest men in the Club at the time but though standing 6ft. 4 ins. he was not heavily built — about fourteen stone and long in the leg, while in addition to having blue eyes and a fresh, ruddy complexion he was full-faced with a mobile expression indicating an active mind and energetic temperament — all in all a handsome man.

H.J. DYBALL - HON SECRETARY

1922 - 1927

In manner he was slightly inhibited as if he had not full confidence in expressing himself. He could also at times be irascible — typical of people who drive themselves too hard. Born a countryman his interests and attitudes were wholly orientated towards business management, and he was above all practical in his instincts, though with an accessibility to general ideas not always found in men of his background and inclination. Routines and processes he saw as means to ends and he had a vein of enquiry and curiosity which, geared to a practical issue, would lead him to probe at times far beyond the commonplace "acceptance-state" of most. Possibly his organizing ability was not absolutely outstanding — though with his immense nervous energy he discharged a volume of Club business in his spare time which would shake most administrators — but strategically it was, subduing all action to the pursuit of a general policy. This was his great quality: everything was made to subserve the overall plan and directing principle. Morale generally in a competitive connection he ignored — or rather thought would take care of itself. It was of course evident at this time that there must be a re-casting of our habitual methods and this naturally gave rise to tensions between the conservatively minded and the forward-looking which were quite as severe as those we have experienced since. There were two burning topics, that of the removal from Blackheath described, and the abandonment of the attitude that it was to be left to new members to come to us without seeking. Of course, he was not alone in appreciating the need for drastic change and it is probably true to say that a majority to a greater or less degree shared this feeling, but a minority, among them Tom Crafter especially, were vehement in its rejection. Ramsay Moir the "Gazette" Editor, and Syd. Taylor especially concentrated on the need to leave Blackheath, while opposition to this came in addition from a few sympathizers with Crafter like Hopper who had lived by Blackheath for so long. Perhaps deriving from a misunderstanding of the Club's reluctance to "poach" him as a member when he had first applied, Dyball nursed a rather irrational notion of an underground prejudice against him which the situation in the twenties aggravated. Of course, Crafter's opposition could be daunting with its accompanying decibels and his lack of inhibition in expressing sentiments, but Dyball was under a delusion as to its extent and he never properly appreciated the impregnability of his position which rested on universal support. He attracted loyal and enthusiastic assistants, but he usually had the tact to leave them their initiative since he had given them his inspiration.

A pregnant suggestion of the moving spirit of the times which the many Blackheath sprinters of that decade doubtless appreciated was in the alteration to Rule 17 recorded thus: "Substitute 'shorts' for 'knickerbockers'." And indeed, it was in the sphere of track and, intermittently, field events that we find strong promise of the successes that were to follow in the thirties as well in the fifteen years following the First World War. The 1920 Olympic 800 and 1500 metres Champion, Albert Hill, had ended his personal triumphs but he became a formidable ally for those of Dyball's mind when he became the Blackheath coach in 1924, not only advising but actually running with them across country. Later he was to foster sprinters of E.L. Page's calibre and find a renewed fame for himself in doing the like for Sydney Wooderson. Actively supporting the Club was his old rival, Henry Stallard, who not only distinguished himself as an Olympic medallist but helped them to many an inter-club victory at this time. An early pioneer of our field events strength today was the British but French-speaking H. Dauban de Silhouette who came second in the A.A.A. Javelin Championship in 1923 and 1924.

We had a sufficiency of County champions, among them the fine sprinter and Summer Captain, G.D. Basan, busy laying the foundations in the mid-twenties for the outstanding performances that were to become almost traditional and himself winning both sprint titles in times that are still more than respectable. R.D. Bell shone repeatedly in mile races, and, finishing 3rd in the A.A.A. Mile of 1928, went to the Amsterdam Olympics for Britain. Good quarter-milers like G.B. Westoby and J.R. Major in the mid-twenties had been inspired by one who was probably the best of our track men at this time, R.A. Lindsay. He overcame the handicap imposed by the war and won the A.A.A. 440 Yards Championship in 1921 at an age when most of his class have given up, after representing Britain at the 1920 Olympics where he won a gold medal as member of the 1600 Metres Relay Team together with a friend of Blackheath, Guy Butler. His support of the Club continued after his active days and he turned up always at Evening meetings and barbecues. At his death his wife presented the Lindsay Salver which today is held by "the member whose example and performance in track or field contribute most to the credit of the Club" and the first holder of which was J.B. Herring in 1959. But the more impressive progress was not now that of individual athletes so much as the teams in the inter-club matches and the large numbers turning out under Dyball's auspices in the Evening Meetings — two dozen in a hundred yards handicap, three dozen in a half-mile handicap — together with an overall rise in standard. The major inter-club meeting was the Woolwich Trophy with Belgrave, Surrey A.C., Polytechnic and Achilles among the dozen clubs competing. Our fourth place in 1924 and 1925 showed as well as anything that we were on the right road and we were first in the Kent Challenge Trophy held in conjunction.

On the face of it the cross-country record of this period is inconsistent and disappointing. The Nicholls Cup Race, which represents a real test of Club as distinct from individual strength, was lost throughout the twenties but this was rather through the increasing power of S.L.H. who had made such excellent recovery from the war than from any stagnation on the Club's part. Still scoring only ten a side they were often close-run affairs by the mid-twenties; in the two years previous to the 1923-24 season the margins had been 73 to 177 points and 67 to 236 but then this narrowed to a gap of 32 points only, and again the following year to 50 points. The numbers were increasing all the time so that in 1926 it became a virtually "all to score" event, that is, each side scoring three less than the total number of starters of the smaller side. Still Blackheath were losing but only by small margins and in 1927 by 47 points, very little indeed with each side now fielding over seventy a side.

Members at this time were well enough aware of a new spirit even without immediate evidence of resounding victories, and today they generally agree that the 1924 race against Ranelagh was the turning point. The field of 72 was almost equally divided between the clubs, disappointing for Blackheath who had expected nearer fifty to turn out for them. Yet over the home course made heavy by rain and on a drizzling day of high wind they won by six points. The margin had been nearly a hundred at the fortieth position but even

"THE 440 YARDS CHAMPIONSHIP OF ENGLAND, 1921."
R.A. Lindsay beating Bevil Rudd.

so the result was enough to gladden their hearts and that of their Grand Old Man Josiah Rampley at the Smoker the same evening, not to mention Jack Reay who had been Referee that afternoon giving tongue to "Phil The Fluter's Ball" and forming a Victorian bridge to that part of the entertainment that had such a flavour of the twenties in John Scott's lightning sketches.

Generally too there was an improvement, though uneven and with many a slip from grace, for example, 19th in the Southern to 10th in 1923; defeated by Ranelagh and Orion in this same year; beating them both for the first time since the war in 1926. The next year they won the Kent and followed this with 4th and 11th places in the Southern and National. By 1928 in the Nicholls Cup with 113 Blackheath and 112 South London Harriers taking the field — the largest ever by any two clubs to that date — and with each side finishing twenty-one in the first forty-two home in a sternly fought contest it became clear that it was only to be a short while before Blackheath put an end to the long line of defeats. Nowhere were there any large time gaps and this is ample testimony to their strength in depth by this time.

CLUB FIGURES BY JOHN SCOTT
From "The Gazette", May, 1924

CLUB GROUP - 1924-25

CLUB DINNER 1923

Not least among them were runners such as Hopper — though he like Crafter was far from enthusiastic about West Wickham — and the evergreen Trevor Davis who ran the 1920 Nicholls Race having also competed in the first of the races for the Cup in 1896. It was in 1922 that Davis' Southern entry was objected to at the scrutiny meeting on the grounds that he had been running since the eighties and the same objection crisply if autocratically dismissed by F.L. Gilbert with the remark that the time of the meeting "should not be wasted with such nonsense". Championship events, though, rest on a small number for their team success and it is evident that we had also acquired a number of runners who could offer contention to the best.

The miler Bell was no more hampered over the country by an arm action imperfect through infantile paralysis than he was on the track and though he tended to fall off over distances greater than seven and a half, which discouraged him, he was useful to the Club in this sphere as he was in singing straight songs. A.G.V. Allen who became captain was very different in that he was at his best usually when the distance was ten and then, preferably, over the tough Hayes country. A strong runner of medium height and build he won the Rowland Cup six times in succession and his greatest ability was to "keep coming" over the last miles of the race. Good backing came from stalwarts like E.J. Castello, H.J. Denyer, D.J. Mobbs, Charles Clowser, Syd. Taylor, R.W. Pattison, C.A. Peachey, B.P. Braund, and even, till 1921, E.F. Judson, by then a veteran, with B.H. Lymbery playing an important part. But the outstanding runners of the early twenties were A.C. Edwards and A.C. Telfer, both cross-country specialists with all its accompanying techniques. With the exception of Sydney Wooderson, Edwards was very likely the finest natural distance runner we have had.

A.C. Telfer, younger brother of the two and a self-styled "country" member, got over[48] a leg wound received in France, returned to take up where he left off, became a pillar of strength to Blackheath and though not the fastest of starters, was a tactician of the first order. In addition he was the prime mover of the now classic fixture with Felsted School whence we derived yet another schoolmaster-member through Telfer's offices, this being P.H. Francis, surely one of our best of all-time. Deceptively frail-looking, he served notice of his ability in the Southern of 1926 finishing 19th then following this with 14th place in the National. The following year he was 8th in the National and was runner-up in the A.A.A. 10 Miles Championships to Ernie Harper who was to finish 2nd in the 1936 Olympic Marathon. Having a Welsh qualification though, Francis missed his international since Wales could not raise a team. More than these achievements, though, are two features of the man: that, being frail — not more than about seven stones — he had some bad times early in his running career, yet was determined enough to persevere, and that, linked with this, he had a loyalty to the Club that was tenacious. He undertook strenuous journeys to arrive in time to race then returned straightaway without further enjoyment of what Blackheath has to offer so much of in the way of social pleasures.

These were members of surely the best team the Club had had up to that time and one to rival most teams since. Blackheath was starting to look outwards much more now and both promoted and won the first South of the Thames Junior Team Race at Hayes, also supplying the individual winner in L.C. Ratcliff who had a meteoric success at this time. Briefly, Dyball spoke a truth which had not always been notably evident but which now placed its emphasis without irony when he said, "Blackheath Harriers is a running club

THE START AGAINST OXFORD UNIVERSITY AT OXFORD, 1929

BLACKHEATH MEMBERS: M. Lindsey (Partly Obscured), J.R. Mullion, H.S. Smith, W.E. Dimes, F.D. Lys, W. Holmes, C. Pollard. The Olympic Middle Distance Runner, Jerry Cornes, is next to Pollard.

and not a social club only".

The unspoiled nature of West Wickham with its picturesque and obstructive elm standing at the cross-roads by "The Swan" and serving as a starting point for two Nicholls Cup races before and after the first World War was no guarantee of preservation against the ravages of creeping suburbia. Unlike Hayes it had no commonland to ensure access to open country beyond and with the electrification of the railway already referred to which was planned for 1926 it was clear that in the foreseeable future it was bound to be "built in". The Blackheath authorities were not going to be caught napping and a small committee were already on the look-out for new quarters in the area. It was apparently T.K. Grant who, Columbus-like, spied out the building which at the present day is our Clubhouse and Headquarters and which is not only our own property but where we have now been for as long as we were at "The Green Man". J. Sims has told the story of the acquisition of the large building and its accompanying cottage in a "Gazette" article: of their former ownership by the Lennard family of Wickham Court, of their being contemporary probably with the opening up of the line from Elmer's End to Hayes in 1882, of the most likely original intention being that of a depot for housing estate development, which came to little more than four or five houses in Station Road, and of their final sale by Mr. A.I. Steer to the Club together with the land for £850 in 1926.

Arthur Israel Steer was a very palpable sort of ghost for Blackheath Harriers since he "haunted" the Club for nearly forty years. Steer was a practical engineer and a property speculator of a sort. He had bought the present Club area from the Lennards in 1923 with the idea that he might put up one or two houses on it and sell at a profit. He apparently gave up this idea and agreed to sell to the Club. Having thus agreed he then, like many a later property dealer, tried to change his mind and back out. The Club held him to his contract and after a bitter wrangle he eventually sold but retained for his own use a small triangle of land behind the cottage, at the end of the garden of 4 Station Road which he also owned and which later was renumbered 54 Bourne Way. On this sunken piece of waste land he built himself a shack of breeze blocks and waste material of various sorts and he used this as a workshop for his engineering activities. It also became apparent in due course that he was actually living in this place for a considerable part of his life. For many years he nursed a

grudge against the Club. Those Club members who were concerned with the management of the Headquarters came to dislike him more and more as he missed no opportunity to create trouble. His appearance alone was quite alarming particularly to anyone who happened to be surprised by him whilst on the property alone. For the most part the Club Stewards or tenants of the cottage lived alongside this eccentric neighbour in a state of silent hostility broken occasionally by his

THE CLUBHOUSE AT HAYES
Before Conversion, 1926.

119

A GROUP AT HAYES, SEPTEMBER, 1966
LEFT TO RIGHT: D.G. Child, E.J.J. Reed, W.P. Whiting,
W.H.M. Vercoe, A.A. Tweedy, G. Waller, L. Norris,
E. Doorbar, B.G. Parrott, G.A. Gardner, J. Collett, A. Nye.

noisy complaints.

In the mid-1950's 54 Bourne Way, which had previously been let, was put up for sale — at a very high price. The house was eventually sold but Steer remained in his shack. Although he was by then quite old he still seemed to spend most of his time in the small area around it and endured all the rigours of winter in these primitive and insanitary conditions. But, although an outcast of society and cut off even from his own wife and family, he was neither penurious nor wretched. He owned more than one property in the neighbourhood and he was able to earn some sort of living at his mysterious 'engineering' work at which he would disappear sometimes for quite long periods. Like other hermits his reputation probably exaggerated his true skill as a smith but there is no doubt that his working activities absorbed and sustained him.

As he grew older his attitude to the club changed. He could still be seen watching our activities silently with a bleak and watery stare but on more than one occasion he was known to have acted as a watchdog and to have frightened inquisitive intruders off the premises. In 1962 and 1963 the club stewards, Leslie Dredge and his wife, a kindly couple, took pity on the old man and began to provide him occasionally with meals. It must have been the first time for many years that anyone had been so kind to him and he accepted their hospitality with gratitude. His hermitage was, however, at its end. His former property at 54 Bourne Way was being pulled down to make way for the modern flats that now occupy the site, there was turmoil from the contractors, he was getting old, well into his eighties, the sanitary officer had made ominous enquiries about fitness for habitation, above all there had been a severe winter and he was far from well: he bowed to the inevitable and

120

agreed to go into an old men's home. On his departure he made over all his possessions in the shack, including some useful and valuable tools, to Leslie Dredge and entered into a deed giving him the property itself. The shack soon collapsed and in due course, after the Dredges had left our service, the Club acquired the triangle of land that had been an eyesore and a source of nuisance for so many years. The acquisition has enabled the Club to improve the entrance to the club grounds and to provide a supplementary parking space. Since then little more has been heard of Steer.

The dilapidated state of the larger "crumbling stable and coachhouse" can readily be seen from the photograph taken before its conversion while its atmosphere can be imagined; it was "about as tumbledown, morbid and depressing a spot as eyes could look upon", they said at the time. Two minutes' walk from Hayes Station, it consisted of half an acre of land with its two substantial buildings, the larger one of two floors, sixty feet by twenty, the other of a cottage of four rooms over a garage. Business and practical action are a particular excellence with Blackheath and this they proceeded to demonstrate. Our member, W.C. Pinhey, acting as Hon. Architect estimated that a further four hundred pounds were necessary to render it suitable, gutting of the interior, disinfection and fumigation ranking as priorities to banish traces of its former occupants. Among these were a firm of breeze-block makers; another of jobbing builders with, as the 1931 "Gazette" correspondent put it, "some seven or eight more (number not guaranteed) "night-dossers" who worked in the local gravel pits and for whom the lack of bathing accommodation and cooking facilities held no terrors". Though what is now the kitchen was first planned as a committee room the members certainly did not intend to emulate the previous tenants but purposed their

THE CLUBROOM AT HAYES.

121

PUNCHBOWL NIGHT AT HAYES January, 1969

122

own catering, only in the cottage across the way and brought up to the clubroom on the first floor by lift and through the trapdoor the outline of which can still be made out on the floor beside the bar. This intention alone was to bring about its own now firmly rooted and proud tradition of the Wine Committee and most of its doings, with its Secretary today the only official privileged to present his report to the Annual General Meeting actually from behind the bar.

Alexander Anderson, who later donated the Presidential collar of office, gave sound legal advice so that the property was in fact purchased by a new body "Blackheath Harriers Headquarters Limited", under whose auspices members were invited to take up debentures of £1. Although subscription was slow the money was raised and the debentures eventually redeemed, by drawing upon donations from Derby Draws and by generous voluntary cancellation or bequeathing of holdings by many of the debenture holders. It was still the policy to discourage any individual member from holding too large a financial interest in the Club and forestall any possible economic domination, but of course this tacit limitation on debenture holdings tended to slow the accumulation of funds. B.H.H.Q. tended for many years — both rightly and wrongly — to be regarded as a body with powers of its own over the members' Club. The change in its function was formally passed at the Company's A.G.M. in 1961, together with a change in the Rules of the Club, altering it from a proprietary Club controlled by B.H.H.Q. Ltd. to a members' Club. This was a change of form rather than substance but it did give recognition to the fact that B.H.H.Q. no longer claimed, as once it could, to have ultimate control over the Club, indeed for a long time past the Directors of the Company had operated as a sub-committee of the Club rather than as a separate body. Paradoxically, it may seem, since 1961 the Company has been more active in its own sphere than for many years before. It has put in hand the major repair of the roof and made small purchases of additional land, to mention two of its more noticeable works.

With money thus short at that time though, it was the efforts of many willing helpers that maintained the fabric, and in particular the work of W.R.J. Clarke, Secretary of the Wine Committee from 1930 to 1948. In addition, though, we have[51] always had many voluntary workers. Dudley Child stands as an example of these not only in scope and persistence of their activities but in their optimistic enthusiasm also — as when, sledge-hammer in hand, he pronounced sentence upon an old air-raid shelter in the Club's ground, declaring that its demolition would occupy but the space of a summer's afternoon — the operation subsequently taking four months.

When in 1948 the last of the debentures was paid off quite palatial bathing accommodation was installed, with electricity following four years after in place of the old gas lighting. No longer could guests like F.L. Ager proclaim as in the thirties:-

"In hip-baths warm, more hot than c.,
You made me lie in ecstasy,
Which soon produced a rosy seat,
But left quite dry my head and feet".

At this time, though, with A.R. Pearson's Treasurer's restraint but with Dyball, as was said, always to be relied on "to turn on the hot tap of optimism" it was all a question of future hopes which the "Special Kop" was himself hardly to see realized for he died in

1931.

It is worth interrupting what flow there is in this narrative concerning the new head-quarters to pay at least a nod to the worth of one who might very well go neglected as must so many deserving others in this history. Pearson was a most definite identity whose character songs, entertaining pessimism and seedy running kit enjoyed both fame and notoriety. He was of that category of members, rare in other clubs but frequently seen in Blackheath, who join after their first youth as he did in 1909. Though nearing the veteran stage by then he took to cross-country enthusiastically. But it was on the executive side that he rendered most valuable service to the Club — in addition to his much-celebrated national contribution as a Special Policeman during the 1914-18 War — and, in especial, as Hon. Treasurer during this crucial period from 1920 to 1928.

The importance of having a clubhouse of one's own can hardly be exaggerated and doubtless even those far-sighted predecessors could not realize the long-term good they were doing. The task of setting their stamp on the new H.Q. went forward apace and all too soon the former aromas were banished in favour of new if not fresh ones, an atmosphere downstairs described by one member as "that happy marriage of liniment, coke and train-tickets, which far travellers like us carry always in the mind's nose", while upstairs there was "badinage, beer and bonhomie" to resort to after the inspiring scent of rotting cabbages always an ingredient of the trails laid by Bill Smith. On December 4th, 1926, the first run took place from Hayes while on the following New Year's Day after an authoritative "All upstairs" from Parrish it was all officially opened in the presence of the Vicar of Hayes and local dignitaries like Sir Henry Lennard. For the more heathen members it was perhaps not fittingly christened until the first social event there which, appropriately, was Punchbowl Night.

Fears that the rapid increase in the size of the Club would diminish its former appeal were not foolish; there was naturally less time to integrate this new membership with the Club as it had existed at "The Green Man" and the new move in a sense both hindered and hastened this process. Certainly by the very fact of the greater numbers people knew one another less intimately than formerly.

There was a more rapid turnover and a wastage that had not been before and all this had the effect of loosening ties and creating a new ethos. Much remained but there was a perceptible modification. The Club became more general and public in character and, by comparison with the old days, less a fraternity and with less central integration. There was a certain amount of internal grouping, an example of which were the Territorial Army members of the London Scottish and the Queen's Westminsters who held runs and races together with social gatherings at Hayes, for many of them were Blackheath members. Already in the West Wickham days they had a name among the locals for forming up outside "The Railway Hotel" after concerts and marching four-deep through the village headed by the pipers, with foursome reels being danced en route by the two Allen brothers, List and Cameron, the party repeating the routine at the station. It was a matter of pride, as the small Jubilee handbook issued in 1924 said, that the Blackheath Harriers was "a Club in the fullest sense of the word," and with its abundance of social gatherings this was no idle boast. No Club dinner would end without its musical turns; concerts and "Smokers" would often start with Eric Reed leading at the piano and Ramsay Moir

Blackheath Harriers.

Grand Bohemian Concert

AT

THE HOTEL VICTORIA

(KING EDWARD VII. ROOMS),

: NORTHUMBERLAND AVENUE :

On Monday, 30th October, 1922

ARTISTES :

DORA SQUIRES
(Contralto)

MIMI COTTET
(Soubrette)

VIOLET PURRY
(Elocutioniste)

STANLEY THOMSON
(Tenor)

RAMSAY MOIR
(Baritone)

A. W. CLAY-THOMAS
(Baritone)

ERNEST HILL
(Entertainer)

ROGER HODGE
(Songs at the Piano)

FRED GOODYER
(Humorist)

HERBERT DAVIES
(Violinist)

CYRIL WARREN
(Pianist and Entertainer)

TICKETS 3/- EACH (including Tax)

Can be obtained from the following—J. P. Amis, F. L. Gilbert, T. K. Grant,
H. G. Hammond, B. H. Lymbery, W. R. Moir, J. F. Ponsford, A. R.
Pearson, R. W. Pattison, T. W. B. Purchase, C. A. Peachey, and H. W. E.
Sercombe; or from the Joint Social Hon. Secretaries.

W. S. A. WINTER, 13, Chalsey Road, Brockley, S.E. 4.

A. T. G. TRUMBLE, 56, Claverton Street, S.W. 1.

FUTURE SOCIAL EVENTS

Dance at Caxton Hall, Westminster, 23rd November, 1922.

Fancy Dress Dance at Blackheath Concert Hall, 7th February, 1923.

WILKINSON BROS., LTD., 37-43, Green Lanes, London, N. 16.—6930.

A NOSTALGIC HANDBILL

maintained a stout tradition with his renderings of "The Lute Player" and "Tommy the Whistler", carrying on after W.A.W.B. ("Henery the Eighth") Purchase had ceased at his death as one of the lingering victims of the Great War. Many and various were the songs of the Club smokers and concerts:"The Company Sergeant Major","Paddy McGinty's Goat", "Maire My Girl", The Prologue from "I Pagliacci" and "I Passed Your Window in the Dead of Night". The efforts to make the clubroom at Hayes the setting it is today all assisted in creating a uniquely sociable and comfortable atmosphere, but reserved to London still were the finest flowerings of the successful Bohemian Concerts together with the Town Dance and Annual Dinner. Aided through his many years by a string of highly efficient organizers of the calibre of W.S.A. Winter and F.W. Parker, A.W. Clay-Thomas was the guiding light especially of the "Bohemians" and, while an audience of two hundred represented the norm, four hundred and more was often the case in the twenties and these concerts supply many of members' fondest memories of the Club. Started before the end of the last century they remained a chief feature of Blackheath life until recently, the final one to date held in 1955 at the Palmerston Restaurant. Apart from our members' talents the fine baritone of Clay Thomas[52] and an occasional cello solo by H.W.E. Sercombe, together with the support of Clay's own faithful circle of artistes regularly including Dickie Hassett and the accompanying pianist, Mr. R. Tonking, there were many well-known names like Naunton Wayne, Elsie and Doris Waters, and Arthur Askey with "A Little Soothing Buffoonery". But whether it was a Town Dance at Caxton Hall, the Fancy Dress Carnival at the Blackheath Concert Hall or an "Alfresco Concert" rained off after a cricket match with the West Wickham Club so that 130 members, ladies and friends had to crowd into the long glass outhouse of "The Railway Hotel" and carry on proceedings there, these events were all greatly enjoyed. No doubt the extreme enthusiasm for such social events at this period was, at least in part, a reaction to the prolonged strain of war, but the pleasure they provided was real and memorable indeed for those who experienced it. The long and friendly relationship with Curlew Rowing Club was maintained and the combined dances continued until quite recently, unlike the traditional Boxing Day matches against Park House R.F.C. ("We lost by the modest score of 26-0").

There were plenty of the traditional ingredients of Blackheath life to be sampled and despite the Club's growth a member from the early days would not have found the scene so very unfamiliar and even the old "Married v. Single" Race persisted into the twenties, but the first race for W.W. Davis' newly presented 7½ Miles Club Championship Cup in 1922 now had to be run in conjunction with one of the journalistically termed "Mob" matches because of the increasing number of fixtures. The Cup's first holder, A.C. Telfer, gained it in what was also the first race for the Pelling-Ratcliff Cup against Ranelagh.

This took place as late as March because of the postponement from January caused by the death of T.M. Gale as he was going out to lay the trail. Gale had been one of the couple of dozen young athletes to join the Club from the South London A. & B.C. in 1881 together with Crafter. It was said that he missed not more than two Saturdays in thirty years and Crafter and he were a familiar pair with their trail bags. Another friend and colleague on the trail with him was A.E. Culver who died in the April shortly after Tommy Gale. There have been many like them in the sense that there is little to convince the unknowing reader of their worth as central influences in the Club so subtle is their presence through

126

A GROUP OF NOTABLES: J.R.D. Cockburn, A.W. Clay Thomas, C. Pollard, W.H.M. Vercoe at Southall, 1962.

the years. What does one do to commemorate such men? Does one set down, as of one such, S.J. Wickham, the trivial yet colourful aspects of the man, "grey-haired even in those days and with his marvellous red nose," as Norman Beyfus remembers him in 1907? Or do we rather single out the marvellous consistency as a runner and his constant and faithful attendance? Doubtless the latter — for it was this quality of "backbone" that is the theme of this passage of Blackheath history when the strengths invoked in the later Club motto were in these post-war years most necessarily called into play.

One other competition deserves mention. From 1922 also dates the Club Five Miles Handicap which closes the winter season. Today it is the only example of an orthodox cross-country handicap retained on our list. Whereas this type of race had been the original staple of cross-country racing the extension of inter-club matches had rendered such handicaps largely extinct.

Because of Dyball's reforms the Club did undergo appreciable modifications which were more easily to be sensed then described, so that some members, even down to today, were to remain unaware that any such modification had taken place. The change was cumulative but its causes occurred in a relatively narrow span of time, with the vast intake of wholly new material in a space of six or seven years. Despite the rather empirical approach of Dyball part of the change was purposed. So far as his "new young men" were concerned he feared the effect of the image of the traditional Blackheath "celebratory" section on them and on their parents. The older Blackheath was comparable to a rugby club in spirit and feeling: a good game no matter who won — the S.L.H. match was an exception — with

127

a gargantuan drinking session and social to follow, and with something more than a smatch of exuberance about it. Many did not like this general spirit, innocent though it was, and Dyball, for no puritanical reason, was among them in his reluctance to deter the quiet, middle-class families whose sons, usually day pupils of grammar schools, he was drawing into the Blackheath circle.

But on the whole high spirits remained the order of the day, though possibly the ale flowed on a less homeric scale than hitherto, and it was a typical "Gazette" report that read: "Thereafter much club crying, singing and bawling generally." while through the streets of Paris in 1924 danced a Blackheath party ostensibly there on Olympic business and including Ramsay Moir of "The Gazette", W.S.A. Winter, the formidably large Captain Leidig of the Irish Guards, so useful in a crowd, and one, D.K. Saunders, all bent on maintaining the irresponsible reputation of the twenties.

In 1928 Dyball was forced to resign office. Already under pressure of his professional job which necessitated his working on Saturday afternoons, the extra burden of business entailed by the new Headquarters — for much of that executive work fell upon his shoulders — must have been decisive. A glutton for work, even he could not cope. Nevertheless he remained a director of B.H.H.Q. till his death; he always turned up at important meetings. His advice was sound and he kept up to date. Blackheath's debt to him is enor--mous — nor did they neglect to show him their gratitude, both during and after his term of office. It was a happy truth that was inscribed on the notice of one Blackheath team's railway compartments: "Mr. Dyball's Harriers". In large and small matters he amazed all — both with the gigantic size of the "Mob" Match fields and with the rapidity of his addition of the scores and the speed with which he produced the result sheet. "The Gazette" rightly said on his retirement, "In five years Dyball has become a tradition". Then, with 657 members on the books, 97 of whom had been elected in the previous twelve-month, he said in his last report, "I shall always look back upon the last five years as some of the most enjoyable in my life". Another five years and he lost his wife suddenly. He himself died prematurely in 1940 at the age of fifty-six.

Besides the severest frost for thirty years with no baths at H.Q., scenes of wreckage in the bar from the exploded bottles, frozen beer and only Guinness to drink,1929 saw the Club's Diamond Jubilee celebrated at the Waldorf Hotel with thoughts no doubt of Club debts centring on their Headquarters somewhere in official minds as Charles Coburn sang of "The Man Who Broke The Bank at Monte Carlo". But times were changing and, whatever misgivings there might be about it all, Blackheath at any rate were prospering, not least of all with a bright new contingent of up and coming men who through their many competitions were moving around much more than formerly had been the case with Blackheath.

The current movement was thrown into relief by the death in this year of Walter Rye which served as a reminder of the furthest days of our sixty years' history.

The rivalries of early days and the attendant jealousies had yielded to the influence of time as our first race with Thames Hare and Hounds the previous autumn indicated. Rye's unique services to the sport of cross-country running were seen in their just perspective and received full appreciation in the lengthy obituary and tribute which appeared in our "Gazette".

THE NINETEEN THIRTIES

"Quod te nescioquis per iurgia dixerit esse exulis uxorem, littora questa tua est . . . . Perfer et obdura: multo graviora tulisti, eripuit cum me principis ira tibi".

(Someone by way of insult has said that thou art "an exile's wife" — of this thy letter complains . . . . Endure — harden thy heart; much heavier things didst thou endure when the wrath of the prince tore thee from me).

(Ovid-Tristia Xl. To his wife from exile).

"And when they were come nigh unto the Farm of Coney there stood two Dear Old Ladies by the Roadside. And one of them said unto the other, Behold these men, are they not surely Acting for the Pictures? And the other answered and said, Yea My Dear. It is the Slow Motion . . . . . . "

("The Gazette" December, 1923).

Thus with the move from West Wickham and the withdrawal of Dyball from the secretaryship the great phase of reconstruction came to an end. Now followed a period in which Blackheath exploited and profited from the new dynamic imparted to its affairs by Dyball's policy. Just as the benefit of rigorous training is felt only after a while so it was with these effects on the Club: the changes were not readily to be observed; it was only when one remembered how things had been after the war and saw where they stood now that the transformation was apprehended. During the 1930's the effects of the First World War began to be apparent in the sphere of the official administration of athletics. As the older type of executive official began to withdraw from the scene as a consequence of advancing years and death there was in more than one quarter a difficulty in finding replacements due to the losses and dislocations of the War. This also was evident in our own Club, but after a time responsibility was assumed by a group of younger men mainly representative of the new management order of the inter-war years. These brought a new spirit of business efficiency to replace the more casual individualism which most private clubs had attempted to cope with their administrative problems and the organisation of routine was vastly improved. There was, however, from the very nature of the case, a certain loss of continuity with the conventions under which affairs had previously been conducted and which in one way or another had a pretty long history. Unromantic though the suggestion may be, the period that was now arriving of individual achievement on the flat really just "happened" in the sense that it was a bonus from the previous decade rather than the product of a deliberate, controlled policy.

Nothing very revolutionary was going to happen. Much remained the same and. recognizably, the Blackheath, not to say national way of life in athletics. J.E. Furniss, who was still going strong on the track after the next war to the extent of finishing 8th in the A.A.A. Steeplechase Championship, says of the thirties, "Athletics was most happily disorganized and very amateur." With the exception of Sydney Wooderson, who at this time was mainly interested in the track, we produced no great cross-country runners in the period up to that war. On the other hand, neither Blackheath nor any other club could ever have had the sheer quantity of competent athletes of the second and third rank that we had at that time. No individual club can be said to have excelled some of the fields, for example, put out against S.L.H. in this decade, fields which could claim to be of a higher average quality than those of today. But of this more later, for though the deep-seated changes belong to the 1920's their effects were to manifest themselves most vividly on the track in successes which were to rival the palmy days of the eighties.

There were significant happenings in the general athletic world too: in addition to the A.A.A. Championships taking place at the White City for the first time, 1932 saw the formation of the British Amateur Athletic Board which replaced the A.A.A. as the British representation in the I.A.A.F. The years immediately preceding the war formed a period of expansion demonstrated most obviously in the trend towards international meetings as distinct from international matches and, together with the increase of competition, an accompanying **seriousness** to match on the part of the athletes concerned. In short, it

ONE OF THE SEVERAL FINE SPRINT RELAY TEAMS OF THE 1930's:
L.W. Ellis, L. G. Parkes, C.A. Wiard, E.L. Page

130

represented the advent of modern athletics as the streamlined and earnest matter it has now become, and a development only retarded by the war.

Certainly in Blackheath, which had so often in the past remained unaffected, usually from choice, by current public trends, the new impetus made itself felt and assisted the stimulus there had been from within during Dyball's period of office. Track, and more surprisingly, field athletics now began to take on an importance not previously experienced by the Club, so much so that by 1932 already C.L. Mobbs was mentioning in his Annual Report as Secretary how it was "becoming increasingly difficult to find matches for everyone to run in", a welcome complaint given point by the number of eighty Club athletes who took part in track fixtures that year. As if to characterize this new lease there was the accession in 1933 of a significantly young President in G.F. McIvor taking over from the 1875 veteran W.W. Davis who said in that Blackheath ceremony that he had thought for a long time a younger man should hold the post. And, while in the matter of recruiting there had been a steep drop in the rate, the steady climb towards the eight hundred mark was to assist the joke in McIvor's anecdote when he in turn retired from office that the Club might take note of Herr Hitler's scheme for ensuring the perpetuation of the race — "received" as "The Gazette" reported, "with great joy by the meeting". Within five years however, they were to take, if not such plans, certainly the planner more seriously.

At the time, however, members were far more disposed to regard the observations of such as McIvor rather than of obscure European upstarts — remarks, for example, such as he directed against the growth of over-commercialized international meetings involving individual athletes which were being organized in order to attract crowds and the accompanying profit at the expense of Clubs and their teams and thus were rendering a disservice to amateur athletics. For, he said, "Clubs must, and in point of fact do, provide facilities for large numbers to engage in healthy athletic pursuits and our governing body must in no way be a party to supporting a policy of simply providing for large numbers to watch". The visit in 1937 of our long-standing member Maurice Bandeville's native club, the "Club Olympique d'Aubervilliers",[54] drew approbation from McIvor for coming over as they did for a training run in such days of intensive and grimly serious international competition. Of course, this was more than a matter of arguing on principle, since invitations to athletes for these international meetings had clashed with some championship events. "We can argue," McIvor concluded, "because we are right".

The Track Captain's message for the new season of 1932 had a far more purposeful note than the usual run of such exhortations which had had so often, winter or summer, conscientious good intentions as their keynote, being acts of faith rather than expressions of realizable projects. New and strange remarks held place in this document, concerning field events for example: ". . . we are unreservedly in favour of giving them a less humble place among our activities". There was an official and credible crispness in "Teams will be entered for . . . " followed by an impressive list of A.A.A. and other Relay Championships. The writer, H.S. Smith, had already been Summer Captain for a year and was to continue for another six, during this time setting a personally active example that was hard to equal, though it was a lesson heeded by a future notable holder of this office, N.W. Page, who, besides gaining his county vest in the triple-jump before the war came, was to be found not only sprinting and discus-throwing but forming part of a large entry of nine members for the Club's "Walter" Cup Steeplechase in 1933 at White City, yet another result of Smith's encouragement. He himself turned out strongly on almost all occasions and regularly ran both one and two miles in matches, winning or being placed in one or both equally regularly. He would turn his hand to any event necessary, running winter or summer the whole range of events from 100 yards to ten miles — steeplechase to high jump. He was indeed an impressive all-rounder, yet was also good enough for a fifth place in the A.A.A. Mile final of 1933.

Now there were javelin, discus, long jump events at the Evening Meetings which themselves increased through demand to three per season by 1935. The signs of development were to be seen in the steady progress to the top of the Southern Track and Field League to which the Club was elected in 1932 and which operated according to a relegation and promotion system. Starting in the 3rd Division of the running and the 2nd Division of the field events league, by the following year the Club was top of the First Division of the latter and by 1935 headed the First Division in track.

A year later the general standard of performance was far better than previously — a reflection of the fact that of 441 ordinary members 294 had joined since 1930, compared with ten Life members of the total of 302 at this date, so that, for example, they could boast some ten half-milers beating two minutes two seconds, very good for that time. Nevertheless, the highest achievement was by individuals of an unprecedented brilliance, certainly, speaking of them as a whole. If Smith was the best all-round athletic and administrative example, then at the start of the 1930's E.L. Page stood as a proud symbol to members of a competitor who after other Blackheath men had for so long failed to attain the highest success could take his place among the best and beat them. Starting a long and consistent line of successes with his Surrey and Southern A.A.A. 100 Yards titles in 1930 and already clocking 9.7 in his first year, he went on to achieve numerous distinctions in international matches as well as the 1932 Olympics and the 1938 European Championships where his sprint quartet were first. The latter was a remarkable climax to an international career which had seen him gain second place beaten only by the Olympic 100 metres Champion, Percy Williams, in the first Empire Games, as early as 1930. Eight years later he beat the stylish sprinter C.B. Holmes to win the 100 yards against France. Despite many such individual successes it was said of him in a "Gazette" of the time, "He . . . . . . always heard the starter's crack for the relay as the call to battle" and it may well be that this is how he would best care to be remembered. And not chiefly in respect of international relay triumphs at that, for the fact is that he formed part of a Blackheath sprint relay strength whose achievements and tradition are unlikely to be excelled. During the 1930's the Club won the A.A.A. Sprint Relay title three times — in 1932, 1937 and 1939 — a feat equalled by few others. The 1932 Middlesex 100 yards Champion, L.W. Ellis, was one of the first winning teams, as was L.G. Parkes, who, like Page, was consistent to the tune of a string of five Kent 100 yard titles in succession up to 1936 when it took a man hardly less brilliant than Page in the form of C.A. Wiard seriously bent on Olympic selection, which he gained, to put an end to his line of wins. Wiard no doubt ranked next to Page in terms of high individual success, but there was keen rivalry and by no means a clear-cut pattern of precedence between them through these years. Other fine performers like the Surrey quarter miler F.S. Whittingham and V.W.W. Beardon with his county sprint placings came in for their share of the cake.

It is to risk a dreary cataloguing of mere names but to accord a due meed of praise to register such as N.D. Cullen, T.W. Cotton, V.S. Ransom and K.M. Torr who also gained A.A.A. Championship winners' medals as members of the relay teams of this period — for these races were not won by the same sprinters each time. So thick was the talent upon the Blackheath ground generally that by 1934 the Club could carry off all the Kent track titles except for the three miles - which omission the winner of the Club's Inter-Schools Race for that year, a youngster, D.E. Reynolds by name, would remedy before long — as well as long jump and pole vault. In 1937 the tally was to improve to a total of seventeen County and Southern Championships held by members of the Club. Among these were the two hurdlers, L.V. Cornish, good enough to win the Southern High Hurdles as he did in 1937 and vulnerable only to a superlative performer like Donald Finlay who reigned supreme in the years before and after the war, and J.C. Oxland, the Middlesex High Hurdles Champion. Cornish performed well over the 440 Yards Hurdles also and both he and Oxland were keen rugby players, Cornish in particular winning Kent County Colours at this sport as well. Another prominent and versatile rugby man was C.S.M. Quigley of the Harlequins 1st XV. and Southern Junior 220 yards winner in 1937. Before him D.F.G. Horwood had been the outstanding junior sprinter, a Kent 220 champion in 1933 and placed 2nd in the British

CLUB CHAMPIONS OF THE 1930s
A.C.J. Poole, E.L. Page, C.A. Wiard, S. C. Wooderson
Sport and General)

SPRINT RELAY TEAM 1937
(by courtesy of South East London and Kentish Mercury)

133

Games 100 yards Under Twenty race. At the same time the Surrey mantle of Whittingham fell upon H.G. Trodd, a worthy quarter-miling successor. In the middle distances, besides S. C. Wooderson, there was in particular A.C.J. Poole who accomplished many fine performances and whose Kent 880 yards record stood till well after the Second World War. In a period when field events were still generally neglected the Club also enjoyed unaccustomed success in this sphere too, H.L. Roache, the Kent pole-vaulter and 2nd in this event in the 1937 Southern, but all-round jumper and thrower also, being the outstanding club man who was also to join in the Club's coaching scheme initiated by Charles Wiard. Internationally, the star was L.D. Butler, triple and long jumper, joining Wooderson and Wiard in the 1934 Empire Games team for both these events. The five years leading up to the war saw progress in attracting an increasing number of useful field performers like E.C. Glaisher and V.A.T. Bignell, the throwers, and high jumpers in G.A.C. Morton, also a discus man, and G.F. Conner, so that if it could not fully match the already powerful track arm the field event strength formed a very useful complementary asset.

Overshadowed as they necessarily were by many of these individual successes the team performances were well up to the standard of this new competitive era the impact of which was indicated in the 1937 comment on the A.A.A. Championships in "The Gazette": "Every half-mile heat is a pre-war final". After meeting Stanley Baldwin on the way out to the 1932 Olympics aboard the "Empress of Britain" ("You're looking very fit") Ernie Page brought back with him a pair of objects called starting blocks which were a sign of a sport that was reaching for change, not stagnating. But this time Blackheath could not be accused of lagging conservatively behind. It was not surprising that with the wealth of talent sketched briefly above a larger measure of team success accompanied it. In addition to the performances in the Southern Track and Field League already noted the team more than held its own in the major national inter-club team and trophy meetings of the day. Chief among these were the Waddilove and Kinnaird Trophy Meetings, the latter dating from 1909 and the gift of Lord Kinnaird with whom we had been associated during the 1890's in the Private Banks Meetings at Catford Bridge. These two competitions always brought the major clubs of the country into contention and to finish 3rd tie in the Waddilove meeting in 1933 and 6th in the Kinnaird in 1934, for example, showed that the Club was no "also ran" as so often in the past. Yet it is an indication of the progress that still had to be made by Blackheath in later years, as well as of the general intensification that has continued since the Second World War that even so, in the 1935 Kinnaird contest three scoring men only – L.G. Parkes, C.A. Wiard and F.S. Whittingham – could carry the Club up a place from the previous year to fifth, and though beaten thus by Achilles, Polytechnic H., L.A.C. and Milocarian – among the best of the time – still finished ahead of good clubs like Surrey A.C., Belgrave, Birchfield and Herne Hill Harriers. By 1937, of these only Achilles headed Blackheath in this ten-event competition of the "big twelve" – as they did also in the "Reading Gazette" Trophy Meeting the same year – even if Harold Smith did have to cut the cards with Surrey A.C. to gain us the runner-up position. Belgrave and Polytechnic were among clubs defeated in matches, and indeed there were few apart from the university and the military forces represented respectively by Achilles and R.M.C. Sandhurst [56] who could best Blackheath at this time. One particular speciality for a club with such sprinting and middle-distance ability was the "Travers-Stubbs" Trophy at Plymouth in which the four-man team would first score in their individual events and then in combination in a medley relay, so that Achilles was in 1935 beaten and in 1936 were tied for first place. By 1938, for example, in the Waddilove meeting, it was possible to tie for 2nd place with L.A.C. and Birchfield even without such an ace points winner like Ernie Page, away winning the hundred yards against Scotland and Ireland. Nor was it all grim, however satisfying gathering of points: there were plenty of events like the Sandhurst match — and even a whiff of the old type of "flower show" meeting, unfortunately so rare today, like the Ravensbourne Meeting with its leisurely programme five hours long and yet with something always to watch in what the long summer of memory recalls as fine weather accompanied by tents, bands and a garden party atmosphere that did not seem at all unfamiliar to the many surviving nineteenth century members of the Club.

"The surprise of the match was the defeat of A.T. Wooderson, of the Club, by his younger brother for third place".
(GAZETTE" Report of the Sutton Valence fixture — Feb. 23rd, 1931.)

". . . . To look at he certainly does not give the impression of being a great athlete".
(Guy Butler – "Sydney Wooderson and Some of His Great Rivals".)

Those who have not cheated this panting saga thus far by reaching to the index will have wondered at the near absence up to this point of a name crucial not only to the period but to the whole record of this Club since he was responsible for gaining many of the points in the competitions detailed above. It is worth stressing this at the outset rather than his world's records and championship — wins — not out of perverseness but because a close examination of the club record of S.C. Wooderson strikes one as remarkable for a man who during his active career was being continuously subjected to the stresses of publicity and competitive demands of which the ordinary club runner remains blissfully unaware. The size and scope of his contribution necessitate a separate section for this man so slight of build. The full record of his achievement is to be found elsewhere, unlike much that this work has concerned itself with and which therefore it has given priority to. Apart from re-stating the main facts of a participation in first-class competition both on track and over the country lasting more than fifteen years, the main purpose here is to offer a Blackheath view of the man which is unknown to the larger athletic world. As for the general public, already the name of Sydney Wooderson has faded from popular memory. Those who "know", however, will readily forget neither what images it conjures nor what that name stands for. From his earliest years in the Club he received praise for his scrupulous support of fixtures and it is a fact that even, for example, during the period 1935-1946 when he was defeated in a handful only of serious contests there was a remarkable intermingling of humbler races with these demanding competitions. Obviously a man as fast as he was will attract notice. That he should for his generation belong to the realm of legend rather than that of celebrity — however forgotten by more recent times — suggests something more than mere speed of movement. He struck a spark in the ordinary Englishman who otherwise had no interest in athletics perhaps by a combination of supreme competitive running ability with an everyday normality and sanity which often maddened journalists avid for copy and which — though it contributed towards the delay in recognition by the cognoscenti outside Blackheath — was nonetheless a potent link with a public who saw in these qualities an image at once of the reticence the English seem to prize above rubies and a projection of their own romantic ambitions of excellence.

135

S.C. WOODERSON WINNING A.A.A. 3 MILES CHAMPIONSHIP.

White City, 1946. (Sport and General)

The spectacles with their suggestion of mortal weakness were significant in forming this image; not less so were the idea of the office worker with such accompaniments as the umbrella and the anonymous suit, the reluctance to stir to sensational utterance thus characterizing the rigidity of that famous portion of British anatomy, the upper lip, and altogether a bewilderingly conformist background of English commuting and suburban life that confounded the sensation-seeking but reassured the public as a whole.

When this figure discarded its camouflage to start in a race the transformation was still something short of god-like. To begin with, his presence in the arena often went unobserved while he was warming up; when on their marks his opponents usually effaced his five feet six inches, and his comparative puniness aided by his customary suit of solemn black prolonged this obscurity even after the race had started, unless he detached himself early from the ruck. It was not until the urge to do so manifested itself that uniqueness was evident for then the slight figure became instinct with fire, the accelerating action was smooth, strong, light and quickened above all with a nervous energy suggesting not training but inspiration. There was no consciousness of size then but rather of total utilization of powers which the user seemed to be intent on consuming absolutely by the time he reached his goal, the high-reaching arms contributing as much as legs to the final onslaught.

Futile no doubt to attempt to record in words the impact of the sight of Sydney Wooderson in fullest motion, yet those who knew it cherish it as something unique not to be rivalled by the smoother beauty of running actions such as that of his great rival before the Second World War, Jack Lovelock. The total commitment of the raking, fiery stride made yet another claim on those who prefer a recognizable humanity of passion to any

136

alien inhuman perfection.

As suggested by the heading of this section his elder, A.T., preceded him into the Club and was a useful performer, as was the third brother, S.J., who had many consistent performances to his credit on track and country, winning the "Rowland" Ten and being first man home for the Southern team in 1939 as well as representing Kent.

Though he had only the previous year won the Inter-Schools Race and the Public Schools Mile in under 4 mins. 30 secs., by 1934 Sydney was running for England in the Empire Games after equalling the English Native Mile Record unofficially as well as beating Lovelock in his first big race as a senior at 19 years of age. In 1935 he won his first A.A.A. mile title, again beating Lovelock and the following year set up a new British record of 4 mins. 10.8 secs. at the Southern Championships as well as vanquishing Lovelock once more in the A.A.A. Mile. "The atmosphere was electric", wrote Bevil Rudd of the latter race, and of the finish, ... "tough as a terrier, he exerted every ounce of energy, and once more led Lovelock by a yard. For two vital seconds neither gained an inch, and then

"THE TOTAL COMMITMENT OF THE FIERY STRIDE".

S.C.W. Winning Inter-Counties Mile, 1939.

(Fox Photos)

Wooderson had breasted the tape . . . . Wooderson's spirit is unconquerable, and if his physique has not suffered he will win at Berlin". The doubt as to Sydney's fitness proved to be a well-grounded fear. He went to the Berlin Olympics but with little hope of a painful injury recovering in time so that he limped through his heat, only after his return discovering several displacements in his left foot and a splintered fibula. 1937 saw some recompense when after another successful defence of his Mile title, several international wins and a new three quarter mile record at the Glasgow Rangers' Meeting he set up a World's Record of 4 mins. 6.4 secs. for the mile at Motspur Park. This was significantly at the Club's own meeting for on both this occasion and the following year when setting up a World's Half-Mile Record of 1 min. 49.2 secs. he preferred to stage them at a Blackheath function rather than at a metropolitan centre like the White City.

SYDNEY WOODERSON CHAIRED AFTER BREAKING WORLD MILE RECORD,

August, 1937.

(Sport & General)

Of the Mile Record "The Times" said, "The run produced the most inspired effort yet made by the British champion. As the slight figure flashed down the home straight officials and spectators alike found it difficult to contain their excitement, and there were remarkable scenes when the time of the run was announced, the young champion being carried off shoulder-high by his admirers". Guy Butler, the "Morning Post" correspondent and a committed Wooderson fan, wrote before the race, "nothing this young runner can do will surprise me. He is a wonder", and afterwards called it "as great a bit of running as I have ever seen". Crafter rose to his feet in the stand and with the remark, "Gentlemen, I think this is an occasion", led the surrounding members in the Club Cry.

Of the 880 Yards Record attempt, John Furniss recalls the whirring of the newsreel camera, and wondering how long he could keep in front of Sydney off 8 yards and whether he would get in his way or trip him up.

"After 50 years' absence the World's Half-mile running record has returned to England", exulted "The News Chronicle". "After the race", reported "The Sunday Express", "Wooderson seemed quite undistressed, and remarked in a matter-of-fact way to his coach, Albert Hill, that 'it didn't seem as fast as all that' ". Joe Binks, a former mile record holder, commented typically in "The News of the World", "His performance was certainly one of the most deceptive I have ever seen in record attempts. Wooderson is an amazing little runner and one never knows what to expect of him next".

Shortly after this came the European 1500 Metres title won with ease at Colombes Stadium, but the last "Gazette" recollection of his 1938 season is to be found in the report of the cross-country fixture at Hayes against the Oxford University 2nd team and their coming across "a solitary figure sitting on a stile and surveying the open country". Wooderson had walked out to Layhams Farm, the furthest point of the seven mile course, to support them.

One of the most impressive performances was the 4 min. 7.4 secs. 1939 Inter-Counties Mile he ran at White City leaving the opposition floundering nearly a hundred yards behind and, after a sub-three minute three-quarter mile record came a visit to America where the press described him as a "slight anaemic-looking sort of chap", which opinion may have been shared by two gentleman he visited at the time — the Olympic swimmer Johnny Weissmuller, by then playing the he-man hero of the screen, Tarzan, and Joe Louis, the Heavyweight Champion.

Throughout the war he continued to run well, even reaching to a 4 min. 11 secs. mile for a new Scottish record in Glasgow in 1940, despite all sorts of handicap, the worst of which came with a serious attack of rheumatic fever which laid him low in 1944. But less than a year after his two months' convalescence he was meeting one of the finest new milers, Arne Andersson, who in neutral Sweden had been enjoying first class competition against the great Gundar Haegg and came against Sydney with a 4 min. 1.6 sec. mile time to his credit. Though doctors had thought he would not run again, Sydney took the lead just before the bell and came near to running the Swede into the ground, a feat which he repeated a few weeks later at Gothenberg when, having told Jack Crump, his accompanying team manager, the time of 4 min. 3 secs. which he planned he met that gentleman's whistle of surprise with the remark, "Well, I'll have to, won't I, to win?". His time — less than a second behind his opponent's—was the fastest of his career—4 mins. 4.2 secs and made one

**WINNING THE EUROPEAN
5000 METRES CHAMPIONSHIP,**
Oslo, 1946.

regret the lost opportunities of the previous four years.

Such niceties of might-have-been never troubled him though and with little experience of the distance he stepped up to the three miles in 1946. He led most of the way in the A.A.A. race and when the fine Dutch runner, W. Slykhuis, stole a four-yard march on him in the back straight, first closed on the younger man round the last bend then let rip with a burst that took him to a new British Record of 13 mins. 53.2 after a last lap of 58.4 secs. When he repeated this feat in winning the European 5000 Metres title he opened the gap of 5.4 secs. on Slykhuis in the last three hundred metres, leaving behind him also such future Olympic Gold medallists as Zatopek and Gaston Reiff.

On his return, once again characteristically despite a troubling tendon which gave way during the race, he staged a record attempt at a Club meeting, this time on the Two Miles but was forced by the injury to abandon the attempt, though not the race, which he won and in which Blackheath took the team prize. This was his last chief track appearance and provided a fitting memory of the man. As the "Gazette" correspondent said of it, "In many ways this race had more dramatic fitness to the man concerned than any brilliant individual triumph could have provided".

In his day a marvel for the sheer range of his performance quite apart from its quality, in 1938 alone he won the "Reay" 440 Cup, the "Barclay-Esson" 880 Trophy, the 7½ Miles "Davis" Cup and was the Club's first man home in the Kent Championship. To the present he is still a self-effacing but dedicated helper of Blackheath whether with his stop-watch or legal advice, while his willingness to help others succeed can be attested by many and by at least one small boy of twenty years ago.

At the dinner in his honour at the Waldorf in 1937 — he was to receive an even more signal tribute ten years later when the A.A.A. held a unique presentation dinner for him — Sydney singled out McIvor and H.W.E. Sercombe for thanks. Sercombe especially gave dedicated support to the Blackheath record holder during the early years when Wooderson's worth tended to be undervalued at large, as well as taking a paternal interest in many other young members. As proof of the latter Harold Thompson recalls his benign appearance and spectacles and thinking at first that Sercombe might be a clergyman: "To me the remarkable thing about him was that in any race . . . . . . he was to be found out on the country, usually where one was feeling bad, shouting encouragement. And more than that — he knew my name!" Sercombe himself preferred cross-country but ran middle distances on the track also. He had a long record of service to the Club up to his death in 1939, having held the offices of Handicapper from 1898 to 1905 and Assistant Secretary also during the nineties, Captain in 1905-06, Joint Handicapper again in 1920-21, culminating in the Presidency in 1931-32. Yet he would probably have been content to be mentioned thus in the same breath as this athlete of a later generation whom he admired so much, for he himself had effect on the Club not by autocratic means but, it has been said, by enthusiasm and persuasion doing more than almost any other member of his time to direct its activities. Like Crafter, he had an encyclopaedic knowledge of Blackheath and an amazing memory for faces. In addition to his official duties and running cross-country he shared the versatility of interests of so many of his age — like Neville Cardus whom he admired — and, a player of the cello, at one time formed a small orchestra among his personal friends. His championing of the champion furnished yet another example in Blackheath history of co-operation and interest between generations.

It is interesting so many years after to observe contemporary reactions to the mani-festations of the new ethos betraying in "Gazette" contributions like the report on the 1930 World Student Games an amazed sense of novelty at Swiss competitors who "persisted in doing muscle-loosening exercises on the green enclosure". They were anxious, though, to show that they were not altogether out of date in recognizing the wearing by competitors of "the now familiar Continental running 'boiler-suit' which was sometimes of startling colours". A more sophisticatedly advanced member like Ernie Page travelling to Canada for the Empire Games the same year remarked on our Dominion athletes donning sleeveless vests with most shorts reaching a point "more than six inches above the knee" and daringly asked how long it would be before the A.A.A. would allow this in Britain.

Today one is familiar with the inquiries and post-mortems that take place after large-scale international festivals like the Olympics, but in the thirties it was the jolting shock of modernity and more rapid advance than had previously been the case — though the signs had long since been there for the observant — which led to serious heart-searching into the new way of sport and the possibility that it no longer exactly matched the British way of life. Harold Rhodes, in a "Gazette" article following the Berlin Olympics of 1936, firstly reported half a dozen meeting after Harold Whitlock's win to discuss a more Russian than English-sounding "Four-years plan" and to form a "Tokyo Club", then went on to offer the larger solution to the conflict of the old amateurism with the new spirit of stress on competitive excellence of a division of athletics into two parts, both to be amateur but one division to be serious "with" as he put it, "a professional outlook"[57].

Perhaps the above better describes the state of affairs at the present time of writing, but certainly as the thirties wore on a consciousness of something of a division between their interests and those of others in the Club came upon many of the keener track men. As a result of generally better performance over the past ten years there was more of a divergence between the more traditional members and the ones who were taking their athletics more seriously than most of their fore-bears. A Club in any case could not thus expand without some effect. There were other kinds of change beside that of the new Ladywell track's adoption as our official training ground. The training of officials as well as athletes was indeed a novel suggestion, and there were smaller innovations like the "re-designing" of the Club medals — though they reverted in fact to something like the old Peckham shape of the Maltese cross at the instance of Adrian Metcalf   or the introduction of Club spoons as awards, replacing as they said, "the eternal biscuit barreis and cake baskets". Rule Number Two had long stated "That the object of the Club shall be the cultivation of athletic sports, especially cross-country running", and something of the new spirit among the track members was evidenced in what A.D. Thwaites called "a good-humoured but nevertheless firm attack" mounted by them which resulted in the deletion of the last three words of that rule. But though there were some signs of dissatisfaction among track athletes at a lack of adequate representation it was far from representing anything like an acute state of unrest and the more notable changes were those compelled by the circumstances of expansion and proliferation of the Club's activities. The treasurer was particularly burdened and compared with former times there were bound to be impossible demands upon single officials under the system of general responsibility as Dyball had already found. So that it was not surprising that by 1934 there was an extension of what would today be called "de-centralization", with the Secretary, C.L. Mobbs, asking for two Assistant Secretaries — one for Track, one for Cross-country — as a regrettable but necessary division. Two years later the responsible sub-committee was recommending the appointment of a non-running team manager, pointing out the necessity of a Field Events vice-captain, and proposing that the Team Secretary, the Captain and Vice-captain should act together as a selection committee.

"......... *the backbone of the Club in its winter activities..... the most deserving and neglected of wayside blossoms and a prince of good fellows".*

(The "Medium" Runner - from "The Gazette ", January, 1939).

Altogether track athletics stole the glamour of this period but may also fairly claim the greatest of the Club's success at this time also. Certainly there were not the same picturesque triumphs over the country, though here many of that era will object to this assessment, recalling as they do, even from so long ago, an excited Mobbs announcing to a packed Clubroom at Hayes the regaining of the Nicholls Cup after twelve years when the sound of their acclaim was heard in the distant neighbouring "New Inn" and, as "The Gazette" said, "The hopes of many years found expression in a minute of bedlam let loose". And, since the Club fielded one hundred and seventeen runners on that day, it is difficult rationally to gainsay our correspondent in his opinion that it was "evidence of healthy state such as the most brilliant individual triumph could not have afforded"

Still, in contrast to the new track phenomenon where the accent had definitely shifted to achievement, things were going on much as usual in cross-country. The growth of strength was noticeable so that although S.L.H. had won yet again in 1930 Blackheath had had twenty-one in the first forty, and there were new faces to be seen too. There was the same unevenness as ever which at times reached the level of seriousness where the English turn such matters into a joke. In 1931, for example, though there were quite reasonable performances in the championships — the Juniors 5th in the newly instituted Southern, the Seniors coming 8th in their race and 16th in the National; with C.E. Clowser, R.F. Cross and R.A.E. Galley leading them home — nonetheless Orion could administer the first defeat for many years. Even as late as 1935, when things had begun to go so well as to show a trio of victories against our three traditional rivals for the first time ever, the team could sink to twentieth place in the National.

Such occurrences at the start of the thirties were all part of the expected pattern of the Blackheath paradox however, together with the usual limited success and the customary warnings against our men's lack of preparation for fast courses such as they came up against in the National Championships. This latter was still second in importance to the Southern as far as Blackheath were concerned. Just as it had been in the previous century so in 1932 the Club still referred to it in almost parochial fashion as "the most coveted honour of the cross-country world". Still, at least now there were signs of the "old brigade" being replenished with new blood after several years' dependence on the same runners, though it was still a situation of promise more than of progress. There were many good runners like L.T Brockway, Rex Cross the Captain, R.E. Walker, and G.H. Wilkinson — the latter possibly the most naturally gifted of all of them but really happier with a pipe and a tankard, being reputed to do no training — but they were all, with the exception of Sydney Wooderson, just short of the calibre of the best of the previous decade. These were backed though by an increasing quantity of runners of a high level of ability and well-led by such as S.A. Field — cross-country secretary in addition to other activities ranging from shot-putting to social organization — and H.T. Aitchison, leader of the medium pack, 2nd Gordon Highlanders, who was later killed at Caen, Normandy, and was said to be able to visit all members of the pack several times in the course of races large and small to encourage his charges.

In keeping with this phenomenon of medium strength the three "all to score" matches were referred to as "the backbone of the season" and certainly the emphasis was on these and on the Camden Cup, for the Club with the first twelve to finish in the Southern, rather than on the National. All in all perhaps runners like Trevor Davis, by the mid 1930's in his fiftieth year of membership and being praised for still running full courses of ten miles, was more typical of Blackheath than the new stars by then appearing.

There was by no means the old complacency however. Notably there was the personal example of the Captain, Rex Cross, who also fused a large body of widely ranging ability into an efficient and disciplined pack system. Just as he had surprised all on joining by following his Novices win at the second attempt with gaining second place in the "Rowland" Ten the same season so he became Cross-country Vice-captain within two years. He is more noteworthy though as an all-round example of Club and general athletic service — as a pioneer of marathon running in Blackheath, a track and country runner, one of the youngest Presidents, in 1937-38, as first President and founder member of the Road Runners' Club after the War, as a director of B.H.H.Q. and a staunch committee man both in the Club and County, and as the designer of the 1939-45 War Memorial in the Club Room after himself serving almost, one would think, uniquely, as Captain in the Royal Engineers aboard a two thousand ton vessel on the run to and from Holland.

In addition there was ample consciousness of deficiencies and the need to repair them. The institution by two Past Presidents, H.E. King and J.M. Morrison of their Cup for Juniors in 1935 — so that for the first time the Junior Five and Senior Ten were held on the same day — was a surface sign of the nurturing of junior talent. It was a necessity which had been apparent in the 1933 Kent Junior, for example, where though the Club had the individual winner in C.T. Pascall, there was no team to back him.

By 1935-37 there was a different story to tell. With Sydney Wooderson a narrow second in the four years-old Southern Junior Championship the team was 3rd; the previously unique feat of winning all three of the large matches was repeated in 1935, and whereas the Nicholls Cup, though wrested from the Irrepressibles' tenacious grasp in 1934, had only left them through the jealously narrow deficiency of 21 points, the next occasion saw the larger margin of 745 points, the victory being achieved on the alien Farthingdown into the bargain in an exhilarating new spirit of optimism. This time the mood was more permanent and the success of the large team matches was carried over into the championships. The Juniors were again 3rd in the Southern in 1937 then 2nd the next year with the miler M.W. Jenkins emulating Wooderson's runner's-up feat and losing by the narrow margin of five yards, while the Seniors climbed to tenth place in the National in 1937. Most of all perhaps there was the healthy indication that, despite the fact that the Club enjoyed the numerical advantage against S.L.H. in 1937 with 106 runners in the field, nevertheless they would still have won under the old ten a-side scoring conditions — a claim they had been unable to make since 1913.

These last years before the war saw reinforcement by still more very useful men like G.F. Brooks, S.J. Wooderson and R.R. Choat enabling the Club to assert superiority in the Kent Championship where often they had had to be content with 2nd or 3rd places behind army teams or the emergent force of Aylesford Paper Mills S.C. And all the time there were the awesomely large teams fielded in the big matches with a record number of 126 Blackheath men opposing S.L.H. in 1938. Even in the depth of winter there were regular "Rowland" Ten fields of forty by 1939 when this race was run for the first time over a course approximating to that of today. Other innovations included the first entry — and victory — in the South of the Thames Championship in 1939, as well as a weak team's venture in the London to Brighton Relay in 1937, while the earlier tradition of long-distance walking was now extended to running with the isolated example of individuals like G.J. Richmond followed more numerously first in 1932 by W. ("Puddy") Holmes, A.G.V. Allen and C.L. Mobbs gaining 3rd place in the Polytechnic Marathon, then by L.E. Hammill winning the individual Kent Twenty Miles title and aiding the winning team of L.G. Toms and G.F. Brooks.

The old controversy about the suitability of the Hayes courses as the best sort of

PRESIDENTS ALL. A GROUP ON HAYES COMMON, 1946:

J.R.D. Cockburn, H.E. King, V.W.W. Beardon, G.H. Wilkinson, G.A. Mullins, A.D. Metcalf, A.D. Thwaites, S.D. Taylor.

preparation for the championship races continued to provide a bone of contention and there is little doubt that, as to this present day also, the Club courses are not only quite different from the typical National terrain but are in any case almost unique in themselves. The Captains sought to correct this by encouraging the country men on to the track for it was true that all too often Blackheath produced the steady and strong rather than the pacy runner able to stand the dash of the big races, to adapt his rhythm to meet sudden challenges, to sprint, and most of all, to run better in the championships than in the rest of the season.

To these time-honoured arguments concerning the Hayes routes was added fresh matter of concern in the further growth of suburbia. Following Eden Park's expansion since 1925 came further threatening defacements in the mid-Thirties, this time along the first rampart of chalk hills from Chelsham to Coney Hall in the form of "garden" suburbs. There was one already at Coney Hall and another was projected between Lodge Lane and Featherbed Lane. "The changes" observed the "Gazette" correspondent for the 1935 Closing run, "mean an irreparable breach of associations".

Such worries no doubt concerned many members as much as if not more than the clouds gathering over Europe. Like the rest of their fellow-countrymen they kept the tenor of their way, for it seemed to most that war could with sense be avoided. So it is; with Club routine that we find "The Gazette" concerned up to the outbreak of war — with innovations in which we now can see signs of the times like the holding of informal dances at Headquarters which had become more frequently accessible, a situation from which we were shortly to reap advantages when it came to holding the Club together in time of war or with peacefully irresponsible trivia mingled with the serious stuff that composes life. In "The Gazette" the mentions of births, deaths and weddings unite with exotica like motor smashes in Rangoon, Philo leaving for Iran, the first rifle match against London Scottish - more peaceful than some of the junketings with Blackheath — missives from R.A. Walker ("M'Bongolwane Store, Zululand"), Tommy Hammond attending his first ever Punchbowl Night in 1937, and Trevor Davis, the Club's Peter Pan as the "Gazette" verse put it, celebrating his 73rd birthday with a walk from London to Brighton, and all this while having remained an Ordinary member giving the benefit of his annual subscription to the Club. Then too, there is E.W. Mullins writing to "The Gazette" in 1932 to know if his pewter can be replaced after its loss in the Smyrna fire of 1922, and the Editor observing gravely that this is the second case of an overseas member losing his pewter by fire: "Members may remember that J.H. Low lost his when his log residence in Canada was gutted". And Mullins' pewter is replaced.

Still, training was more of a pleasant, sociable event as B.L. Purton and others have recalled it and Blackheath life in general continued on its healthily extrovert way. If they were aware of the source of the Club's motto quoted at the start of this section Blackheath widows might spare a smile at the irony of its address to an abandoned wife from an absent husband. As for members there were always people like the Brothers Clowser to enliven existence if life threatened to become dull — "lovable clowns", R.A.E. Galley calls them; Charles in particular "always looked most impressive with bowler hat, rolled umbrella and not another stitch on". In 1938, after the election of A.D. Thwaites as President, members adjourned to the local cinema to bask in the reflected glory of a film showing of Sydney Wooderson's feats.

But that presidential appointment was to last for the seeming lifetime of the second world war.

PART FOUR 1939-1969

"VIEW HALLO"

THE SECOND WORLD WAR
THE POST WAR PERIOD 1946 – 1968
TO THE PRESENT DAY
ROAD RUNNING
CROSS COUNTRY

"Evening News" 15th April, 1940.

(by courtesy of the London Evening News)

CLUB GROUP 1938

THE SECOND WORLD WAR

"We have no doubt that all members feel with us a sense of relief and thankfulness that we are to be spared the havoc' and horror of another European or world war . . . . we remember with pride and gratitude those older members who kept the Club alive during the years 1914-18, but ask yourself whether such self-sacrificing achievements would be possible today? Another war would affect the Club even more, and only a person of vivid imagination can picture what might have happened in London and its environs had hostilities broken out".

(Editorial by A.D. Thwaites, "The Gazette", October, 1938).

"I am glad that Queen Victoria did not live to see this. She would have been very angry indeed".

Old Lady surveying bomb damage in the
Bayswater Road, 1940 .

In common with others in whom the British efforts at appeasement had raised high hopes the Editor of "The Gazette" was deceived and what had seemed avoidable became inevitable. But as President for the duration of the War he was to prove himself wrong in the above expression of its consequences upon the Club, though not, alas, of those upon the capital. That he should do so was in large measure due to the man himself, for it was Thwaites who held the Club together and provided the focal point and energizing force not only to encompass its survival but to ensure its flourishing continuance so that Blackheath, unlike many similar bodies, was able to pass into the peace in a state virile enough to grapple with the new problems that were to succeed those of the war.

Just under a year after the Editorial quoted above, with the outbreak of war, the following announcement appeared in "The Gazette": "For the present runs will take place every Saturday throughout the winter season; perhaps even a few small matches will be arranged. The only known factor to prevent this will be destruction by enemy aircraft of local house property, when our premises will be used as a temporary home for homeless". There followed details of other arrangements: the setting-up of an Emergency Committee to conduct the affairs of the Club for the duration of the War, together with plans for training runs at which serving men and their friends were to be especially welcome, while an open invitation was made to members of Orion, Ranelagh and S.L.H. to use facilities at Hayes. "The Gazette" was to continue at less frequent intervals but was to be kept going for the same invaluable purpose it had performed for men away from home during the First World War.

The Annual General Meeting in that fateful autumn was necessarily brief and only about forty members were present. Its business, like that of their 1914-18 forebears, was digging in and preserving as much continuity as possible in the affairs of the Club. There were no changes: the Committee was re-elected en bloc and the Emergency Sub-committee made responsible for management. The same was true of subsequent Annual General Meetings of the war: they were very largely a formality but all the same the work was being done. There were visible signs of the new emergency in the Clubhouse in the shape of A.R.P.

impedimenta and a large pile of palliasses in the dressing room, and in fact, Headquarters served a useful function for outsiders, for by the beginning of 1941 some 75 locals had sought shelter there for periods up to eighteen days, in addition to a couple of R.A.F. parties.

In contrast to the 1914-18 War, however, there was a very active continuation of Blackheath activities; like that other famous — though different — institution, the Windmill Theatre, we never closed. Many clubs had to, but Blackheath not only survived but quit the ordeal of war at least as strong as it entered it. The track section, with its sprinters away in the forces, was not so well off as the years wore on, but the cross-country runners maintained a strong state.

Arthur Thwaites was to perform the office of a Crafter in leading the Club and in fact, Crafter, on the point of death in October 1939, made two special journeys to Hayes to advise Thwaites and urge him to ensure that above all the Club did not go out of operation. Crafter never had the same kind of affection for the Blackheath homes of West Wickham or Hayes that he had had for "The Green Man" and this twilight gesture of love and concern towards what he and his companions, among whom he was nearly the last, called "the old Club", therefore must rank among the finest impulses of this man of sentiment so large and generous.

Both Thwaites and "Nobby" Clarke were elected to the board of directors of B.H.H.Q. in 1939. The latter, a giant in himself, was a pillar of support in these years as in others in his masterly government of the Wine Committee and together with them and the help of the ever-faithful Mrs. Dodson he waged his private war against food rationing in which he did more than win on points. [58] It is an indication of the efficacy of his endeavours that by 1943 the sales were up by £41, in 1944 by £55. When in 1942 there were 110 runners at Hayes for one of the war-time series of Southern Counties Cross-Country team races tea was made available to 150 — at some sacrifice of members' personal rations — with the Clubroom holding men in the uniforms not only of the armed forces but also of Home

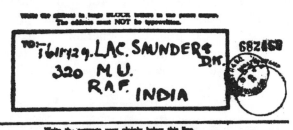

AIRGRAPH LETTER
A.D. Thwaites to D.K. Saunders

Guard, Air Raid Wardens and the Fire Service. The latter had started to share Hayes as their H.Q. under the aegis of A. Dale, our member.

Of course, much had to be foregone. In effect, the fixture list was cancelled, though this was to be offset by emergency arrangements; Catford Bridge could not be used for midweek training any longer; there were no entertainments. Vic Beardon as Summer Captain sent his message via "The Gazette": "I look forward to the next summer season under peaceful skies", while from the Winter Captain came word "As he is busy guarding the air, learning army language (if still unknown to him) the message is short and to the point: 'Carry on!' " On the Blackheath home front Dick Cockburn, H.A. Wilkinson, who had already achieved nearly twenty years of unbroken editorial office and now continued until 1946, L.E. Hammill, Syd Taylor and E.G. Lymbery did yeoman service, the latter — until his unlucky death through a direct hit on the gun-site he was guarding in 1943, having already lost a son and with another taken prisoner — performing the duties of Treasurer, Secretary and Editor.

In the early spring of 1940 L.A.C. convened a meeting of S.L.H. and Blackheath at which combination was agreed upon and the T.C.C. — "The Combined Clubs" — came into being. There were three members from each club forming a sub-committee with executive powers and as a result a large number of successful fixtures was subsequently held. A considerable debt of gratitude was owed to Cyril Jones of the L.A.C. for his work in this connection. Later in 1940 they could rightly claim, as "The Gazette" said, "Whatever the future history of the Club, the first year of this war will rank always as one of its greatest years of achievement, for despite the absence of so many of our best men in the services, curtailed and erratic travel facilities, blackouts, rationing and blitzkriegs, both the summer season and the previous winter season were carried through to a successful conclusion".

Over the country the original intention was for the Club and S.L.H. to unite against Orion and Ranelagh but in the event Blackheath was pitted against the rest, and won, with Sydney Wooderson first home, both brothers — Stanley was there also — looking, they said, "positively burly" with wartime weight. In these early years, George Brooks, Laurie Hammill and Harold Thompson were consistent performers. The Kent Championships were held as were the first Southern Team races for which special medals were struck. In addition to matches against Cambridge University and schools such as Sutton Valence where the difficulty was not so much the race as gaining access to a defence area, even the Kent Twenty was held at Hayes, with Acting Captain Hammill coming second.

Enemy action took tiles off the roof of Headquarters, brought down part of the ceiling of the cottage and placed incendiaries in the car park while the far graver blitz of London destroyed among so much else an old Blackheath landmark in the "Devereux" where so many committee meetings had taken place in the past. Trail-laying was dealt a foul blow by the act of wasting paper constituting a war-time sin, but lime became an adequate though unflattering substitute, as K.N. Wilcockson found when passing an irreverent group of airmen who christened him "Floury Fred", having none of the traditional Blackheath reverence for the august body known as the Trail Layers. For the future Chief of these, indeed, it was a hard year, for even when he forsook trail laying for the less-demanding pursuit of racing as at Chingford in 1941 he was driven to speak against the faintness of the trail, though himself destined later to suffer from unfeeling complaints of the same nature. "Punch" commented in its humorous fashion on the fact of Sydney Wooderson coming under the command of Lieut. General Alexander but were unaware of their common Blackheath membership; Sydney himself was push-biking to fixtures from where he was stationed at Aldershot in addition to running miles under 4 mins. 12 secs. more than once; Vic Beardon burned "gallons of midnight oil" in poring over handicap form; T.C.C. were winning most of their matches — 23 in 1940, 14 in 1941 — with 2500 spectators at the 5-sided match at New Southgate, and in 1940 at Grove Park against Kent they also watched the "dog-fights" going on overhead at tea-time.

From the very start of the war there had of course been serving members — familiar names linked with unfamiliar titles: Gunner G.H. Wilkinson, Pilot Officer R.G. Cross, Flight Lieut. G.F. McIvor. As the war continued there came a steady stream of news from serving members and others caught in the vortex. Wilkinson tasted the bizarre quality that seemed to epitomize so much of this war for many:[60] "I am on guard tonight and have just heard the nightingale. What a war!". Arms were broken on assault courses; lemons from George Tye in Tunis helped raise "Gazette" funds in a raffle at an evening meeting; there were overseas complaints about the absence or quality of beer; B.P. Braund's duties were heard of as constituting, among other things, "Officer in charge of rats and mice". There was of course more serious news also: Brian Lymbery, Harold Smith and J.W. Cockburn, the acting Secretary's brother, all killed flying; Bob Pattison having a close escape in flying his damaged machine back from a sortie on the Pas de Calais; D.H. Trumble getting his wife and child away from Penang to Australia during the Jap invasion, then he himself hiding in the jungle and escaping to Java; S.H. Dewdney, who had for some time been a missionary, helping to evacuate women and children at the Japanese invasion of New Guinea, and returning to Papua by 1944 notwithstanding. There were A.A. Roberts who had escaped from Dunkirk and others like George Wilkinson, R.E. Walker, R.F. Cross, S.A. Bliss, wounded when a "55" went through his tank turret, Will Vercoe and M.W. Jenkins all in North Africa and variously engaged from Algiers to Cairo, from Alamein to Tunis, and, after, in Italy; David Crump on the Russian convoys; H.E. Allanson taking 18 days to do 480 miles in a car on Burma roads, while his brother K.E. died tragically on a torpedoed Japanese boat in which he was a prisoner; Frederick Scholes killed in the Normandy landings after D-Day, 1944. By the end of the war forty-four members had died on active service, a percentage painful still to contemplate.

Others were held[61] in prisoner of war camps and the names of Stalag VIII B and Oflag VIB became familar to "Gazette" readers. The latter establishment saw J.G. Lymbery and J.H. Sewell competing in a brigade sports meeting and for these and others Syd Taylor, remembering his own experience of the previous war, did what he could to ease their situation — by corresponding and by a successful Blackheath Prisoners of War Fund.

While there were many others, as already indicated, doing their share in sustaining the Club, Arthur Thwaites and Syd. Taylor together seem to form a pair both in this war-time period and in other respects. They were both members before the First World War in which both had served and been wounded; they had shared not only a love of cross-country running but each held in time the Club offices of Hon. Treasurer, Editor and President. They were both actively engaged in maintaining the Club's life-line during the Second World War and for years they lived in the vicinity of the Club and within a few hundred yards of each other, while they died in June, 1965, within hours of each other. Thwaites has rightly been called one of the great servants of athletics, for not only was he something of a financial

152

wizard for Blackheath, but also for bodies like the E.C.C.U. and the A.A.A. His chief task in respect of B.H.H.Q. was to see a balance preserved between the needs of that body and those of the Club; care over this evolving process was no more of a sinecure than his war-time responsibility. He was always in demand and among other things took great pride in his selection as a Track Judge for the 1948 Olympic Games and the Empire Games of 1958.

Syd Taylor was a resident of West Wickham for over forty years and as such had been one of Blackheath's earliest settlers in the area as well as keeping open house for members when they ran from "The Railway Hotel". It was said that he knew and was known by more members than any other of his time. He was back in running harness very soon after his four years as a prisoner of war, representing Blackheath in the Southern and National. In addition to his joint Editorship of "The Gazette" his chief impact was as Chief Trail Layer in which he was not only meticulous in the more obvious aspects of this activity but as a local man succeeded in forging strong links with the farmers and landowners who allowed the Club use of their land which was not open to the general public. His was a painstaking work of relations and liaison, the most important and evident symbol of which is now the traditional

WINTER AT HAYES

153

Farmers' Walk that he fostered and which takes place before each Christmas and visits each person to whom we as a Club owe thanks. Initiated by Arthur Thwaites about the mid-Twenties and continued by them both together, the custom originated in the visit to Mr. Boreham, gamekeeper at the now-vanished Dog Farm [62] to convey seasonal messages of good-will since it was to him the Club was indebted for briefing about shooting syndicates' plans for the following Saturday so that trail-layers were warned. From this emanated the custom of Thwaites being appropriately accompanied by the Chief Trail Layer and other colleagues as well as other visits stretching over some ten miles in all to Mrs. Crowe of Rouse Farm, Farmer Levitt of Wickham Court Farm, the Cresswells of Layhams Farm who were re-nowned for their "alarming shooting parties", "Darky" and Mrs. Saunders, celebrated for their onions and elderberry wine and many other names such as Legge, Winterflood and Still.

The latter in particular was a time-honoured figure at another Club institution invol-ving the owners of land over which the Blackheath courses run, namely "Farmers Night" at which, in addition to "drinking people's healths", as Farmer Still used to put it, "until one's own is slightly affected" we make some attempt to repay hospitality like that of Farmer Levitt, who would arrange gaps and spread sacking across barbed wire to protect runners, by entertaining them to dinner at Headquarters with the traditional fare of an apple tart and a roast.

This was a link with peace that they found possible to continue during the war and in 1940, for example, there were present a dozen farmers and some fifty in all — though "Nobby" Clarke voiced his disappointment at the Club's failure to keep up with the times by the inclusion of Land Girls.

Of drawbacks and losses there were all too many reminders but even when, as in 1943-44, there were signs of things improving such as the revival of the Inter-Schools Race with seventeen schools taking part, there were trials yet to come for the home front in the shape of the especially sinister and treacherous flying bomb menace. This together with the previous bombing experience, led to the devising of special precautions and safety routes avoiding the open space of the [63] common. When such crises occurred even the most dignified of trail layers was forced to seek temporary rest in a ditch "after which", as one "Gazette" reported, "the usual search for mushrooms was resumed". In such circumstances runners had to develop an eye for the air as well as for country.

The flying bombs badly affected the London track season and caused many cancella-tions, including our own evening meetings, but for the rest and further out towards the country the war could be forgotten occasionally. Fresh corners of the Hayes region were discovered and pastures new delighted in; there were some quiet, even idyllic nights, while there is a description of one occasion when the President was "observed having a quiet afternoon browsing among the Club archives and so peaceful was the Club-room that the war seemed far away".

There were interesting enough consequences of that war at Hayes: American Army uniform was seen for the first time there in 1944 — "You fellows sure enjoy taking your punishment!" — while when a Canadian scion of the Crafter family arrived in the form of Tom's son, Bob, he was included by Keith Wilcockson in his party for a series of exclusive historical and agricultural "invitation runs" which explored in leisurely fashion all the district's stopping-places of interest. Of course, the average age of the runners going out was increasing and remarks were heard like the small boy's "Fancy making those poor old men run like that!". Yet though summer runs had been curtailed and the "doodle bugs" were modifying joy on the home front at the advances being made in France, the appetite for a run at Hayes again of many away from home was whetted by the rare appearance of a photo in "The Gazette" taken by Syd Taylor of D.J. Tingey, "Baggy" Hargreaves and H. Coldwell going up the leafy lane of a full-blown English summer towards the Common — a nostalgic sight which gave rise to correspondence from overseas betraying surges of homesickness.

Many members have since referred to the Club's inspiration in "keeping them going through the dark years", and Len Towers spoke recently for many in recalling it as "a wonderful experience to find week by week that more and more of my old colleagues were returning to the Clubhouse". As holder at the outbreak of war of the "Bennett" Cup he was responsible, as he said, for retaining it under heavy fire in the Blackheath area in his understairs cupboard. Among those returning were the prisoners of war, including S.D. Gittings, liberated by the Russians and on his way home by April, 1945.

The many already spoken of would not return. To them, on the 27th March, 1948, was dedicated a Memorial flanking that of the First War. In the presence of a large number the Rev. W. Telfer, then Master of Selwyn College, Cambridge, assisted by the Rev. A.N. Daniel, both Club members themselves, conducted a brief service . . . " Grant that we may walk worthy of their fellowship . . . . "

Others though returned would not run again because of wounds and other consequences of the war. It was Dick Cockburn in his Secretary's report at the first post-war Annual General Meeting who timely and rightly reminded them of Blackheath's capacity to offer more than active athletics. Now others could take up the reins together with these men who had done such a service for the Club: Thwaites, Clarke, Taylor, Beardon, Cockburn and Hammill. Just as a new generation of young athletes had arisen represented by D.G. Child, R.G. Richardson and J.H. Scott-Wilson, the first three home in the 1945 Kent Junior Cross-country Championship, so the Club as a whole would go on unhampered by the late disaster to capitalize on its good fortune in retaining the use of its headquarters under a constant threat of requisition, in its members returning whenever possible, even though it was for a few hours only, and, above all, in its officials.

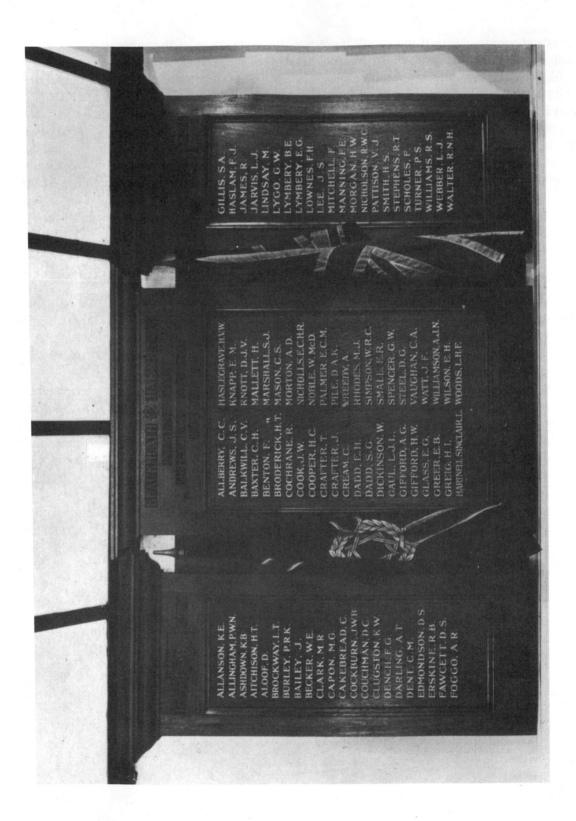

ROLL OF HONOUR

THE POST-WAR PERIOD
1946-1968

".........to those of us who can help the Club through these dark days strength and courage will increase as the task gets stiffer, and the strength and courage will not disappear when the days become brighter. A platitude, we know, but it's worth a little thought".

("The Gazette" - Oct. Dec. 1939)

The years that followed were hardly to lead to the "sunlit uplands" hoped for by Churchill at the time of Dunkirk but for Blackheath it was to be no period of "austerity", then the term applied to the state of the country as a whole. Though in Europe and elsewhere the suffering was not to end with the War, the Club now reaped the reward both of its good luck during the previous four years and of the perseverance of Arthur Thwaites and his fellows, so that as a result of, in particular, their energetic recruiting we were in 1946 one of the strongest clubs in the country and remained so for some time.

The first Annual General Meeting of the new peace that was to be so uneasy reminded those already home that the names that had passed away during those years were not confined to serving men or contemporary athletes: time as well as war had taken its toll — notably of John Metcalf, member since 1872, who had died at the great age of 94, H.F. Pash who had joined in 1896, while a year later the notable Tommy Hammond followed them. The Club's realization of the debt to Thwaites was reflected in the extraordinary response for a presentation to him; members who had not been heard of for years joined in this acclaim, and rightly so, for his contribution had been outstanding among the many signal services he had performed not only for the Club but for national athletics also. Even now he was not to escape into retirement or thankful obscurity for in the absence of Hammill in the army he acted as Hon. Secretary. His stalwart companion and Hon. Treasurer Syd. Taylor at this same first meeting with the sobriety of his kind gave warning against complacency, but the popular sentiment among mere Club laymen was that Blackheath had never been stronger, reinforced as it was with great power of returning servicemen, among them new members drawn to the sport by the enforced taste they had had in military and physical training of the joys of hard running. The subscription might have to be raised from a half to one guinea — a step probably unique in Club history but the sum had remained fixed for over half a century and in any case now was only following the pattern of post-war inflation. In every other respect Blackheath was on the move — not only in performance but in general consolidation. So much so that in 1948 the outstanding Headquarters debentures amounting to £385 were redeemed and the Clubhouse became indeed our own. There too shortly followed changes. Mrs. Dodson, who had been with us for twenty years, died, though her place was taken by her daughter. The next year, 1948, saw "the transition to the higher plane" of Club Presidency of the self-described head cook and bottle-washer W.R.J. Clarke, after eighteen years of diligent service much enjoyed by members as leader of the Wine Committee. Not only did he continue to make his presence felt by the chairs on which he stood to lead the Club Cry for others but equally available was his advice deriving, Victor Beardon has observed, from "an unfailing, sound commonsense approach

LAYHAMS, FEBRUARY 1946.

The last of the series of Matches between Blackheath and the combined clubs during the War Period.

By courtesy of the Times)

and appraisal of all matters".

In 1945, however, the immediate aim was to get things re-started, despite the fact that the process of resettlement in civil life was going on so slowly that it seemed few members under thirty would be available. Nonetheless, an ambitious programme was arranged and what looked at the time like an act of faith ushered in a new era of success. Momentum came gradually, of course. To begin with, Club Championships were revived while, with the incentive of a "token" Southern Cross-country Championship, the Captains urged members into training straightaway, a point well urged since members new to Blackheath during the war years had not raced above 7½ miles. Dick Cockburn was organizing a traditional stroll in June and the following month there was once more a Club Evening Meeting, a small programme put on at New Beckenham to "assist revival", and though there was little more than a hundred yards, 440 and two miles races, yet the eggs in the ladies' spoons were real, supplied from ducks by the resourceful Neville. In August before a packed crowd at the White City Sydney Wooderson in his attempt to run the towering Swede, Arne Andersson, into the ground gave public witness of Blackheath vitality, but privately and in a domestic way so did a working party in the same month in setting their House in order. A cameo which to those who know the men involved perhaps epitomizes this period of renewal is that of a small group — Eric Reed, Douglas Tingey, George Brooks and Dick Cockburn — taking the traditional summer run, this time over the old "Five", and, not to sentimentalize a casual event, embodying a testimony to the enduring fixity of human nature in its desire to hold fast to the things which are good in their return to the well-tried paths of peace after the ordeal of war.

158

Well might the "Gazette" Editor say at the end of 1945, "Hayes is well and truly alive": the signs were increasing all the time. The following August saw the revival of a major Club Open Meeting worthy of the old "Blackheath Day" gatherings, while previous to this in the spring an attendance of well over two hundred had showed the traditional "Bohemian" to be by no means a thing of the past. With the opening run of the next year calling forth a hundred members it was not surprising that, already in 1946, in the last of the "austerity" fixtures we were fielding more than the forces of Orion, Ranelagh and S.L.H., combined against us. As always, Blackheath was not relying upon its "active" members to sustain its reputation either, public evidence of which came in our supplying four officials at the 1948 Olympic Games: Arthur Thwaites, as Track Judge, J.C. McPhail, Deputy Referee of Field Events, Cyril Starnes, Field Events Judge and Ernest Neville as Walking Judge and Master Timekeeper for the Marathon.

But whereas recruiting at first went forward satisfactorily so that, with 834 members in 1947 and over half of the new ones juniors, the number by 1949 was disappointingly low with only 17 juniors joining that summer. In 1954 though numbers were being maintained 311 of these were Life members and the 50 new members made the lowest total since the war. This had not of course gone unnoticed by the Club authorities. The Junior subscription was halved in 1949 and a most happy innovation, a New Members' Night, was introduced in 1948 and has persisted for the twenty years since. In 1950 one of the difficulties hampering junior recruitment — National Service, whereby often brand-new members were whisked away for two years — was alleviated by the franking of their subscription for their period of service. At the 1949 Annual General Meeting A.J. Brent pointed out

2 MILES TEAM RACE, CLUB OPEN MEETING,

Motspur Park, 1946. Blackheath & Sydney Wooderson, team & Individual winners, on inside.

(Sport & General)

159

that there was a big gap in the Club membership between seniors of twenty-seven to thirty and the Juniors of about twenty. Certainly the effect of National Service was unsettling.

Still, for the time being we were to capitalize strongly on our returning seniors, especially over the country. Thwaites' end of war message to members had been "Turn out and run for the Club although you are some years older. Remember the strength of the Club has always been the "middle" pack". The result must have gladdened his heart; indeed, the Trail-layers might have been said to have had a more difficult task than the Winter Captain G.H. Wilkinson through the intensified cultivation of the land. But the runners showed no signs of resulting inhibition: new member H.N. Nunns, won the individual Kent title, while D.G. Child emulated him in the Junior race before going into the Navy and so all too soon became lost to class competition. The senior team won easily and later came 4th in the Southern as well as in this race carrying off the "Camden" and in the National, the "Otway" Cups. Here they finished 5th and R.R. Choat, the future Captain who was to lead the teams so successfully, came 18th, higher than any Club member except P.H. Francis in forty years. One of the Olympic torch carriers in 1948, he performed like figurative service for Blackheath until the fifties and though he finished in the first ten of the Inter-Counties Race, our general team success was a greater achievement still, aided by D.E. Reynolds, his vice-captain and later to succeed him. Most of the matches and all three of the large ones at this time were won and though we lost to the newly arisen force of Aylesford Paper Mills in the Kent the next year our 3rd position in the Southern was the highest since 1891. Our fourth place in the National was our best ever,

THE GREAT ARTHUR WINT COMPETING IN BLACKHEATH OPEN MEETING
Motspur·Park, 1946   (Sport & General)

only to be bettered in 1948 when we were 2nd in the Southern and 3rd in the National with Sydney Wooderson winning both individual titles, the latter by twenty yards after a gruelling uphill finish at Sheffield. Brilliant though his success was it had first-class backing by a team of real spirit; not only he but G.E. Monshall gained Internationals in 1947 and behind them came runners of dedication beside those already mentioned: J. Braughton, the deceptively frail-looking W.F. Spencer, and A.J. Brent. There were some eight capable of finishing in the first fifty of the English Championship and justly could their Captain boast of the most successful seasons ever. Such a high standard is hard to sustain, but the subsequent decline was far from disastrous and the success in Club matches continued, most being won. Though most of the stalwarts of the mid-fifties had in effect retired from the scene, others like L.J. Atkinson, who in 1950 finished 22nd in his first National, helped us maintain a respectable place in cross-country society, as did J.H. Scott-Wilson who gave yeoman service both during and after a distinguished and protracted Oxford running career. The rugged T.J. Betteridge, 15th in the 1951 National Junior race, was prominent together with R.D Fletcher and A.V. Hayday who subsequently succeeded to the key office of Hon. Secretary. One of their team mates, G. Scotting, was one of our best as well as of Surrey in the fifties but a loss too early for us, his friends, by his death at thirty, his ashes scattered at his wish upon Hayes Common.

CROSS-COUNTRY TEAM 1947-48

STANDING: E.V. Beaton, H. Smith, E.R. May, H.N. Nunns, J.P. Clark, W.F. Lake, A.E. Beedle, C. Busby.
SEATED: J. Braughton, S.C. Wooderson, R.R. Choat, G.H. Wilkinson, D.E. Reynolds, W.F. Spencer, A.J. Brent.

161

All these and many more were to be led home time and again by the man who succeeded Reynolds and remained Cross-country Captain for the next five years, in this as in other offices, creating an impression of integrity, understanding and dedication not readily matched. Alan Brent's first Club win was in the Club "Closing Five" of 1946 with an allowance of five minutes which in the light of the twenty years of achievement to follow now appears amusing. By 1947 he was finishing well up among the best in the country and in the early sixties he only seemed to increase his work load when competing as Club first team member as well as Veteran. Throughout this period he ran regularly for Kent in the Inter-counties Races. More impressive even than his consistent running has been his continuing industry for the Club — together with his wife's similar efforts on our behalf — and for athletic associations like the Schools' and the South of the Thames Cross-country of which Associa-

G. SCOTTING   A.J. BRENT & L.F. FLETCHER

London to Brighton relay 1951

162

tion he was President in 1966, though more often appearing behind a measuring wheel than in any superior glory. He was largely instrumental in directing the Club's attention to this latter body which, although founded before the end of the last century, only received serious attention by Blackheath after the last war, having since made up for past omission by winning the Championship more than once despite the fact that a six years' disqualification from the race accompanies a team's victory. A Vice-President of the E.C.C.U. he is at the present time of writing President-Elect of the Southern Counties Cross-country Association. Many both within and outside the Club can testify to his encouragement of youth not only officially or on coaching courses, but morally, and always, cheerfully. It is also not inappropriate to mention at this point the help given over the last twenty years by the pupils of his school, Hawes Down, in marking road races and Club matches for schools.

No less indispensable both during and since this time was G.F. Brooks, who having made an exceptional return to running after the war with a ninth place in the Kent though he was in his forties, then became the most skilled handicapper to be wished for the Club both summer and winter, while for many runners he was their favourite and most ardent supporter. Typifying this man's calibre is the story, no more than four years old, of how, asked to officiate as an outsider at the Salvation Army's Centenary Sports at the new Crystal Palace Centre he arrived to find the Army there in battalions but no other officials than himself and three W.A.A.A. ladies. With no more than these and some unskilled aides he got the large programme under way with no starter, no gun, no "clapper" substitute — though the Track manager produced a hunting horn. "Thus", said "The Gazette", reporting this in sanguine fashion as nothing more than what was to be expected from a Blackheath Harrier, "George saved the honour of the A.A.A. and won himself an honourable mention in "The War Cry".

A third vital influence was the highly efficient D.J. Tingey who discharged the duties of Cross-country Secretary, but whose best-known achievement probably is the organisation and stage management of a whole series of the Club's Inter-Schools' races as well as those for novices.

The "Parrish" Cup given for the Schools Race was first competed for in 1946 and arose from a bequest to the Club by W.J. Parrish, its devoted servant for many years. As such it is perhaps unique in the history of athletic trophies and an outstanding instance of the disinterested loyalty which Blackheath has been capable of inspiring.

William James Parrish, the Club's attendant, trainer, adviser and usher from 1908 to 1932, is still impressively remembered by old members. A fatherly figure who had the Club's welfare at heart is how one such recalls him and indeed his concern for Blackheath extended far beyond his official retirement until his death in 1944 when he was in his ninetieth year. The description Ratcliff applied to him — a grand old Englishman" — was no sentimental cliche. Parrish was a chip of the old England and many of his obiter dicta on life and athletics were of a Shakespearian order. Subjects under his firm palm on the massage table at the Crystal Palace might tind themselves advised sternly to "give it a break for a bit — you ain't got 'arf the belly you 'ad, sir," He always went with the British Olympic teams but his whole heart lay with Blackheath for whose members he was himself a proverbial institution.

The first post-war Race had already attracted 17 schools, marginally less than before 1939. Now the competition became very popular with teams coming from as far afield as Derbyshire like Repton as well as locally and, eventually, a limit had to be placed on the number invited, since by the 1950's entries commonly exceeded 25 schools. Our member, R.A. Gordon-Smith, presented the "Rags" Trophy for this race which, since 1964, has served to encourage local schools in the face of severe outside competition. Thus have combined the time-honoured Club tradition of encouraging the sport in the public schools and that begun by Dyball in the twenties of fostering local talents.

The early fifties may have seen an inevitable falling-off from the high standard set by the masters of the forties but it was not one of which we were depressingly aware for a more than respectable level was maintained. 1952 saw a new record of seven teams entered for the three Kent Championship Races; most straight matches were being won, as well as the three big ones, and though S.L.H. was closing the gap all the time, by 1953 we had levelled scores. So that, all in all, the regaining of the Kent Championship in 1955 for the first time since 1949 seemed to characterize a strength that was more often dormant than absent, a contention substantiated by our defeats of S.L.H., a club which nonetheless at this time could win all three National team titles on one day. More new names were appearing, prominent among them being a novice winner, B.F. Pearce, who later showed his mettle over great distances on the road, and N.F. Everard, the younger of two brothers, both of them runners of class, the elder to reach his peak in 1957-58.

In 1961 the veterans composed 40% of the field in the Club ten miles championship. This strength of runners above forty years of age has been fostered by a policy of veterans races with Orion, Ranelagh, S.L.H., and the Veterans A.C. since 1955 and this helped to correct an uncharacteristic tendency to weakness in our medium pack. Some of these veterans were running on the bonus of several years of rigorous training and racing over long distances on the road, this form of competition now taking on a new seriousness both nationally and within the Club.

Led by the early example of C. Busby in 1947 with but little backing while Sydney Wooderson was helping the relay teams to victory, the teams formed by L.E. Piper, D.E. Reynolds and G.J. Gosling struck a new competitive note from 1948 onwards, when in the space of four years they won every major long-distance honour on the road and crowded that period with more success than almost the whole of previous Blackheath history. Here more than elsewhere it is difficult to resist the temptation of mere cataloguing — not only was the quantity of competition increasing but they were winning it, from ten and fifteen miles to marathon, thirties, fifties and one hundred mile races. They were, in effect, the pioneers of the developments which have continued since in road running, both in their example and organizationally, for once again Ernest Neville enters our story, as the inspirer in 1951 of the now immensely strong and popular Road Runners' Club with its world-wide membership. Together with him was the R.R.C's first President, Rex Cross, himself a forerunner in Blackheath long-distance, while Lew Piper later succeeded to the same office. By the same way of influence the welcome given to Hardy Ballington, the South African Road champion and London-Brighton record holder, at Hayes in 1953 was to bring about the return visits of British competitors to South Africa and its Comrades Marathon. These are long-term effects of the kind Blackheath had always helped to engineer but in this period of the early fifties it was the immediate feats that claimed the attention as the record of the 1951 season amply witnesses with wins in the Cambridge and Wigmore 15 mile races, the Kent '20', Peterborough and Polytechnic Marathons and the S.L.H. '30'. Chief among these victories was that in the first London to Brighton. This race was sponsored by the R.R.C. and was the immediate reason for that organisation's establishment. Blackheath also supplied the individual winner in Lew Piper, as they had done in the Peterborough race in C. Busby. These two had backing from stalwarts like B. Foster and G.O.J. Grier, not to mention L.E. Hammill who had helped them to an early 2nd place success in the 1949 Wigmore '15' in addition to the other debts owed him by the Club and, in particular, B.H.H.Q.

The full extent of their triumphs is on record already and they are too numerous to mention even in summary, but the greater distances are worth dwelling on, together with their chief performers. The two protagonists, Piper and Reynolds, need no one to champion their courage, either of the kind required to put through the programme of thousands of training miles they underwent during these years or of that they drew on in putting that preparation to use. If they did, perhaps their steel would be sufficiently suggested by Reynolds' first enquiry upon recovering consciousness when wounded in the North African campaign as to whether his legs were all right, and Piper's perseverance not only in recovering from the road accident necessitating the removal of a knee-cap in 1953, but in demonstrating that recovery in subsequent distance races which included the hundred miles which admitted him to that select band, the "Centurions". Reynolds had long been a distinguished Club and Kent Champion, and after leading the post-war cross-country teams

D.E. REYNOLDS & L. E. PIPER, S.L.H. 30 MILES ROAD RACE, 1951.

(By courtesy of H.W. Neale)

for a while, had then graduated to these longer races with the encouragement of Neville. He followed Piper's example and won the London to Brighton the following year himself in record time with Piper 3rd and Gosling 5th, did the same for 40 and 50 miles at Motspur Park taking over twenty minutes off Fowler-Dixon's 1884 and Edgar Lloyd's 1913 figures and the following year repeated the trick with 4 hours 19 mins. 20.4 secs for forty and 5

ROAD RUNNING TEAM, 1950-1951

| A.C. Dashwood | F.W. Parker | D.E. Reynolds |
| C. Busby | (PRESIDENT) | L.E. Piper |

hours 30 mins. 22.4 secs. for fifty miles. While at Hayes Ballington had warned them to look out for his compatriot W. Hayward who in 1953 came to England and competed successfully against Reynolds in a record twenty four hours race, again at Motspur. The Blackheath man covered 154¾ miles, having beaten Arthur Newton's performance. No less impressive in the circumstances though 50 miles less was Reynolds' run from London to Brighton and back, especially in the terrible weather which dogged them from the start and the drenching the runners took, yet he covered 104 miles 1,130 yards in 14 hours 54 mins. 59 secs. A tall runner with an economical stride considering his height, his chin well up, it was not for his performances alone that we recalled and mourned him at his early death in 1962, but for his calm, modest and gentle manner backed by great strength of conviction.

One recalls the rugged Piper and the rest of the team in full maturity, not as young men, since they came to running after the interruption of years of war, or, as in Lew's case, for the first time then. Perhaps the dominant impression they left on us was of their great and relaxed enjoyment of running.

Finally in discussing their heyday, it seems fitting to place here mention of Ernest Neville, whose energies reach throughout the elapsed portion of our century, so much so that it is an historian's puzzle where chiefly to place him. Possibly here among distance men of this later generation is what would best please him since he, like the perennial Clay Thomas and his fine Norfolk jacket or the youthful Starnes, appears to age by degrees only of the gentlest kind. His athletic genesis has been recorded in this story just as his genius has been celebrated in more than one dinner in his honour: on his 80th birthday at the House of Commons, by the Road Runners' Club — itself flourishing today with over 3000 members — or by the Road Walking Association in recognition of his office as a founder. Indeed his services as an inaugurator must, one thinks at times, have been enjoyed by most athletic foundations, so pervasive has his influence been. A "Centurion" with, too, a lifetime of athletics organization behind him he is that rare phenomenon, a man of action as well as of inspiration. He has flourished since the first years of this century and well into these 1960's has remained something of a powerhouse of ideas put into execution. Memories of him will always be strongly human ones, like that observed at the 1953 24 hours Run where, as the "Gazette" correspondent remarked, "He seemed to be continually appearing at the starting post announcing with a great voice 'Another New Record!' then disappearing into a little hut, where, it appeared, was the very necessary store of refreshments".

Since then the heart of Neville has been gladdened by those who have maintained also the traditions of his first love, long-distance road-walking. The spirit of Schofield and Hammond and the long-standing links between Blackheath and Surrey Walking Club have been upheld in signal fashion not only by Piper but by such as W. J. Traer and ex-Surrey W.C. President, Gerry Rhodes. These two became Centurions 290 and 292 respectively in 1959 between London and Brighton. Often they would lead with them efficient but blind walkers like Les Dennis. Bill Traer in particular has proved his worth to both clubs as Racing Hon. Secretary to Surrey W.C. and as a redoubtable treasurer and popular President to Blackheath. In more recent years H.N. Nunns has followed in their steps along the Brighton road in addition to his raids upon the Johnson Bowl. In this latter period also an inspiration and active participant has been the Club's former Hon. Secretary N. Dudley, among other things a perpetual plotter of road runs and walks. Many of their performances have been based on a dedicated preparation unsurpassed by other Club men though they have usually gone unsung by comparison with more glamorous feats.

In the unprecedented achievement of our men in these long-distance road events we had under our noses a sign of changing times and attitudes. The post-war world was like the earlier one no more in athletics than in other respects. Just as road racing in any quantity was a new phenomenon, so too was the approach to it and to other branches of our sport by the more earnest of its devotees in the new spirit of seriousness that was more or less total in its dedication, a lesson which, desirable or not, athletes in Britain were slow in learning — though some like Gordon Pirie of S.L.H. could profit — even after the crucial display of one of its high priests, Emil Zatopek, at Wembley in 1948 who showed no vestige of gentlemanly style, but who nevertheless won. So that even athletes like Bannister and Chataway who were best placed to observe contemporary trends were still as late as 1952 receiving shocks at the hands of better-conditioned men than themselves at the Helsinki Olympics. After 1945 England began to lose the International Cross-country Championship more often than before and it was evident that athletic growth elsewhere was going on, and more quickly. More hopeful signs like the first appointment by the A.A.A. in 1947 of a National Coach, Geoffrey Dyson, were all too isolated, though the previous year the A.A.A. Coaching Scheme had been initiated. Small wonder that a Club that prided itself upon its traditions should experience some little pains of adjustment to an athletic world that was more harshly competitive than that of previous ages. The 1946 Club Meeting with a crowd of 7000 squeezing its way into Motspur Park to see its heroes, Wooderson, Wint, and MacDonald Bailey, had flattered to deceive. Blackheath's problems expressed in losses on such meetings of over £150 were a phenomenon all organizers of big meetings were to find confronting them in succeeding years.

There were good legacies from the war years of older members like C.A. Wiard, E.L. Page and Victor Beardon plentifully available to help younger members with advice after their own active days were over; there was the welcome "Four Clubs" Match deriving from the wartime "Combined Clubs" institution, and individually the Club was represented in the 1948 Olympic 5000 metres by J. Braughton.

This man was one of the most relaxed and graceful movers the Club has ever had and a great asset on track, road and country. The outstanding distance runner of the Club track team in this period he possessed the smooth inexorability of leg action that one associated with the superlative Finnish distance runners and performed with distinction over a variety of distances from the half mile to the marathon. Apart from some fine runs in the London to Brighton Relay he was one of the only ones ever to attempt to challenge the overwhelming supremacy of Jim Peters and Stan Cox at the marathon. He was also one of the few runners directly following the war to see the necessity for British distance men to increase their training in order to match the performances of continental athletes like Zatopek. But there was always a hard-headed commonsense and realism about this northerner which recognized a limit to what amateurs like himself could achieve in this coming age of full-time athletics.

There were plenty of successful track fixtures and a quantity of county champions: sprinters like P.B. Smith and A.D. Coote, quarter-milers like A.G. Chappell, three-milers like Gordon Monshall setting up a Kent record, with many juniors coming along such as K.M. Horn, our Kent Junior Long Jump Champion followed by E.J. Malone doing the same and adding the High Jump title, both in 1949, and even a steeplechaser in J.E. Furniss, 2nd in the Southern Counties and, as has been mentioned, 8th in the A.A.A. Championships. Then there were over a thousand pounds' worth of Olympic tickets sold among members in 1948, while Secretary Beardon's appeal for younger men to fill the gaps left by the war years – "There may be a difference in years between us but we are all Blackheath Harriers" – brought a quick response of 15 nominations for places on the General Committee. Altogether there was plenty to be cheerful about, but looking back at this period one is conscious chiefly of far-reaching developments coming into play.

Surveying the pattern of Club competition from 1950 onwards one notes a sharp increase in quantity and intensity. Of Blackheath it is probably true to say that since this date there has been an all-round development unprecedented and probably unequalled in respect of diversity by any other club. What it may have lacked in terms of competitive drive at periods in its past it seems now to some degree to have remedied, while it remains unrivalled in its hospitable provision and spirit of fellowship. One is tempted to think that

there has been more competition since the last war than in the rest of our history and it was significant of the way a corrective to the old social rather than competitive tradition had been administered that the Hon. Secretary's Annual Report of 1957 voiced a complaint about a decline in Ordinary Runs – the life-blood of former days' activities – but gave recognition to the good support of Club Championships. In short, people were competing on Saturdays now rather than training. Plans were announced for revitalizing Pack running, but it seems that the movement of the times was against even so sociable a club as ours succeeding in other than a piecemeal fashion in this intention. The mounting volume of competition was quite simply taking the body of regular runners away to more arduous pursuits elsewhere and leaving fewer Saturdays for social running. Another pressure was that of the more serious attitude to training of the Zatopek–Pirie tradition mentioned above, which caused such runs to go out of fashion, though pack running as being an over-gentle pursuit for useful purposes is today something of an exaggerated superstition and in fact among our faster runners has often only been relegated to Sunday morning.

J. BRAUGHTON
Olympic Distance Runner.

But, so far as this Club was concerned, with its special character, the immediate effect at this time was to create a greater gulf than could ever be thought to be desirable between competitive and social runners. It was not a phenomenon in the many other clubs which had always been competitive in emphasis — often to the exclusion and discouragement of merely recreational running — but to those who held responsibility for the welfare of Blackheath it was a matter of some concern.

In 1957 the then Club Coach, J.H.M. Cole-Powney, wrote in "The Gazette" about resistance to new methods of training, lamenting the fact that members of the Club had, evidently, not proved sufficiently receptive to such doctrines: "Just trudging over the heath in slow packs and fast packs does not provide a means to top-class performance up to 10,000 metres or for that matter racing over the country or road racing". Of course, this call to action had been sounded before in Blackheath but now, as elsewhere, it came to assume a more stringent and — at times — a more strident tone. In the same article he referred to the formation of a coaching body from among retired and semi-retired Club athletes for the purpose of looking after our large numbers. This was something extremely valuable, as it had proved in the past more than once, while today it is a formidable advisory body with consultation possible for every event and several persons responsible for each event.

The great problem since 1950, then, has been that of adaptation to a world of modern athletics which was itself undergoing very rapid and revolutionary change. Already the athlete in his teens starting today can hardly appreciate the extent and volume of the changes that have come about in his life-time. To him it must seem that the present high-powered situation was always so. But a Club with a lengthy past knows that it is otherwise. Such a club in a situation of rapid change is bound to undergo tests of a kind that will not worry younger clubs which have come into being and grown up with the new ethos — an ethos that pertains not only to athletics but which is general and social in nature and is of such scale and influence that even now we cannot see its end and long-term effect. No doubt many older members were taken by surprise by these developments and doubtless they had difficulty in grasping what was in the minds of the generation that was growing up. Had an outsider to guess at the likely future of such an institution in the years that followed he might have been forgiven for prophesying a destiny similar to that of the unadaptable dinosaur. Yet this would have been to ignore the past record of Blackheath Harriers, a body with a tradition, certainly, but a tradition of adaptation — a framework of flexible potential, not a design of rigidly planned permanence. Once again its powers of absorption, digestion and exploitation of new experience were called upon. It is the Club's great fortune that there were men of the calibre of V.W.W. Beardon and J. Sims to guide it through its difficulties. Victor Beardon followed his successful athletic career not only with an industrious period of office as Secretary but with one equally proficient as a starter. It was he who, at the 1960 Annual Dinner, referred to the rapid rise to the Club's highest office of Jack Sims, whose quiet yet imposing presence is well-known in both athletic and rowing circles. He was earlier a noteworthy Entertainments Secretary who, despite the waning of the "Bohemians" at that time, arranged a full programme of other parties, dances and concerts. The chief debt to him, however, is probably for his eternal vigilance over the Club's best business interests, of which the 1962 Fund-raising scheme for the Headquarters roof is a good example.

CLUB GROUP 1951

TO THE PRESENT DAY

The speeding-up process acquired momentum about five years after the end of the war which was when the quality and quantity of competition started to intensify. The immediately impressive success of the Club in the early 1950's was, as we have shown, in long-distance road-running, but the most striking long-term development was to be in track athletics. In 1947, Charles Wiard, in his Track Captain's message had said, "I have appointed N.W. Page as a kind of Father Confessor to you all — I know he will take a great interest in you". Looking back over the last twenty years one can find little reason to modify that description; for that is what the new Track Captain of 1950 has been for so many members, as well as acting as a kind of catalyst and focus of the strength that was to flourish consistently in track and field in the years that followed. During that time he has had many capable and industrious helpers — men like K.L. Jobson, who assumed Page's office for a spell of two years. T.T. Sullivan, R.E. Taylor, J.R. White and P.J.G. Baigent as well as the co-operation of many older helpers — men of sterling quality like the ex-Kent half-miler Arthur Nye. Yet these would be the first to endorse the fact of his vital inspiration. In his first message as Captain he gave clear indication of purposes that were to be no empty exhortation to himself or others: ". . . it is my aim to see Blackheath well on the way to re-establishing themselves as one of the leading track clubs in the country", and, going on to define this more precisely, ..."and that, by the time spikes are hung up at the end of this summer". Lack of assurance is never his fault: as a "Gazette" correspondent noted, "When talking to Norman Page half-way through one of these Trophy Meetings, one is surprised by his confidence in the team". And the most surprised were always the athletes who, having heard amazing prophecies concerning themselves blandly declared, gaze hidden behind superior veiled eye-lids, then have sallied forth to fulfil or — at times when the Captain's prophetic powers have been inaccurately off-form — even to exceed that seer's predictions as to their placing and performance. After which, returning for compliments to the source one would be met instead by further sibylline judgments as to a more remote future delivered like, not to speak it profanely, a clergyman pronouncing benediction, but with hands clasped benignly across unholy writ of programme or mill-board. It is true, as he himself said, that he is "interested in each individual, however good or bad a performer he may be" — and truly, though one was only a member of the team, he always made one feel as if you alone were the one who could and would win the match. From details like commending an assiduous supporter like Eric Reed to himself making fifty per cent of a Club Javelin Championship field as in earlier days, he has been a first class example of practising his own fluent — and when writing, — underlined in red biro, preaching. The famous late arrival and characteristic mopping of the brow belie a formidably sanguine outlook where members and team potential are concerned. A recent appearance at a track will be re-called in the entirely characteristic beeline he made for the Dorking Trophy Meeting on the same day that he came out of hospital in 1967 despite considerable physical discomfort. Since he is a realistic romantic, it is not surprising that two of his other interests are the Stock Market and Classical music. Champion telephone user and dogged in persuasion, master of the grand design and spacious declaration, a typical ending to his annual Captain's message is "In conclusion, I salute my team . . . . " Many team members will return the compliment, for the story of the growth of our track strength over this period is largely his story also.

ACCUSTOMED ROLE: N.W. PAGE, TRACK CAPTAIN.

GROUP OF MEMBERS AT WHITE CITY
G.L. Gosling, A.F. Nash, E.J. Sawkins, P.J.G. Baigent, A.J. Humber

173

Truly the Club will remain in his debt — no doubt in more senses than one.

In 1950 the junior membership began to increase, while the all-round standard improved; the sprint team of A.D. Coote, the Kent Champion, A.W.O. Webb, J.B. Spence and J.F. Toal won the Southern Relay title while a hint of the future came in our Southern Discus Junior winner D.G. Pooley, as well as in junior milers like T.J. Betteridge and A.S. Smith. The following year with J. Le Masurier as coach, there was already discernible the promise of harvest: in nine first places in fourteen triangular matches; in many Junior successes in the Kent Championships, significantly both in track and field; in a first-class junior sprint relay team coming second in the Southern and third in the A.A.A. Championships. The field event weakness called for remedy, since in a contest like the Metropolitan Police and Milocarian Match, though we could lead the track score by 17 points, in the full match we still lost by 12½, so that versatile athletes like the cheerful and long outstanding E.J. Sawkins who on occasion would compete in half a dozen events in addition to his speciality of hurdles and achieving a 14.9 secs. Junior Highs in 1951 could find their individual versatility discounted by that of clubs more evenly powerful.

The year of Le Masurier's field event coaching was followed by the work of Franz Stampfl. The influence of this blue-eyed and twinkling Austrian ex-skiing and javelin throwing international was no less powerful for lasting only a couple of years before he emigrated to Australia. Although he was a field event specialist his impact as a personality was felt by all sorts of athletes and not least by runners. Blessed with the ability rare even among coaches to persuade people to perform feats they believed themselves incapable of and to enjoy the process into the bargain he was a man who no one who met him will forget. Maxims like his injunction, quite seriously meant, "You don't have to limp — it's only pain", his promises of improvement ending with a confident "you will SURPRISE yourself!" and his agonized or exultant shouts as his charges stormed round the tracks of England — no matter whether to 5 or 4 minute mile performances — will also long remain in the memories of those athletes whose good fortune it was to encounter this Svengali of the cinders. His great psychological effect on the athletes contributed, with Norman Page's added concentration, to a strong and continuing progress. As a result, since then we have been able to boast of many fine jumpers and throwers. Already by 1952 — when, incidentally, the old "Walter" Steeplechase Trophy race was revived as Page had promised — there were signs of hope and the three years succeeding saw Kent Discus champions in the massively staunch C.D. Purves, still going strong today, and H.A. Abbott; javelin winners in T.M. O'Reilly who was good enough to win both senior and junior titles in 1953 and another consistent performer, C.M. Brand, who set up a Junior Championship best in 1954 as well as winning senior titles in 1957, 1958 and 1959, jumpers like D.R. Bell, placed in the Junior Southern, and B.E. Le Sage.

Probably the greatest pleasure of these and later years was the improvement in our Junior strength of which several of those just mentioned were such notable examples. They were certainly the outstanding feature in 1952 when they carried off the Chesham, Loftus Tottenham and Reading Standard Trophies — feats which they were to repeat in following years. By 1955 they were strong enough to take five Kent titles as well as other places and regain the Grenville Trophy which they had lost the previous year after winning it in 1953, with the seniors 3rd in the accompanying Waddilove Competition. They also gained 3rd place in the Junior A.A.A. Sprint Relay Championship, coached by Norman Page and raising

GRENVILLE TROPHY 1953

M. Tilley   C.M. Brand   L. Jones   N. Everard   D.A. Pinckard   J.B. Herring   B.G. Stone   P. McCarthy   H.J. Willis
K.L. Jobson   N.W. Page   E.J. Sawkins   J. Frost
Front: P.R. Davis   J.H. Sewell (Capt. Crystal Palace F.C.)   T. O'Reilly   T.T. Sullivan

A.A.A. JUNIOR 440 YARDS RELAY CHAMPIONSHIP, 1956.

Blackheath (I.R. Smith) 1st, Cambridge H. (Extreme right) 2nd, London A.C. (K.4)
3rd, Southgate H. (E 4) 4th, Wimbledon A.C. (Behind Southgate) 5th.

175

hopes of future victory which they confirmed the next year, equalling the record of 43.8 secs. In this the trio of D.J. Fournel, A.H. Gedge, and D.J. Hahn was completed by a very fine sprinter I.R. Smith who in 1955 won the Junior A.A.A. 220 yards and was placed third in the Hundred. In 1957 Gedge and Hahn repeated the dose aided by D.R. Livett and the up and bustling Ross who was to become such a fine quarter-miler with a 3rd place behind another member, P.G.R. Lyon, 2nd in the Southern Junior 440 yards, Ross as a senior gaining international honours in the same event by 1960. This time they bettered the record with 43.5 secs. The junior performers of class in this period of increase are too numerous for justice to be done to the fine achievements of these years, but among them were P. Duffy who, as well as becoming the first holder of the Wooderson Junior Mile Club Trophy, made his 880 yards mark of 1 min. 54.8 secs. at a White City meeting – a time which though good enough to win many Senior titles in the past was to become common-place in the crucible of modern athletics; D.J. Fournel, Southern Long Jump winner with 21ft. 9 ins. in 1956 and W.D. Jenkins, winner of the Southern high hurdles.

The most eye-catching junior success, and one to rival that of the long-distance men at the same period, was that of the milers where a number combined to form a virtually unbeatable combination at the time, while several were to go on for many years as prominent athletes and officials. Regularly they would win Championship and trophy team races, often filling all the top placings, as in the Reading Standard Trophy of both 1952 and 1953. In the Grenville Trophy races and the Kent Championship they would fill the individual first place by turns, even if it became necessary to heave the chosen one over the line. Chief among these were J.B. Herring and B.G. Stone, the former destined for international success but already distinguishing himself with County Mile titles and with second places in Southern and A.A.A. Junior Miles in times around 4 mins. 20 secs. Stone, however, claimed more immediate attention, for, in addition to being a strong anchor man in this fine team with times regularly well below 4 min. 30 secs., in 1953 as well as winning the Club's Inter-schools Race he carried off the Southern Youths Cross-country Championship. There is little doubt that in more recent years he could still have been turning in first-class performances had it not been for his work as Cross-country Captain as well as his other activities. These two had excellent backing from their team mates, the small and powerful T. Sullivan, who was to become so valuable a middle-distance man and Club track official, L.L. Jones, P.A.V. Broome and D.A. Pinckard who in 1953 became the third man of the season to break 4 mins. 30 secs. This group, together with the sprint relay teams, were by no means the least of the glories of the period.

1953 showed the first density of general track success, particularly in the demanding special inter-club invitation contests, so that by the following year we were up to a standard represented by 5th place in the Waddilove Trophy, 3rd by 1955 and in the 1956 L.A.C. Relays winners for the first time together with a reminder of former days in becoming holders of the Herbert Pash Memorial Trophy. The outstanding seniors of 1952-54 were R.A. Morley, W.A. Aylett and, still, with successes like his second place in the Southern 3 miles, Jack Braughton, though he was to show himself a long way from finished as late as 1955 when, for example, he would turn in a 13 mins. 50.6 secs. three miles just after running quick time in the Polytechnic Marathon. Roy Morley had been a late joiner and was already a middle distance runner of international class, though too often having to be satisfied with second places behind great performers like Bannister and the Olympian Arthur Wint beside whom he

**A.A.A. JUNIOR 440 YARDS RELAY CHAMPIONS, 1957, IN BEST CHAMP.
TIME OF 43.5 SECS.:** D.R. Livett, A.H. Gedge, D.J. Hahn, I.M. Ross.

was one of the very few whose stride did not look silly. Ill-success came to him on such occasions as the A.A.A. 880 yards final of 1951 when, certain of a place, he fell — though he claimed our own A.C.J. Poole's Kent 880 record in 1952 after it had stood for 18 years. By then his half-miling career was drawing to a close and with an eye on the Helsinki Olympics he turned to steeple-chasing with a win in the Southern race and still in 1954 was among the first half-dozen nationally in this event. After this he was to enjoy success as the Club's premier cross-country runner and also to perform creditably in marathon and other road events. He has been a great asset to the Club whether as a team member or wielding a paint brush. But those who have known him from his first Blackheath days will long recall that majestically long and raking stride.

Aylett was similarly tall and impressive but with a more lanky and rangy style which carried him close to 1 min. 50 secs. for the half-mile and to Kent and Southern titles and international representation in 1954, his best season, when he was placed third in the A.A.A. 880 final and set up an English Native record of 2 mins. 10.5 secs. for 1000 yards. The team successes were certainly maintained by a formidable body of individual talent many of whom, however diminished by modern pressures and other more brilliant clubmates, were, by any standards, class performers. They tend to be ignored except by grateful connoisseurs like

Page but their service was and is invaluable. Prominent among these and perhaps as an example of one who is deprived of highest honours by the intensity of modern competitive conditions is L.F. Fletcher who through the fifties and well into the sixties was a consistent performer and gainer of points. As early as 1950 we find Norman Page saying of him that during the season he had hardly ever been out of the first two places in inter-club half and one mile events. Such was his most important contribution to Blackheath as typified by his thrustful upright action even though his perseverance was occasionally rewarded by runs like his 4 mins. 14.4 secs. for 4th place in the 1955 Southern mile. Doubtless today he finds greatest satisfaction in the total record as represented by the facts that at one time or another he has held every Club Championship from half to ten miles and in 1956-57 had six Club Championship Cups in his possession at one time. A versatile stalwart of road, track and country events he is the kind of competitor no club can ever have enough of.

From 1956 onwards it was the Youth Section that began to compete for the "improvement stakes" and in addition to an abundance of such young good class material they claimed ample individual success, especially — and how it showed the changing pattern of things — in field events where we had Kent and Surrey Youth Shot Champions in B.M. Shapcott and P.R.R. Jackson and, in 1957, the Southern Youth Long Jump winner, B.C. Harding. Shapcott in particular was later to show up well in good all-round achievements like his 1958 A.A.A. Junior Championship places of 3rd, 5th and 6th in Shot, Discus and Hammer.

D.J. Harker and E.J. Sampson were regularly beating 50 secs. for the quarter mile already by 1955-56; 4th in the 1957 Inter-Counties Championship G. Hickey in 1956 had been the first Blackheath high jumper to clear six feet. By 1962 he had cleared 6ft. 2 in. 29 times and went on to 6ft. 3 ins. for Essex County titles and consistently high places over the years. Over a similarly lengthy period D. Gale also distinguished himself at sprints, hurdles and jumps alike. Even cross-country men were at last induced regularly on to the track so that in 1958 surprising victories were gained like A.A. Everard's in the Kent Steeplechase and J.R. Baldwin's in the same event at the "Brockman" Trophy. The old order had indeed changed and by that same year the Club was winning nearly all of its numerous matches with, in the big contests, 3rd in the Brockman, 7th of twelve leading clubs in the Sward, and 3rd in the Ryder, while we won the "Reading Gazette" Trophy for the first time. This overall strength was the chief source of satisfaction but there was again ample

B.M. SHAPCOTT

cause for pride in the feats of individuals. J.C. Whall was beginning to make a name for himself as a triple-jumper as well as a fearsome and floor-piercing trainer with weights to such good effect that the following year he set up an English Native record of 49 ft. 2¾ ins. — for jumping, that is, rather than for floor-cracking — as well as claiming Blackheath's first A.A.A. title since Wooderson's last and our first field event title ever. Though cursed with injury in this strenuous event he later cleared 50 ft. while representing Britain in Finland, and also in these years competed for Britain against France, Germany, Poland and the U.S.S.R.

E.J. Sampson's longer career reached its peak in 1958 when, after first and third placings in Kent and Southern Championships the previous year, he reaped the reward of much hard winter preparation in a fine season climaxed by places in both Commonwealth and European Games 440 squads. In addition to a best personal performance of 46.8 secs.[66] in the second round of the Empire Games 440 yards which stood for a short while as a Games and for longer as an English Native record, he was a member of the quartet who gained 2nd in the Commonwealth Games Mile Relay and 1st place in the European 1600 metres Relay, the latter in record time.

Equally pleasing in its way in 1958 was the enterprise of the Club's first full-scale "holiday with athletics" abroad with a match that was tied and a visit that was a social success, thanks largely to the organizer, Len Fletcher. There were many evidences of a keen team spirit so often invoked but less often seen as on occasions like that remarked by Norman Page when the team was late at the 1959 Ryder Trophy Meeting and Jim Day the vaulter seized his pole, ran half a mile to the track for an event already twenty minutes in progress and finished third. Blackheath won this contest for the first time and this 1959 season was fairly described[67] as the greatest in Blackheath track history, since the Ryder numbered among a dozen team trophies won in the course of the year. They also came a close 2nd in the L.A.C. Relays, 4th in the Sward Field events competition, and, including the Kent 20 Miles Championship, secured exactly half of the available titles in the County, together with four 2nd and four 3rd places, while the Youths won the Southern Sprint Relay Championship. This high level of achievement was generally sustained the next season with Ian Ross individually continuing where Sampson had left off and securing 9th place in the Ranking lists with his 48.2 secs quarter mile best, while a namesake of the former but unrelated — J. Sampson — held 11th place in these lists for his 151 ft. 1 in. Discus performance. Naturally, there was bound to be some falling-off, but the decline was only slight since the groundwork was sure and Page there to urge as he would do when given the slightest reason to do so: "Forward still to greater triumphs". In 1960 and 1961 with plenty of encouragement from Vice-captain Hickey's example of a Southern High Jump victory came international long jump honours for J. Lissaman, also an industrious "Gazette" Editor; a 13 mins. 35.8 secs. Inter-Counties three miles from John Herring — time which represented some 20 seconds better than Sydney Wooderson's 1946 European record; places in the A.A.A. Mile Relay and Junior Sprint Relay Championships and trophies like the Coventry Godiva "Ashby" being gained for the first time. Blackheath were also back in the Kinnaird since we were now well able to cope with such formidable competition again, and both Captain Page and team had little to be dispirited about.

SOUTHERN A.A.A. 440 YARDS RELAY CHAMPIONSHIP, 1962:
D. Bryant, G.C. Thomas, J.E. White, J.J. Day.

John Herring's was to be the most notable individual improvement to distinction in the following years. Never at his happiest over the country, his short, even mincing steps considering his length of leg, were best suited to the more level progression of the track and it was here and in these years, despite many fine runs over country, that he was at his best. For, in the following year, 1962, in addition to fathering twins, he achieved a Championship best time in winning the Southern 3 miles in a hard-fought finish, doing 13 mins. 29.8 secs. which placed him equal 5th in the British ranking list. It was obvious therefore that if he was to obtain Olympic selection which became thus tantalizingly close he would have to improve still more. It was a measure of the "Kipper" spirit that he succeeded in this and by the most conscientious preparation made his way into the team for the 1964 Tokio Olympics in the face of most intense competition.

In the nature of this work the more recent events must have least said of them — they are too close for true historical perspective and they are least likely, at present, to be forgotten. A brief summary of the last five years must suffice therefore.

Briefly then. The trend of competitive emphasis has continued and shows little sign of a halt. Even more team trophy contests have been entered and won. In 1965, for example, even under such pressure of competition as was by then the custom, as late as mid-June the

J. WATTS, ENGLISH NATIVE RECORD HOLDER
FOR THE DISCUS, 1968.

J.B. HERRING WINNING 3 MILES, SOUTHERN
CHAMPIONSHIPS, 1962

in 13 mins. 29.8 secs. M. Batty, Thurrock H. 2nd.

JIM DAY - CROYDON 1964

G.L. HAMLYN, BROCKMAN TROPHY,
WIMBLEDON, 1966.

team found itself still undefeated. There are not only further brilliant quarter milers like G.C. Thomas and B. Shurmer and sprinters of the calibre of J. White, the latter of whom, together with others like the workmanlike and speedy R.E.D. Taylor, quarter and half-miler, is not afraid to combine active competition with the demands of Club office, but others of international standard like the 4 mins. 2 secs. miler and 1 min. **48 secs.** 880 yards runner, Jim Baker, and others of international class or potential: G. Hamlyn, A. Wadhams and P.J. Hudson in the jumps, John Wright scoring over 6000 points in the Decathlon, David Wright, an all too regular 1 min. 50 secs. half-miler and member of our victorious A.A.A. Mile Medley Relay team in 1966, a 229 foot Javelin thrower in M. Turner and the recent breaker of the United Kingdom Discus record, J. Watts. The Club Track and even more its Field power is greater today than at any previous period and represents a far cry from the old days as much as does the 1963 circumstance — under the inspiration of Jim Day — of our furnishing eight out of the total Kent entry of seventeen for the pole vault. And surely we may believe that such a phenomenon would have gladdened the hearts of our old 6 a.m. risers in the days of the Peckham meets at the ground behind "The Rosemary Branch" more than we today might give them credit for. While, finally, more than in all previous times and forms of competition, our heavy summer fixture list — not forgetting the extension into the Winter months since the inception in 1960 of the highly successful annual February meeting — makes more onerous and time-consuming demands on those members who officiate at these meetings, so that it is proper that the last mention of this prosperous track and field era should relate gratefully to that dedicated body.

R. HARKER - CHISWICK 1968

ROAD RUNNING 1952 — 1968

The Club's first tentative entries into road relays like the exciting London to Brighton contests in the thirties were to increase correspondingly with the new popularity of this branch of the sport after the Second World War, one of the most noticeable aspects of athletic expansion in these recent years. From one or two such events held more by way of a casual relief and sandwiched between the cross-country and summer seasons road relays have become a feature in their own right both of the spring and autumn seasons as well as other times. Today the Club takes part in many of these and holds, as a result of Alan Brent's and John Herring's suggestion in 1961, an important large one of its own supported by many major Clubs.

The successes of the long-distance team of the early fifties may have over-shadowed those of the road relay teams but these were not inconsiderable. As early as 1947 the Club was occupying first places for both 'A' and 'B' teams in races like the Cambridge Harriers' Bexley Road Relay and second place in the most important race in this branch of running, the London to Brighton Relay, with Wooderson setting up a new record for the last leg into Brighton. Feats like these were to be repeated more than once in the ensuing years, though, as has been observed above, there was something of a lull after the great climax of road success at the beginning of the decade. Nevertheless, for the Club to finish 1st, 4th, 6th and 10th teams in a single road relay as they did in the 1950 Bexley race remained typical of our strength. In the London to Brighton Relay we generally finished in the first dozen and this amid the new vigorous expansion of road running was something to pride ourselves on.

Another feature of this period both generally and within our own Club has been the increasing participation of track and cross-country men in the longer distances on the road — a development already heralded for us when the 'B' team of Braughton, Brent and Scotting gleefully defeated the 'A' team "specialists" in the Mitcham 15 Miles race of 1952. Braughton in fact was to progress competently to the marathon distance, finishing as high as 6th in the 1955 Polytechnic classic for example, while at the same time, in this period of comparative lack of success, he was a member of the Club's winning team in the same race. With him was J.E. Withers, the small, compact and very light runner who always seemed to move with great ease and who was for some years to be a staunch member of the long-distance team, winning the Kent 20 Miles Championship in 1956 and helping the Club to several team victories in this and in the Southern Marathon in 1957 while until recently he himself was the fastest Blackheath performer over the latter distance. For the rest, George Gosling of the old team continued to enjoy success, especially at the greater distances. A welcome addition to our forces was the South African, J. Mekler, a worthy successor to the record-breaking Hayward and six times a winner of the formidable "Comrades" Marathon, who joined and ran for us in several major races such as the A.A.A. Marathon of 1955 when he gained third place in a shade temperature of 81 degrees, while in 1960 he was to break the London-Brighton record of his fellow-countryman Hayward in finishing first.

For the next five years things were leaner by comparison; in 1958, for example, there[68] was little success and only a few seemed to be interested, a ray of relief being Roy Morley who, running the marathon as well as the gamut of other athletic distances, won the "Lalande"

Trophy for the first novice home by finishing 16th in the Polytechnic Marathon and represented Kent in the Twenty Miles Road Championship which now formed a scoring part of the Inter-Counties Summer Championships. The road relay position was better, with regular placings, but while we retained the Kent 20 Miles Championship the general picture was not so good. There was now always stiff opposition wherever one competed and no success could be easily gained.

Yet the relay men of the early sixties formed a team of great distinction with whom one could be proud to be associated and several of them were certainly among the best cross-country and road performers we have had in the last twenty years. Herring was to become the real short-distance road specialist, but regulars like Brent and Fletcher, together with M. Weller, P. Jackson, R.J. Webber and J.R. Baldwin contributed to many good results and carried the Club well up into the first half dozen in the London to Brighton Relay. Paul Jackson perhaps was another at his best on the road. Tall, thin and wiry with an action that did not help the foot trouble he fought against manfully for several years, he was a Club Champion at distances from three to ten miles and it was a tragic irony that he should be killed in a road accident in 1964 depriving us of a most amiable companion as well as an able competitor. The equally cheery Dick Webber, later to become Hon. Secretary of the Buckinghamshire A.A.A., and Maurice Weller, than whom there was none more consistent in backing the leading scorers, were both long-standing runners who at many times in the past would have been winners more often than modern standards of competition allowed. Another of this generation who was to excel at short and long-distances alike on the road — often both within the space of a few days — was B.F. Pearce, running in all kinds of races from road relays to marathons and from London to Brighton races to the taxing special skill of the Ben Nevis contest which in 1962 became a venture several times since enjoyed — so they have said — by Club members. Five of these, for example, made the long journey there the following year undismayed by Pearce having broken an arm the day before their inaugural venture in surveying the course, though this did not prevent him from competing in the race. No doubt it is this spirit which has since seen to his achieving more than respectable performances in the London to Brighton and Exeter to Plymouth Races, the latter yet another Blackheath inspiration through its organizer P.W. Johnson in 1965.

Chief among Club officials, however, in what may nowadays be termed our road section has been D.H. Hopgood, the Secretary, for he has nurtured a strengthening force over the years of this decade immediately preceding our Centenary One may fairly say that it is largely due to him that road running, so long regarded by Blackheath as a cinderella, has become effective as an independent yet linking activity with cross-country and track middle and long distance running. The record speaks of a steady stream of success under his leadership down to the present, though there is space here to refer to only a few. The success of organization in our own Road Relay was matched by our winning it for the first time in 1965 against the stiffest opposition, having come second in 1962. An equal organizing success was our staging of the 1964 Road Runners' Club Marathon for the "Rex Cross" Salver at Hayes, in torrid conditions ameliorated by the first-class work of a team of some sixty Blackheath members. In carrying off the Bracknell and Walton Ten Mile team races in 1965 also we were beginning to win our first real successes at this road distance for several years past. The same year we were first club home in such relays as the Ilford and

FOX HILL, NEAR THE TOP.

(by L. Norris)

Bexley, the latter for a new course record, as well as regaining the Kent Twenty Miles title from Cambridge Harriers after a break of four years. Indeed, that autumn the Club was never out of the first four places in the by now considerable number of events entered. Yet it was too often the case that mature athletes carried the teams, with too little youth of good enough standard to displace them as witnessed by the Belgrave Relay team in which eight of the twelve were over or near to thirty years of age, with two of them actually being veterans. Still, in gaining fourth place in this major contest there was nothing to complain about for the present and as the "Gazette" correspondent observed, the outlook was very bright for the next London-Brighton Relay. This was not to be though for the promoters of the race, "The News of the World", were forced to withdraw support that by now seemed traditional for this favourite event among athletes. The Belgrave event replaced it as the Southern Relay Championship which that Club organized with characteristic efficiency. In 1967 this was matched by an official National Relay Championship destined for a permanent central venue at Leicester.

Apart from such individual successes as those of B.W. Heaver and Baldwin especially the latter's 4th and 2nd places in the frighteningly large field of the "Hog's Back" Race — and not to forget such exhibitions as the then sixty-four years-old Eric Reed's "finest two hours" in covering the Mitcham Fifteen — the most pleasurable aspect in this[69] division has been the quantity of its participants, often furnishing several teams for one event and a host of stalwarts of all standards: from A.M. Davis, running 1 hour 50 minutes for twenty miles, to equally versatile road men game for any distance from three to twenty six miles-and-the-extra-bit on the road like E. Pepper, I.C. Wilson and G. Jex. Perhaps the best inspiration for future individual and team success though, has been the appearance of the most encouraging marathon prospect for years in Bob Richardson, who has, at first attempt achieved 2 hours 24 minutes in the A.A.A. Marathon of 1968. Nowadays too there is a growing tradition of Veteran participation to match that of cross-country, as Roy Morley supplied ample evidence of as recently as 1965 in gathering Veterans' awards on every hand.

CROSS-COUNTRY   1955 — 1968-69

It was Morley who received the mantle of Cross-country captain from Brent in 1955 after his five years in office and both he and his successors Allan Wood — President of the South of the Thames Cross-country Association in 1968 — 69 and John Baldwin continued along the competent lines of example he had laid down. Nor was Alan Brent by any means to decrease in usefulness to the Club but was to go on to new success as an alarmingly formidable veteran, winning some races by as much as five minutes or more since he was for many years to challenge far younger men for a place in the Club's first teams.

There was certainly present an unevenness typical of some periods of Blackheath team history so that while, for example, in 1958 despite first-class runners like A.A. Everard, we could lose the Nicholls Cup and the matches with the two older universities we would none-theless win nearly all our inter-club fixtures the same season as well as the Kent Champion-ship and the South of the Thames, come 6th in the Southern and only one place lower in the National. No doubt such a paradox is to be explained partly at least by the effect of the pressures and quantity not only of modern competition but of our increasingly competitive society and the pace of life. It seems to be more and more necessary to devote oneself single-mindedly to one pursuit if one is to attain the heights — yet more and more im-possible to do this, if it does not concern one's living. The turnover of athletes, as Derek Hogg observed when Secretary, is greater today and members are no longer to be regarded as belonging permanently to the Club once they have joined as at one time they were.

It could be contended that almost all subsequent seasons have been disappointing but this view is only possible by ignoring the change of conditions already outlined in these pages. It is perhaps enough at this point to remark the increase in the size of the field of the National Cross-country Championship: over 500 in the 1955 race; 700 in 1957; 800 in 1963; 900 in 1965. The very full, possibly even too demanding fixture list is also a witness to the changed times to which we have had to adjust ourselves as a club and for which even we have given ourselves often little enough credit, preferring to notice the disappearance of the last steam trains at the start of this decade which were wont to bear us towards Chingford for our biennial visit — "another link with the more leisurely past swept away". We frequently choose to ignore the significant phenomena which have produced willy-nilly the contem-porary situation so many loudly but indiscriminately deplore. Not only were we all too frequent victims to the compact but powerful Aylesford team led by the redoubtable but always enjoyable and generous opponent Frank Sando, as well as to the more numerous S.L.H., but what had always in the past been our great strength, the medium runners, appeared now strangely to diminish. Whether as a result of modern competitive stress or not is hard to say, but the trend did seem for a while to be very much towards more first class team run-ners and away from our traditional "middle" strength, though a better balance has lately been achieved.

Yet for the time being this new trend had its compensations, and by 1963 teams were showing a more determined attitude so that whereas 1962 had seen us 15th in the South of the Thames we had climbed to 5th place by the next year, in addition to going up fif-teen places in both Southern and National to seventh and twenty-sixth respectively. 1962 represented the nadir of our post-war fortunes and since 1963 we have continued the climb steadily though hardly with a plenitude of class runners to enable us to reach the ultimate heights. Still, those we had were very good. There was by 1963 an outstanding junior in Brian Heaver who, though overshadowed then by our second-claim member J. Farrington, winner of the National Junior title that year, came sixth in the Southern and fourteenth in the National. Two years later he had joined Baldwin and was runner-up to the latter in the Kent Senior when all three of our teams — Senior, Junior and Youths — finished second. Essentially a "power" runner, barrel-chested and reaching forward all the time with his legs he is a runner who one feels has not yet realized his best though he has shown intermittent brilliance, a notion substantiated by his most recent National performance of 46th in 1967 achieved despite injury. He is only the second man in the Club history to have won all three Club cross-country cups in a single season.

Though the Youths were doing better there was still not much comfort for the future from that direction and while 1964 saw the Seniors and Juniors winning the Kent for the third time in succession, the Club was endeavouring to encourage its younger members by, for example, the first organized Club training weekends held that year. There were signs of up and coming talent in R. Richardson who came 25th in the National Youth Race and gave promise of better still when his small frame had filled out, but he lacked really solid backing despite the Youths' undoubted improvement in both Southern and National races. Known from the first as "Young Richardson" he has gone from strength to strength. After narrowly missing a place in the first three in the Southern he improved to 8th place in the National Junior in 1966 as a result of which he gained his first E.C.C.U. representation. In his first senior National he finished 58th and in the second in 1968, 32nd, justifiably disappointing himself because of ill-health, since not only had he been the first Blackheath Harrier to score an individual win in the Nicholls Cup for ten years but had already gained 3rd place in the Southern. He also took an impressive runners-up position in the demanding Mitcham '15' and won the Kent Championship the following April. His ability to rise to the occasion and to run above himself — the mark of class — are already beyond question and he seems to possess the necessary qualities to stand among the best the Club has had.

The only one to challenge him for achievement in this latter period has been the former Captain, John Baldwin, who like many of our worthiest performers of the past has been able to combine his duties with excellent personal performance. One may wonder though whether he might not have done better in the crucial balance of international selection had he been permitted to concentrate more single-mindedly on that taxing goal. But this is perhaps only to expect more from one who has achieved so much already: if he does nothing more he will have earned a name for himself as one of the Club's foremost distance runners since the Second World War. His season of 1966 was enough to demonstrate this when he won both Kent and South of the Thames Championships. The team were first and second respectively in these and went on to win the latter the following year. John finished 7th in the Southern and effectually missed his international by an attack of cramp near the finish of the National, though he did subsequently represent the E.C.C.U. in Milan.

The year was good for the team in general, for the improvement of the previous three seasons was now consolidated. The Youths, for example, were no longer a limping force as so frequently in the past and had climbed from 38th to 11th place in the National. The concentration on fixtures against local schools and organizations at Hayes had stimulated the Youth and Boy sections of the Club by giving them more competition and had also helped

OUTSTANDING CLUB DISTANCE MEN

J.R. Baldwin leading R. Richardson and I.C. Wilson in the Club mile championship at Beckenham in 1966.

recruiting. There were five such fixtures with fields that ranged satisfactorily from fifty to just over a hundred.

At the other end of the scale Brent and Gordon Monshall led the veterans' team to victory against the Veterans A.C. and this pointed to something of a resurgence in our one-time weakening medium strength so that this and our powers in general led to the regaining of the Nicholls Cup after a lapse of seven years. This, with a further win the following year made the score twenty-nine all. With characteristic quirkiness we were to lose the Pelling-Ratcliff Cup to Ranelagh this season, and though this was for the first time since 1924 it was no accident, for the growing might of that ancient club with whom we have enjoyed so long a friendship as well as with Orion and the "Irrepressibles" has been a phenomenon from which we have been able to derive pleasure as well as suffering in defeat.

The performances of Baldwin and Richardson were not the only individual successes of the season. I.C. Wilson showed promise of better things to come in gaining his Kent vest at his first senior attempt and there was ample backing from men like Weller, "Rowland" Cup winner that year, who yet again scored in the National team. To be ranked with these too are the efforts of both officials and trail layers who coped with a crowded programme of more than sixty races under the guidance of D.L. Gregory to whom is due credit for three years of work as Captain and who now found a capable successor in Brian Stone aided by one of equal experience in the erstwhile "Davis" Cup holder, G.R. Last

1967 saw further advances with all three of the big matches won, though not with ease, with the Kent Championship, with a second place in the re-christened Greater London Championship, and a successful match with a visiting Belgian Club, Union St. Gilloise. Now, with a team that was a blend of youth and experience, there was an improvement out of the customary place in the twenties — not in itself to be sniffed at in these days of fields of runners a thousand strong — and up to eleventh place in the 1967 National after gaining sixth in the Southern. The juniors, and in particular, R. Hawtin representing Kent in the Junior Inter-Counties Championship which had come into being, were also on the upgrade. These achievements have set a new norm which should make it more difficult to retain some of the more modest satisfactions of the recent past, demonstrating as they do a vigorous spirit of competition that in no wise vitiates the old traditions of participation for the sport's sake.

PART FIVE
"FULL CRY!"

SYDNEY WOODERSON: THE CENTENARY PRESIDENT.

(L. Norris)

TODAY
THE MEMBERS AND CHARACTER OF BLACKHEATH HARRIERS
FOR THE FUTURE

THE PYLON FIELD
by L. Norris

192

TODY

In speaking of recent times the historian is in danger of an inhuman narrative of statistical achievement as well as the more obvious one of an inaccurate perspective. The modern increase of competition implies a bulk of fact at the expense, if one is not careful, of a sense of the continuing life-blood of an institution. Beneath an array of exploit lies the flourishing activity which is the chief justification of Blackheath, providing as it does satisfaction of such various kinds to its members, so that this account of the post-war years would be incomplete without some reference, however brief, to those happenings which do not find their way into less human histories than this.

In his Annual Report of 1964 the then Hon. Secretary, D.F.E. Hogg, observed, "Years ago members joined in their late 'teens and their twenties and ran on into their fifties. Nowadays they tend to join at thirteen and are spent at twenty-five". Expectedly there is a larger turnover of members today than in the more settled past with its smaller and therefore more intimate nucleus. Yet there does of late seem to be an increase in the number of men who linger on long after their active days — to continue running in a less strenuous way, to take Club office or simply to enjoy the social life of Blackheath. Certainly there is a widening circle of participants in a variety of social activities and Headquarters today is used more than at any past time — not only for mid-week and Sunday training, both of which are post-war developments responsible for maintaining the old pack running habits today far more than is done on Saturdays which are reserved invariably now for races — but for regular dances, parties, barbecues and Bonfire Nights with toffee apples and baked potatoes for the children. In the late Fifties Ladies Nights were revived, and most happily so, making informal and pleasant occasions, while more recently there have been moves to enable more frequent visits. Such female participation had been a feature during the greater part of Blackheath history and happily we seem to be too traditional in our tastes to assist fossilization by neglect of the female kind and thus do violence to a long-standing custom of hospitality. Girls are therefore today encouraged to become interested in Blackheath Harriers, a process assisted by enterprising functions like the Riverboat Dances organized by E. Doorbar in 1963 and 1964, the "Gay Nineties" Dance in 1959, the barbecues laid on by such ace caterers as Richard Edmonds where carcasses still roast outside even if all else is driven within by the first wet Saturday of the summer.

The early venture into Kent for the weekend mentioned above was soon extended to "Holidays with athletics" on the Continent. Tours like the first of 1957 in Switzerland organized by Len Fletcher and termed by a member of the party "one of the most happy events in the Club's history" became an almost yearly occurrence with Italy visited in 1959, the Rhineland in 1961 and Switzerland again in 1963. On these, Club members have masqueraded under the various guises of 'Blackhaerth", "Blackenham" or "Blackhat Harries" with, apart from athletics, multifarious activities involving sauna baths, Jack Sims walking, thick heads, Jack Sims rowing, sightseeing, swimming and shopping. All these have lent a new dimension to Club spirit — in addition to other kinds of achievement, as suggested in one Gazette report: "Some energetic parties blazed their way through passes in the day while others made passes at parties in the night". Typical has been the bridging of generations in groups whose ages have ranged from two to sixty-five.

There have been other pursuits hardly less colourful as, for example, shooting matches at Bisley with London Scottish of old Blackheath connection in 1959 and 1960 as there had been in the 1930's. Even more exotic was the visit to a blonde bombshell in a West End theatre of a Blackheath team — "a blend" as "The Gazette" said, "of looks, youth, dash and experience". Here they collected a torch which they then tore themselves away to bear down to Crystal Palace — the old Club stamping-ground where today we once again disport ourselves since the opening of the National Centre — to mark the revival of the Crystal Palace Firework Displays and to aid local charities. Another kind of revival was staged in the euphemistically called "strolls" in which younger members have sought to emulate former Hammonds and present Traers through the night to Brighton just as Starnes and his companions had done half a century before.

By way of happy innovation but now set fair to become an institution has been the Vice Presidents' Supper, the happy invention of that demon energizer, Laurie Hammill, started in 1962 at "The Two Chairmen", Westminster, and annually the organizing responsibility of the junior Vice President. The traditional Annual Dinner has of course continued its success as in bygone years, becoming more memorable on more than one recent occasion in its venue of the House of Commons where in 1959 the chief guest was Harold Macmillan, the then Prime Minister, who in his speech made the most of his connection with us through his constituency of Bromley, noted that we had no lady members, remarked that his House was not similarly fortunate, and ended with his opinion that Club loyalty such as ours helped form what was best in our character as a nation.

CLUB TOUR — SWITZERLAND 1958

CLUB GROUP 1967

THE MEMBERS AND CHARACTER OF BLACKHEATH HARRIERS.

"I run socially for Blackheath"
(Member).

What follows may seem a strange inclusion in a work of historical pretensions but the thoughts and opinions of individual members of all ages and from different periods which have been offered to assist the present writers, taken together in themselves represent a kind of description of the peculiar nature of the Club which perhaps cannot be improved upon. Some of them had not been to the Club for forty years, but in these as well as others one recognized, though it was independently expressed, the same warm remembrance:

"Fellowship is the answer . . . . . . when I joined Blackheath in 1919 as a young man I was at once made to feel one of the Club and everybody talked of Blackheath as "The Club" without affectation or boasting".

Another wrote, "It was the welcome and friendliness . . . . . . which made me become a Life Member". Friendship is their constant theme, together with the care given to novices and new members, so that they never felt neglected but were introduced to many different people. This is a feature testified to as recently as 1963 by a correspondent newly joined and writing of New Members' Night, adding "If ever a Club was founded on the high ideal of voluntary service it is Blackheath Harriers . . . .   fellows who but a brief hour before were sweating with one up Fox Hill turning to behind the bar and serving sausage and mash".

Some are more flippant, another Club characteristic, so that E.J. Castello's comments are representative of a certain vein familiar to regular readers of "The Gazette": "I did badly in the Poly Marathon but no one could have had such beautifully symmetrical blisters" and he finishes with the anecdote of himself out training dressed in ancient battle dress and reported by a doctor's receptionist as an escaped Broadmoor prisoner. Older members can recall the Blackheath packs leaving "The Green Man" on their Saturday training run and watching this spectacle "with something akin to reverential awe". Others by no means young single out more recent events like "the welcome incursion of wives, lady friends and children of members" into the Clubhouse. There are boasts of Novice Pewters still gracing mantle-pieces long after the last run has ended; there is pride in continued subscriptions paid annually instead of as a single one for life, so that the Club receives the regular benefit of the sum; there are memories like that of hurried consultation between lofty officials like Crafter, A.R. Pearson and the Hon. Secretary at the end of which the new member lining up for his first race in his sleeveless vest was hurried back to the dressing room and given one with sleeves.

Most of all, there are the reminiscences of the sport itself:

"The exhilaration of running, the feel of the cold fresh air, the soothing and invigorating hot bath and cold shower respectively gave one a feeling of well-being and fitness which enhance the enjoyment of life from one week to another and from which one feels the bene-fit long into middle age and the sixties and seventies". Younger than Leslie Pendered but speaking to the same effect, — Tony Oldfield recalls: "We seemed to run for an apparently interminable period and I was soon gasping for breath. I have a clear recollection of my sense of wonder when Derek Reynolds dropped back and chatted to me in a normal conversational tone. Clearly Blackheath consisted of maniacs and supermen!" To all comes at least one proud memory as it did to him:

"After three miles of the Orion match I found myself leading the race, the entire force of Blackheath strung out behind me. The whole race had gone off course".

The race may be an ordinary friendly match but it can still call forth for its participants the thrill of the largest championship event:

"The ascent to the famous cliffs of Dover covered on one occasion with snow; the exhilarating ice cold air and the dramatic three hundred foot plunge down a nearly vertical hill to the finish by the school pavilion. It is in these away fixtures that one gets to know one's fellow Heathens". In like manner the chief memories of many are of the Nicholls Cup races and times when it has been regained after a lapse, rather than of events of more public athletic importance.

Haphazard though these examples may be they lead to a contemplation of something in Blackheath which is not of individual men, though it is man-made, which pervades their talk, their feelings and the accounts from the earliest days when men started to feel that they belonged to a tradition as well as to a Club, and which to contemplate in accumulation gives one an uncanny sense of presence when a common sentiment unites men. It is that abstraction which the late Derek Reynolds was seeking to voice when as Chairman of the Punchbowl Night of 1958 he spoke of "the influences which the Blackheath Harriers exerts

R. RICHARDSON

leads Ian Stewart European and Commonwealth Games Champion

upon the lives of those who remain members for any length of time". The blending of generations which takes place within our ranks, as well as the mingling of aims and interests and so many temperaments inevitable in so large a club is — one may state it without over-much exaggeration — by way of being a tiny English miracle, and, like all miracles, tending to the unique. No Club can be better off for willing hands nor count itself more fortunate in its advantage of possessing quantities of assistance and support from those whose active days are over. It is the quality and abundance of this service which are perhaps the most readily observable and constant evidence of the truth that members like the above have sought to express in bearing witness to the greatness of Blackheath Harriers as an institution.

**CENTENARY GOBLET. ONE HUNDRED OF THESE WERE ENGRAVED
IN CELEBRATION**
(B.M. Shapcott)

198

FOR THE FUTURE

"Whether as sports they afford as much healthy and quiet enjoyment as of old may be doubted. The young athlete of the present day often takes his pleasures rather sadly, at the cost of more self-denial and trouble than they are worth perhaps. His pastime is more like a serious business than a light and agreeable recreation".

("The Sporting Gazette" circa 1876)

"We of the Blackheath Harriers KNOW about these things".

(Tom Crafter).

The tone of the remarks with which the previous section concluded can rightly be said to be self-congratulatory; indeed, the chief danger of a history written by members to signalize the occasion of the Centenary is inward-looking complacency and resulting inaccuracy; no one has been more conscious of this besetting bias than the present writers. Certainly truth is the only diet for men and the strength of an institution is to be tested by robust analysis — not by sentimentality and blindly total approval. Many of the comments proffered during the preparation of this work have shown that many, often the staunchest and most responsible members, themselves have criticisms to make of the Club as it has developed and as it stands today. Were it otherwise it would not only be surprising but unhealthy in a living and constantly developing organism such as Blackheath Harriers. Where the writers have seen such signs in the history of past events they have tried to show them in their true significance.

As for the present and future it could be argued that they have no place in the writers' brief, but, excusing our presumption, it would be inhumanly strange if the experience of composing this History did not call forth a personal response from us, as well as possibly furnishing a sea-mark for those whom we hope will be future historians of this Club.

Competitive athletic achievement today has moved much nearer to the frontiers of the possible. This is not to say that record-breaking is at an end but that it is rapidly becoming more difficult to excel without a total dedication that must exclude much else that constitutes the normality of life. In this we find an expression of the competitive ethos of society at the present day so that in other fields than athletics there are signs of a certain wearying of this pressure. Consequently, a parallel phenomenon is the major change in the direction of relaxing from the neurotic compulsions of an excessively competitive society.

In our own limited orbit of athletics, if competitive emphasis is thus laboured finally to an uncomfortable extreme, interest must then shift to other factors or the whole sport will die an unnatural death. In such a system which tends to encourage the excellent rather than the ordinary performer it may well be that Blackheath with its widely based recreational provision, including the enjoyment of running for exercise's sake, will satisfy where others fail in a society where "rat-races" are more the custom than recreational ones. Certainly, with its comprehensive provision of walking, track, field, cross-country and road competition, its participation in all kinds of other sports from rowing to hill-walking, its social facilities both catering and companionable in its own Headquarters, its wide range of association and fellowship, the efficiency of its administration and its corporate pride and sense of identity Blackheath Harriers will be well equipped to develop along any line that its future members may wish to take.

Then there is another contributing factor which is less sensational in character but no less vital to the Club. We have seen how in the latter quarter of the last century with the growth of competitive racing there was a difference of attitude between the athletes of then and now. Even today there are two generations who really do not speak the same language in respect of cross-country, for example. The old paternalism of Frederick Reed and his world may be gone for ever but many members today have discovered, as many no doubt have in the past, that, principally in the foundation known as the "Blackheath Harriers," they have in common much more than they have in differences. This in itself, it appears to us, is an aspect worth comment in an age that is not renowned for sympathy of feeling between young and old. No doubt a special contribution has been made in the later years of the Club's history by the mature athletes who, starting late and continuing longer as a result of the last war, have helped to form a bridge between the generations.

In "The Gazette" nearly twenty years ago and writing of the Dyball era it was observed "All organized interests and institutions depend for their survival upon two basic needs which appear at times to conflict: the need for a unifying tradition and for the capacity to adapt to changing circumstances". The future is by definition uncertain, the only assured things being difference and change. For the authors, as has already been suggested, the writing of this History has been not simply a commemorative matter but a signal lesson that perpetuation depends upon adaptability, as throughout man's evolution. One must be prepared to change — even if it implies an alteration foreign to the present. Just as we have had to move in the past so we may have to in the future: the fixity of the Hayes Headquarters is no more permanently assured in the long term than was that of "The Green Man". This age of the motor car implies the necessity — but the means also — to move out, as we have done more than once in the past. Many pride themselves on the permanence of the Club's identity, its personality, but to equate this tradition with immutability is a vain delusion, and there would have been no celebration of the Centenary had our predecessors believed so. Indeed, one of the chief characteristics of Blackheath's past has been empirical commonsense. This too we have attempted to demonstrate as aspects of, for example, the moves from Peckham to Blackheath, from Blackheath to West Wickham, from West Wickham to Hayes, while, constitutionally, the built-in safeguards are but a different face of the same coin.

We should be unworthy of the legacy we have inherited if we did not perpetuate this tradition.

EPILOGUE

"I have trod the upward and the downward slope,
I have endured and done in days before . . . ."

He sits alone, the Old Member. Evening now. Darkening in the Club Room but outside where in this September it is summer and autumn together there is mellow sunlight still. Within, it is the lull, the quiet spell between tea and supper. Some have gone home but will return. There are a few talking there by the bar . . . . . and two over there . . . . Now dies the day, now lengthens the year . . . soon the fire will burn bright in the great hearth, so hot no one will stand close to . . . . Soon, soon the falling leaves, soon the winter . . . .

Pleasant now to sit by this window . . . . quiet here for once . . . even that usual rowdy group in the bar corner subdued . . quietly they talk . . . ("Rarely, rarely comest thou, Spirit of Delight") . . . Is that chap going to draw the curtains? Pity to shut out the sun, the last of the day . . . not the curtains . . . no, he lays the cloth. Sounds from the dressing room below ("You hear this fellow in the cellarage") . . . one or two coming in late from the Common, or beyond . . . ploughland sable, sandy on hillside, wind over Nash Farm. There has been a race that afternoon for schoolboys — good to see a young crowd doing what we have so long done . . . some have asked about joining . . . and some of the fast pack were here too — a rare thing nowadays — always racing somewhere — it has been good to see them . . Now they have gone, the runners are gone. They are gone home.

Light, shadow and sunset. Slanting sword striking now of sun in glass of photo frames. Images of the dead. Gone, gone. Tablecloth gleams white in twilight, dark wood of chairs and polished table glooms. Swaying branches softly outside narrow windows shimmer leaf spangles within, swaying, shifting, reflections to and fro . . . . "In light and shadow both" . . . reflects on ceiling flickers the leaving light . . . ("which now for your delight the leaping light discovers . . . ") . . . . Music in the air. Ghosts of lengthening age? No, the old piano sounding . . voices from the past released by the old tune, sentimental per-haps but right for his present mood, stealing they come . . . . Rowland, "Shrimp", Eddie Nicholls, Crafter, Derek, Syd . . . . . twilight . . . but sun-flames aslant photos . . memories.
. . . Memories — " . . . . looking upon the happy autumn fields,
And thinking of the days that are no more . . ."
Tennyson? The Old Member thinks so . . . memory not so good — a ragbag now: a relay baton signed with Olympic names; crunch of cinders; evening scent of green turf and shadowed, close-cut grass; a Sevres vase, tokens, a handful of ribbons for judges, their colours faded pale . . . haunted Peckham paths with friendly ghosts, a cemetery and gas-lit roads . . . . a Roll of Honour . . . "walk worthy of their fellowship" . . . . . Allanson, Cooper, Erskine, Gifford, Lymbery, Small, Walter and Williamson. Memories.
" . . . . So sad, so strange the days that are no more". All gone. The runners are gone, generations gone. Leaves fall . . . like his friends they go. They are gone home. The leaves fall and are gone, gone are the champions, the runners all gone home . . .
"Time breaks the threaded dances and the diver's brilliant bow . . . ."
The long stride is shortened, the runners go to the long clay of the plough they have beaten with their feet . . . Some of us are left. My friends have gone. Gone home . .

201

. . . Yet these are here. Those over there in the corner. That one — he has the look of . . . .? It is so long ("Old men forget . . .") And there are still friends here.

One comes from the bar to the window, bends across the table to where he sits, smiling speaks quietly . . . the Old Member starts from reflection, "What's that? Penny for . . . . .? Oh!" . . . a laugh . .

"Feel a hundred years old! Autumn thoughts, autumn thoughts".

"Plenty of time for those," says the other, "Here's a jug . . . or is it a gin for you?"

PERFER ET OBDURA

PART SIX
CENTENARY YEAR
THE NEXT TWENTY YEARS

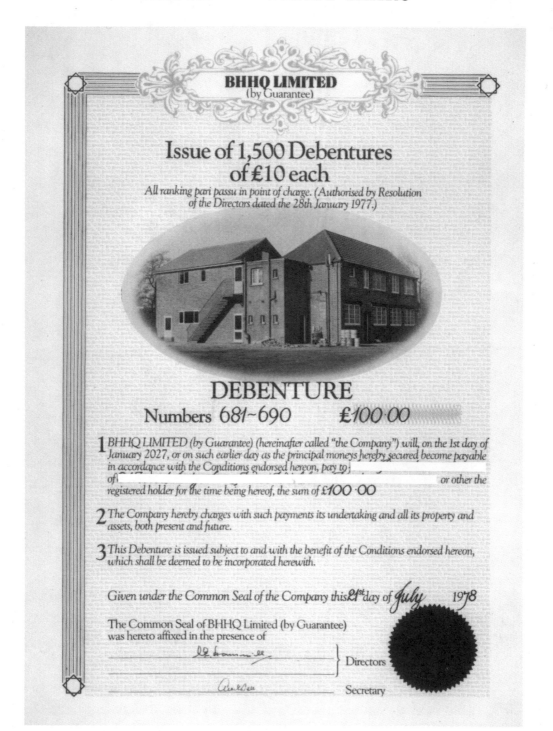

BHHQ LIMITED
(by Guarantee)

Issue of 1,500 Debentures of £10 each

All ranking pari passu in point of charge. (Authorised by Resolution of the Directors dated the 28th January 1977.)

DEBENTURE

Numbers 681~690   £100·00

1 *BHHQ LIMITED (by Guarantee) (hereinafter called "the Company") will, on the 1st day of January 2027, or on such earlier day as the principal moneys hereby secured become payable in accordance with the Conditions endorsed hereon, pay to* _____ *of* _____ *or other the registered holder for the time being hereof, the sum of £100·00*

2 *The Company hereby charges with such payments its undertaking and all its property and assets, both present and future.*

3 *This Debenture is issued subject to and with the benefit of the Conditions endorsed hereon, which shall be deemed to be incorporated herewith.*

Given under the Common Seal of the Company this 21st *day of* July   1978

The Common Seal of BHHQ Limited (by Guarantee)
was hereto affixed in the presence of

_____ } Directors
_____

_____ Secretary

CLUB GROUP, OCTOBER 1988

"In the market place of world athletics there has to be wheeling and dealing, and the secretaries of Blackheath Harriers, Stretford Ladies and Birchfield Harriers who represent the sport from a different era may have to accept it."

This extract from a 1989 Guardian newspaper article by John Rodda on the latest eruption over payments and subventions to star athletes may have struck Blackheath members as the sort of inverted compliment they had become accustomed to down the years. In the light of current developments and successes it may seem out-dated. At the time of the Centenary this traditional image may well have been an accurate picture of Blackheath. By now in 1989 the general view is doubtless that the Club has achieved perhaps the most satisfactory balance to date of high-class individual or team perform-ance and social provision for its thousand members, including those like the one who years ago described himself as "running socially for Blackheath".

Like this present addition the Centenary History was researched and written under some pressure of time. One of the anxieties for its authors was that haste would result not just in inaccuracies but distortions. In retrospect, one of the things they seem to have got right was the forward view contained in the concluding piece, 'For the Future'. The authors thought the Gazette extract of two decades earlier had been equally correct:

"All organized interests and institutions depend for their survival upon two basic needs which appear at times to conflict: the need for a unifying tradition and for the capacity to adapt to changing circumstances."

Naturally, there can be no skipping of the main text to arrive at this present climax of 1989. To do so would be not just to miss some deathless prose and many pages thrown together in haste in the late 'sixties, but many other facets of Club life which still endure yet which must be taken as read in this terse narrative condensing the twenty years which followed the Blackheath Centenary and its celebrations. Such items are numerous: the annual awards of Club trophies, some of them continuously now for more than a hundred years; awards for fifty years of membership; the annual rowing race; Punchbowl Night, lurching between the outrageous and the innocuous; the Johnson Bowl Walk or Maryon Wilson Swimming races; the Vice-Presidents' Supper of roast beef organized by Mike Peel which regularly attracts a field of forty.

Such omissions may not matter greatly: "We of the Blackheath Harriers know about such things", as Crafter used to say. In 1969, at any rate, the aim of members was to do justice to a unique occasion and, as Churchill said of another signal event, to permit themselves "a brief period of rejoicing".

There was plenty of that. Already, in advance of Centenary Year, the select band of historians researched all the surviving hostelries that had played a sustaining role, from Peckham to Blackheath to West Wickham. They were in time to visit The Green Man for a last drink before its demolition hard on the heels of the Centenary.

For many members the year remains a welter of memorable events. It was inaugurated by a Press Supper and a Special General Meeting, commemorated by a Centenary Club Photograph of 150 members and a grand dinner at London's Mansion House, memorialized by a Thanksgiv-ing Service at West Wickham Church which was attended by representatives of the A.A.A., E.C.C.U. and our fellow clubs. This last was one of P.P. Harold Thompson's ideas. At the

Clubhouse tea afterwards someone said that on this occasion at least Heathens had belied their name.

There were the Centenary Match at Crystal Palace against Kent and the Southern Counties A.A.A.; the Centenary Cross-country race won by the E.C.C.U., the Club coming second, followed by S.L.H., French, Belgian and Thames Hare and Hounds teams. More leisurely were the Peckham-Blackheath-West Wickham-Hayes Commemorative Run, the Peckham to Blackheath Stroll, the Centenary Ball at the New Inn, Hayes. And 'Dicky' Green and Humphry Nunns celebrated in their own way by walking the London to Brighton.

A key event was the opening one of Centenary Year, the 100 x 1 Mile Relay, an inspiration of Ernest Neville, held in April at Croydon Arena. Cambridge, Belgrave and Croydon Harriers joined the long battle. Through the connection with the Stevens brothers there was to have been a fifth, remoter club, the Scottish Harriers in Wellington, New Zealand, though they only postponed their independent effort till the July. Sydney Wooderson ran his leg at the half distance and commented that he had been ''more photographed and interviewed than in his heyday''. The Club finally won from Belgrave, but it was a gripping contest, the gap often less than a lap, the lead changing four times in the last ten miles. Reporting for the Gazette, D.K. Saunders said he was convinced an event like this is ''of more real value to the cause of amateur athletics, involving as it does general participation at all levels of ability, than much which, as they say, 'makesnews'''.

Make news it did, however, and the Club's higher profile in years following may be said to date from this Centenary publicity. R.C. Falconer, an Australian member, pronounced the Relay ''a bonza experience''. ''To Australian eyes,'' he wrote, ''this interest of past members, as competitors as well as officials, is our most outstanding experience of British Athletics''.

The year saw the passing of one past member of distinction from Green Man days: Field Marshal the Earl Alexander of Tunis who had joined in 1912. Two happier Centenary commemorations were the planting of a red oak on Hayes Common and the presentation by the Club of a Division One Trophy to the new British Athletics League, launched in 1969. An abstract sculpture commissioned from David May, this made a striking emblem of their progressive, not merely traditional outlook. The Club itself appeared in the competition before withdrawing in the face of superior odds to prepare more rigorously for this top level of performance.

The 100 x 1 Mile Relay became a regular occurrence, together with variations of 25 and 50 mile events. As a national contest, there were simultaneous competitions at different venues: in 1976, for example, 4493 ran on the day, the event being stoutly organized by Chris Haines and Andy Frankish, with Blackheath fielding two teams. Subsequently, such events were adopted and varied by others nationally – for example, in racing 100 x 400 metres. For the Club, these and various other activities have been giant undertakings which demand enormous energies and concentration, whether to raise necessary funds, to coach and field quality teams, to re-furbish or re-build. At times – for these ventures continue – it is almost as though Club organizers and administrators vie to surpass previous ambitions.

''A strange year for the Club –'' was the Secretary's enigmatic comment after the shindigs were over.

President for the 101st year was George Brooks who, still today a lynch-pin of Club officialdom, appealed then for more members to share the numerous burdens. It was and it remains a real complaint, since the growth of both jogging and veteran athletics, which really date from the end of the sixties, has inhibited the supply of officials.

CENTENARY DINNER SKETCHES – John Scott

The Secretary's Report observed that George had taken office at a time when the fortunes of the Club were in ''a rather critical state ... we could wish for a healthier financial situation and better representation by more of our active members''. Many members would not agree with this severe view, he thought, but with hindsight we must side with him. Certainly, with the expansion, if not explosion of these 1980's, the previous decade now appears to have been a period of containment. Annual recruitment of Boys, Youths or Juniors numbered no more than two dozen for any one of these groups. This was aggravated by a regular loss of young members within two or three years of joining.

Though the bridge from junior into senior ranks remains weak today, the mid-seventies saw the start of a progressive climb which has only the Dyball era of the 1920's to rival it. In 1970 and 1976 the membership stood at 600. In 1978 it was 673. The following year the evergreen Past President Brooks was presented with a watch inscribed,

''George. Thank You For Your Time.''

At the 1989 National he was still to be seen, though faintly in the murk, taking care of dry clothes and soaked athletes.

In those years of the previous decade, however, others were lost to the Club: Clay Thomas, founder-member of the Concert Artistes Club, vocalist and ''megaphone steward extraordinary'' of a pre-electronic era; J.M. Scott of Curlew Rowing and Lewisham Swimming Clubs whose last sketches are reproduced here; P.P. Freddie Parker, wounded veteran of the Somme in 1916, one of the members by whom Black-

GEORGE BROOKS

heath enjoyed its 'special relationship' with London Scottish; the welcoming and cheery P.P. Cecil ('Brown Boots') Pollard whose sketch of Eric Reed and piano appear at the conclusion of the History; at the age of 91 years, P.P. Cyril Starnes, field events judge at the 1948 Olympics, ex-President of the Northern Counties C.C. Association. And, for sure, Blackheath could ill afford the loss of P.P. Jack Sims whose sudden death in 1974 while on a long-anticipated Himalayan holiday not only shocked members but left them without a most able, dedicated administrator, a holder of Club offices widespread, various. His service is on Gazette record, including his many generous but untrumpeted projects: for example, the restoration and framing of the Club's collection of photographs and other pictures. He is, of course, remembered also in the Jack Sims Salver. Already these twenty years have witnessed a variety of Gazette styles, all lively, under a number of Editors; it has changed without becoming unrecognizable. The increase in quantity of results has made the problem of efficient publishing no easier, in terms either of space or delay. In 1969 P.P. Ian Smith introduced the duplicated Centenary 'News-sheet' Five years later he developed this news sheet into the 'Courier' which continues even more comprehensively today under the human word-processor, Bill Clapham. This has been all to the good, since the Gazette Editor was wisely determined not to run the risk of its becoming "a statistical encyclopaedia of out of date athletic news". At the same time, the next Centennial historian should note the implications for his researches of this resolve not to be "duty bound to print match results in detail". The Courier's informality, the Gazette's elegance are complementary. In recent years the latter has collected prizes for best U.K. athletic magazines. Today, due largely to the work of Gordon Wright, it sports many more photographs of better quality than was formerly possible. Its most recent chief, Les Roberts, stated his resolution quite sternly in 1983 when he took office: "Factual accounts laced with points of interest should still be our stock in trade". Setting his face against "heading towards Rag Mag status", he introduced a range of innovations, from advertisement pages for Club members to help support costs, to a series of personal profiles. Editorial policy was seen to be justified by an episode in 1989 after two letters had been sent to an elusive life member, followed by a strong third which insisted on acknowledgement, failing which, it promised, the Club would assume he no longer resided at the listed address. This time the Editor was rewarded with a response:

"... We have lived at this address for ten years and Mr — did not live here before then. I have written before this but must add I have enjoyed your magazine immensely and as a pensioner/jogger will miss it. Many thanks.

Kath Cotter.''

With characteristic Blackheath humanity to all sexes it was decided to continue sending the Gazette to this address.

The publication ought to remain the Club's archive; awareness of such resources and their value certainly increased as a result of the Centenary. In the 1980's arrangements were made for the most valuable of the records to be placed in the safe-keeping of Bromley Public Library with the irreplaceable nineteenth century manuscript books on micro-film.

In the Clubhouse's Jubilee Year of 1977, Laurie Hammill, so it is recorded, complained that the tempo of the Club Cry acclaiming the new President was "too slow". Keeping pace with Past President Hammill and his projects had long been a challenge for fellow members: the Centenary History itself was largely his fault – "a bright and breezy brochure," he suggested. When he retired from the chairmanship in 1988 after forty nine years of service to B.H.H.Q. Ltd. the Gazette rightly recorded the end of an era. He was the instigator of so many of the Clubhouse's improvements and works. After the 1939-45 War he played a vital role in paying off the debentures raised to purchase and convert the Headquarters in 1926. He was made a director in 1960 and soon after became Chairman, continuing for the next twenty seven years. Already, no doubt, his successor P.P. Peter Baigent has experienced increased challenges and the greater need for long-term planning. The Roofing Fund had ensured that the building was watertight again by 1965. Next, in 1974-75 came a large modernization programme including new boilers, showers and heating system. In 1976 a Development Sub-committee proposed the building of a major extension, with athletic facilities on the ground floor and a Steward's flat above at an approximate cost of £24000. Even with a Sports Council grant the Club had to find £16000 and raised most of it with a debenture issue like that of 1926.

That the extension opened in 1979 owed much to Hammill's guidance. His deceptively modest tongue continued to coax forth donations for the fire escape and the new drainage system, popularly known as the Cess-pool, completed at the end of 1987. His years of service to the Company are unsurpassed; his inspiration of other ventures like this History is acknowledged. He is the only Past President to attend and chair the Vice Presidents' Supper by right as its founder.

It is a 1978 letter from him to the Gazette Editor that reminds us of the planning and hard work put into the Headquarters fabric, in this case by George Brooks and Gordon Hickey, but, of course, continually by numerous people, whether for re-wiring at a cost of £2000 in 1981, or for the re-roofing of the cottage in 1989. In 1983 P.P. Jim Day writes to the Editor thanking all who "contributed so generously to my appeal for the Main Drains Fund". And the Editor thanks Jim Day, apparently without irony, for "his initiative that got the thing off the ground and", he continues, "maintained its incredible momentum".

This fragrance of high-flown metaphor was no doubt justified by the ever-mounting use the premises were put to: Bonfire Nights or table-tennis, weight-lifting or Wine Committee functions which in 1980 averaged nearly two per month. Already in 1973 Brian Stone was reporting perfectly gross statistics of 1640 suppers served, with close on six hundredweight of meat, including 152 lbs. of steak and kidney, 1218 lbs. of potatoes – i.e., 4000 peeled spuds – 616 lbs. of other vegetables, 1903 cakes – not counting the one baked for 'Nosey' Howard and Leslie Pendered in their 61st and 51st years of membership, and Nobby Clarke, one of our oldest Past Presidents like Cyril Starnes who also had a slice for his 88th birthday.

Small wonder the '200' Group was fully booked up and providing a regular income of £1200 for the Club before the end of the decade: with so much financial demand from the dozens of sprouting schemes, it had to. More jargon, as when one of its members attempted his 1985 explanation of this Group's investments and profit:

"... Thus any discrete configuration mode maximises the probability of project success and minimises the cost and time required for the acquisition of the aforesaid pecuniary rewards."

Well, with that sort of impressive chat, a lottery couldn't help but be a success.

With the increased use of the Clubhouse the Wine Committee's responsibility grew likewise. Its greater turnover caused the Committee to be registered for V.A.T.; a separate treasurer became necessary to see to the extensive accounts and the number of bills. It funded the running of the Clubhouse, its heating and fittings, the running repairs.

When 1977 marked the anniversary of fifty years at Hayes such hard work seemed to justify the celebration on New Year's Day. The Golden Jubilee of the opening of Club Headquarters saw a short Thanksgiving Service and the presence of a crowd containing some sixteen who had been members for the whole of that period or more, as well as fourteen who joined before the 1939-45 War. J.H. Allanson wrote a letter of thanks ('Dear Taylor') to the President:

"One looks to the future and applauds the foresight and drive of those in charge today..."

J.H. Kitton, Cross-country Captain 1923-27, recalled how at the time of the move from West Wickham their fortunes had been at a low ebb. Interestingly, he remarked on the gulf there had been between older and younger and between summer and winter members.

Care of the Clubhouse and its fabric has been a constant pre-occupation. At the 1976 A.G.M. the Secretary related, "A high point of committee business was achieved in January when B.H.H.Q. Ltd. reported that, in addition to the new Stewards in residence, emergency lighting installed, heating system fully operational, 'the leak in the ladies toilet had finally been sealed'." This last was a more crucial triumph than may appear, so baldly stated. These facilities were not only for the odd female visitor escorting Saturday males. The formation of the Blackheath Social Club had followed the 1973 A.G.M. where ways were discussed "in which it would be possible for ladies to take a fuller part in Club life –" though, less ambitiously, the statement continued, "– particularly with reference to table-tennis where mixed teams are very common."

Social Club membership was expressly forbidden to any person eligible to be a Blackheath Harrier. With the sexes thus honourably segregated, conformable to Blackheath tradition, the first Chairman (yes) was that star worker and supporter (again, yes) Brenda Brent. Aided by Margaret Haines and doubtless spurred by that generous concession that enabled "ladies to compete in the local Table-tennis League under the Club's name", in the following years they proceeded to raise sum after sum for Blackheath needs. By means of barn dances, jumble sales, tombola, raffles and Christmas fairs, the Club kitchen was furnished to the tune of £600 in 1978, with a further £400 promised; shortly after came a donation of £800 to equip the new extension; in 1983, after ten years in being the supply of money was unstinting still: £700 for equipment and tiling in the Jubilee Kitchen; kitchen units for the Caretaker's flat; £1000 for the new drainage system. The Gazette extolled the value of Social Club membership, without apparent irony:

"... Benefits? An opportunity to join a happy hard-working band and a night out once a year..."

Hardly possible to exaggerate not merely the gratitude owed to this generosity of effort but also the vital importance of these moneys. In his 1980 Treasurer's Report, Pete Shepheard was urgent for fund-raising ideas. Income had increased, but only because it had been swollen by the recent phenomenon of sponsorship. It was not just problems such as the increase of the rateable value of the Clubhouse from £500 to £1088 and expenditure rising by 25 per cent: the whole scale of things was growing. Within five years membership had increased from six to seven hundred, the financial turnover from £1750 to £9000. These were unignorable signs of change. The remainder of this account deals largely with athletic performance, growth and success, yet it cannot be forgotten how much is owed by members to the ground rock of work and planning, less glamorous than athletic achievement and executed by a numerous, industrious body. Without that base, none of the rest would be possible.

The story both of the Club's relative failure at the start of the 1970's and of the subsequent climb to success is illustrated by the record of Track and Field for the period. To begin with, what was happening was masked from uncritical eyes by the celebration of the Centenary and the buzz it engendered, by the projects going forward as well as by individual performances like those of internationals Wadhams, Hamlyn, Hudson, Gower, Watts and Richardson. Nonetheless, "We rarely managed to field an adequate team" was the Secretary's stark A.G.M. comment of 1969-70. Though they won the Sward Trophy, the League team was relegated to Division Three. Perhaps more than with cross-country or road, the scoring pattern of the Track and Field League is vivid and inexorable: each year the team is promoted or demoted, or holds its place. The Blackheath League tale of these years is a neat graph showing the team's continuing descent and its subsequent climb back in five successive seasons. The British Athletics League Programme tells it nicely, sensitively:

"Blackheath Harriers.

Founder member of B.A.L. in 1969, placing 6th in Div. 1. Left B.A.L. after 1972, re-qualified in 1980, winning promotion in successive seasons to reclaim their premier status in 1984. Best League position: 4th in 1986; best Cup: 4th in 1982."

Behind that laconic outline lies the richer story of a deal of management, recruiting, competition and coaching, together with the central name of Andy Frankish, as surely linked with these latest years as those of Gary Botley with cross-country and of John Powell with the young athletes. Certainly it is a name to stand with other Track Captains, not least that of Norman Page. Norman died in 1986, but not before he had seen successes dear to his captain's heart. Moreover, the first League team represented the tip of the iceberg. The Club came to have great strength in depth also, with teams in Divisions One and Four of the Southern League, promotion in 1988 for the third team and an additional one for Division Seven in 1989. None of which should make us lose sight of the fact that to single out names like the four above is to run the risk of forgetting others: in 1971-72, for example, John Baldwin and Tony Oldfield, respective organizers of the Club Open Cross-country Relay and the Schools Cross-country Race, or Bob Taylor, whose Winter Track Meeting was as successful as ever.

Nor should the gloom of League demotion in the 1970's obscure the many individual successes. From the extended Tables in this Second Edition it will be seen how they had A.A.A. Champions: medallists also in Martin Carroll for Junior 400 metres hurdles; Ken Tonkin, Junior 3000m. Walk; Nick Burrows, Youth Triple Jump; a third place in the A.A.A. Junior 4x100m. Relay, all in 1972. By 1978 new names had arrived: Nick Brooks, with two English Schools Championships, already a sub-1 min.50 sec. performer while still a junior and 7th in the A.A.A. Senior Championship; Julian Spooner, another half-miler, Schools and Junior International with Southern and A.A.A. titles to his credit. No, the first name was not so new: he was George's grandson, while Gordon his father can claim the unusual pedigree of joining the Club as an official.

By 1977 the Secretary could change his tune: "a very encouraging season". The Club enjoyed its first League win ever and soon followed it with another. The drive and enthusiasm of Mike Mahoney and Frankish were praised. These were seasons of anticipation, with field events and greater all-round strength major factors in the growth. Trevor Llewelyn, Welsh record holder and 6th in the U.K. all-time list, high-jumped against West Germany and Finland, was 1st in the Home International, 7th for Great Britain in Tokyo, while Tim Foulger also figured in the U.K. High Jump listings at 9th. A stalwart of these and later years, both by performance and example, was shot-putter and Commonwealth Silver medallist, Mike Winch who, joining in 1977, in addition to his international appearances, for example, competed for the Club in every League match as well as numerous minor events. In 1981 he was rewarded by his first A.A.A. outdoor title for the Club and he holds the record for the most 'A' string wins in the British League. Perhaps the first real belief in success took hold in 1979. The League season began with a win; two days later there were victories for all three teams, Senior, Junior and Youth, in the Gordon Pirie Trophy Meeting. In the Southern League the team was 2nd overall; in the Qualifying Match for the British League at Haringey the field events section scored 198 out of a possible 224 points: the Club finished 1st overall. More heady stuff was on the way. By 1981 the growth of the Club meant that many were unable to find a team place, so that a third was formed, for Division 6 of the Southern League. There were further acquisitions like the decathlete and sprinter, Luke ('Buster') Watson, later to represent Great Britain at the Los Angeles Olympics. In 1982 Blackheath had ten individual members in the A.A.A. Championships, the largest number for some years. At the Commonwealth Games in Brisbane, Peter Yates, U.K. Javelin Champion, was 6th; Mike Winch, 2nd in the Shot; Watson reached the 200m. final; Llewelyn was 13th for Wales in the High Jump.

The first team was promoted to Division 2, having won three of the four fixtures, while the other two held their places in the Southern League. In the G.R.E. Cup Final 3rd place was missed by half a point, but the Club won the G.L.C. Championships, with five individual places. Unsurprisingly, these developments brought their own pressures. It was no longer sufficient, said the 1982 Gazette Editor, "to have an 'A' string and another to collect one or two points. Matches are won by placing the majority of the team in the first three places at the very outside".

Still, more than one spoke of 1981 or 1982 seasons as the best ever. More modestly, Secretary Bill Lake said, "We hope to have a small building near the track very soon". For by now there was indeed a track – all-weather, as they now called it – at Norman Park. The 'Shed' came soon after, courtesy once more of the B.H. Social Club who provided a sum of £2500, paying for both the base and fabric, together with equipment for refreshments at the track. Field event facilities were imminent, with floodlighting to follow. The new building was ready in 1983. It was surely a fitting landmark in Club affairs when, in addition to the first sub-four minute mile at Norman Park, a special award was made there to P.P. Victor Beardon, distinguished athlete and former President, Kent A.A.A., retiring after long service as a starter. The award: a sampler made by Brenda Brent.

The same year saw the Club move up to Division Four of the Southern League, then narrowly miss promotion the following year. But the first team gained 5th place in Division One and have determinedly stayed there since. In the same year Blackheath were 5th of the finalists in the G.R.E. Cup, were 3rd in the Kinnaird and won the Sward. As significant in their own way, perhaps, were the six first places and three runners-up in the nine races for all age groups in the Kent Relays.

One who would undoubtedly have relished all this was genial P.P. Arthur Nye who died in 1981. A devoted official, most often as time-keeper, he was President, Kent A.A.A. and of Sevenoaks A.C. when that club re-started in 1978. Holder of the Kent Half Mile title in 1932, he was always an encouraging coach of young athletes. Other losses of this period were the Centurion Humphry Nunns, eleven times winner of the Johnson Bowl in fourteen years; A.G.V. Allen, Club Cross-country Captain, 1927-29, Rowland Cup winner six times in succession, well-known for quick, late changes into racing gear on the Hayes train; Tommy Mountford, with 105 years total membership of Blackheath and his other club, Herne Hill. Not least of these was P.P. Bill Traer who had been a dogged Centurion and distinguished Treasurer, both of the Club and Kent A.A.A. Another of the valued 'cross connections' of our past was Jack Stevens, as old as the century and dying in 1986. A keen and able rower, he was a Past President of the Curlew Club and a 'Kent Krawler'. Stanley Field who died in the same year was also a walker, including the London to Brighton. Our 1952 President, he was an Alderman of the City of London. The Rev. P.H. Francis was not merely the most distinguished athlete of this group but one of the best half-dozen cross-country runners that Blackheath has seen. Runner-up in the 1926 A.A.A. Track Ten Miles, he was 8th in the 1927 English Cross-country Championship. His Gazette obituary said how in his day he "blazed like a meteor across the athletic sky". Youngest of these was Norman Dudley who died in 1985 after a long illness. A member of Coventry Godiva, in 1947 joining S.L.H., in 1949 Blackheath, he ran for the opposition in the Nicholls Cup but always entered for the Blackheath handicap in that race. He too was a Johnson Bowl winner and did much to encourage Club walking. A first-claim member from 1955 on, he had a reputation as an inaugurator of odd but thoroughly respectable encounters, among them the Veterans' Self-handicap, the Tooting Hospital match, the entry of Ultra-senior teams for the Sunday Times Fun Run. He had organized the Centenary Peckham-Hayes Run and he also had a hand in initiating the Four Clubs Veterans Mob Match.

A kindred spirit, surely, is Garry Spencer who with Andy Frankish devised the 'Dreamers' Mile' series in 1985, with trophies for the most improved runner and the series winner on points. This kind of mass encouragement was most valuable, attracting for the first competition some thirty members of all standards with, of course, the time-keeping support of George Brooks. In 1987 the same man dreamed up another, different mile race – one to celebrate the fiftieth anniversary of Sydney Wooderson's World Record. The central feature of the International Athletes Club 'Miller Lite' Grand Prix Meeting at Crystal Palace, it followed the original handicap form when Sydney had been off scratch. The Club was represented by Alan Guilder, Dave Heath, Mike Laws and Chris. McGeorge, winner of the Emsley Carr Mile the following year. They opposed world-class runners like Kenya's Mike Boit, with Jack Buckner and Steve Crabb, the last-named winning off scratch in an exciting, well-staged handicap. Many senior Blackheath colleagues of Sydney were present, including Stanley Wooderson and John Furniss from the original 1937 field. Film of Sydney's run was shown on the stadium's giant screen as well as on television, and the most famous Heathen of them all was introduced to the crowd.

To celebrate his 75th birthday and filling a long-standing gap, a book of photographs, 'Sydney Wooderson – Forgotten Champion' by David Thurlow appeared in 1989. Fittingly for one of the last great amateurs the book was devoted to a worthy cause, being published by the British Sports Association for the Disabled. There was a link with the more distant past the previous year when Wooderson unveiled a plaque in Calne, Wiltshire, commemorating the other great Blackheath miler, W.G. George and his 1886 record of 4 mins. 12¾ secs., in the town of his birth. And Sydney was the only one present at the dinner who had met the Victorian champion. Equally pleasing, and matching Sydney's own support for disabled athletes were the funds raised by Blackheath competitors in the London Marathon: in 1988, £4000 for the Seoul Paralympics; in 1989 £15000 for the Marjorie McClure School at Chislehurst for children with severe handicaps.

In the 1986 British League the Club were fourth, their highest placing to date. The second and third teams were 15th and 16th respectively in Divisions One and Four, Southern League. And national and international successes continued to come, individually: Peter Yates, 3rd U.K. Closed Championships Javelin; Graham Savory, 1st and 2nd, U.K. Discus and Shot, and both representing England and Great Britain. Brad McStravick competed for Scotland in the Commonwealth Games Decathlon and placed 4th behind Daley Thompson. Daryl Brand was 4th in the Commonwealth Javelin, before taking New Zealand citizenship. One of Blackheath's select Celts, Phil Davies, 1st in the 1986 Welsh 100 metres, 7th A.A.A. 100 metres, finalist in both 100 and 200 in the U.K. Closed Championships, has continued in the top flight and has been unlucky to coincide with the current flourish of British sprinting talent.

In the last three years the levels of team performance have been well sustained: 5th place in Division One in 1987 and 1988, 6th in 1989, promotion to Division 3, Southern League, in 1988, continued victories in Sward and Reading Gazette Trophies, in 1989 the first ever Kinnaird Trophy win and two further appearances in the G.R.E. Cup Final. In the latter the Club colours were seen on television on every event when the team finished sixth in 1989. The latest encouragement has been the entry to Southern League Division 7 of a fourth Blackheath team. Lost to the Club in this year of track success was an early builder of their fortunes, former Captain and quarter-miler, Charles Woods, who happily had been reunited with colleagues two years before at the Wooderson Anniversary Mile.

"For a Club whose traditions are so firmly established in winter activities, it is ironic that in recent years its achievements on the country, or lack of them, have contrasted so starkly with those of the track section in their rise to British League Division One status in the top eight clubs in the country. It is the Winter Captain's pleasure to record that the cross-country department is now back in business!".

The defiant optimism of this salvo in Captain Botley's 1985-86 Review indicates the general pattern of Club cross-country in the past quarter of a century, namely, one of recent, dramatic improvement but following behind that of the Track and Field section. Tantalisingly uneven also, for there were successes throughout the period which often flattered to deceive. This uncertain thread must be traced through the labyrinth of the Gazette where, in any case, reports of important races like the National Championships often occupy a fractional space. Where they occur team victories tend to shine out quirkily, almost unaccountably, until one remembers the quality and service of runners like Richardson, Baldwin, Coles; the 3rd team placings in the Southern Championships of 1970, 1972, 1976; the 1969 National Youths 4th place; the wins of 1971 or 1976 in the G.L.C. Championship and South of the Thames.

More often there is no evident pattern, only some sense of puzzlement, for instance, at teams veering between 4th and 18th positions in the 1974 and 1975 Southerns, or else finishing 54th in the 1975 National. All the more so, since there was more than one clean sweep of Mob Matches in the early '70's, together with individual achievements like Martin Hore's 3rd place in the 1969 National Youth Championship, the team coming fourth; Coles and Richardson finishing 2nd and 3rd in the South of the Thames, 8th and 12th in the Southern.

Bob Richardson continued for some years as a backbone of Blackheath after his 1969 highpoint when he was 5th in the National and 19th in the International Cross-country as a member of the winning English team. And speaking of high points, 1969-70 was the most successful season for some years with 2nd and 3rd places in Kent and Southern, 4th in the G.L.C. Championship, 1st in the South of the Thames and a commendable 9th National placing, with Gary Botley 9th man home behind hardy perennials like Ian Wilson, Chris Haines, Pete Horwood, Joe Clare and John Baldwin.

One seemingly immovable feature of Club cross-country was the Chief Trail-layer, P.P. Keith Wilcockson. He died in the evening at home after laying the Hayes trail for the 1977 Nicholls Cup race. Irreplaceable, he was nevertheless worthily succeeded in his office by another, future President. 'Johnson's Redcoats' got their trail-laying name from the all-weather anoraks they trooped out in.

Jealously watched? In a 1983 Gazette notice some dishonesty was gently hinted at in London Marathon marshals who had borrowed these garments: "Due to the popularity of this exclusive sect the supply of distinctive jackets is insufficient to meet the demand".

Following the new litter laws, the 'paper chase' had disappeared, together with the laying of paper trails. Since 1977, however, it has been reinstated as a Boxing Day event by dint of the enthusiasm of Mike Peel and Peter Hannell and an unoffending scent of flour and soluble confetti across Hayes Common and the surrounding farms. Hares and Hounds disguise themselves as humans in fancy dress and after, the whole Pack are regaled with cocktails and prizes from the President for the best dressed in a Clubhouse crowded with four Heathen generations.

Perhaps, after all, the general feeling about the 1970's was more of frustration at varying between 9th and 54th, 13th and 27th placings in the National or at having several fast individuals without the thrust of others competing for team places. At times it did seem as though individual runners had to carry the whole weight, but no doubt that was an illusion of the ambitious.

One man who ran a full team's worth by himself was Mike Hampton who in 1978 left Keswick at 8.00p.m. one June evening and returned at 6.56 p.m. the next, after the Lakeland Circuit of 72 miles and 27000 feet up mountain and down hill for the 93rd successful attempt since the first in 1932.

The 1979 season typified the decade, with the disappointment of 16th in the Southern but 28th in the National where they were 9th Southern club home. The promise of breakthrough was always there: the following year was more cheering – 5th in the Southern, 20th in the National. Yet still, as the 1980 Secretary's Report lamented, there were no juniors moving up, no junior teams in either Southern or National. And they lost the Nicholls Cup race, so that there were also complaints about turn-out in respect of the masses. Still, they did finish second in their own Open Cross-country Relay and though the old pattern persisted into the early 1980's – 12th, 10th, 10th Southern places, 33rd, 30th, 39th in the National in successive years – there were other, newer signs. They might lose to S.L.H. still, but now there were more solid placings, in the Kent, for example, by the Juniors and Youths, both teams finishing third, with the Seniors runners-up in their Championship. "This day saw the emergence of a new enthusiasm in cross-country running in Blackheath Harriers." Faced with this sort of rhetoric from the Captain, most members had no choice, so that the 1984 Nicholls Cup saw a Club record of 130 runners.

One inspiration of the same Captain was to donate inscribed vests to the 50th and 100th Blackheath men home in this race. An even more cunning incentive was culled from the Tour de France by Les Roberts: the 'Lanterne Rouge' for last Club scorer.

**R. COLES AND W.O'DONNELL
CLUB '5'**

No apologies for this welter of statistics – they provide a dramatic picture of events: the shift, within the two years of 1985 and 1986 from 93rd position to 20th in the National; from 15th to 1st in the Southern. "An historic day for the Club," said a letter from P.P. Hammill of this latter occasion. For Richard Coles, too, who found a long-awaited exhilaration in success. With thirteen successive National appearances no one deserved this late fortune more. The Secretary's 1971-72 Report had mentioned "a youth who was 29th in the Inter-counties race." Richard's career is therefore long as well as distinguished. It is a sign of a tough Blackheath competitor to win all three winter championships in one season, as he had done in 1979, only the third in Club history to manage it. When the team finished 15th in the 1985 Southern, he had been first home; now, in 1986 he was fifth scorer for his gold medal. New blood was coursing through the veins: the average age of this winning team was twenty five years.

Yet, with a Heathen quirkiness, still they lost, not just to Orion but away to their rivals in ancientry, Thames Hare and Hounds. The Secretary claimed the latter to be the result of "a clever bit of gamesmanship – 'Do not bring more than fifty – our changing accommodation is limited'". A sign of the times was their poor fifth in the 1986 Kent Championship, accounted for by the fact that several first team members were not eligible for the County. No matter: the season's success was no flash in the pan. In 1988 came 3rd place in the National at Newark behind Birchfield and Tipton Harriers and in front of over 220 other teams. The scoring six of Jerry Barton, Tim Nash, Alan Guilder, Bill Foster, Mark Jones contained the ever-green Coles. And despite the ravages of the October hurricane the previous year, tree-clear courses were devised and all three mob matches won. Against S.L.H. it was the fifth successive win. Before the start they planted a yew tree on Farthing Down as an emblem of regeneration.

Hopes were naturally high for the next National Championship. 516 points had been enough for their third place in 1988, but now, in a fiercely fought team race eight clubs scored less than 500. Some were disappointed with Blackheath's seventh position and 483 points, yet it would have delighted almost any other previous team. In a field of close on two thousand they were also the only club with all nine runners in the first two hundred. That evening there was more than enough to celebrate in a remarkable gathering of past and present team members at a Club 'National' Supper. Present were not only the complete team from that day but P.P. Roy Morley heading others from the sixties and seventies. During the evening, one of the 3rd placed team of 1948, Gordon Monshall, phoned his good wishes from Australia. Their captain, Dick Choat, was present, together with several of the others: Sydney Wooderson, Jack Braughton, John Clark and Alan Brent.

It was hard to tell exactly what the last named was celebrating that night, for, apart from the reunion with his team of forty years earlier, he was wearing his chain of office as E.C.C.U. President after a meticulous organization of the thousands of runners that the modern Championships attract. Moreover, during the evening there was a special presentation to him for his services to the Bromley Sports Council. He had, of course, held numerous other offices outside Blackheath. Laurie Hammill had become the first of the Kent A.A.A.'s annual presidents in 1969; ten years later Alan held the same post, to be succeeded in turn by D.F. Millgate, I.F. Smith and V.W.W. Beardon. Since 1969 there have been three Blackheath Presidents of the South of the Thames C.C. Association – Ian Wilson, Martin Athawes and, for a second time and for the Association's own 1987 Centenary, Alan Brent, who had received the Queen's Jubilee Medal in 1977. Like Brent, Ian Wilson was a President of the Southern Counties C.C. Association and he has played a regular role in managing teams. At the World Cross-country Championships at Stavanger in 1989 he was manager of the Great Britain team, as was Head of the New Zealand Delegation, Alan Stevens, of his own country. In such ways Blackheath has continued to serve the sport, as it has done from its organized origins in the 1880's.

At the time of their own Centenary Blackheath had only London Athletic Club and Thames Hare and Hounds for company. Since then, several others have reached their centuries, among them, Ranelagh, Birchfield, Herne Hill – all Harrier clubs. In 1983 the English Cross-country Union had celebrated theirs at Birmingham. The prominent part played by the Club in its formation was commemorated by a plaque bearing badges of both E.C.C.U. and Blackheath. The Club reciprocated by sharing in a new trophy presented to the Union by the eleven original clubs for the first of these to finish in future Championships.

Blackheath was flourishing. What brought this about, in addition to the factors of organization or athletic enthusiasm and quality? Evidently, there were external influences for which the Club can claim only the credit of seized opportunity. Soon after the mid-1980's the membership had swelled to a thousand, following the common annual pattern of about a hundred deletions or resignations balanced by a similar number of elections. This may be seen as a combined effect of the London Marathon and the 'Jogging boom'. Many of the new members were aged between thirty five and forty five, in Blackheath commonly referred to as the 'Wednesday Nighters' and largely interested in marathon running. Ernest Neville would have been delighted, as he was by Joe Clare's 1970 win in the London to Brighton Run pursuing the tradition of Lew Piper and Derek Reynolds. Our oldest member, Ernest died in 1972. Founder of the Road Runners Club, judge at the 1936 Berlin Olympics, he had been largely responsible for the restoration of walking to the Olympic programme in 1928. While still in his teens he walked to Brighton and back.

On the road there were team successes too at this time: in 1972, 1st team in the Kent '20', 2nd in the A.A.A. Marathon, thanks to a fine trio of Bob Richardson, Chris. Haines and Chris. Woodcock. Road relay performances were solid, not brilliant, but in 1974 and 1978 at least, the team were good enough to qualify for the National Road Relay Championship. In this latter year the Club lost one of its staunch road runners in one of Nature's cruel accidents. After Ted Pepper had gone off course and died of hypothermia in the Three Peaks Race the Committee decided on an open Memorial Race. Generously backed by the Social Club, the annual event is organized by Mike Peel.

The growth of popular road running had of course begun before the first London Marathon, held in 1981. The effect on the Club was evident before the end of the seventies. In 1979 numbers increased to 700, by 1983 to 800. Of the membership that year nearly half had joined in the past five years, but most of the rest had been members for much longer. Fifty four had over 50 years – a further eighteen, more than 60 years membership. Less consoling remained the significant turn-over of other sections, mostly young athletes who moved – to other areas, to other sports – or life. Some fifty Blackheath runners finished in that first London Marathon, three in under two and a half hours for the first time since 1972. Since then there has been a matching explosion of pithy commentary in the Gazette:

"...Only my second marathon, but at least I'm one up on Pheidippides..."

"...Anyway, I did come in ahead of both halves of the cow..."

"– Trying to keep up with those nice girl runners made me stiff."

The Club had been involved in the 'London' from its inception when it was still a twinkle in Ranelagh Harrier Chris Brasher's mind. He approached Ian Smith and Tony Oldfield for discussion and help with experimental starting arrangements on Blackheath. Don Hopgood, who has given so many years of sterling service to the Club's road runners, remains the Blackheath Marshal for the 'Blue Start' of the race. The Club's own entry quickly doubled in these fields of thousands. So did their involvement in the large-scale preparations, the Club contribution itself being organized by Tony Oldfield, then for several years by Mike Williams, now by Mike Martineau. Les Roberts became first holder of the Club Marathon Trophy held in conjunction with the event, while Vice-Presidents Braughton, Shepheard and Peel have completed all nine of the races. One of the best London memories must be that of the blind ex-race walker, Alan Pickering, helped by Mike Peel to finish among the host in just over four hours. Bill Lake opined then that the London Marathon was "the best thing that ever happened to athletics". Which may be true, yet it may turn out to be better for runners than for the clubs, tending to encourage individual road running rather than athletics as a whole and the organizations which are its backbone.

This is not to deny its benefit to Blackheath. A Gazette letter by Don Gillate in 1984 drew attention to "the apparent renaissance of a form of life previously thought to be as rare as a mob match victory". A daisy-picking, geriatric quartet had reported sightings in the Common of the species 'Pacrunna' – "an agglomeration of some ten to twenty disparate members into a coherent, queue-like mobile whole by common elements of speed, sociability and a thirst for new or risqué narrative". With the rescue of this species, the writer confidently anticipated "an era of ordered success that must inevitably ensue". The 1989 President appears to have been correct. Elsewhere on the road in the 1980's there was improvement reflecting if not matching that on track and country, whether it was second team places in both Kent and Open '20' races or, as in the Tonbridge '10', eleven Blackheath teams and a different set of twenty runners next day in the Worthing '10'.

In addition to training holidays abroad there were continental racing forays by members of all ages from youths to veterans, and assaults on America by Les Roberts, as in the 1984 New York Marathon when he finished 179th of 17000 starters. His 38th place in the Boston Marathon, 3rd Veteran home, gained him the sum of 500 dollars. Mentions of commercial cash like these remind us how far we had travelled from former days in these few years. They were further signs of the times, reported in Gazette columns. Not individual prizes alone, either, but for the Club in general, Gazette headlines now:

"Sponsorship Deal Goes Ahead",

when, following the line of the English Schools and Milk Marketing Board collaboration, Blackheath obtained Express Dairy sponsorship for the Kent Cross-country Championships at Sparrows Den, together with added benefits, from certificates for Colts and Boys to a pint for each at the finish. Of milk. 1986 brought a 'Minolta Copiers' coaching grant of £1000 enabling help for fifty young athletes per session. No sponsorship, however, in 1987 for a valiant team headed by Jim Bennett on the John O'Groats to Land's End road. Ten over-60 veterans ran a relay, paying their own way and raising £1200 for the Rotary International 'Polio-Plus' Campaign. They ran 131 stages of six to eight miles. Two wives provided food and chauffeuring.

By 1988 Blackheath was up to 3rd place in the Southern Road Relay, behind Aldershot and Haringey. In 1989 a fine Blackheath team ran out winners. Other excitements included first team in the A.A.A. 10 Kms. Road race and, in the following year, runners-up in the National Cross-country Relay, 12th in the National Road Relay. And, however patronizing it may be to Blackheath's 1989 individual Southern Cross-country Champion, Jerry Barton – who certainly had seen how tough life is at the top – all this was done without athletes of the absolute top rank. Not yet.

The feminist movement had been on the march some years before the Centenary. There have been a number of mentions of the other sex in this brief narrative: remarkably so for an all-male club. None of these has been to do with our sharing the new Norman Park track with the unignorable presence of Bromley Ladies A.C., young compared with Blackheath, yet already a leading national team. The Development Sub-committee set up in 1986 had a wide-ranging commission. Spurred on by the response to a questionnaire to all members older than thirteen years, the Committee requested this group to focus on coaching, the relation of Blackheath Harriers to Bromley Ladies A.C.; the possible change of the Club's name, sponsorship, finance and the Committee structure. Next, following a Special Committee Meeting, the creation of a coaching scheme was proposed, together with the setting-up of a joint committee with the Ladies' Club to examine common athletic and administrative interests at Norman Park. There was a determination to persevere in seeking sponsorship for the Club. On the change of name no action was proposed.

This dialogue was not an isolated passage. Two years earlier, a letter from Geoff. Crowder, staunch veteran and supporter, had appeared in the Gazette at a time when, interestingly, the Blackheath results of the London Marathon were listing what must be termed associated women with the male Club finishers. "There is...one major area," he observed, "in which we are sadly lagging behind." The fact that Blackheath lacked a women's section was an anachronism in 1984. He reminded members that a number of families were involved with the Club; he regretted that not all the active athletes in those families could be members of Blackheath. In the same year came the death of Elizabeth Daniels who with the help of her family had catered for Christmas and other suppers, with numbers above a hundred at a time. Which was like another aspect of the same argument.

In 1986 Crowder returned to the charge, pointing out in a second letter what a dramatic change in numbers there had been of women competing, also in the range of those competitive activities and the standards they were now achieving. "We are bound to take note of the state of our sport in 1986," he said. The majority of clubs throughout the country had recognized this and now had male and female sections. Junior recruitment was the key to continuing success and it was increasingly likely that parents with sons and daughters of athletic potential would look for a club which made provision for both sexes: those without that facility would suffer. On the question of a change of name, and bringing to mind the shift of title as well as of ground from Peckham to Blackheath, he thought it "intriguing that, on the basis of tradition, there should be resistance to modifying our name. Our ancestors had no such inhibitions."

The Secretary's Annual Report appeared, consciously or otherwise, to lend support at least to the thrust of his principle: "Some members," it said, "have evinced concern over the mere discussion of such issues. However, the Club has been in existence since 1869 and has survived, whilst others have disappeared off the athletic map, by having the perspicacity to foresee the changes happening in our sport and acting in advance of, rather than responding to them." When these concerns were brought before the body of members at the 1988 A.G.M. some more 'evincing' was done. As for these present mentions, they are less for today's readers than for Blackheath successors. Finally, another Gazette correspondent, contemplating the disadvantages of such increase of membership, plumbed, sniffily, leaden depths of irony:

"By doubling that Wednesday attendance, we might even bring back the therapeutic benefits of ankle-deep sewage now so sorely missed."

As with women's participation in athletics, so too with Veterans. Generally, there was a growth here also. Beginning before the Centenary, it was large-scale and certainly another factor in the Club's expansion and all-round strength – in terms of mob matches, marathon running, special veterans events and much more. Of course, these athletes prolonging active life had the same adverse effect on the supply of officials, together with other disadvantages already mentioned. Overall, however, most would hold the gains to have outweighed such effects. A large number competed, seriously, enjoyably, finding satisfaction in individual endeavour or in being part of a team. Blackheath veterans figured prominently in track and field events throughout the period. There have been National title-holders such as record-breaking David Gale in the Long Jump; pole-vaulter Jim Day, notorious for regular retirement after twenty, thirty years, twice National Champion, five times Southern and Kent Champion; Gordon Hickey who held the High Jump record in 1978 at 1.75.   In addition Colin Brand was Southern Decathlon Champion in 1981 and '83.

In the 1984 European Veterans Championships held in this country, Gazette Editor, Les Roberts, won the 5000 metres and was second in the 10000; Peter Hannell, Chris Ellis, Jim Day had 3rd places in the 5000m. Walk, Discus and Over-50 Pole Vault.   The World Veterans Championships in Rome the next year numbered four members among its four thousand competitors: Peter Baigent, with years of sprinting technique behind him, reached semi-finals, achieving 13.65 for the 100, 28.6 for the 200 metres; Peter Hannell came 8th and 10th in five and ten km. Walks; Chris Ellis, later to create a national discus record of 48.44 in 1987, here won the bronze medal, while Les Roberts carried off the gold in a 5000m. of 14.40.3 after an inspired last lap of 61 secs. Among other talented performers on road, track and country was, still, Jack Braughton ''– the flying phoenix from the roaring forties'' with so many first class performances, from 5000m. to marathon. He regularly placed in Over 60 and Over 65 Southerns and Nationals, toughened no doubt by his nine London Marathons. His junior, John Baldwin, has enjoyed even more success as a veteran. In his presidential year, still he finished 100th in the National Senior: no problem, presumably, for an organizer of the '200' Group and the Club's Cross-country Relay, a Minutes Secretary, Officials Secretary and B.H.H.Q. Director. Now, among autumnal distinctions he has been Southern and National Cross-country and Southern 10000 metres Track Champion. In 1983 at Perpignan he won the World 10 kms. over 45 Road Championship and was runner-up in the 25 kms.

Veterans teams have done well also.   In the 1980's they have regularly won or come second in the Southern Cross-country Championship, have fielded several teams at a time in the Kent and placed third or fourth in a number of National C.C. Championships.   At Wolverhampton in 1984 the Club won its first National Cross-country Championship in any age group with the combination of new blood and experience of Richard Pitcairn-Knowles, Ron Foreman and former historian, Tony Weeks-Pearson.   With 61 points they beat Hallamshire by 13 and Tipton by 26 points for the Over 50 title.   The next year saw two more notable team wins: the Bruges 25 kms., with Les Roberts, John Baldwin and Ian Wilson; the Southern 10 miles Road Race, with Les Roberts as individual winner, Chris Woodcock and Peter Anderson.   In National Road Relay Championships, the 1988 7th place out of 82 teams by the over-forties and 15th of 32 teams by the over-fifties have been typically creditable performances.   In 1989 Blackheath fielded teams in 40, 50 and 60- year age groups.   However, by this date some difficulties lay in their path that were not of their making.

During these years the lack of unity of the various athletic organizations grew worse rather than better.   The Southern Veterans Athletic Club registration scheme, for instance, made many Blackheath veterans reluctant to compete under a regime they felt to be inappropriate and which is still unresolved by the formation of a single body.   The Veterans Mob Match, the central team race for the mass of members, has been unaffected by such considerations, and with varying success the Club has kept its end up: 3rd, for instance, in 1987, 2nd, to Orion, in 1988, with Pete Hamilton, latest trail-blazer to arrive on the scene, the individual winner.   Since 1972, the Peter Driver Cup has been the trophy for this race, in memory of the fine Empire Games 6 Miles Champion of 1954 who died so early.

BLACKHEATH GERIATRICS 1983

Many of these veterans excel – all are marvellous for their age: a few are amazing. The 'Blackheath Geriatrics' were not, as other members first inferred, a Clubhouse pop group but a select, sprightly team of over sixties expressly formed for assault upon the massed thousands of the annual autumn race in Hyde Park. Ill-named – for the Sunday Times 'Fun Run' is, in fact, a deadly earnest contest, more perilous than any National. Instigated by Johnny Walker, abetted by Norman Dudley, the team has competed for the past twelve years. And Jack Parrott has run eleven of these races. Expectedly, this élite équipage contains other extraordinary people: from a Dignity of Past Presidents like Alan Brent, Bill Lake and ultra-distance star Lew Piper to Olympian Braughton and the late Gus Tweedy who in 1973 ran this course when 73 years of age. The team finishes well up – in the first baker's dozen of well over fifteen hundred teams. For their next trick, they will field a 70-plus scoring six in addition to the juvenile pensioners.

''The supervision, training and maintaining of interest of our younger members,'' Secretary Dave Amner attested in 1977, was ''the crux of the Club's future.'' He found no one to contradict his claim. He remarked also on the small number of supervisors of young athletes: so much depended on Don Clouston, John Baldwin, Gary Botley, Mike Peel, and parents. The story of these years is the escape from such difficulties to success. This achievement and its subject, the Young Athletes who can guarantee the Club's future, appropriately occupy the final section of this short review.

Enough has been said already to suggest the general standard of junior performance in the 1970's, but with the arrival of one who, as is generally agreed, was more than a 'supervisor', John Powell, the Club experienced a discernible shift of fortunes and spirit in 1979. The cross-country performances had remained disappointing; there had been only individual early promise like that of Robert Weeks-Pearson 2nd in the 1978 Kent Junior, 5th at 17 years in the 1977 Club '5'. Now came the outstanding Robert Farish, first in the Schools Inter-counties Cross-country, 7th in the National Schools. Still not a team. But stirring signs came later that Spring in the Medway A.C. Relays where the Colts finished 1st, the Youths 3rd. Overall, the Boys were the strongest team. In 1978 the youths had been relegated to Division 2 of the National Track League, Southern area: 1979 found them winning four of five matches, scoring a new Division points record of 276 points in one afternoon, and promoted to Division 1. The Boys won the S.E. Counties League, the Colts were 4th; in the Combined League they were 2nd, but only by one point. In addition to Farish, 2nd in both Southern 1500 and 3000 metres, there were the blossoming talents of Paul Ashen, 1st and 2nd in Southern 100 and 200 metres;

Paul Austridge, 1st, 80 metres Hurdles; John Hunter, 3rd, High Jump. To speak of just one Championship meeting.

In the same year, to meet these refreshing challenges, a Young Athletes Management Committee for the under 17's was formed of parents and Club representatives, including the President. In 1980 there were a Parents Social Evening with more than a hundred athletes and parents, and the first ever Young Athletes Section Dinner attended by over eighty athletes, parents and guests. John Powell had been a member only one year before he was so enthusiastically and firmly in charge of the Young Athletes. At the same time, the debt owed to Gary Botley is undisputed. He did so much basic work in the 1970's, in terms of encouragement and the securing of coach Charles Elliott's services.

After these two swelling years it was a steady march of success from season to season: in their main winter competitions, Herne Hill's Young Athletes C.C. League and the Kent Boys and Colts' League, the 2nd and 3rd team places in the 1979-80 became typical, while Robert Farish's Southern Counties Boys win at Parliament Hill in 1980 was the first individual title since Brian Stone, in 1953. By 1986, though there was no Junior team in the Kent, the Colts were 3rd, the Boys and Youths both sixth, and, in the H.H.H. League, 3rd.

Spectacular team and individual successes came in track and field: in 1980, 3rd in Southern Division I of the National Y.A. League, 1st in the Boys and Colts S.E. Counties League, then, appearing for the first time in a national final, 8th in the Auxiliary Final. This season set a pattern which stretched over the next decade: the National Young Athletes Final saw them three times runners-up – in 1986, 1987 and 1988. The Boys and Colts won the Kent League competition in 1983 as well as the Overall first place; and then retained both Boys and Overall titles with maximum points. In 1986 and 1987 they headed the Eastern Premier Division of the National League, as well as retaining the three Kent Boys and Colts League titles.

There was a constant clink of medals, individual or relay championships were won, records broken indiscriminately. In 1986, for instance, Colts teams won both 4x100m. and 4x400m. in the Kent Relays. In the first, Bassey Essein, Matthew Pearson, Sergio Chambers and Roger Lashley were second fastest British team ever; in the second, Matthew Pearson, Darren Stickles, Nick Durham and Joe Staples went one better in a record 4.13.1. So did Andrew Bailey, Laurence Rogers, Richard Bolt and John Forrest who set a fastest Boys time of 1.37.4. over 4x200m. Winners of the Colts and Boys Medley Championships were Jonathan Murray, Sergio Chambers, Matthew Pearson, Joe Staples; John Forrest, Matthew Griffiths, Andrew Bailey, Richard Bolt.

As with teams, so with individuals in these 1980's. Robert Farish continued to fulfil his early promise: in 1980, Southern Youths 1500 m. winner in 3.58.5, 2nd in both English Schools and Home International. Interesting also to note in passing how he has perpetuated one of the early Blackheath traditions of competing at water-polo like Crafter and the rest, for he played in the 1988 Centenary Match against Ranelagh. Others, however, will have to meet the challenge of the re-match in 2088. Paul Ashen was Southern runner-up in both 100 and 200 metres, returning 22.4 in the latter. Robin Ashdown won the Kent 400m. and came second in the Southern, with 53.2 at 14 years. In 1986 Vaughan Corless won the Southern Youths 400m., John Forrest the Boys, with Richard Holt runner-up. Wayne Evans and Jim Overall gained 3rd places in High Jump and Shot.

While these words were being written the 1989 Young Athletes League Final was fought out at Birmingham. The news has come that after the years as runners-up Blackheath are champions. With the outcome in doubt into the final straight of the last relay, the Club won by six points from Shaftesbury Barnet, themselves winners for the two previous years. There were individual wins in some twenty events. They are too numerous for this short space, but even by modern standards they include performances that are beyond many seniors – the 55.0 400m. Hurdles by Jamie Quarry, 1989 English Schools Champion, for instance. Yet one of the things Blackheath athletes 'know' is that competitions are won not just by the best individuals like Jason Mulcahy, the brilliant thrower, but by every team member. The credit due is widespread. Everything about this latest triumph, including the U.K. record of the Colts 4x100m. relay team, speaks of justified hope for a competitive future. And among the talk is word of Europe and a new challenge for Blackheath juniors to represent their country as a team.

Alas, these must serve as instances before both readers' and historian's heads are dizzied. The names are reassuringly numerous; they give reason for optimism about the next eighty years. In respect of these and the whole Club it is only when facts and figures are marshalled that one is properly impressed by the full magnitude and ambition of Blackheath's present operation.

Time only for brief, last words. Let them be from P.P. Ian Smith when, as Secretary in 1976, he characterized the Club as:

''...alive and healthy, forward-looking despite our valuable traditions and well worth our investment of time and money.''

YOUNG ATHLETES TEAM 1989

NOTES TO MAIN TEXT

Note 1 Page 10
It was not that the working classes or indeed many business people were very secure economically but the establishment of an effective and disciplined police force and the absence of external dangers made for a certain sense of stability.

Note 2 Page 12
Published by Longmans Green and Company 1888.

Note 3 Page 12
These date at least from 1852.

Note 4 Page 13
Blackheath members visiting Shrewsbury School before the First World War became acquainted with the particular paper-chase ritual there — though not, fortunately, at first hand, for not only did it cover ten miles but it entailed the application of a most material "whip" to ensure that the pace was maintained.

Note 5 Page 14
The third of their Peckham Public house headquarters, the first two being "The King's Arms". Peckham Rye, and "The Heaton Arms", Rye Lane. All three are happily still open today.

Note 6 Page 17
Darnell appears to have handled routine financial matters.

Note 7 Page 17
Since re-named Southampton Way. "The Rosemary Branch" possibly connected with the much earlier "Rosemary Bush", is still functioning as a public house. Part of its premises formed a music hall stage in Victorian times and beside it still are traces of the old ground — tennis courts, a hard games pitch, play-ground and public gardens.

Note 8 Page 18
By then things were organized to the point of their having twenty-two Club rules ("no member can grumble at not getting enough for his money," said the press). Subscriptions were half a guinea for active members and "not less than" 5/- for male Honorary members and 2/6d for ladies.

Note 9 Page 19
Until 1891, it is believed.

Note 10 Page 20
The Club medals today still take the form of a cross though it is of a different design.

Note 11 Page 22
A lady member of the Club, it should be noted.

Note 12 Page 22
There may have been a gap of a generation between the decline and fall of Corinthian sport and the emergence of the gentleman amateur though there are some discernible connecting threads. Corinthian sport, of course, developed round the personal challenge and the associated wager — sometimes for a contest between the principals and sometimes between their clients, usually professionals. The wager, as distinct from organized betting for profit, is the gesture people whose occupations are not prudential are apt to enjoy as giving spice to an occasion. The wager, especially where horses and pugilism were concerned, helped to encourage organized gambling which became almost a disease among the 18th Century aristocracy, led to many scandals, attracted riff-raff and was eventually discredited when the middle classes imposed their ideas on society. So the old sort of patron cum professional sport sank further into the mire for want of responsible patronage.

Note 13 Page 23
H.F. Pash said Griffin was the only correspondent to address him in four colours.

Note 14 Page 27
Immediately prior to the Blackheath move the Peckham Committee were hoping that coloured trail paper would help to lessen confusion.

Note 15 Page 27
This continued to operate until well after the Second World War.

Note 16 Page 35
There is a bare possibility that S. Collins, one of the original eleven members known to have belonged to Peckham Hare and Hounds, had some part in founding Blackheath Hare and Hounds, but the evidence is slender.

Note 17 Page 35
Very possibly a derivative of the kind referred to already of the Rectory Field Cricket and Football Club.

Note 18 Page 36
Probably not more than a dozen were active runners.

Note 19 Page 42
Some were very vehement about it. "The future of paper-chasing is doubtful. The evils of importing members solely to run in match teams, of running matches round enclosed courses for gate-money, and of winking at, if not tolerating, regular bettings by lists, have taken firm root, and have injured it greatly as a sport. The mechanic, artisan, or labourer, who used to be barred from competition with gentlemen, is now not only allowed to run, but, if fast, is a welcome member of all country, and many London, Clubs, there being only one which insists on all its members being gentlemen by profession and education."
(Walter Rye in "The Badminton Library - Athletics and Foot Ball" (1888).

Note 20 Page 43
The previous year London Athletic Club had won a match in Ireland which is taken to be the first international match.

Note 21 Page 44
Writing in 1967 after the death of his brother, Gillie,

wno had been an outstanding Surrey cricketer of the early 1920's, C.R. Reay said "from childhood we were all reared on the B.H. and L.A.C.".

Note 22 Page 44
Probably Reed's influence became little greater because of this change than it had been during his chairmanship. Yet it did mark an alteration in the character of the Presidential office, a serving official for the first time being chosen instead of a non-participating patron and this was a real change which has persisted.

Note 23 Page 44
"Did Mr. Pash, or indeed anyone else, ever see Val Hunter in anything but a silk hat?" (R.R. Conway, Gazette).

Note 24 Page 46
It probably is the oldest in the sense of a strictly inter-club cross-country team race pure and simple without any intrusion from hare and hounds conceptions.

Note 25 Page 48
George actually ran a mile time-trial in 4 minutes 10¼ seconds in 1885. The distance was afterwards found to be 6 yards too long, so his time was even faster.

Note 26 Page 49
Founded by a Londoner, H.M. Oliver (not related to the Peckham A.A.C. Oliver family) usually referred to as "father of cross-country running in the Midlands."

Note 27 Page 51
Some of the modern field events had not been developed then; events like discus and javelin came in by classical analogies with the Olympic Games; throwing the hammer and putting the weight — already included in the A.A.A. Championships — derived from Scottish and Irish Games and thus chiefly attracted those nationalities up to 1914. The jumps were apparently not well supported but the standard of the best performances was low.

Note 28 Page 52
Despite its faded condition this is reproduced on page 54 but only F.H. Reed and one or two others can now be identified.

Note 29 Page 52
It seems to have developed spontaneously among members before 1884 and was a sign of the growing corporate enthusiasm. The complete uniform of the present day was officialy proposed by D.T. Mayson, 6th May 1884, at a Special General Meeting: "That the Club uniform be black jersey and knickerbockers with Club badge (two entwined squares) in light blue and white on the left breast and that members be expected to wear it."

Note 30 Page 59
But already in the 1880's the first public convenience in London had been sunk by King Charles's statue in the roadway of Trafalgar Square; thus the notices "Decency Forbids" were to become redundant, while by the early 'Nineties the first electric advertisements winked out their important messages: "Vinolia Soap", "Nestles Milk" and "Sapolio".

Note 31 Page 63
In the thick of the protracted exchange of views between the clubs we find recorded in the minutes a communication from future members of both clubs Mr. A.W. Clay-Thomas of South London Harriers "offering to sing a song or two." The offer was accepted "with many thanks."

Note 32 Page 64
Like Reed, St. John Mathews was a member of Thames Rowing Club. He was also an ardent politician and Tariff Reform campaigner, making fifty-four speeches to crowded audience all over the country in 1910. He was an all-round sportsman — anything from rugby and soccer to otter-hunting and sea-fishing — and a much travelled Fellow of The Royal Geographical Society.

Note 33 Page 66
A founder and first Secretary of Lewisham Swimming Club 1885; won Senior Veterans' Race 1931 and 1932.

Note 34 Page 66
The first winner of a Club Pewter was H.D. Thomas.

Note 35 Page 68
Its addition of "Club Record" was perhaps taken over from early journals but is most likely accounted for by analogy with Blackheath's previous custom of allowing newspaper reports to stand as a record of Club doings.

Note 36 Page 69
The scoring arrangements were laid down by the donor and remained unchanged until after 1926, i.e. the first ten in each club home scored, as they finished, without elimination of non-scoring places betweeen-the method applied in the so-called "varsity system".

Note 37 Page 69
The clock until recently in the dressing room bore this firm's name.

Note 38 Page 73
The 1905 "Blackheath Day" Meeting had an entry of 600.

Note 39 Page 78
The first recorded Open "London to Brighton" Race was in 1886.

Note 40 Page 78
He promoted the first race from London to Brighton in 1902.

Note 41 Page 78
Neville is "Centurion No. 7". Hammond and Harold Rhodes senior were the second and third Blackheath Centurions respectively.

Note 42 Page 82
Strangely enough we know little about this group. The earliest reference to it is in 1886 when Club Minutes were not being kept and the first person we know to have been associated with it was H.J. Barclay. Its chief purpose seems to have been the provision of adjacent training facilities for those north of the river but they had some competitions of their own and the main "Green

Man" contingent paid them "Official" visits. It apparently fell into desuetude in the first years of the new century.

Note 43 Page 86
A.C. Telfer's elder brother Canon W. Telfer was not his equal as a runner but gained distinction in the field of scholarship and in the 1914-18 War. He was Master of Selwyn College, Cambridge, until his retirement in 1956 and Treasurer of Cambridge University Hare and Hounds for over thirty years. He also instituted the Club's match with King's College, Canterbury.

Note 44 Page 88
The so-called "Mob" matches against S.L.H., Ranelagh and Orion are still run under these conditions today.

Note 45 Page 88
There had been one in 1898, with Lea Harriers and United Hospitals Hare and Hounds joining in.

Note 46 Page 107
Their success owed most to W.S.A. Winter and his friends John Scott, Leo W. Harris and J.S. Goodman.

Note 47 Page 107
Blackheath had provided a clear run-in which was not possible at West Wickham. After one or two attempts to find a satisfactory equivalent the practice was abandoned. Crafter walked away from "The Railway Hotel" saying "They are ruining the Club!"

Note 48 Page 117
He also bestrode nocturnal railway engines on the Hayes line as Clay Thomas could bear witness.

Note 49 Page 119
Removed early in 1935.

Note 50 Page 120
A reminder not only that the occupants of the cottage have so often also been stewards to the Club, but that Blackheath has enjoyed great fortune in attracting the services of a succession of the most amiable and competent people in this work.

Note 51 Page 123
One of the Club's most popular members, "with unfailing good humour and cheery nature," was F.L Gilbert, first Secretary of the Wine Committee. This was only one of a wider range of duties he performed, however.

Note 52 Page 126
St. George's Day, 1913 – gave a recital of songs at the Aeolian Hall. St. George's Day 1953 – celebrated 70th birthday and recovery from more than one serious illness by giving two-part recital of forty-two British songs.

Note 53 Page 129
The Ovidian motto of Blackheath was suggested by H.F. Pash in 1929.

Note 54 Page 131
Apart from providing a notable social occasion two of the French runners were good enough to beat Birchfield H. as they had done shortly before. The Club was the best in France, and among them were five international nations. "The Gazette" correspondent was suitably impressed.

Note 55 Page 132
The fastest time for this series of the 1930, was 42.9 secs. in 1937.

Note 56 Page 134
The Military Academy are longstanding rivals in one of our oldest and most enjoyable fixtures at their pleasant track – a fixture fostered by our pre-1914 member and middle distance performer M.C.C. Harrison.

Note 57 Page 142
It was Hitler who nailed down the amateur coffin at international level for he was the first deliberately to exploit sport for political advertisement. The fruits of this are evident today.

Note 58 Page 150
He died the following month.

Note 59 Page 150
For the benefit of our younger readers "points" was the name associated with the system of war-time rationing.

Note 60 Page 152
By 1943 these numbered 283 and by the end of the war just over 330. This includes Home Guard but not A.R.P. and Fire Services which of course were often just as dangerous.

Note 61 Page 152
Exactly the same number as in World War 1.

Note 62 Page 154
A trail-layer's nickname for a gamekeeper's cottage properly known as "The Larches" and never actually a farm.

Note 63 Page 154
The Hayes cross-country course was in the vortex of some of the fiercest air fighting in the 1940 Battle of Britain. Nearby Biggin Hill was a key "Sector" Station in Fighter Command, i.e. An H.Q. from which a group of squadrons from other airfields were called to readiness and directed on to incoming enemy formations. The hill below Layhams Farm towards Furze Bottom and the long valley towards Leaves Green were something like a 1914 battlefield with chain-linked bomb craters at the end of the war.

Note 64 Page 172
And a considerable specialist too, able to beat 50 secs. for 440 yards. He held the Sandhurst 220 yards track record for thirteen years.

Note 65 Page 178
Even today few more than a dozen British high jumpers have bettered 6ft. 6 ins. Hickey performed well at other jumping events as his 43ft. 7ins. Triple Jump performance demonstrates.

Note 66 Page 179
This still figures in the British Best Performances List.

Note 67 Page 179
Inspiration passed on to good effect as the fact of both A.A.A. Pole Vault representatives v. Cambridge University in 1968 being Blackheath men demonstrates. Those were L. Jones and J. Faircloth, the latter achieving 13 ft. in 1968 and winning both Junior and Senior Kent titles on the same day.

Note 68 Page 184
Mekler in turn was followed by another South African member, Jon Lang, a more than useful marathon performer (2 hours 27.08 best) of whom members today still have very pleasant memories.

Note 69 Page 187
1924 - 74th v. Ranelagh H.
1966 - 79th v. Ranelagh H.

Appendix One

**The Origins of Peckham Hare and Hounds with some general
notes on the background and the sources consulted.**

No circumstantial account of the inception of the Peckham Hare and Hounds pack has survived either by way of oral tradition or in any written record which has yet come to light. As mentioned in the main text of the History, the date of the inauguration of the pack in October, 1869, rests upon a bare statement by the late F.H. Reed in a letter to a local paper in May, 1872, and the confirmation provided by the contemporary press notice in "Bell's Life" of the actual event. Nevertheless at the cost of some rather laborious investigation it has been possible to restore a good deal of the background, and, since the details are somewhat involved and raise certain general problems which cannot be solved in the present state of our knowledge, it has seemed advisable to relegate a discussion of these topics to an appendix which can be consulted by those interested without interrupting the more general narrative in the main text.

In order to put the whole matter in perspective it seems advisable to preface a sketch of the state of amateur athletics as these had developed by the late 1860's. It is common ground with most of the readily accessible authorities that the sport had reached quite an advanced stage of development in the course of the sixth decade of the 19th Century; and that a number of important specialised or semi-specialised clubs had been formed. These rather uninformative generalisations, however, conceal some very interesting facts which are probably little known to modern readers, and, although somewhat outside the brief of a Club History, an account of the situation nationally in 1868 and 1869 can perhaps be justified on the grounds of the unfamiliarity of the details alone.

The greatest surprise to a modern reader who has pictured the athletic world of a century ago from the summary statements in various selective essays is likely to be the geographical diffusion of important amateur promotions nationally at that date and the indications here and there of a higher degree of integration in these activities than is provided simply by the promotions of individual clubs. Geographically, the range is almost nation wide, though as might be expected, the chief meetings are found in the main centres of population, in the metropolitan area, the midlands and the industrial north west. But before 1870 major promotions are noted as far apart as Douglas, Isle of Man, Lincolnshire and South Wales. In the London area in 1869, there is competition at Kennington Oval for a county trophy, the Surrey County Cup, and about this time too a regional representative side, the Northern Counties Clubs, visited the metropolis. By way of illustration of the general character of the contemporary programmes, a few of the principal meetings and the clubs from which competitors were drawn may be noted at random.

Taking London first, besides the L.A.C. and A.A.C. meetings which eventually provided the basis of the A.A.A. Championships, Richmond Cricket and Athletic Club promoted a two day meeting in April, 1869, at which it is of more than passing interest to note that a certain W.G. Grace was an entrant in the steeplechase event. Other London Cricket clubs holding major athletic sports at this time were South Norwood Cricket Club and Lewisham Cricket Club both of some years standing by 1869. It is to be regretted that the Lewisham event seems to have provoked a scandal, for it is recorded that a Mr. Simpson of that club subsequently lapsed from virtue – and turned professional. Although it was from the larger rowing and cricket clubs that the growth of the sport in 1860's seems mainly to have derived, they were not alone. Lausanne Football Club, frequently mentioned in the Peckham domestic records, was holding a status athletic meeting in 1869 and the promotion was then evidently well established. Likewise, the German Gymnastic Society promoted a big event at Tufnell Park in that year, as did West London Rowing Club, the Thames Rowing Club,[3] the Red Rovers Football Club and the West Kent Football Club. Competitors from the Flamingoes Football Club are noted not infrequently.

In the provinces, the sports at Douglas, Isle of Man, already alluded to, appear to have been an established attraction by 1868 and 1869. On Merseyside, the Liverpool and Birkenhead Cricket Club (or Clubs) staged a major promotion which drew entries from leading athletes in other parts of the country. In this context a Mr. F.G. Reynolds is spoken of as "a cross-country runner of great local reputation". His specialism seems to have been the steeple chase and this early use of the term cross-country runner invites some intriguing speculations.

Of considerable interest is the reference to Haslingden Athletic Club as a nursery of northern runners of quality at this time. Haslingden lay almost on the fringe of the East Lancashire industrial region within ten miles or so of the Yorkshire border, near a moorland feature known as Rossendale Forest, in surroundings described somewhat lyrically in a Gazetteer of 1842 as "alpine". The town was not a large one and fairly remote from the great urban centres of Liverpool and Manchester on the other side of the Palatine County; it had once been a centre of the domestic woollen manufacture financed and managed by the capitalist middlemen of Rochdale and appears to have become famous as a sporting rendezvous on account of its traditional horse race meeting. Whether the vigour of athletics locally owed anything to the popularity of professional "pedestrianism" in the neighbouring West Riding of Yorkshire is perhaps a question not to be asked.

As samples of contemporary meetings elsewhere, finally, one may mention Stamford Football Club in Lincolnshire and Cadoxton Cricket Club, near Swansea, in South Wales. Both these promotions attracted or produced local runners of high ability. A. Powles, the second Honorary Secretary of Peckham A.A.C. who succeeded F.H. Reed in 1876, gained high reputation as a runner with Monmouth Cricket Club before 1870, came to London and joined South London Harriers in 1872 – and ascending yet higher in grace became a member and official of Peckham A.A.C. as indicated, some years later.

It is surprising also to discover that these early athletic events were promoted at all times of the year. The meetings appear to have originated in two principal ways: as gala social events in summer and as a means of maintaining interest in the winter season for members of cricket and rowing clubs whose principal activities were confined to the summer months. It is clear that such meetings ante-dated the specialized athletic clubs by some years and the London Athletic Club is said to have adopted its definition of the "gentleman amateur" from the rule laid down by the West London Rowing Club which held athletic meetings in the winter of 1861/2 for the purpose indicated above. How far back this particular line of development in amateur athletics can be traced is somewhat speculative but it appears to be the case that the Boltons Cricket Club also held athletic sports at Christmastide 1861 and again in February, 1862 and it is stated that W.M. Chinnery. the outstanding miler of the 1860's, made his debut in senior running at the 1861 meeting of this club. It is possible to construe this reference as implying that the Boltons meeting was already well established by 1861, but the evidence is rather too tenuous to support any positive conclusion about this.[4]

Whatever reputation "cross-country" runners may have gained in the late 1860's as instanced by the reference to the Lancashire runner, Reynolds, it is regrettably the case that the pundit of "Bell's Life" writing in 1873 held the paper chasing routines in no unduly high estimation, for referring to H.S. Larette, one of the outstanding distance men of the day, he remarks that since 1872 this runner had confined himself to hare and hounds competitions[5] and "it is not considered these events are such as to merit recapitulation". He concedes however that Mr. Larette's achievement in covering 29 miles across country in under 4 hours including periods of rest, does at least invite passing notice.

The athletic world into which the small Peckham pack made its modest entry in the autumn of 1869 was thus a mature and strongly established one. If fully specialized athletic clubs were still not numerous there were many powerful organizations, most commonly cricket clubs, which had devised some kind of ad hoc subsidiary body for carrying on regular programmes of athletic sports. The success of the leviathans bred emulation among the minnows and to complete the[6] sketch of the background in the year of our club's inception it has to be borne in mind that below the great world of senior amateur sport was another of small private, sometimes quasi-residential cricket, football and rowing clubs etc., whose existence, usually ephemeral, bore tribute to the success of the more powerful institutions.

If the scant respect for hare and hounds was anything more than the individual prejudice of one of the "Bell's Life" contributors, it is perhaps rather a stroke of luck that a notice of the Peckham pack's inaugural outing ever found its way into public print, the more since the undertaking does not seem to have originated among any senior athletes of the time. On the contrary, examination of the details preserved in the notice, our sole authoritative document for any matters affecting the Club prior to the spring of 1870, suggests that the pack was not at all unlike the various small private clubs of other kinds already mentioned and which appear to have been fairly common in the Peckham and South London area at the time.

As is well known, the notice was not discovered until 1908 or later as the result of correspondence between F.H. Reed and H.W.G. Haslegrave and the consistent tradition of the Club's origin in 1869 appears to have been preserved orally prior to that correspondence. In the circumstances, it is not perhaps surprising that determined sceptics have sometimes cast doubts on the authority of the documentation, and it is therefore with satisfaction that the authors are able to record that the notice has been verified among the files of the British Museum at Colindale in course of preparing this History and the bona fides of our forbear are fully vindicated.[7]

The notice appeared, to repeat unavoidably what has been said elsewhere, in "Bell's Life" on Wednesday, 27th October, 1869 and bears some signs of having been set in type rather hurriedly, presumably from a MS. report supplied by a member of the pack. As less than four days had elapsed between the run itself on the late afternoon of the 23rd and the appearance of the notice on the morning of the 27th and the weekend intervened, this, with a minor item of news submitted on the eve of publication, is not very surprising. The errors are mostly of a trivial kind, the omission of initials before a surname and very probably the incorrect spelling of another; but the most tiresome consequence of casual sub-editing has been that the peculiar arrangement of the names of the participants was disguised and a fruitful line of investigation remained for long unexplored. It is obvious at first glance that some alphabetical arrangement of names has been in the mind of the author of the notice; but it is not at all obvious that the arrangement is in fact very systematic indeed, and in the circumstances one need not wonder that those who examined the notice sixty years ago remained content with establishing confirmation of the traditional date of October, 1869.

It was in course of the preliminary work on the present History some years back that the so-called "double-listing" of the names first came to notice and that comparison with the MS. journals of the Club's activities from 1870 onwards disclosed that the 1869 press notice was drafted on the same principle as that which became common form in the domestic journals for a number of years.

The principle was not of course radically different from notices prepared for other clubs at that early time save in one significant respect. After considerable search not one instance has yet been found of any other club using the strictly alphabetical sequence in listing the names of members of the pack present on the·day which was consistently followed by· the Peckham scribe. [8] It is not therefore a common form imposed by press conventions but a strictly domestic idiosyncrasy.

The "Bell's Life" notice of October 1869 records that the "following gentlemen were present : C. Black, Cornell, A. Johnson, W.H. Williamson, S. Collins, A.H. Darnell (Trafalgar C.C.), J. Dryden (Hope R.C.), J.H. Easthie (Argyle C.C.), W.H. Hawke (German G.S.,), W. Henman (Croydon A.C.), F.H. Reed (Thames R.C.)" — and one may as well add here that it is further stated that Black and Easthie were the hares. The first four names are in alphabetical order; and so are the last seven: but the printers' space-saving device of running the names straight on without any direct indication of the presence of two groups or categories produces an impression of confusion where in fact there is order in a high degree. Tabulated the list breaks down:-

List A.   C. Black, Cornell, A. Johnson, W.H. Williamson

List B.   S. Collins, A.H. Darnell (Trafalgar C.C.), J. Dryden (Hope R.C.),
                J.H. Easthie, (Argyle C.C.), W.J. Hawke (German Gymnastic Society),
                W. Henman (Croydon A.C.), F.H. Reed (Thames R.C.)

The basis of discrimination is then evident. The names in priority List A have no other club indicated after them. Those in List B do have this qualification in each case, for Collins is only apparently an exception. Reference to the 1870 MS. Journals will satisfy the extreme sceptic that where names in sequence all refer to the same parent club, the club appears in parenthesis only after the last name in the series. And this indeed is the case with notices of other clubs of the time, abating the peculiarity of the alphabetical sequence which is Peckham's alone. It may be pointed out here too that while List A. affords no scope for refinement, in List B. where there are two names beginning with the same letter the ordinary index method is applied, "Da" Darnell precedes "Dr" Dryden, and "Ha" Hawke precedes "He" Henman: and this meticulous order of presentation is also followed in the MS journals from 1870 onwards. [9]

The problem is to discern on what principle the discrimination between List A and B really rested. At a later time there would be no doubt: the priority list is always of club members, other categories corresponding to List B. (visitors, guests introduced and so on) being regularly distinguished by the name of the club or other institution to which those named belonged and presumably recorded as evidence of their credentials as gentlemen amateurs. In the context of an inaugural run, one can hardly assume that the distinctions of a later time applied in quite the same sense; and it may as well be admitted here and now that while one may attempt a credible guess at the basis of discrimination in October, 1869, the evidence is not firm enough to establish a positive conclusion. At any rate, a useful lead for further study was disclosed and the next step was obviously to try to discover anything possible about the individuals named and, where List B was concerned, the clubs with which they were associated before joining Peckham pack on its formation.

It would be tedious to detail all the processes of a search involving consultation of contemporary directories and a very useful sketch map of round about 1865 preserved at the Dulwich Library though for those engaged these had all the fascination of a piece of detective work. In fact, it was chance rather than systematic study which disclosed the next lead of importance. W. Henman, No. 6 in List B., is easily picked out as the only one of the whole eleven with an unequivocal geographical affiliation and it was natural to attempt to discover if anything were known of the Croydon Athletic Club to which he belonged in 1869. Examination of a local directory of that year failed to disclose anything of the club (by analogy it is pretty obviously a derivative of the local cricket club on the lines already discussed) but it did produce the information that in 1869 a Mr. Charles Henman, F.R.I.B.A., Chartered Architect and Surveyor, was living at No. 7 Bedford Villas, East Croydon, the only one of the name in Croydon and, it may be added, the only one of the name in the contemporary London Postal Directory as well. And Mr. Charles Henman was an ornament of the profession which F.H. Reed afterwards followed and to which he may even then have been an articled pupil.

The results of subsequent search are given in the text but may as well be repeated here. F.H. Reed's address as Honorary Secretary of Peckham A.A.C. was preserved in the early MS records as 110 Grange Road, S.E., and although there were two Grange Roads in the S.E. postal district, Fred's habitat was eventually established as in Bermondsey. The Post Office Directory for 1869 disclosed the following details: 86 Grange Road, John Eastty; 110 Grange Road, Hayter Thornton Reed; 113 Grange Road, Alfred Bevington; 124 Grange Road, Procktor and Bevington, Glue makers and in Upper Grange Road, turning out of Grange Road proper: 65 Upper Grange Road, William Darnell Junior; 89 Upper Grange Road, Hayter Reed. So much for the residential or "Court" category as H.M. Post Office somewhat grandiloquently defined private householders as distinct from business firms and shops etc.

The business sections of the directory were equally informative. The firm of Hayter Thornton Reed and Sons, Corn and Coal Merchants, did business in Mill Street, Dock Head, Bermondsey, at Bermondsey Wall, and the New Corn Exchange, Mark Lane, E.C. John Eastty was a member of the firm of Edwards, Eastty and Company, Merchants on the Baltic Exchange; and in Bermondsey Wall again was the establishment of William Darnell and Son, Granary Keepers. Although not included in the eleven present on the 23rd October, 1869, Bevington is of course the name of the first President of Peckham A.A.C. appointed in 1871. Eastty presented something of a problem since the name is spelt "Easthie" twice over in the press notice. But both spellings are highly unusual and the chances of two corruptions of a name unusual in itself co-existing in the same restricted area of South London seem to be very remote indeed. And a member of the Eastty family, F.H. Eastty, was certainly interested in running for he appears as a competitor at the Peckham (Social) Club Sports in June, 1872. He then appeared as a member of INO Rowing Club.

List B. began to emerge in outline as a coherent social group nearly connected by residence and business interests. Subsequently, it was found that S. Collins, No. 1 in List B., lived at Fort House, Grange Road, Bermondsey.[12]

Of the clubs named, apart from the well known ones, Thames Rowing Club and German Gymnastic Society, Hope Rowing Club, to which Dryden belonged, was discovered by the Honorary Secretary of the Amateur Rowing Association, Mr. J.H. Page whose patience and courtesy we gratefully acknowledge, to have been a small private club situated in Rotherhithe; and Trafalgar Cricket Club was clearly identifiable with a residential area astride the Surrey Canal between the Kent Road and North Peckham or Peckham Park as it then was and which still retains vestiges of its original character as a level area of meadow land drained by willow lined ditches and dykes. In each case within an easy walk of Grange Road.[13]

Argyle Cricket Club, it is regretted to report, seems to have disappeared without trace of its locale into mists as opaque as those which veil the peaks of its Dalriadic godparent.

Finally, the addresses of the remaining two members in List B were provisionally established. In 1865 a J. Dryden was living at 2 Hebron Terrace, Grove Lane, Camberwell, and in 1869 a J. Hawke at 3 Brockley Villas, New Cross. Both are peripheral to the Grange Road nucleus, but within orbit, and both are the only representatives of their respective names (neither very common in the London Directories as a whole) recorded in the South London area.

The focal centre of List B pretty evidently was provided by F.H. Reed and his family associations, and it is rather difficult to accept that he appeared at the inaugural run simply as an individual "invited" or as a "visitor". Rather it seems List B was an organized contribution to the enterprise.

It was natural to hope that some equally useful information about list A would be forthcoming but this has not so far been the case. Late in the 1870's a G. Black, living in Grange Road, joined the Club and it may be he was a relative of the C. Black present in 1869; but no family of the name is recorded in the 1869 Directory. Cornell, regrettably,[14] disappears into limbo with not even his initials bequeathed to posterity. A.[15] Johnson rejoined the club in 1870 and his address was then that of a business firm in Southwark Street. It is rather to be feared he may also be the same A. Johnson who was summarily ejected from the Peckham (Social) Club Sports in June, 1872, because he had in the meantime accepted a professional engagement with the Surrey County Cricket Club. Like the deplorable Mr. Simpson of Lewisham C.C. already stigmatised he may not have been proof against the fleshpots of Egypt in the hour of temptation and so ceased among gentlemen amateurs of the true grain.

The remaining member of the four in List A., W.H. Williamson, is of far greater importance and the failure to trace anything definitive about him is most unfortunate. W.H. Williamson or W.H. Williamson, Junior, as he usually signed himself was the first Captain and Chairman of Peckham A.A.C. from April 1870 to midsummer 1871, and it is evident both from the position of leadership he assumed then and the fact that he is a member of the priority List A. in 1869 that he was a key member and very possibly the key member in organizing the whole undertaking. It seems most probable both from the seniority of his position at the time and his early resignation which may credibly be ascribed to marriage in 1871, that he may well have been somewhat older than the members in List B. Reed was only just 20 years of age in 1869 and a novice in the senior sporting world as will appear later and Williamson's signature on the minutes is that of a mature and assured personality. [16] All that can be said of him at present is that he appears to have been at one time interested in gymnastics in some way and that in 1882 a William Henry Williamson, the only one of the name with the right initials, was living at "Celia Cottage", Queen's Road, Peckham.

The general impression given by List A. however is of some precedence in hare and hounds expertise. Black was one of the hares, a specially responsible position. Johnson, the fastest runner in the pack on the day and Williamson's general pre-eminence has been indicated. Given the priority of the group evidenced by their being in List A. at all it is natural to assume that their status referred to participation in the "unofficial" run which Reed mentions in his letter to Haslegrave in 1908 as having taken place in the first week in October, 1868. Reed, it will be recalled, does not appear to write of this from first hand recollection, though he speaks of the run itself as a known thing. The possibility of such an unofficial run at that date conflicts with received opinion and this will be discussed later. It is difficult, however, to find a more credible explanation of the presence of this priority group in October 1869.

To return to firmer ground, the future lay with List B. and F.H. Reed in particular and some biographical details of one who is always spoken of as the Founder of the Club will be helpful to an understanding of these early problems.

Frederick Henry Reed was born on the 24th September, 1849, the third and youngest son of Hayter Thornton Reed and Ann (nee Wanostrocht), his wife. The parents were then living at No. 8 Grove, Blackheath and the birth is registered in the parish of Greenwich. It is of considerable interest to note that No. 8 Grove may have stood and perhaps stands, within 100 yards of the portals of the "Green Man" Hotel, just across the green facing our eventual headquarters, and it may very well be that Reed passed his boyhood in that vicinity. [17]

Hayter Thornton Reed was well forward in middle life when his youngest son was born. At his death in the spring of 1881 his age is given as 81, [18] so that he must have been born himself in about the year 1800 and would be upwards of fifty in autumn 1849. The character of the father suggests a strong personality and one of which we would gladly know more, especially since it is recorded that he always manifested a keen interest in the Club which provided his son's life interest; but he does not seem to have been the sort of man to seek public notice, and no informative obituary can be traced. Nevertheless he was a business man of substance and authority and in 1853 became Master of the Worshipful Company of Saddlers, and so of course a leading figure in the City of London. Both genealogically and in the by-ways of economic history he challenges interest beyond the scope of the historian of athletics. With two given names, both manifestly family surnames, there is a hint of a family history of considerable interest. The combination of the corn and coal trade is also intriguing for such as are attracted by economic trivia. Pretty surely the coal business was associated with the dying coastal trade between Whitby and Tyneside and the Port of London which was being superseded by rail carriage in H.T. Reed's lifetime, and he may have developed the grain importing business as a substitute for the original family concern.

It is not known at what date Hayter Thornton Reed decided to remove from the salubrious uplands of Blackheath to the far less attractive environment of the residential fringe of Bermondsey but it must have been for business reasons. Why with two elder sons in the business and in partnership with himself he should have thought this necessary is a matter for speculation. Possibly the business itself had moved or been reorganised and anyway he was a masterful man who liked to have his eye on things. But from this decision however arrived at it can be said that it came about that the Blackheath Harriers as we know it originated in the No Man's Land between industrial Bermondsey and residential Peckham and not, as might just possibly have occurred had the Reeds continued at Blackheath, in its eventual home.

The Reed family evidently had sporting inclinations and on 23rd February, 1869, Fred Reed was proposed for membership of the Thames Rowing Club by his elder brother H.M. Reed and seconded by E.H. Scovell, a prominent member and at one time Honorary Secretary of that club. H.M. Reed, of whom little more is known, was a regular member of the Thames Henley crews[19] and evidently a good deal older than his younger brother who was only just over 19 years of age in February, 1869. This seems to have been Fred's initiation into senior amateur sport (he was elected in the March but in the event does not seem to have shown much interest in rowing), and all things considered this seems to militate against the possibility of his having taken the lead in forming the Peckham pack though he may well have recruited a group of friends of his own age to support the venture. Nor does it seem likely he took any part in the "unofficial" run of 1868.

Whether we should see in the elder brother H.M. Reed the essential link between the group of older local men in List A. on the one hand and the interests of the greater world of amateur sport on the other is a fascinating speculation which must be left to later research or researchers. So far as the Peckham enterprise went F.H. Reed became its life and soul from 1871 onwards at least, though family support and social connexions were probably of much greater importance than can now be appreciated.

To conclude, a few remarks on some of the general problems[20] suggested by the foregoing details may be offered.

If the account given by Reed to Haslegrave in 1908 is correct it is not at all easy to fit the emergence of the Peckham pack into the accepted background, which in effect confines formalised hare and hounds to a limited number of public schools with perhaps some occasional imitators in the provinces, and holds that with the exception of one school, Blackheath Proprietary School, there was little of this pastime in the London area prior to the inception of Thames Hare and Hounds in October, 1868.

It is long enough from October, 1868 to October 1869 for the last-named initiative to have diffused itself to sportsmen in South London, but if Reed's account is true in its essentials, there was not enough time for such a process of imitation to develop in the same autumn of 1868 when the "unofficial" run which anticipated the formation of Peckham

Hare and Hounds is said to have been held. And on any terms it is surprising to find an obscure group of junior sportsmen mainly from clubs of a very minor order as the first to respond to the influence of events at Roehampton.

Reed's statement is of course uncorroborated[21] and it is most unlikely that now it can be; and he himself speaks of the unofficial run without the air of recalling the event at first hand — rather curiously he is positive on the week and the month ("the first week in October") but can only be hesitant about the year ("I believe, in 1868"). One need not labour this point: if he was right about the month, 1868 is the latest possible date and any earlier one only makes the problem more difficult. The simplest way of disposing of it is to assume that, writing forty years after the event, his memory had played him false. This is not the place for a dissertation in the psychology of recall and in fact Reed did in this correspondence confess to a failing memory and did also fall into some demonstrable errors in detail. The significant thing about the errors, however, is that these are not citations of things which never happened or existed but transposition or lapse of details accurate in themselves in relation to matters of proven authenticity — the secondary and unfamiliar title of a publication is recalled for instance but not the main one and a date with the day of the month is accurately quoted but assigned to the wrong year, or seems to be so for the wording is rather loose. These are usual phenomena associated with recall and the case against an unofficial run cannot be made out on grounds of defect of memory alone. That is as far as one can fairly go, bearing in mind once again that it is only by assuming some sort of preliminary experimental association that the double listing of the members present at the inaugural run in October, 1869 can be really convincingly explained.

A further point ought to be made here for it is a measure of belated[22] justice to Reed himself. It has been widely believed in our own Club that in the teeth of the evidence he spent his life maintaining a seniority for the Peckham venture to which it was not entitled. The authors have to report that not merely have they been unable to find any evidence at all so far of his having advanced such pretensions but on the only known occasion where he is on record on the subject he said directly the opposite. Speaking at the Annual Dinner of the Club in 1882 Reed stated publicly and was so reported in the press that the Blackheath Harriers was the second oldest cross-country club in the country, only Thames Hare and Hounds being older by exactly one year. If he subsequently retracted what is now known to be the exact truth the evidence of it has not yet come to light. The misapprehension seems to have originated in hasty inferences drawn by Club officials sixty years ago as to the import of the unofficial run in 1868. It is quite true that the date or origin of the Club in 1869 has been criticised but this was on rather recondite grounds relating to the constitutional changes made in its organisation and administration in 1870 and 1872. The precise distinction between a hare and hounds pack and a fully formed club of the normal kind as such things existed a hundred years ago is not quite certain. Several of the early packs called themselves clubs but in certain details of finance (if the rudimentary arrangements in force then can be dignified by the name) and of the conditions of membership they seem to have differed a little from fully established clubs of the accepted sort. But the existence or otherwise of a continuing entity at Peckham from 1869 onward does not seem to have been the real issue in the controversy.

If a prima facie case for the spontaneous creation of a hare and hounds pack in

South London in a period roughly between 1868 and 1869 is admitted there is some difficulty in accepting the view that hare and hounds, at any rate as a casual and intermittent activity of London sportsmen, was a rarity at the time. It may as well be said at once that so far no evidence of any connexion between our founding members and the Blackheath Proprietary School has been discovered, despite the fact that Reed himself was born at Blackheath. South Bermondsey itself seems hardly the most likely place on any terms to inspire such a venture in the absence of fairly general practice elsewhere in the London area; nor is a small private club the most likely vehicle for a pioneering effort of the kind.

One can of course exaggerate the unsuitability of the environment. The very mention of Bermondsey conjures up visions of dockland, crowded alleyways, evil smelling tanyards fell-mongers' warehouses, and slum dwellings. It was not as bad as all that and forty years earlier the areas beyond the waterfront and the industrial concentration immediately backing on to it were quite open, and residential amenities could be found only a stone's throw from some of the worst evils of haphazard commercial development. The monks no doubt had found the Bermondsey basin a lonely enough place, a water[23]-logged level between the river and the Norwood Hills, congenial to their calling to settle in desert places and labour while they prayed. An embankment, first erected it seems by the Romans, protected the flats from periodic inundations of the Thames; the monks and other improvers after them set about draining the marsh which by the beginning of the 19th Century was a region of level meadows, market gardens and residences of landed proprietors attracted by open country in the vicinity of the capital city or associated with the many victualling depots. Willow lined ditches and drainage cuts, still remembered in local place names, abounded bordered by field paths now converted to passages and entries. The rural genius was still not quite dead round Grange Road a hundred years ago — if the Reeds had Messrs. Prockter and Bevington's glue factory as a neighbour (an enterprise less sweet of savour than new mown hay perhaps) and the river breeze carried the unspeakable stench of the tanneries to their doors, still in Grange Road was yet the Grange reminiscent of the monastery and, if the directory[24] is to be believed, the establishment of a cowkeeper. Kent Road beyond the "Bricklayers Arms" railway depot seems still to have been open and residential and beyond the Surrey Canal aristocratic Peckham Park yielding before the implacable onslaught of the much abused armies of clerkly commuters still provided a link with rural Peckham, the Rye and Dulwich Common and the wholesome hills of wide aspect over the Ravensbourne basin: A Cockney's traditional playground but still recognisable country and only half an hour's walk or less from Grange Road. Sporting facilities seem to have been reasonably ample but in none of this was the district in any way distinguished from a score of others on the semi-rural outskirts of the metropolis, and of insistent reminders of the life of the fields and field sports there cannot have been many. A hunting pink would not often brighten the banks of the Surrey Canal and not by the back gardens of Grange Road did "The huntsman loosen on the moon ' a gay and wandering cry.' " If challenge and response are the prerequisites of a new departure in activity of this kind Bermondsey and Peckham had nothing special to offer — rather one would think the reverse.

But was hare and hounds quite the rarity that has been implied? If we venture to express doubts our authority is no less than the novelist, Charles Dickens, who, of all people has an explicit reference to hare and hounds by that name in the seventeenth chapter of

"David Copperfield", where he writes: . . . . these Wednesdays were the happiest days of Mr. Dick's life . . . How often at hare and hounds have I seen him mounted on a little knoll cheering the whole field into action . . . " "Copperfield" was published in 1850 and as is well known it is very largely autobiographical in its general character. Dickens in translating his personal memories into creative fiction would necessarily preserve a considérable element of direct recall in detail and the image cited here has specific qualities implying direct reminiscence. No man who has ever lived was less interested in sporting specialisms than Charles Dickens and it may be taken as fairly certain that he is here reporting a matter of general observation arising out of the recreational routines of his day. The period of the novel is not perhaps very clear for imaginative literature is not documented history. It is certainly "pre-railway" and assuming as is most probable that Dickens was recalling a boyhood memory the date could be anywhere between, say 1820 and 1830. It is clearly the fully developed sport[25] which is described, the correct terms are used, and the reference is not to a public school like Rugby but to Dr. Strong's private academy for young gentlemen in the good city of Canterbury. It is true Canterbury is not London but it is only fifty miles or so away and there seems to be no very obvious reason why the many academies similar in character to Dr. Strong's to be found on the outskirts of London should have followed a different routine in their pastimes. If then hare and hounds was a regular pastime of schools in the first half of the 19th Century one may wonder if it was quite such a novelty to the London sportsmen of the 1860's as has been alleged. At least, the point merits a little examination and it may be the "unofficial" runners of 1868 were not quite so unique as might appear.

Note 1 Page 229

The most easily accessible source of information in these matters is a series of articles published in Bell's Life in 1873 reviewing the athletic careers of a number of the leading amateur runners who were prominent in 1872. The authors were enabled by the courtesy of the A.A.A. to consult a book of cuttings in which these articles are preserved. The files of "Bell's Life" at the British Museum can of course also be consulted.

Note 2 Page 229

Big enough to warrant press Notice at least.

Note 3 Page 230

Most of the events both in London and elsewhere are specifically referred to 1869 in our authority. Sometimes 1868 or earlier is indicated but it would be rather tiresome to be precise in each case, even if time and opportunity had been afforded to make the necessary notes. 1869 is the norm of reference in nearly all cases.

Note 4 Page 231

Of another runner born in 1851 it is stated that his abilities might be inherited since his father had been a sprinter of exceptional powers. The paternal prowess can hardly have been demonstrated in a competitive vacuum and presumably his active career must go back before 1850. There seems to be scope for some research in these matters.

Note 5 Page 231

Larette came from Lincolnshire but appears to have established his reputation as a distance runner during his period of residence in South Wales. Later he came to London and fame as a member of South London Harriers and Spartan Harriers. In passing, it may be added that G.A.F. Syers, another outstanding distance runner attracted to S.L.H. in that club's formative stage and who became the first captain of the club, had been a member of South Norwood Athletic Club. Later on he became a member of Thames Hare and Hounds also.

Note 6 Page 231

The conjoint "cricket and athletic" club is by no means unknown even today as any examination of programmes attracting large entries nationally or regionally will attest. Rather confusingly many of the early ad hoc organisations are referred to simply as athletic clubs though their dependence on a parent body such as a cricket club is usually evident enough.

Note 7 Page 231

Haslegrave had originally copied the notice quite accurately, but in course of periodic reproductions some minor errors in the spelling of names had crept in. These have now been corrected in the present work. The original is of course available for public inspection at Colindale.

Note 8 Page 232

Latterly the hares were not usually included in the alphabetical sequence but only the members of the pack by categories as members, visitors and guest by invitation. In the 1869 press notice the hares too are taken into the alphabetical scheme.

Note 9 Page 232

There is an instance in the latter of an interlineation out of sequence but this was clearly an afterthought. The main list had been drafted on the usual principle.

Note 10 Page 233

Upper Grange Road has now been obliterated by redevelopment, but Grange Road remains a main thoroughfare.

Note 11 Page 234

Easthie cannot be found anywhere in dictionaries of surnames, or directories, nor can the most probable geographical original as Easy Hay or East Hey be identified in the Gazetteers consulted. Only one dictionary of surnames available out of half a dozen examined quotes the name at all with variant spellings as Easty, Eastey and Eastty, all taken from the London Postal directory. The authority suggests, not very confidently, that the village of Eastry near Sandwich in Kent is the original of the name. Another member of the Bermondsey family, Stephen Eastty, J.P. was living at Wellesley House, Croydon in 1869, not very far from Charles Henman, as it happens.

Note 12 Page 234

The identity of Fort House is preserved today by a public house on the east side of Grange Road.

Note 13 Page 234

The association with Nelson apparently originated with the naming of an inn or alehouse in the Kent Road which stood at the head of a field path leading to a crossing of the canal as an early map clearly shows.

Note 14 Page 234

The Directories did not necessarily account for all residents at that time however and the alphabetical lists are certainly not comprehensive.

Note 15 Page 234

It is a City surname according to some authorities, a corruption of Cornhill.

Note 16 Page 235

It was after Williamson's retirement that the Club invited Captain S.L. Bevington, a non-playing member of senior status to become the first president. Captain Bevington it should be added was of another branch of the prominent Bermondsey family from the A Bevington who lived near the Reeds. He was the son and successor of the owner of a firm of organ builders in Soho, which incidentally provided several of the church organs in Peckham. He died with the rank of Lieutenant Colonel in the West country early in the present century.

Note 17 Page 235
"Grove" as such has disappeared but a surviving wing of it (or so it is assumed) now known as Westgrove is immediately opposite the "Green Man". The orientation as "West" seems to be fully justified by the situation.

Note 18 Page 235
The Saddlers' Company to whom we are indebted for some of this information have his first name Hayter in its original and incorrupt form of Haytor on their records, i.e. as the name of a topographic identity in central Devonshire. As H.T. Reed also gave the name to one of his sons, probably the eldest, it had evidently considerable family significance. Thornton is probably North Country and Yorkshire at that.

Note 19 Page 236
For these details we are greatly indebted to the researches of Mr. Jackson of Thames Rowing Club who very kindly examined the minutes of that club at our request.

Note 20 Page 236
On a flying visit to the Bermondsey area in the present autumn, one of the authors noted the name of J.C. Oastler, the Club's second President, on a plaque or foundation stone inset in one of the Bevington family's business premises, thus confirming the close knit character of the social grouping from which the early Club derived its sustaining force.

Note 21 Page 237
Oral tradition especially in the negative sense is not a very reliable guide, but it is certainly the case that from first to last there seems never to have been any suggestion that the institution of the Peckham pack owed anything to emulation. Walter Rye himself does not appear to have suggested as much and there are grounds for thinking he was unaware of the rival pack's existence earlier than the winter of 1870/1 when the Peckham runs began to receive regular notice in the sporting press.

Note 22 Page 237
The nature of the unofficial run is not of course known but it can hardly have been other than some form of paperchase.

Note 23 Page 238
Even today there is a surprising amount of open ground in the Grange Road area little more than a quarter of an hour's walk from the foot of London Bridge. Many of the mid-Victorian villas now sadly tarnished remain in Grange Road itself.

Note 24 Page 238
Presumably the 18th Century buildings mentioned in various authorities. Grange Road itself is part of the Abbey precinct. If the date on some buildings not far from the Reed's home corresponds to the date of its establishment on that site, it is of passing interest that the depot of the Alaska Trading Company was established in Grange Road in 1869. The U.S.A. had purchased Alaska from Russia only two years previously.

Note 25 Page 239
According to some authorities the primitive form of hare and hounds was a game called "hunt the fox" which is said to be mentioned round about 1800. It could be much older if the authors' guess that this game or something like it is alluded to at the end of "Hamlet" Act IV Scene 2 is right. But excursions into such byways of Shakespeare scholarship are decidedly beyond the competence of mere historians of athletics.

Additional Note

Further information of great interest relating to F.H. Reed's family has been discovered while the History was in the press. The wharfing business on the Surrey shore of London River existed as early as 1817 and may be considerably older; it still exists as Reeds' Wharf Ltd. in its original situation in Dock Head, Bermondsey. The family connexion with the Saddlers' Company is also very long standing and of its kind must be almost unique, Reed's grandfather, Hayter Reed was Master in 1814 and 1828; his father, Hayter Thornton Reed in 1853 and 1865; and his elder brother, Hayter Marsh Reed, who introduced him to Thames Rowing Club, in 1882 and 1905. In 1817 Hayter Reed was in partnership with his father as Reed & Son and it is quite possible the father was the John Reed who was Master of the Livery in 1792 and 1811. Of later generations Mr. Hayter Langton Reed was Master in 1925 and Leonard Lewis Reed in 1929. A descendant, Mr. John Hayter Reed, C.B.E. still represents the family it is believed.

The Hayter family connection which was evidently of great traditional significance seems to have been well represented in the City at the beginning of the last century. Thomas Hayter was the deputy and eventual successor of Samuel Pepys, the diarist, at the Navy Office and a Thomas Hayter, a goldsmith, was in business near Wood Street in the City circa 1800. The connection with the Reeds is not established by the authors but it is certainly not without interest as a possibility.

Even more interesting, especially in a sporting context, is the maternal background. Anne Wanostrocht was a first cousin of Nicholas Felix Wanostrocht, the cricketer, who represented the Gentlemen v. Players on a number of occasions in the period 1830-1850 and has been described as the first of the great left handers. The family, of Flemish origin, settled in England in the 1780's when Nicholas Wanostrocht was appointed French tutor to the Earl of Bathurst. Later he established a school near Camberwell Green known as Alfred House School in association with a nephew, Vincent Wanostrocht. Nicholas Felix, the son of Vincent carried on the school which afterwards moved to Blackheath. He was a man of colourful personality, a gifted artist and a good classical scholar and the author of an early cricket classic, "Felix on the Bat". He played in first class cricket under the pseudonym of "Nicholas Felix".

The local standing of Reed's family and the background of sporting interests must have a bearing on the Club's earliest history which has been lost to view in the passage of years and perhaps partly on account of the sudden infusion of new blood early in the 1880's.

APPENDIX TWO

BLACKHEATH HARRIERS LIST OF OFFICERS –
1869 – 1969

Year	President	Hon. Secretary	Ass. Hon. Sec.	Hon. Treasurer	Captain	Handicapper	Editor
1869-1870		F.H. Reed			W.H. Williamson		
1870-1871	S.B. Bevington	F.H. Reed			W.H. Williamson	F.H. Reed	
1871-1872	S.B. Bevington	F.H. Reed			A.H. Peniston	E.E. Smith	
1872-1873	S.B. Bevington	F.H. Reed			A.H. Peniston	F.T. Pridmore	
1873-1874	S.B. Bevington	F.H. Reed			A.H. Peniston	F.T. Pridmore	
1874-1875	J. Oastler	F.H. Reed			A.H. Peniston	F.T. Pridmore	
1875-1876	J. Oastler	F.T. Pridmore				F.H.Reed	
1876-1877	J. Oastler	F.T. Pridmore W.H. Brooker				W. Rowland	
1877-1878	J. Oastler	W.H. Brooker Committee (Pro tem)				W. Rowland	
1878-1879	J. Oastler	A. Powles				H.D. Thomas	
1879-1880	J. Oastler	D.T. Mayson				H.D. Thomas	
1880-1881	J. Oastler	D.T. Mayson				H.D. Thomas	
1881-1882	J. Oastler	D.T. Mayson	C. Cattlin			H.D. Thomas	
1882-1883	F.H. Reed	J.C. Milligan	J. Vickers-Smith				
1883-1884	F.H. Reed	J.C. Milligan					
1884-1885	F.H. Reed	J.H. Birkett	H.R. Ball T. Crafter	J.H.A. Reay			
1885-1886	F.H. Reed	J.H. Birkett	T. Crafter C.A. Morgan	F.H. Reed			
1886-1887	F.H. Reed	T. Crafter H.J. Barclay	C.A. Morgan H.G. Jackson	F.H. Reed			
1887-1888	F.H. Reed	H.J. Barclay	C.A. Morgan H.G. Jackson	F.H. Reed			
1888-1889	F.H. Reed	J.J.C. Esson	J.F. Ponsford A.G. Holmes	F.H. Reed		T. Crafter T.M. Gale	
1889-1890	F.H. Reed	J.J.C. Esson	J.F. Ponsford A.G. Holmes	F.H. Reed		T. Crafter T.M. Gale	
1890-1891	F.H. Reed	J.F. Ponsford	J.J.C. Esson C.T. Morris	F.H. Reed			
1891-1892	F.H. Reed	J.F. Ponsford	C.T. Morris W.F. Esse	F.H. Reed		T.M. Gale	
1892-1893	F.H. Reed	J.F. Ponsford	C.T. Morris W.F. Esse	F.H. Reed		T.M. Gale	
1893-1894	F.H. Reed	J.F. Ponsford	W.F. Esse H.E. King	F.H. Reed		T.M. Gale	
1894-1895	F.H. Reed	J.F. Ponsford A. Cook (Pro tem)	H.E. King A.V. Morris	F.H. Reed		T.H. Warland	
1895-1896	F.H. Reed	A.V. Morris	H.W.E. Sercombe W.H. Lilly	F.H. Reed		A. Cook	
1896-1897	F.H. Reed	A.V. Morris	H.W.E. Sercombe E.W. Edwards	F.H. Reed		T.H. Warland	
1897-1898	F.H. Reed	E.F. Nicholls	H.R. Hopper G.E. West	F.H. Reed		H.W.E. Sercombe	
1898-1899	F.H. Reed	E.F. Nicholls	H.R. Hopper G.E. West E.J.D. Ratcliff	F.H. Reed	G. Hoare	H.W.E. Sercombe	H.R. Hopper
1899-1900	F.H. Reed	E.F. Nicholls	G.E. West E.J.D. Ratcliff	F.H. Reed	G. Hoare	H.W.E. Sercombe	H.R. Hopper

Year							
1901-1902	F.H. Reed	E.J.D. Ratcliff	W.G. Suffield H. Bull	F.H. Reed	E.J.D. Ratcliff	H.W.E. Sercombe	H.R. Hopper
1902-1903	F.H. Reed	H.W.G. Haslegrave	A. Metcalf G.H. Bull	F.H. Reed	T.C. Davis	H.W.E. Sercombe	H.F. Pash
1903-1904	F.H. Reed	H.W.G. Haslegrave	A. Metcalf G.H. Bull	E.F. Nicholls	T.C. Davis	H.W.E. Sercombe	T. Crafter
1904-1905	F.H. Reed	H.W.G. Haslegrave	A. Metcalf G.H. Bull	E.F. Nicholls	G.L. Hopkins	H.W.E. Sercombe	T. Crafter
1905-1906	C. Val Hunter	H.W.G. Haslegrave	G.H. Bull H.G. Johnson	A. Metcalf	H.W.E. Sercombe	H.W.E. Sercombe	M. Cavanaugh
1906-1907	H.J. Barclay	H.W.G. Haslegrave	T. Morgan E.H.C. Hitchings	A. Metcalf	M.P.S. White	M.P.S. White H.F. Pash	T. Morgan
1907-1908	J.H.A. Reay	H.W.G. Haslegrave	W.A. Dewsnap J.C. Johnson	A. Metcalf T. Morgan (Asst.)	E.R. Small J. Loveys, Jun (Vice)	E.R. Small H.F. Pash	H.F. Pash W.L. Allden (Sub)
1908-1909	W. Rowland	H.W.G. Haslegrave	J.C. Johnson W.D. Lancefield	A. Metcalf T. Morgan (Asst.)	C.A. Glaeser C.W. Starnes (Vice)	E.R. Small H.F. Pash	C.A. Glaeser A.H.L Knapp (Sub)
1909-1910	R. St. J. Matthews	H.W.G. Haslegrave	J.C. Johnson W.D. Lancefield	C.A. Morgan F.L. Gilbert (Asst.)	C.A. Glaeser R.W. Davis (Vice) S.J. Marshall	E.R. Small H.F. Pash	H.R. Hopper
1910-1911	R. St. J. Matthews	E.J.D. Ratcliff	J.C. Johnson W.D. Lancefield	C.A. Morgan	R.W. Davis C.A. Glaeser (Vice) S.J. Marshall	E.R. Small	H.C. Cooper
1911-1912	C.G. Wood	E.J.D. Ratcliff	J.C. Johnson F.L. Gilbert	C.A. Morgan	R.W. Davis L. Latreillex (Vice) W.D. Lancefield	E.R. Small	H.C. Cooper
1912-1913	E.F. Nicholls	E.J.D. Ratcliff	J.C. Johnson F.L. Gilbert	C.A. Morgan	R.W. Davis C.H. Baxter (Vice) F.T. Browne	E.R. Small	E.J. Denney
1913-1914	E.F. Nicholls	E.J.D. Ratcliff	J.C. Johnson F.L. Gilbert	R.W. Davis	C.H. Baxter H.C. Cooper (Vice) F.T. Browne	C.A. Glaeser E.R. Small	E.J. Denney
1914-1915	T. Crafter	E.J.D. Ratcliff	J.C. Johnson I.W. Nicholson	R.W. Davis	H.C. Cooper A.D. Morton (Vice)	C.A. Glaeser E.R. Small	E.J. Denney
1915-1916	T. Crafter	E.J.D. Ratcliff	J.C. Johnson I.W. Nicholson	R.W. Davis	H.C. Cooper A.D. Morton (Vice) H.J. Dyball	C.A. Glaeser E.R. Small	E.J. Denney
1916-1917	T. Crafter	E.J.D. Ratcliff	J.C. Johnson I.W. Nicholson	R.W. Davis	A.D. Morton (Vice) H.J. Dyball	C.A. Glaeser E.R.Small	G.D. Gray
1917-1918	T. Crafter	E.J.D. Ratcliff	J.C. Johnson I.W. Nicholson	R.W. Davis	A.D. Morton (Vice) H.J. Dyball	C.A. Glaeser E.R. Small	H.R. Hopper
1918-1919	T. Crafter	E.J.D. Ratcliff	J.C. Johnson I.W. Nicholson	R.W. Davis	H.J. Dyball	C.A. Glaeser E.R. Small	H.R. Hopper
1919-1920	T. Crafter	E.J.D. Ratcliff	I.W. Nicholson F.L. Gilbert	R.W. Davis	A.C. Edwards B.H. Lymbery (Vice) H.J. Dyball	H.W.E. Sercombe H.J. Dyball	H.R. Hopper
1920-1921	E.J.D. Ratcliff	F.L. Gilbert	C.A. Peachey R.W. Pattison	A.R. Pearson	A.C. Edwards C.A. Peachey (Vice) R.A. Lindsay	H.W.E. Sercombe H.J. Dyball	W.R. Moir S.D. Taylor (Sub)
1921-1922	W.W. Davis	F.L. Gilbert	P.E.D. Glaeser C.H. Sercombe H.J. Dyball	A.R. Pearson	A.C. Edwards B.H. Lymbery (Vice) R.A. Lindsay C.H.W. O'Brien (Vice)	H.W.E. Sercombe H.J. Dyball	W.R. Moir H.A. Wilkinson (Sub)
1922-1923	T.C. Davis	H.J. Dyball	F.L. Gilbert P.E.D. Glaeser	A.R. Pearson	S.H. Claydon C.H.W. O'Brien (Vice) A.T.G. Trumble G.D. Basan (Vice)	B.H. Lymbery H.J. Dyball	W.R. Moir H.A. Wilkinson (Sub)
1923-1924	J.F. Ponsford	H.J. Dyball	W.S.A. Winter N.L. Davis D.K. Saunders	A.R. Pearson	J.H. Kitton W.C. Colegate (Vice) R.H. Coblan (Vice)	B.H. Lymbery H.J. Dyball	W.R. Moir H.A. Wilkinson (Sub)
1924-1925	H.A. Munro	H.J. Dyball	W.S.A. Winter N.L. Davis D.K. Saunders C.L. Westley	A.R. Pearson	J.H. Kitton A.E. Bagi (Vice) G.D. Basan R.H. Gollan (Vice)	F.L. Gilbert H.J. Dyball	G.F. Datlen H.A. Wilkinson (Sub) S.D. Taylor (Sub)
1925-1926	T.K. Grant	H.J. Dyball	N.L. Davis C.E. Clowser D.K. Saunders V. Harris	A.R. Pearson	J.H. Kitton A.E. Bagi (Vice) G.D. Basan G.B. Westoby (Vice)	F.L. Gilbert H.J. Dyball	C. Lowen H.A. Wilkinson (Sub) J.W.M. Norman (Sub)
1926-1927	H.F. Pash	H.J. Dyball	R.F. Barclay N.L. Davis V. Harris D.K. Saunders	A.R. Pearson	J.H. Kitton A.E. Bagi (Vice) G.D. Basan G.B. Westoby (Vice)	F.L. Gilbert H.J. Dyball	C. Lowen H.A. Wilkinson (Sub)
1927-1928	C.A. Morgan	W.S.A. Winter	V. Harris C.L. Mobbs R.W. Pattison	A.R. Pearson J.M. Scott (Asst.)	A.G.V. Allen and J.S. Horsley E.M. Saville (Vice) C.G. Royce J.W. Orr (Vice)	F.L. Gilbert R.W. Pattison	C. Lowen H.A. Wilkinson (Sub) D.K. Saunders (Sub)
1928-1929	A. Metcalf	V. Harris	C.L. Mobbs R.W. Pattison F.W. Parker	A.D. Thwaites J.M. Scott (Asst.)	A.G.V. Allen C.E. Clowser (Vice) C.G. Royce J.W. Orr (Vice)	D.K. Saunders	C. Lowen H.A. Wilkinson (Sub.) D.K. Saunders (Sub)
1929-1930	A. Anderson	V. Harris	F.W. Parker C.L. Mobbs J.W. Orr	A.D. Thwaites J.M. Scott (Asst)	C.E. Clowser R.F. Cross (Vice) C.J.R. Woods V.W.W. Beardon (Vice)	D.K. Saunders	W.E. Dimes H.A. Wilkinson (Sub) D.K. Saunders (Sub)

Year	President	Hon.Secretary	Ass.Hon.Sec.	Hon Treasurer	Captain	Handicapper	Editor
1930-1931	H.E. King	V. Harris	F.W. Parker C.L. Mobbs J.W. Orr	A.D. Thwaites J.M. Scott (Asst)	C.E. Clowser R.F. Cross (Vice) C.J.R. Woods H.S. Smith (Vice)	D.K. Saunders	J.D. Rogers H.A. Wilkinson (Sub)
1931-1932	H.W.E. Sercombe	C.L. Mobbs	F.W. Parker L.R. Clowser R.A. Wearn	A.D. Thwaites J.M. Scott (Asst)	R.F. Cross R.E. Walker (Vice) H.S. Smith E. Anslow Wilson (Vice)	D.K. Saunders C. Waller	J.D. Rogers H.A. Wilkinson (Sub)
1932-1933	W.W. Davis	C.L. Mobbs	F.W. Parker R.A. Wearn	A.D. Thwaites J.M. Scott (Asst)	R.F. Cross R.E. Walker (Vice) H.S. Smith C.A. Wiard (Vice)	D.K. Saunders C. Waller	J.D. Rogers H.A. Wilkinson (Sub) E.J.J. Reed (Sub)
1933-1934	G.F. McIvor	C.L. Mobbs	R.A. Wearn L.R. Clowser	A.D. Thwaites J.M. Scott (Asst)	R.F. Cross R.E. Walker (Vice) H.S. Smith S.J. Loader (Vice)	D.K. Saunders C. Waller	H.L. Roache H.A. Wilkinson (Sub) E.J.J. Reed
1934-1935	J. Morrison	C.L. Mobbs	L.R. Clowser R.A. Wearn S.A. Field	A.D. Thwaites J.M. Scott (Asst)	R.E. Walker R.J. Philo (Vice) H.S. Smith S.J. Loader (Vice)	D.K. Saunders V.W.W. Beardon	H.L. Roache H.A. Wilkinson (Sub) E.J.J. Reed (Sub)
1935-1936	W.D. Whiter	G.F. McIvor	R.A. Wearn S.A. Field J. Morrison L.D. Lee	C.J. Woods J.M. Scott (Asst)	R.E. Walker R.J. Philo (Vice) H.S. Smith A.C.J. Poole (Vice)	D.K. Saunders V.W.W. Beardon	H.L. Roache H.A. Wilkinson (Sub) E.J.J. Reed (Sub)
1936-1937	H.J. Staines	G.F. McIvor	S.A. Field (C.C.) R.A. Wearn (Trk) J. Morrison L.D. Lee	C.J.R. Woods J.M. Scott (Asst)	R.E. Walker R.J. Philo (Vice) H.S. Smith A.C.J. Poole (Vice)	D.K. Saunders V.W.W. Beardon	C.L. Mobbs A.D. Thwaites H.A. Wilkinson G.H. Wilkinson (Sub)
1937-1938	R.F. Cross	G.F. McIvor	S.A. Field (C.C.) R.A. Wearn (Trk) J. Morrison L.D. Lee	E.G. Lymbery J.M. Scott (Asst)	R.J. Philo T.S. Crawford (Vice) C.J.R. Woods A.C.J. Poole (Vice) J.C. Oxland (Vice)	R.F. Cross V.W.W. Beardon	C.L. Mobbs A.D. Thwaites H.A. Wilkinson G.H. Wilkinson (Sub)
1938-1939	A.D. Thwaites	G.F. McIvor	J.R.D. Cockburn (C.C.) R.A. Wearn (Trk) L.D. Lee	E.G. Lymbery J.M. Scott (Asst)	G.H. Wilkinson T.S. Crawford (Vice) V.W.W. Beardon A.C.J. Poole (Vice) V.A.T. Bignall (Vice)	R.F. Cross H.S. Smith	H.A. Wilkinson G.H. Wilkinson E.J.J. Reed (Sub)
1939-1940	A.D. Thwaites	C.F. McIvor E.G. Lymbery (Acting)	J.R.D. Cockburn (C.C.) R.A. Wearn (Trk) L.D. Lee	E.G. Lymbery J.M. Scott (Asst)	G.H. Wilkinson T.S. Crawford (Vice) V.W.W. Beardon A.C.J. Poole (Vice) V.A.T. Bignall (Vice)	R.F. Cross H.S. Smith (Killed in action 29.5.40.)	H.A. Wilkinson G.H. Wilkinson E.J.J. Reed (Sub)
1940-1941	A.D. Thwaites	"	"	"	"	R.F. Cross	"
1941-1942	A.D. Thwaites	"	"	"	"	"	"
1942-1943	A.D. Thwaites	E.G. Lymbery (Killed in action 1.6.43.)	"	E.G. Lymbery (Killed in action 1.6.43.) S.D. Taylor (Acting)	"	"	"
1943-1944	A.D. Thwaites	G.F. McIvor J.R.D. Cockburn (Acting)	"	S.D. Taylor J.M. Scott (Asst)	"	"	"
1944-1945	A.D. Thwaites	"	"	"	"	"	"
1945-1946	G.A. Mullins	G.F. McIvor	J.R.D. Cockburn (C.C.) V.W.W. Beardon (Trk)	S.D. Taylor J.M. Scott (Asst)	G.H. Wilkinson R.R. Choat (Vice) V.W.W. Beardon	J.R.D. Cockburn V.W.W. Beardon	H.A. Wilkinson G.H. Wilkinson E.J.J. Reed (Sub)
1946-1947	S.C. Wooderson	V.W.W. Beardon	J.R.D. Cockburn (C.C.) A. Dale (Trk)	S.A. Field D.J. Tingey (Asst)	R.R. Choat D.E. Reynolds (Vice) C.A. Wiard A.C. Chappell (Vice) G.A.C. Morton (Vice)	R.E. Walker C.A. Wiard	G.H. Wilkinson E.J.J. Reed (Sub)
1947-1948	G.H. Wilkinson	V.W.W. Beardon	W.F. Dew (C.C.) A. Dale (Trk) K.J. Johnson (Ent)	L. Pendered D.J. Tingey (Asst)	R.R. Choat D.E. Reynolds (Vice) C.A. Wiard A.G. Chappell (Vice) G.A.C. Morton (Vice)	G.F. Brooks C.A. Wiard	R.E. Walker E.J.J. Reed (Sub)
1948-1949	W.R.J. Clarke	V.W.W. Beardon	W.F. Dew (C.C.) G.A.C. Morton (Trk) K.J. Johnson (Ent)	L. Pendered D.J. Tingey (Asst)	R.R. Choat D.E. Reynolds (Vice) C.A. Wiard R.W. Goldsmith (Vice) G.A.C. Morton (Vice)	G.F. Brooks G.F. Brooks	R.E. Walker E.J.J. Reed (Sub)
1949-1950	S.D. Taylor	V.W.W. Beardon	W.F. Dew (C.C.) G.A.C. Morton (Trk) J. Sims (Ent.)	L. Pendered D.J. Tingey (Asst.)	D.E. Reynolds A.J. Brent (Vice) N.W. Page R.W. Goldsmith (Vice) G.A.C. Morton (Vice)	G.F. Brooks G.F. Brooks	J.G. Lymbery E.J.J. Reed (Sub)
1950-1951	F.W. Parker	V.W.W. Beardon	D.J. Tingey (C.C.) A.C. Brill (Trk) J. Sims (Ent)	L. Pendered W.F. Dew (Asst)	A.J. Brent H.J. Bishop (Vice) N.W. Page A.W.0. Webb (Vice) G.A.C. Morton (Vice)	G.F. Brooks K.L. Jobson	J.G. Lymbery K.L. Jobson (Sub)

Year	President	Hon.Secretary	Ass.Hon.Sec.	Hon.Treasurer	Captain	Handicapper	Editor
1951-1952	C.W. Starnes	V.W.W. Beardon	D.J. Tingey (C.C.) A.C. Brill (Trk) J. Sims (Ent.)	L. Pendered W.F. Dew (Asst)	A.J. Brent H.J. Bishop (Vice) N.W. Page J. Lindblom (Vice) G.A.C. Morton (Vice)	G.F. Brooks K.L. Jobson	E.J.J. Reed A.V. Hayday (Sub)
1952-1953	S.A. Field	V.W.W. Beardon	D.J. Tingey (C.C.) A.C. Brill (Trk) J. Sims (Ent.)	L. Pendered W.J. Traer (Asst)	A.J. Brent H.J. Bishop (Vice) K.L. Jobson K. Loveday (Vice) C.D. Purves (Vice)	G.F. Brooks D.G. Child	E.J.J. Reed A.V. Hayday (Sub)
1953-1954	C.A. Wiard	J. Sims	D.J. Tingey (C.C.) A.C. Brill (Trk) B.G. Parrott (Ent)	W.J. Traer G.H. Smith (Asst)	A.J. Brent R.A. Morley (Vice) K.L. Jobson K. Loveday (Vice) C.D. Purves (Vice)	G.F. Brooks D.G. Child	H.J. Bishop R.H. Thompson (Sub)
1954-1955	R.E. Walker	J. Sims	D.J. Tingey (C.C.) L.G. King (Trk) B.G. Parrott (Ent)	W.J. Traer G.H. Smith (Asst)	A.J. Brent R.A. Morley (Vice) N.W. Page K. Loveday (Vice) C.D. Purves (Vice)	G.F. Brooks D.G. Child	R.H. Thompson A.J. Woodrow (Sub)
1955-1956	K.N. Wilcockson	J. Sims	D.J. Tingey (C.C.) L.G. King (Trk) B.G. Parrott (Ent)	W.J. Traer G.H. Smith (Asst.)	R.A. Morley A.W. Wood (Vice) N.W. Page K. Loveday (Vice) A.J. Brent (Vice)	G.F. Brooks A.J. Brent	R.H. Thompson A.J. Woodrow (Sub)
1956-1957	W.H.M. Vercoe	J. Sims	D.J. Tingey (C.C.) G.F. Brooks (Trk) J.R.D. Cockburn (Ent)	W.J. Traer G.H. Smith (Asst)	R.A. Morley A.W. Wood (Vice) N.W. Page A.F. Nash (Vice) A.J. Brent (Vice)	G.F. Brooks A.J. Brent	R.H. Thompson A.J. Woodrow (Sub)
1957-1958	C.H.R. Williams	J. Sims	A.J. Woodrow (C.C.) G.F. Brooks (Trk) J.R.D. Cockburn (Ent)	W.J. Traer G.H. Smith (Asst)	R.A. Morley A.W. Wood (Vice) N.W. Page A.F. Nash (Vice) A.J. Brent (Vice)	G.F. Brooks A.J. Brent	R.H. Thompson A.A. Oldfield (Sub)
1958-1959	V.W.W. Beardon	J. Sims	B.J.C. Sanders (C.C.) K.J. Johnson (Trk) J.R.D. Cockburn (Ent)	W.J. Traer G.H. Smith (Asst)	A.W. Wood R.J. Webber (Vice) N.W. Page J.B. Herring (Vice) G. Hickey (Vice)	G.F. Brooks A.J. Brent	R.H. Thompson A.A. Oldfield (Sub)
1959-1960	J. Sims	N. Dudley	A.V. Hayday (C.C.) K.J. Johnson (Trk)	W.J. Traer G.H. Smith (Asst)	A.W. Wood R.J. Webber (Vice) N.W. Page J.B. Herring (Vice) G. Hickey (Vice)	G.F. Brooks A.J. Brent	R.H. Thompson A.A. Oldfield (Sub) J. Lissaman (Sub)
1960-1961	J.R.D. Cockburn	N. Dudley	A.V. Hayday (C.C.) K.J. Johnson (Trk) P.E. Sims (Ent)	G.H. Smith J.V.F. Bennett (Asst.)	A.W. Wood G. Scotting (Vice) N.W. Page J.B. Herring (Vice) G. Hickey (Vice)	G.F. Brooks A.J. Brent	R.H. Thompson A.A. Oldfield (Sub) J. Lissaman (Sub)
1961-1962	C. Pollard	D.F.E. Hogg	T. Sullivan (C.C.) R.E.D. Taylor (Trk) K.J. McSweeney (Ent.)	G.H. Smith J.V.F. Bennett (Asst)	A.W. Wood J.R. Baldwin (Vice) N.W. Page J.B. Herring (Vice) J.E. Day (Vice)	G.F. Brooks A.J. Brent	R.H. Thompson A.A. Oldfield (Sub) J. Lissaman (Sub)
1962-1963	L.E. Hammill	D.F.E. Hogg	A.A. Oldfield (C.C.) R.E.D. Taylor (Trk) E.J. Malone (Ent)	A.E. Ball J.V.F. Bennett (Asst.)	J.R. Baldwin B. Heaver (Vice) N.W. Page I.M. Ross (Vice) J.E. Day (Vice)	G.F. Brooks A.J. Brent	R.H. Thompson J. Lissaman (Sub) D. Fiddes (Sub)
1963-1964	D.K. Saunders	D.F.E. Hogg	A.A. Oldfield (C.C.) R.E.D. Taylor (Trk.) E. Doorbar (Ent)	A.E. Ball J.V.F. Bennett (Asst)	D.L. Gregory J.R. Baldwin (Vice) N.W. Page I.M. Ross (Vice) J.E. Day (Vice)	G.F. Brooks A.J. Brent	R.H. Thompson J. Lissaman (Sub) B.D. Lee (Sub)
1964-1965	W.J. Traer	E. Doorbar	A.A. Oldfield (C.C.) R.E.D. Taylor (Trk) A.D.R. Filby (Ent)	A.E. Ball J.V.F. Bennett (Asst)	D.L. Gregory J.R. Baldwin (Vice) N.W. Page I.M. Ross (Vice) J.E. Day (Vice)	G.F. Brooks A.J. Brent	R.H. Thompson J. Lissaman (Sub) B.D. Lee (Sub)
1965-1966	R.H. Thompson	E. Doorbar	G.R. Last (C.C.) R.E.D. Taylor (Trk) R. Pinder (Ent)	A.E. Ball J.V.F. Bennett (Asst.)	D.L. Gregory B.G. Stone (Vice) N.W. Page M.W. McFarnell (Vice) J.E. Day (Vice)	G.F. Brooks A.J. Brent	J. Lissaman P.J.G. Baigent (Sub) W.P. Whiting (Sub)
1966-1967	A.J. Brent	A.V. Hayday	G.R. Last (C.C.) R.E.D. Taylor (Trk) R. Pinder (Ent)	A.E. Ball J.E. White (Asst)	B.G. Stone R. Richardson (Vice) N.W. Page M.W. McFarnell (Vice) J.E. Day (Vice)	A. Nye L.F. Fletcher	P.J.G. Baigent W.P. Whiting (Sub) I.C. Mackley (Sub)
1967-1968	D.G. Child	A.V. Hayday	G.R. Last (C.C.) P.J. Hudson (Trk) B.G. Stone (Ent)	A.E. Ball T. Cavanagh (Asst)	B.G. Stone R. Richardson (Vice) N.W. Page R.E.D. Taylor (Vice) J.E. Day (Vice)	A. Nye J.E. White	P.J.G. Baigent I.C. Mackley (Sub) G. Botley (Sub)
1968-1969	D.G. Child	B.G. Stone	C.R. Haines (C.C.) P.J. Hudson (Trk) R.A. Michell (Ent)	A.E. Ball T. Cavanagh (Asst)	C.P. Woodcock D. McIver (Vice) G.E. Monshall (Vice) N.W. Page R.E.D. Taylor (Vice) J. Philip (Vice)	A. Nye R. Hawtin	P.J.G. Baigent I.C. Mackley (Sub) R. Richardson (Sub)

Year	President	Hon. Secretary	Ass. Hon.Sec.	Hon. Treasurer	Captain	Handicapper	Editor
Apr 69-Apr 70 S.C. Wooderson Centenary President							
1969-1970	G.F. Brooks	B.G. Stone	C.R. Haines (C.C.) J.E. Philip (Trk) R.A. Michell (Ent)	R.J. Edmonds F.G.W. Dudman (Asst)	A.N. Mandeville (C.C.) (Trk)	A. Nye (C.C.) R.E.D. Taylor (Trk)	P.J.G. Baigent I.C. Mackley (Sub) R. Richardson (Sub)
1970-1971	G.F. Brooks	B.G. Stone	– (C.C.) I.M. Ross (Trk) – (Ent.)	R.J. Edmonds F.G.W. Dudman (Asst)	R.I. Hawtin (C.C.) I.M. Ross (Trk)	A. Nye (C.C.) R.E.D. Taylor (Trk)	P.J.G. Baigent I.C. Mackley (Sub) I.C. Wilson (Sub)
1971-1972	P.J.G. Baigent	I.F. Smith	F.C. Rogers (C.C.) I.M. Ross (Trk) E.M.H. Pepper (Rd)	R.J. Edmonds F.G.W. Dudman (Asst)	R.I. Hawtin (C.C.) J.C.W. Friend (Trk)	A. Nye (C.C.) R.E.D. Taylor (Trk)	G.B. Botley B.M. Shapcott (Sub) C.R. Clarke (Sub)
1972-1973	R.A. Morley	I.F. Smith	F.C. Rogers (C.C.) I.M. Ross (Trk) E.M.H. Pepper (Rd)	F.G.W. Dudman W.P. Whiting (Asst)	I.C. Wilson (C.C.) J.C.W. Friend (Trk)	D.G. Child (C.C.) R.E.D. Taylor (Trk)	G.B. Botley B.M. Shapcott (Sub) M.B. Hamlin (Sub)
1973-1974	A.A. Oldfield	I.F. Smith	F.C. Rogers (C.C.) A.W. Frankish (Trk) C.P. Woodcock (Rd)	F.G.W. Dudman M.G. Hampton (Asst)	I.C. Wilson (C.C.) J.C.W. Friend (Trk)	D.G. Child (C.C.) R.E.D. Taylor (Trk)	G.B. Botley B.M. Shapcott (Sub) M.B. Hamlin (Sub)
1974-1975	A.E. Ball	I.F. Smith	F.C. Rogers (C.C.) A.W. Frankish (Trk) D.H. Hopgood (Rd)	F.G.W. Dudman M.G. Hampton (Asst)	I.C. Wilson (C.C.) J.C.W. Friend (Trk)	G.F. Brooks (C.C.) P.J.G. Baigent (Trk)	D.R. Gillate T. Cavanagh (Sub) T.F.P. Phillips (Sub)
1975-1976	J.R. Baldwin	I.F. Smith	F.C. Rogers (C.C.) A.W. Frankish (Trk) D.H. Hopgood (Rd)	P.E. Shepheard R.S. Savery (Asst)	I.C. Wilson (C.C.) P.R. Horwood (Trk)	G.F. Brooks (C.C.) P.J.G. Baigent (Trk)	D.R. Gillate T. Cavanagh (Sub) T.F.P. Phillips (Sub)
1976-1977	R.E.D. Taylor	D.W. Amner	F.C. Rogers (C.C.) A.W. Frankish (Trk) D.H. Hopgood (Rd)	P.E. Shepheard R.H. Savery (Asst)	I.C. Wilson (C.C.) M.J. Mahoney (Trk)	G.F. Brooks (C.C.) P.J.G. Baigent (Trk)	G.R. Last A.A. Oldfield (Sub) T.F.P. Phillips (Sub)
1977-1978	T.T. Sullivan	D.W. Amner	I.K. Young (C.C.) A.W. Frankish (Trk) T.C. Mallott (Rd)	P.E. Shepheard R.H. Savery (Asst)	I.C. Wilson (C.C.) M.J. Mahoney (Trk)	G.F. Brooks (C.C.) M.L. Peel (Trk)	G.R. Last A.A. Oldfield (Sub) J.C.W. Friend (Sub)
1978-1979	C.M. Brand	D.W. Amner	I.K. Young (C.C.) M.J. Carroll (Trk) T.C. Mallott (Rd)	P.E. Shepheard R.H. Savery (Asst)	T.J. Souter (C.C.) A.W. Frankish (Trk)	G.F. Brooks (C.C.) M.L. Peel (Trk)	A.A. Oldfield P.G. Stenning (Sub)
1979-1980	B.G. Stone	D.W. Amner	I.K. Young (C.C.) M.J. Carroll (Trk) T.C. Mallott (Rd)	P.E. Shepheard	T.J. Souter (C.C.) A.W. Frankish (Trk)	D.H. Hopgood (C.C.) J. Wilkinson (Trk) J.E. Day (Fd)	G.B. Crowder P.G. Stenning (Sub) J.C.W. Friend (Sub)
1980-1981	I.F. Smith	F.G.W. Dudman	I.K. Young (C.C.) M.J. Carroll (Trk) M.L. Peel (Rd)	R.D. Ebbutt	T.J. Souter (C.C.) A.W. Frankish (Trk)	D.H. Hopgood (C.C.) A.W. Frankish (Trk) J.E. Day (Fd)	J.V. Powell P.G. Stenning (Sub) J.C.W. Friend (Sub)
1981-1982	I.C. Wilson	W.F. Lake	R.P. Cliff (C.C.) M.J. Carroll (Trk) M.N. Williams (Rd)	R.D. Ebbutt	T.J. Souter (C.C.) A.W. Frankish (Trk)	D.H. Hopgood (C.C.) A.W. Frankish (Trk) C.S. Ellis (Fd)	S.H. Cluney L. Roberts (Sub) C. Woodcock (Sub)
1982-1983	J.E. Day	W.F. Lake	R.P. Cliff (C.C.) C.J. Bird (Trk) M.N. Williams (Rd)	R.D. Ebbutt	R.J. Coles (C.C.) A.W. Frankish (Trk)	D.H. Hopgood (C.C.) R.E. Green (Trk) C.S. Ellis (Fd)	S.H. Cluney L. Roberts (Sub) C. Woodcock (Sub)
1983-1984	M.A. Walker	W.F. Lake	R.P. Cliff (C.C.) R.D. Ebbutt (Trk) M.N. Williams (Rd)	I.K. Young	G.B. Crowder (C.C. Vice) A.W. Frankish (Trk)	D.H. Hopgood (C.C.) A.W. Frankish (Trk) J.A. Wakeman (Fd)	L. Roberts D.W. Dunn (Sub) T. Llewelyn (Sub)
1984-1985	L.E. Piper	W.F. Lake	D.W. Dunn (C.C.) R.D. Ebbutt (Trk) A. Nana (Rd)	I.K. Young	G.B. Botley (C.C.) A.W. Frankish (Trk)	D.H. Hopgood (C.C.) N.F. Ebbutt (Trk) J.A. Wakeman (Fd)	L. Roberts D.W. Dunn (Sub) P.E. Shepheard (Sub)
1985-1986	W.F. Lake	D.W. Dunn	B.W.J. Grant (C.C.) R.D. Ebbutt (Trk) A. Nana (Rd)	I.K. Young	G.B. Botley (C.C.) A.W. Frankish (Trk)	D.H. Hopgood (C.C.) N.F. Ebbutt (Trk) J.A. Wakeman (Fd)	L. Roberts P.E. Shepheard (Sub) N.J. Keogh (Sub) N.J. Davidson (Sub)
1986-1987	D.L. Gregory	D.W. Dunn	B.W.J. Grant (C.C.) R.D. Ebbutt (Trk) A. Nana (Rd)	I.K. Young	G.B. Botley (C.C.) A.W. Frankish (Trk)	M.J. Cronin (C.C.) N.F. Ebbutt (Trk) J.A. Wakeman (Fd)	L. Roberts N.J. Keogh (Sub) N.J. Davidson (Sub)
1987-1988	P.G. Stenning	D.W. Dunn	B.W.J. Grant (C.C.) S.G.M. Parsons (Trk) A. Mothersole (Rd)	I.K. Young	G.B. Botley (C.C.) A.W. Frankish (Trk)	R.P. Coe and G. Spencer (C.C.) N.F. Ebbutt (Trk) J.A. Wakeman (Fd)	L. Roberts N.J. Keogh (Sub) N.J. Davidson (Sub) W. Clapham (Sub)
1988-1989	K.J. Johnson	D.W. Dunn	B.W.J. Grant (C.C.) S.G.M. Parsons (Trk) A. Mothersole (Rd)	J.E. Hill	G.B. Botley (C.C.) A.W. Frankish (Trk)	A. Nana (C.C.) N.F. Ebbutt (Trk) J.A. Wakeman (Fd)	L. Roberts N.J. Keogh (Sub) N.J. Davidson (Sub) W. Clapham (Sub)
1989-1990	D.R. Gillate	J.R. Baldwin	M. Martineau (C.C.) S.G.M. Parsons (Trk) A. Mothersole (Rd)	J.E. Hill	G.B. Botley (C.C.) A.W. Frankish (Trk)	A. Nana (C.C.) – (Trk) J.A. Wakeman (Fd)	J. Phelan N.J. Keogh (Sub) N.J. Davidson (Sub) W. Clapham (Sub)

Appendix Three
BLACKHEATH HARRIERS TROPHIES

TROPHY AWARDED FOR
CROSS-COUNTRY

	FIRST PRESENTED
CLUB	
5 Mile Challenge	1880
DAVIS	
7½ Mile Championship	1922
ROWLAND	
10 Mile Championship	1895
KING MORRISON	
5 Mile Junior Championship	1936
PAUL JACKSON MEMORIAL	
3½ Mile Youth Championship	1966
BROWNING TANKARD	
10,000 metres Veteran Championship	1974
BENNETT MEMORIAL	
Points Handicap for season	1930
PONSFORD PEWTER	
1st Veteran to finish v S.L.H.	1956
SCOTTING SALVER	
Handicap Winner in S.L.H. Mob Match	1962
FOOKS	
1st member in Kent C.C.	1928
RAPLEY	
1st member in Southern C.C.	1904
MUNRO	
1st member in English C.C.	1957
ROGER SMITH TANKARD	
1st Veteran member in Kent Veterans Championship	1978
D.K. SAUNDERS CUP	
Winner of 'Closing 5'	1975
JACK SIMS SALVER	
Outstanding example and performance in cross-country	1976
PARRISH	
1st School Team in 3½ miles Inter-Schools C.C. race	1946
R.A.G. SMITH (RAGS)	
1st School Team within 10 miles radius of Hayes (except Parrish winner) in 3½ miles Inter-Schools C.C. race	1964
NICHOLLS	
Inter-Club Mob Match v S.L.H.	1896
PELLING-RATCLIFF	
Inter-Club Mob Match v Ranelagh H.	1922

ROAD

A.G.V. ALLEN CUP	
Marathon Championship	1982
REYNOLDS PEWTER	
1st member in Kent 20 mile road race	1966
TED PEPPER TROPHY	
Winner of B.H. 7 mile open road race	1979
BROMLEY ADVERTISER	
Winning Team in B.H. open relay	1963
CHIEF WHIP'S TROPHY	
1st member in Ted Pepper race who has competed in all three mob matches (S.L.H., Ranelagh H., and Orion H.)	1986

TRACK AND FIELD

RAMPLEY	
100 metres Championship	1896
WOOD	
200 metres Championship	1912
REAY	
400 metres Championship	1909
BARCLAY-ESSEN	
800 metres Championship	1890
PASH	
1 mile Championship (first claim members only)	1900
MORGAN	
3000 metres Championship	1929
REYNOLDS BOWL	
5000 metres Championship	1965
BRICKWOOD TANKARD	
10000 metres Championship	1970
WALTER	
2000 metres Steeplechase Championship	1896
SCHOFIELD	
100 metres Junior Championship	1956
BURLEY	
400 metres Junior Championship	1948
HOWARD	
800 metres Junior Championship	1924
WOODERSON	
1 mile Junior Championship	1956
PAT CHURCHER	
Most improved runner in the Dreamer's Mile	1989
LINDSAY SALVER	
Oustanding example and performance in Track or Field	1959
PONSFORD	
Member scoring most points in any seven of the Senior Club Field Event Championships	1955
HORNAL	
Best performance in Club Junior Field Event Championships	1954
JOHN POWELL YOUTH TROPHY	
Most significant contribution to team in team manager's opinion	1985
BROWNING TROPHY	
Junior or younger member contributing most by example and performance in Track or Field	1975
JOHN POWELL I AND D TROPHIES	
Awarded for Improvement and Determination in each category to a member who has received no other award	
Youth 1983 Boy 1983 Colt 1984	
LESTER CUP	
Youth who has contributed most to Senior Track Teams	1989

OTHERS

JOHNSON BOWL	7½ mile Road Walk	1902
MARYON-WILSON	66 yard Swim	1893
ST. JOHN MATTHEWS	Club v S.L.H. Rowing Race	1903
FRANKEISS		
Club v Ranelagh H. v S.L.H. & Others Rowing Race		1929
LEE BRAND TANKARD		
Youngest member of Club Rowing Crew		1979
R.E. WALKER BOWL		
Held by President for use on Punch Bowl Nights		1961
PONSFORD SALVER	Held by President	1955
PRESIDENT'S CHAIR		
For use by the President at Club H.Q.		1957
CECIL POLLARD CANDELABRA	Held by President	1975
CECIL POLLARD TANTALUS		
For use by the President at Club H.Q.		1977

Appendix Four

BLACKHEATH PERFORMANCES IN SOUTHERN CROSS-COUNTRY CHAMPIONSHIP

Compiled by G. R. Last and P.J.G. Baigent

Year	Venue	Date	Points	Position						Scoring Runners						
1883-84	Hendon	2 Feb 84	149	3rd	F.W. Monk	3rd	C. Cattlin	12th	H.A. Spain	16th	C.C. Rengger	30th	T. Stockham	84th		
1884-85	Sandown Park		204	5th	F.W. Monk	10th	M. Hill	21st	C.A. Morgan	23rd	C.C. Rengger	36th	J.T. Terry	49th		
1885-86	Sandown Park		227	4th	F.W. Monk	11th	C.A. Morgan	34th	J.B. Nash	35th	G.P. Manson	40th	E.R. Rapley	60th		
1886-87	Kempton Park		256	6th	J.F. Ponsford	12th	H.C. Pritchard	30th	H.B. Godbold	30th	C. Luxon	53rd	J.B. Nash	69th	J.B. Nash 112th	H.A. Spain 110th
1887-88	Kempton Park		217	6th	J.F. Ponsford	11th	H.C. Scard	29th	J.B. Nash	32nd	C.A. Morgan	40th	T.C. Davis	22nd	W.J. Spring 92nd F. Denman 74th	H.B. Parkinson
1888-89	Kempton Park		184	5th	T.C. Davis	14th	J.F. Ponsford	37th	A.B. Godbold	38th	T.C. Davis	40th	H.C. Pritchard	41st	J.P. Fortman 107th P.G. Butten 87th	C.E. Turner - Retired
1889-90	Croydon Racecourse		210	6th	H.C. Scard	9th	J.B. Nash	33rd	A.R. Cooper	38th	C.H. Ellis	46th	H.J. Whitefield	52nd	J. McLoughlin 99th P.G. Butten 83rd	W.J. Luxor - Retired
1890-91	Kensal Rise		167	3rd	A.R. Cooper	20th	J.F. Ponsford	21st	F. Stephens	22nd	R.N. Frazer	27th	J. Young	46th	F. Denman 74th T. Carter 54th	C.A. Hardiman
1891-92	Ickham Near Ripley		126	4th	G.M. Harris	4th	J.F. Ponsford	17th	H.J. Whitefield	20th	R.W. Frazer	25th	J.B. Nash	31st	S.H. Seargent 87th C.A. Morgan 54th	C.A. Lowry
1892-93	Oakham		245	7th	L.O. Keer	11th	G.E. West	26th	H.R. Cooper	22nd	H.C. Scard	50th	T.C. Davis	27th	G. Follet 89th J. Young 41st	
1893-94	Wembley		245	7th	G.M. Harris	22nd	H.J. Whitefield	33rd	J.B. Nash	37th	G.M. Harris	52nd	F. Stephens	55th	E.R. Rapley 98th C.H. Ellis 85th	
1894-95	Wembley		not known	11th											F. Stephens 60th	H. Oldfield 89th
1895-96	Wembley		"	10th	NOT KNOWN										G. Harris 79th	G.B. Harris - Retired
1896-97	Wembley		"	9th											F. Nicholls 45th	B. Baddry 53rd
1897-98	Wembley		"	10th											H.C. Scard 75th	L.O. Keer 41st
1898-99	Lingfield Park	18 Feb 99	370	10th	E. Ratcliff	39th	H. Bull	57th	W.G. Suffield	60th	E.A.S. Young	66th	S.T. Pyrke	78th	H. Bull 81st J. Baker 89th	B. Baddry 92nd
1899-1900	Wembley		297	9th	W.H. Manning	32nd	W.G. Suffield	38th	E.A.S. Young	41st	E.F. Nicholls	60th	W.H. Barnett	62nd	H.G. Johnson 72nd G.E. West	E.C. Good 93rd
1900-01	Wembley		451	10th	E.F. Judson	46th	E. Ratcliff	58th	H. Bull	63rd	W.G. Suffield	81st	W.H. Manning,	118th	A.E. Culver 73rd G.W. Hansfield	
1901-02	Lingfield Park		630	15th	T.C. Davis	48th	E.F. Judson	84th	W.H. Barnett	104th	W.H. Barnett	128th	T.S. Brooks	136th	G.W. Hansfield 144th H.G. Johnson 152nd	H.G. Johnson 158th
1902-03	Lingfield Park		522	13th	T.C. Davis	49th	J.E. Fisher	56gh	T.S. Brooks	78th	W.H. Barnett	92nd	H.G. Johnson	133rd	H.W. Hadegrave 154th W.G. Suffield 101st	C. Hyland 154th
1903-04	Lingfield Park		399	11th	E.F. Judson	31st	M.P.S. White	52nd	G.L. Hopkins	60th	H. Bull	114th	G.L. Hopkins	89th	H. Pash 176th C. Ashby 140th	W.S. Smith 177th
1904-05	Lingfield Park		396	8th	E.F. Judson	27th	H.W.E. Sercombe	52nd	H.W.E. Sercombe	67th	T.C. Davis	100th	T.C. Davis	108th	H.G. Johnson 176th O.D. Hopkins 101st	C.E. Deacon 176th
1905-06	Imber Court		523	8th	R.G. Herbert	38th	E.F. Judson	41st	M.P.S. White	77th	G.L. Hopkins	61st	E.G. Lymbery	151st	E.R. Small 145th P. Kerry 124th	F.C. Carnaghan 139th
1906-07	Imber Court		635	17th	E.F. Judson	64th	M.P.S. White	80th	P.A. Openshaw	105th	H.W.E. Sercombe	85th	E.R. Small	143rd	W. Smith 191st E.V. Norman 127th	C. Hyland 142nd
1907-08	Wembley Park		526	12th	E.F. Judson	10th	C.A. Glaeser	42nd	C.A. Glaeser	83rd	T. Davis	131st	J. Lovey	138th	E.V. Hollingworth 169th P. Kerry 169th	R.H. Blackwell 193rd
1908-09	Epsom		48,	10th	H.E.J. Southwell	30th	E.F. Judson	76th	E.R. Small	81st	E.V.Hollingworth 134th		J. Lovey	119th	E.V. Norman 178th E.H.J. West 147th	E.G. Lymbery 190th
1909-10	Epsom		562	15th	H.E.J. Southwell	29th	C.A. Glaeser	36th	C.H. Baxter	113th	R.W. Davis	98th	C.H. Baxter	102nd	E.V. Norman 150th E.J. Jeminey 166th	H.H. Prior 192nd
1910-11	Lingfield		610	18th	E.F. Judson	51st	C.A. Glaeser	78th	C.A. Wickham-Jones	95th	E.R. Small	129th	R.W. Davis	151st	S.J. Wickham 161st W.K. Fry 165th	E.V. Norman 166th
1911-12	Hillingdon		706	19th	J.R. Barrow-Clough 31st		W. Kirk	54th	R.W. Davis	134th	J.R. Barrow-Clough 113th		C.H. Baxter	138th	E.R. Small 174th R.A. Baldrock 126th	S.J. Wickham 181st
1912-13	Camer (Kent)		602	11th	C.A. Glaeser	43rd	C.H. Baxter	83rd	A.P.L. Johnson	115th	L. Barnes	150th	A.R. Small	178th	C.H. Baxter 167th S.D. Taylor 153rd	E.V. Norman 174th
1913-14	Guildford		362	8th	A.C. Telfer	22nd	H.C. Cooper	45th	C.A. Glaeser	56th	B.H. Lymbery	72nd	T.W. Purchase	127th	A.R. Morton 144th A.P.L. Johnson 167th	F.L. Gilbert 180th
1915-16	No races owing to war														L. Barnes 173rd E.R. Small 173rd	Only eleven ran S.J. Wickham 191st
1919-20	Kenley		416	11th	A.C. Telfer	8th	B.H. Lymbery	46th	E.F. Judson	58th	R.W. Pattison	81st	T.W. Purchase	100th	W.E. Dawe 92nd E.F. Judson 188th	H. Morgan 203rd
1920-21	Chingford		393	11th	A.C. Edwards	13th	A.C. Telfer	20th	E.F. Judson	55th	B.H. Lymbery	63rd	W. Layfield	131st	C.H. Baxter 202nd T.W. Purchase 214th	E.V. Norman 235th DNF
1921-22	Uxbridge		424	10th	A.C. Telfer	23rd	A.C. Edwards	34th	E.J. Castello	46th	H.J. Danyer	58th	B.P. Braund	130th	A.R. Pearson 173rd W.E. Dawe 92nd	A.P.L. Johnson 205th
1922-23	Rochford		490	12th	A.C. Telfer	22nd	E.J. Castello	42nd	W.C. Colegate	85th	W.G. Kilby	106th	C.H.W O'Brien	120th	W.E. Dawe 100th L.A. Liddon 134th	F. Dawe 179th
1923-24	Boxmoor		667	19th	D.J. Mobbs	71st	A.C. Radcliff	74th	J.H. Kitton	110th	C. Whittington	126th	J.H. Kitton	115th	F.H. Gladwin 138th L.A. Liddon 141st	A.H. Watkins 175th
1924-25	Beaconsfield		603	11th	P.H. Francis	59th	A.C. Telfer	100th	F.B. Mallinson	105th	C.E. Clower	116th	P.H. Francis	131st	C.A. Peachey 190th G.F. McIvor 141st	E.B. Slatter 142nd
1925-26	Rye House Hailsyburg		492	10th	D.J. Mobbs	19th	C.W. Colegate	87th	C.E. Clower	89th	S.H. Dewdney	122nd	R.D. Bell	116th	B.H. Kitton 189th D. Taylor 193rd	F.H. Gladwin 177th
1926-27	Horton Kirby		272	4th	R.E. Walker	19th	D.J. Mobbs	27th	C.E. Clower	29th	D.J. Mobbs	56th	W.C. Colegate	73rd	C.H. Peachey 178th A.E. Bagi 192nd	M.L. Davis 186th
1927-28	Shenfield		690	19th	C.L. Mobbs	75th	W.C. Colegate	83rd	W.F. Dines	93rd	L. Pendred	126th	C.E. Clower C. Pollard R. Langdale	157th	A.T.H. Pritchard 184th E. Preston 138th	D. Whittington 192nd
1928-29	Horton-Kirby		554	12th	W.E. Dines	52nd	R.E. Galley	86th	H.S. Smith	90th	C.L. Mobbs	97th	S.H. Dewdney	108th	R.F. Barclay 159th E. West 129th	E.V. Norman 205th D.K. Saunders 161st
1929-30	Brighton Racecourse		607	12th	C.E. Clower	67th	C.L. Mobbs	81st	A.G. Allen	102nd	A.G. Allen	119th	C. Pollard	130th	R.F. Barclay 172nd A.C. Telfer 138th	H.W. Lloyd Martyn 225th
1930-31	Shenfield		383	8th	R.F. Cross	48th	A.G.V. Allen	53rd	C.E. Clower	62nd	R.E. Walker	69th	P.W. Glover	78th	H.C. Pollard 185th J.H. Kitton 138th	J.S. Horsley 186th
1931-32	Beaconsfield		469	10th	J.W. Norman	45th	R.E. Walker	62nd	A.G.V. Allen	73rd	C.L. Mobbs	80th	H.S. Smith	104th	W.C. Colegate 74th J.H. Kitton 113th	C.L. Mobbs 151st
1932-33	Chingford		359	9th	A.G.V. Allen	26th	H.S. Smith	32nd	R.F. Cross	51st	H.S. Smith	86th	R.E. Walker	77th	S.H. Dewdney 166th G.Q. Pollard 169th	J.W. Norman 144th
1933-34	Teplow		360	7th	L.T. Brockway	40th	R.E. Walker	42nd	A.G.V. Allen	63rd	R.F. Cross	71st	A.G.V. Allen	82nd	P.W. Glover 137th A.N. Daniel 185th	M. Lindsey 142nd
1934-35	Hassocks		386	8th	R.E. Walker	40th	R.J. Philo	45th	A.G.V. Allen	57th	R.F. Cross	58th	H.S. Smith	114th	G.J. Richmond 211th A.N. Daniel 165th	A.H. Walter 172nd
1935-36	Sandown Park		414	—	G.F. Brooks	49th	G.H. Wilkinson	55th	H.S. Smith	66th	D.E. Reynolds	88th	R.J. Philo	48th	G.J. Roberts 135th P.W. Glover 167th	W. Walters 173rd
1936-37	Horton Kirby 1st race		322	7th	G.F. Brooks	29th	A.C.I. Poole	38th	G.F. Brooks	—	D.E. Reynolds	—	S.J. Wooderson	46th	A.N. Daniel 158th L.T. Brockway 135th	H. Smith 144th
1937-38	Ascot	26 Feb 38	322	7th	G.H. Wilkinson	29th	G.H. Wilkinson	33rd	D.E. Reynolds	55th	S.J. Wooderson	67th	L.G. King	76th	L.I. Brockwell 137th A.G.V. Allen 161st	J.W. Norman 140th
1938-39	Apsley	25 Feb 38	389	8th	S.J. Wooderson	29th					R.E. Walker	113th	H.S. Smith	121st	A.G.V. Allen 160th L.G. King 133rd	H.S. Smith 146th
1939-40	Hayes	9 Mar 40		Unofficial Race - 7½ Miles											P.J. Barnwell 103rd H.E. Starnes 110th	J.D. Woodrow 156th

Race declared void - Blackheath team who ran were R.J. Smith - H.S. Smith - R.E. Walker - G.H. Wilkinson - D.E. Reynolds - A.C.I. Poole - A.G.V. Allen - G.F. Brooks - L.E. Hammill
R.F. Cross - H.D.M. Charleson and H.E. Starnes. The Club did not compete in the 're-run' on 27 March 1937

Cross Country Championship Results

Year	Venue	Date	Points	Position
1945-46	Wimbledon	23 Feb 46	195	4th
1946-47	Ascot	22 Feb 47	203	3rd
1947-48	Aylesford	28 Feb 48	113	2nd
1948-49	Camberley R.M.A. (Sandhurst)	26 Feb 49	230	6th
1949-50	Eastbourne	25 Feb 50	218	3rd
1950-51	Cockfosters	24 Feb 51	232	4th
1951-52	Hadleigh	23 Feb 52	331	5th
1952-53	Aylesford	21 Feb 53	262	4th
1953-54	Parliament Hill	27 Feb 54	488	9th
1954-55	Brighton	19 Feb 55	351	4th
1955-56	Windsor	18 Feb 56	382	6th
1956-57	Epsom	16 Feb 57	355	5th
1957-58	Parliament Hill	15 Feb 58	355	6th
1958-59	Aylesford	14 Feb 58	423	9th
1959-60	Parliament Hill	13 Feb 60	606	9th
1960-61	Ewell	18 Feb 61	556	8th
1961-62	Reading	17 Feb 62	1009	22nd
1962-63	Parliament Hill	16 Feb 63	649	10th
1963-64	Parliament Hill	15 Feb 64	423	7th
1964-65	Brighton	13 Feb 65	522	9th
1965-66	Parliament Hill	12 Feb 66	797	14th
1966-67	Parliament Hill	11 Feb 67	358	6th
1967-68	Parliament Hill	10 Feb 68	774	15th
1968-69	Reading	8 Feb 69	383	8th
1969-70	Parliament Hill	7 Feb 70	259	3rd
1970-71	Parliament Hill	13 Feb 71	387	8th
1971-72	Parliament Hill	12 Feb	225	3rd
1972-73	Parliament Hill	10 Feb 73	289	6th
1973-74	Parliament Hill	9 Feb 74	256	4th
1974-75	Parliament Hill	8 Feb 75	976	18th
1975-76	Parliament Hill	31 Jan 76	217	3rd
1976-77	Windsor	12 Feb 77	377	5th
1977-78	Parliament Hill	11 Feb 78	504	16th
1978-79	Parliament Hill	10 Feb 79	827	16th
1979-80	Parliament Hill	9 Feb 80	359	5th
1980-81	Trent Park	14 Feb 81	618	11th
1981-82	Parliament Hill	13 Feb 82	555	10th
1982-83	Trent Park	12 Feb 83	681	10th
1983-84	Parliament Hill	11 Feb 84	1232	26th
1984-85	Trent Park	9 Feb 85	782	15th
1985-86	Brighton	8 Feb 86	207	1st
1986-87	Parliament Hill	10 Jan 87	355	5th
1987-88	Trent Park	9 Jan 88	356	8th
1988-89	Basingstoke	14 Jan 89	292	4th

Scoring Runners (name and individual finishing position)

1945-46: R.R. Choat 8th; H.H. Nunns 16th; D.W. Smith 19th; D.E. Reynolds 45th; A. Dale 52nd; A.C.I. Poole 55th; G.H. Wilkinson 63rd; G. Ness 71st; C.O. Davies 95th

1946-47: S.C. Wooderson 5th; G.E. Monshall 15th; W.F. Spencer 16th; H.G. Wilkinson 50th; R.R. Choat 54th; A.C.I. Poole 54th; A.D. Kennedy 70th; W.F. Dow 83rd; R.J. Dangey 118th

1947-48: S.C. Wooderson 1st; R.R. Choat 11th; J. Braughton 18th; G.E. Monshall 25th; A.J. Brent 29th; W.F. Spencer 33rd; J.P. Clark 63rd; J.P. Clark 87th; A. Dale 120th

1948-49: S.C. Wooderson 14th; R.R. Choat 20th; W.F. Spencer 22nd; E.R. May 31st; A.J. Brent 69th; A.C.I. Poole 74th; D.E. Reynolds 102nd; J.P. Clark 107th; E.V. Beaton 133rd

1949-50: H.N. Nunns 16th; R.R. Choat 26th; J. Braughton 28th; G.E. Marshall 39th; A.J. Brent 42nd; E.R. May 67th; A.C. Brill 103rd; H.H. Nunns 11th; A.C. Brill 119th

1950-51: A.J. Brent 15th; J. Clark 33rd; R.R. Choat 35th; A.C. Brill 47th; R.R. Choat 50th; J.P. Clark 52nd; L.J. Atkinson 70th; C. Busby 111th; C. Busby 138th

1951-52: J. Braughton 20th; J. Braughton 29th; A.C. Brill 42nd; E.D. Reynolds 55th; J. Withers 50th; J. Withers 77th; E.D. Reynolds 72nd; P.G. Stenning 113th; P.G. Stenning 117th

1952-53: G. Scotting 16th; G. Scotting 20th; J.E. Withers 89th; H.J. Bishop 77th; A.E. Ball 90th; J.E. Withers 77th; H.J. Bishop 104th; L.H. Childs 136th; H.J. Bishop 119th

1953-54: A.A. Everard 38th; A.J. Brent 47th; J.E. Withers 104th; A.C. Brill 108th; A.E. Ball 81st; A.J. Brent 104th; A.C. Brill 118th; G. Godling 134th; A.E. Ball 149th

1954-55: A.J. Brent 30th; H.N. Nunns 50th; T.D. Payne 86th; D.G. Child 110th; T.D. Payne 74th; R.J. Webb 110th; D.G. Child 89th; J.P. Clark 121st; D.E. Reynolds 132nd

1955-56: A.J. Weeks-Pearson 11th; R.A. Morley 28th; D.A. Bentley 104th; D.H. Hopgood 138th; D.H. Hopgood 82nd; D.H. Hopgood 138th; D.H. Hopgood 153rd; D.E. Reynolds 122nd; A.C. Brill 160th

1956-57: L.F. Fletcher 30th; A.J. Brent 49th; G.R. Last 42nd; A.A. Everard 145th; G.R. Last 53rd; A.W. Wood 145th; H.N. Nunns 94th; A.C. Brill 150th; D.G. Child 154th

1957-58: A.J. Weeks-Pearson 41st; T. Sullivan 43rd; A.W. Wood 72nd; G. Scotting 141st; A.W. Wood 74th; M. Weller 77th; G. Scotting 87th; H.N. Nunns 187th; D. French 147th

1958-59: M. Weller 25th; A.J. Brent 51st; M. Weller 118th; R.J. Webber 218th; M. Weller 72nd; R.J. Webber 85th; R.J. Webber 111th; G.E. Greer 199th; A.C. Dashwood 163rd

1959-60: J.B. Herring 13th; P.D. Jackson 73rd; A.J. Baldwin 88th; E.O. Driscoll 128th; D.A. Bentley 69th; D.A. Bentley 128th; P.E. Baldwin 141st; F.O. Driscoll 218th; R.J. Webb 196th

1960-61: J.R. Baldwin 47th; J.R. Baldwin 47th; R.J. Stevens 79th; W.S. Hill 141st; M. Taylor 101st; M. Taylor 149th; W.S. Hill 113th; P.E. Baldwin 138th; R. Whitlock 177th

1961-62: J.R. Baldwin 116th; G. Cross 117th; R.A.G. Smith 163rd; D. Gregory 161st; D. Hopgood 217th; M. Taylor 161st; J.R. Baldwin 145th; B.D. Underhill 111th; A.W. Wood 194th

1962-63: A.N. Mandeville 62nd; R.J. Webber 90th; D.S.I. Peode 108th; G.E. Greer 145th; F.C. Rogers 74th; D. Hopgood 217th; G. Scotting 133rd; D.I. Currie 113th; A.J. Woodrow 196th

1963-64: J.R. Baldwin 18th; K. Mitchell 36th; J.S. Cutting 67th; T.J.W. Mandeville 128th; J. Roberts 144th; P.W. Cately 144th; A.J. Brent 231st; J.E. Witkers 147th; A.W. Wood 178th

1964-65: J.R. Baldwin 5th; B.W. Heaver 12th; A.J. Weeks-Pearson 70th; G.L. Jex 149th; J.S. Cutting 185th; A.J. Brent 281st; D.L. Gregory 337th; R.J. Webber 156th; R. Whitlock 205th

1965-66: J.R. Baldwin 7th; M. Weller 86th; F.C. Rogers 69th; T. Mandeville 161st; M. Weller 144th; E. Pepper 213th; R.A. Morley 190th; R.A. Morley 131st; L.F. Fletcher (DMF)

1966-67: J.R. Baldwin 18th; M. Weller 24th; A. Davis 153rd; G. Jex 281st; B.G. Stone 74th; J.B. Herring 51st; A.J. Brent 195th; T. Mandeville 282nd; D.A. Bentley 303rd

1967-68: R. Richardson 3rd; W. Wade 88th; A.J. Weeks-Pearson 57th; J. Heren 162nd; J.B. Herring 189th; D.W. Wade 74th; G. Weller 282nd; B. Stone 233rd; D. Fildes 337th

1968-69: R. Richardson 3rd; I. Wilson 30th; C. Haines 134th; G. Jex 225th; P. Horwood 99th; W.S.E. Hill 110th; A. Mandeville 131st; R. Hawin 160th; D. Fildes 373rd

1969-70: R. Richardson 7th; I. Wilson 25th; P. Horwood 49th; R. Shepheard 225th; M. Willis 54th; M. Willis 63rd; A. Mandeville 160th; R. Hawin 256th; L. Rogers (ONF)

1970-71: R. Richardson 8th; J. Clare 47th; I. Wilson 53rd; A. Davis 283rd; C. Haines 72nd; R. Barker 112th; A. Mandeville 184th; R. Hawin 277th; E.M. Pepper 201st

1971-72: I. Wilson 11th; J. Clare 18th; R. Richardson 27th; E. Pepper 301st; J. Baldwin 30th; E. Pepper 84th; P. Shepheard 158th; F.C. Rogers 312th; D. Fildes 233rd

1972-73: R. Richardson 6th; I. Wilson 27th; J. Clare 53rd; B. Heaver 227th; R. Horwood 66th; G. Botley 73rd; G. Botley 154th; B.F. Pearce 234th; R.A. Morley 232nd

1973-74: R. Richardson 10th; I. Wilson 18th; J. Baldwin 43rd; W. Hill 160th; J. Clare 65th; E. Pepper 78th; B. O'Gorman 166th; G. Browning 195th; L. Foster 261st

1974-75: P. Hamilton 61st; I. Wilson 112th; J. Baldwin 147th; C. Haines 85th; M. Athawes 190th; C. Haines 117th; C. Haines 184th; T.J. Mandeville 190th; R. Foster 272nd

1975-76: R. Coles 8th; R. Richardson 8th; J. Baldwin 21st; C. Bird 254th; S. Knowles 40th; R. Savory 249th; J. Nash 132nd; R.A. Morley 195th; A.E. Ball 270th

1976-77: R. Coles 6th; A. Edwards 6th; P. Hamilton 12th; I. Wilson 113th; J. Clare 78th; W. Hill 91st; E. Pepper 250th; C. Bird 197th; C. Woodcock 463rd

1977-78: R. Coles 9th; S. Knowles 9th; J. Baldwin 27th; M. Athawes 101st; I. Wilson 82nd; S. Knowles 96th; S. Knowles 113th; T. Mandeville 254th; C. Haines 155th

1978-79: R. Coles 14th; A. Frankish 14th; I. Wilson 63rd; R. Cliff 122nd; E. Pepper 141st; R. Cliff 149th; R. Cliff 158th; E. Pepper 321st; M. Athawes 187th

1979-80: R. Coles 9th; W. Foster 9th; I. Wilson 128th; A. Davies 169th; P. Shepheard 212th; T. Soutar 169th; T. Soutar 231st; B. Heaver 169th; B. O'Gorman 123rd

1980-81: R. Coles 12th; J. Baldwin 52nd; I. Wilson 116th; I. Young 175th; B. O'Gorman 117th; P. Shepheard 296th; G. Spencer 317th; M. Athawes 324th; M. Wilkinson 170th

1981-82: R. Coles 10th; L. Roberts 50th; W. Foster 67th; M. Athawes 196th; P. Shepheard 177th; B. O'Gorman 178th; P. Barrington-King 353rd; C. Haines 365th; C. Woodcock 269th

1982-83: R. Coles 10th; J. Baldwin 91st; F. O'Gorman 136th; L. Roberts 209th; A. Davies 175th; J. Young 141st; J. Beck 250th; J. Beck 261st; M. Athawes 334th

1983-84: R. Coles 37th; K. Pike 148th; G. Martin 216th; M. Colpus 209th; R. Cliff 288th; R. Cliff 207th; P. Betts 266th; S. Fitzcosta 274th; P. Betts 321st

1984-85: R. Coles 43rd; W. O'Donnell 120th; C. Haines 157th; A. Tilley 186th; R. Cliff 78th; P. Calnan 74th; K. Coe 194th; K. Coe 197th; A.J. Woodrow 255th

1985-86: W. Foster 12th; T. Nash 30th; W. O'Donnell 35th; McGee 269th; K. Coe 16th; P. Calnan 40th; K. Pike 194th; R. Coe 204th; P. Betts 276th

1986-87: J. Barton 21st; T. Nash 36th; L. Roberts 70th; P. Ward 90th; J. Barton 83rd; R. Coles 209th; C. Lord 186th; G. Spencer 217th; J. Phelan 351st

1987-88: J. Barton 10th; A. Guilder 53rd; M. Jones 62nd; D. Heath 245th; M. Colpus 80th; M. Colpus 137th; P. Ward 90th; K. Pike 205th; M. Watling 339th

1988-89: J. Barton 1st; A. Guilder 13th; W. O'Donnell 39th; M. Trinca 123rd; M. Watling 88th; R. Coles 140th; P. Barlow 476th; R. Coles 178th; N. Newport 178th

249

BLACKHEATH PERFORMANCES IN ENGLISH CROSS-COUNTRY CHAMPIONSHIP

Compiled by G.R. Last and P.J.G. Baigent

(Note: Until 1924 the Club competed only when the race was held in the South, though individual members took part.)

Season	Venue	No. of Runners	Blackheath Points	Blackheath Team Position	Club Placings
1875-76	Buckhurst Hill	32	–	DID NOT COMPETE	
1876-77	Roehampton	34	–	DID NOT COMPETE	
1877-78	Roehampton	33	–	DID NOT COMPETE	
1878-79	Roehampton	41	–	DID NOT COMPETE	
1879-80	Roehampton	88	148	4th	W.W. Davis 15th
1880-81	Roehampton	106	163	4th	G.M. Nehan 5th
1881-82	Roehampton	104	201	4th	G. Cattlin 15th
1882-83	Roehampton	89	225	4th	A.H. Davies 21st
1883-84	Sutton Coldfield	56	–	DID NOT COMPETE	
1884-85	Manchester	66	–	DID NOT COMPETE	
1885-86	Croydon	58	–	5th	
1886-87	Sutton Coldfield	54	–	DID NOT COMPETE	
1887-88	Manchester	88	–	"	T.C. Davis 10th
1888-89	Kempton	82	–	7th	
1889-90	Sutton Coldfield	80	–	DID NOT COMPETE	
1890-91	Rock Ferry	88	–	"	
1891-92	Ockham	91	–	6th	
1892-93	Redditch	81	–	DID NOT COMPETE	
1893-94	Blackpool	83	–	"	
1894-95	Wembley	149	–	"	
1895-96	Water Orton	104	–	"	
1896-97	Trafford Park	98	–	DID NOT COMPETE	
1897-98	Horton (Northants)	80	–	"	H. Bull 64th, W.G. Suffield 75th, W.H. Manning 85th, J. Baker 89th, E.C. Good 98th, T.C. Mills 99th, G.N. Sturgeon 100th, H.G. Johnson 417th, E. Ratcliff –, S. Wilkinson –
1898-99	Wembley	116	510	22nd	
1899-1900	Rotherham	93	–	DID NOT COMPETE	
1900-01	Leicester	113	–	"	
1901-02	Lingfield	159	–	"	
1902-03	Haydock	146	–	"	
1903-04	Wolverhampton	114	422	9th	M.P.S. White 44th, E.F. Judson 62nd, G.L. Hopkins 69th, T.C. Davis 71st, P. Kerry 88th, E.R. Small 93rd, A. Robins 101st, E.V. Norman 109th, F.D. Carr 113½
1904-05	Lingfield	125	–	DID NOT COMPETE	
1905-06	Haydock	162	–	"	
1906-07	Colwall Park Gt. Malvern	186	–	"	
1907-08	Newbury	252	834	22nd	E.F. Judson 79th, H.E.J. Southwell 105th, C.A. Glaeser 138th, A.H. Woodhouse 154th, A.H.L. Knapp 178th, S.J. Wickham 187th, T.C. Davis 194th, E. Hough 202nd, F.D. Carr 207th, R.W. Davis 412nd, I. Loweys (Jnr.) –
1908-09	Haydock	163	–	DID NOT COMPETE	
1909-10	Derby	247	–	"	
1910-11	Taplow	240	775	21st	E.F. Judson 93rd, C.A. Wickham-Jones 119th, C.A. Glaeser 125th, C.H. Baxtor 136th, A.P.L. Johnson 150th, T.W. Purchase 169th, E.R. Small 183rd, S.J. Wickham 187th, T.C. Davis 192nd, R.W. Davis 197th, A.R. Pearson 209th
1911-12	Haydock	173	–	DID NOT COMPETE	
1912-13	Wolverhampton	211	–	"	
1913-1914	Cheltenham	273	–	DID NOT COMPETE	
1914-15 until 1918-19 – No Races					
1919-20	Windsor	271	716		A.C. Telfer 15th, B.H. Lymbery 101st, C.A. Peachey 137th, S.D. Taylor 138th, T.W. Purchase 138th, A.H. Atkins 157th, W. Layfield 168th, A.D. Thwaites –, L.A. Lidden 202nd, E. Snelling 207th, J.C. Stevens –, W.R.J. Clarke –
1920-21	Doncaster	205	–	DID NOT COMPETE	
1921-22	Hereford	236	–	"	
1922-23	Beaconsfield	327	1039	24th	W.G. Kilby 135th, W.C. Colgate 151st, C. Whittington 174th, D.K. Saunders 197th, S.H. Clayton 250th, 268th
1923-24	Doncaster	219	–	DID NOT COMPETE	
1924-25	Hereford	245	–	"	
1925-26	Wolverton	331	517	13th	P.H. Francis 14th, D.J. Mobbs 83rd, S.H. Dewdney 132nd, R.D. Bell 96th, C.L. Mobbs 149th, E.M. Saville 162nd, R.F. Barclay 165th, J.W. Norman 168th, J.H.K. Hon 207th, J.S. Horsley 228th, A.E. Bagg 229th, J.H. Kitten 231st, R.F. Barclay 241st, R.F. Barclay –
1926-27	Crewe	429	606	11th	P.H. Francis 8th, A.G.V. Allen 61st, J.W. Norman 127th, D.J. Mobbs 161st, W.E. Dimes 170th, A.C. Barclay 179th, E.M. Saville 191st
1927-28	Leamington	375	988	21st	C.L. Mobbs 129th, J.S. Horsley 152nd, W.F. Dimes 162nd, J.W. Norman 163rd, H.S. Smith 177th, W.F. Street 205th, D.K. Saunders 231st, J.E. Ashmore 243rd
1928-29	Beaconsfield	247	670	17th	W.F. Dimes 59th, C.L. Mobbs 100th, M. Lindsay 114th, Dewdney 121st, A.G. Allen 137th, C. Pollard 139th, H.F. Smith 145th, F.D. Lys 152nd
1929-30	Sheffield	334	634	16th	A.G.V. Allen 80th, D.J. Mobbs 93rd, C.E. Clower 94th, Pollard 115th, R.F. Cross 123rd, H.S. Smith 129th, P.W. Glover 141st, N.L. Burt 147th, J.W. Norman –

Season	Venue	No. of Runners	Blackheath Points	Blackheath Position	Club Placing (counting runners)								
1930-31	Kettering	348	649	16th	C.E. Clower 87th	R.F. Cross 98th	R.A.E. Galley 110th	W.E. Dimes 117th	C.L. Mobbs 118th	A.G.V. Allen 119th	R.E. Walker 123rd	P.W. Glover 127th	H.S. Smith 226th
1931-32	Wolverton	289	864	24th	A.G.V. Allen 121st	R.E. Walker 134th	C.L. Mobbs 138th	H.S. Smith 146th	J.W. Norman 160th	W. Holmes 165th	P.W. Glover 191st	G.J. Richmond 194th	R.J. Cross 219th
1932-33	Alderley Edge	344	679	19th	P.W. Glover 90th	P.H. Francis 102nd	L.T. Brockway 111th	C.L. Mobbs 112th	H.S. Smith 128th	R.F. Walker 136th	R.E. Walker 160th	R.J. Philo 197th	Polland 207th
1933-34	Himley Park	297	608	14th	L.T. Brockway 58th	R.E. Walker 76th	P.W. Glover 114th	R.F. Cross 115th	R.J. Philo 116th	H.S. Smith 129th	A.N. Daniel 151st	V.L. Mobbs 197th	W.G. Mills 201st
1934-35	Beaconsfield	295	773	20th	R.J. Philo 80th	P.W. Glover 125th	R.J. Philo 133rd	H.S. Smith 139th	A. Roberts 145th	H.S. Smith 151st	G.H. Wilkinson 155th	P.W. Glover 174th	L.G. King 182nd
1935-36	Alderley Edge	285	704	15th	H.S. Smith 64th	R.F. Cross 94th	G.F. Brooks 101st	R.R. Cross 135th	H.S. Smith 136th	W.F. Dew 174th	L.D. Butler 205th	P.W. Glover 174th	R.F. Cross 195th
1936-37	Stratford-upon-Avon	315	510	10th	H.S. Smith 43rd	H.S. Smith 54th	G.H. Wilkinson 82nd	A.C.J. Poole 88th	R.E. Walker 120th	G.H. Wilkinson 123rd	H.E. Starnes 154th	L.E. Hammill 180th	R.E. Walker 155th
1937-38	Reading	288	513	13th	A.C.J. Poole 58th	A.C.J. Poole 74th	H.E. Starnes 81st	H.E. Starnes 59th	G.F. Brooks 100th	A.G.V. Allen 105th	L. King 120th	A.G.V. Allen 123rd	R.E. Walker 155th
1938-39	Worsley	392	787	19th	G.H. Wilkinson 76th	P.J. Barnwell 81st	H.E. Starnes 128th	R.E. Walker 158th	W.F. Dew 158th	G.F. Brooks 169th	H.S. Smith 172nd	L.E. Hammill 183rd	G.F. Brooks 200th
1939-40 until 1944-45 No Races													
1945-46	Leamington Spa	239	289	5th	R.R. Choat 18th	D.E. Reynolds 33rd	D.E. Reynolds 50th	A.E. Keopax 61st	A. Dole 62nd	H.N. Nunns 65th	D.W. Smith 70th	A.C.J. Poole 98th	A.D. Kennedy 113th
1946-47	Apsley	279	255	4th	S.C. Wooderson 7th	R.R. Choat 9th	J. Braughton 29th	W.F. Spencer 64th	A.J. Brent 66th	G.E. Monshall 56th	G.H. Wilkinson 102nd	D.E. Reynolds 144th	A. Dale 171st
1947-48	Sheffield	402	183	3rd	S.C. Wooderson 28th	R.R. Choat 28th	J. Braughton 30th	W.F. Spencer 45th	A.J. Brent 32nd	D.E. Reynolds 53rd	D.W. Smith 138th	E.R. May 66th	G.E. Monshall 121st
1948-49	Bromford Bridge B'ham	449	501	12th	J. Braughton 41st	W.F. Spencer 45th	A.J. Brent 48th	R.R. Choat 73rd	A.J. Brent 146th	E. Beaton 148th	D.E. Reynolds 56th	D.O. Smith 320th	A.J. Brent -
1949-50	Aylesbury	493	343	7th	L. Atkinson 22nd	H.H. Hunns 50th	A.J. Brent 56th	W. Spencer 57th	J. Clark 70th	R.R. Choat 88th	G. Monshall 129th	G. Monshall 129th	D. Reynolds 166th
1950-51	Richmond (Yorks)	350	574	10th	A.J. Brent 57th	J. Withers 83rd	H.H. Nunns 89th	R.R. Choat 91st	J. Clark 91st	R.R. Choat 148th	P. Stenning 181st	L.E. Piper 218th	G. Grier 278th
1951-52	Gt. Barr B'ham	418	729	17th	R.R. Choat 60th	R.R. Choat 112th	J.E. Withers 115th	A.E. Ball 119th	I. Clark 120th	A.J. Brill 143rd	A. Brill 165th	L.M. Childs 198th	J.P. Clarke 259th
1952-53	Caversham Pk. Reading	473	526	9th	J.E. Withers 77th	H.N. Nunns 83rd	A.J. Brent 83rd	A.J. Brent 109th	H.H. Nunns 119th	D.E. Reynolds 123rd	T.D. Payne 149th	A.E. Ball 153rd	D.G. Child 165th
1953-54	Arrowe Pk. Birkenhead	419	819	17th	A.J. Brent 50th	A.A. Everad 101st	A.J. Brent 165th	A.J. Brent 165th	H.N. Nunns 165th	R.R. Choat 178th	D.A. Bentley 212th	D.H. Hopgood 216th	R.J. Webb 235th
1954-55	Cardington, Bedford	544	762	13th	A.J. Weeks-Pearson 11th	D.A. Bentley 128th	H.N. Nunns 140th	H.N. Nunns 133rd	A.C. Brills 178th	P.E. Baldwin 182nd	T.D. Payne 187th	T.D. Payne 216th	A.J. Brent -
1955-56	Warwick	509	570	9th	R.A. Morley 26th	A.J. Weeks-Pearson 33rd	A.J. Brent 86th	G.R. Last 123rd	D.A. Bentley 129th	A.C. Brills 173rd	A.W. Wood 174th	A.J. Woodrow 258th	F.L. O'Driscoll 307th
1956-57	Parliament Hill London	717	710	10th	A.J. Weeks-Pearson 14th	A.J. Brent 65th	D. Bentley 139th	D. Bentley 153rd	G. Scotting 164th	H.H. Nunns 165th	A.W. Wood 176th	A.C. Dashwood 417th	
1957-58	Arrowe Pk. Birkenhead	574	536	7th	A.J. Weeks-Pearson 11th	A.J. Brent 64th	M. Weller 175th	M. Weller 176th	T.T. Sullivan 122nd	R.A. Morley 133rd	B.D. Underhill 168th	G. Scotting 223rd	J.B. Herring 224th
1958-59	Peterborough	617	1377	24th	A.J. Brent 117th	L.F. Fletcher 176th	A.W. Wood 176th	A.W. Wood 176th	P.D. Jackson 269th	G. Scotting 428th	G. Scotting 428th	D. Bentley 280th	
1959-60	West Bromwich	662	1037	16th	A.J. Weeks-Pearson 78th	L.F. Fletcher 147th	A.R. Stevens 149th	A.J. Brent 157th	P.D. Jackson 231st	G. Scotting 275th	D.L. Gregory 275th	A.W. Wood 281st	A.W. Wood 395th
1960-61	Parliament Hill London	796	1054	15th	J.B. Herring 77th	F.C. Rogers 285th	A.J. Brent 158th	M.A. Taylor 195th	R.J. Werber 223rd	D.L. Gregory 262nd	R.A. Morley 281st	A.W. Wood 311th	M. Weller 467th
1961-62	Blackpool	696	2009	41st	P.D. Jackson 259th	F.C. Rogers 285th	F.C. Rogers 325th	B.J. Pearce 349th	O. Fildes 374th	A.W. Wood 417th	F.C. Rogers 316th	A.W. Wood 473rd	
1962-63	Cambridge	857	1376	26th	J.R. Baldwin 118th	A.J. Brent 216th	A.J. Brent 235th	A.J. Brent 245th	P.W. Catley 246th	A.J. Brent 316th	B.F. Pearce 366th	R.J. Webber 460th	T.J. Mandeville 468th
1963-64	Leicester	853	1341	23rd	J.R. Baldwin 89th	A.J. Weeks-Pearson 141st	L.F. Fletcher 185th	F.C. Rogers 282nd	J. Roberts 286th	A.B. Pearce 286th	F.C. Rogers 499th	J. Webber 496th	J. Farrington -
1964-65	Parliament Hill London	838	1636	27th	B. Heaver 39th	A. Davis 251st	J.R. Baldwin 303rd	B. Stone 308th	F. Rogers 360th	J.S. Cutting 358th	A.J. Brent 429th	J. Roberts 540th	
1965-66	Sheffield	808	1495	25th	J.R. Baldwin 17th	I.C. Wilson 229th	M. Weller 255th	B. Stone 309th	A. Davis 316th	D. Gregory 369th	A.J. Brent 375th	D. Gregory 384th	G. Jex 575th
1966-67	Norwich	753	617	11th	J.R. Baldwin 28th	J.B. Herring 46th	R. Richardson 58th	J.B. Herring 124th	I.C. Wilson 170th	A.J. Weeks-Pearson 191st	P. Horwood 191st	C. Haines 286th	
1967-68	Sutton Coldfield	856	1351	24th	R. Richardson 32nd	C. Haines 264th	A.J. Weeks-Pearson 191st	C. Haines 264th	D.W. Wade 270th	P. Horwood 286th	C. Haines 385th	B. Stone 286th	P. Shepheard 509th
1968-69	Parliament Hill London	901	820	16th	R. Richardson 5th	I. Wilson 95th	J.R. Baldwin 215th	P. Horwood 181st	C. Haines 213th	W. Wade 297th	A. Davis 260th	A. Davis 488th	A. Mandeville 330th
1969-70	Blackpool	931	745	9th	R. Richardson 32nd	C. Haines 70th	I. Wilson 154th	C. Haines 156th	P. Horwood 163rd	J. Clare 170th	R. Hawin 232nd	R. Hawin 238th	G. Botley 415th
1970-71	Norwich	851	1089	20th	R. Richardson 34th	C. Haines 114th	J. Clare 120th	J. Clare 147th	R. Hawin 328th	G. Botley 346th	A. Davies 416th	A. Davies 524th	
1971-72	Sutton Coldfield	887	925	17th	R. Richardson 87th	I. Wilson 90th	J. Baldwin 131st	C. Haines 162nd	J. Clare 196th	G. Botley 259th	M. Hamlin 380th	M. Hamlin 492nd	
1972-73	Parliament Hill	1070	819	13th	R. Richardson 56th	J. Clare 116th	J. Baldwin 130th	J. Baldwin 182nd	P. Horwood 270th	C. Haines 348th	R. Hawin 336th	M. Athawes 340th	B. O'Gorman 364th
1973-74	Sheffield	968	1136	21st	R. Richardson 47th	I. Wilson 111th	J. Baldwin 132nd	C. Haines 227th	P. Shepheard 283rd	A. Frankish 348th	C. Woodcock 336th	P. Shepherd 616th	R. Hawin dnf
1974-75	Luton	1053	2646	54th	I. Wilson 262nd	N. Rust 395th	M. Athawes 415th	M. Athawes 504th	P.W. Catley 528th	K. Daniel 322nd	C. Woodcock 542nd	I. Young 508th	
1975-76	Leicester	1214	1107	21st	R. Richardson 29th	S. Knowles 100th	J. Clare 147th	J. Clare 147th	G. Botley 270th	B. Swift 400th	R. Savory 585th	M. Athawes 611th	W. Wade 453rd
1976-77	Parliament Hill	1368	1779	36th	A. Edwards 111th	I. Young 243rd	I. Young 323rd	C. Haines 341st	C. Haines 380th	G. Martin 331st	W. Wade 369th	K. Pike 732nd	R. Coles dnf
1977-78	Leeds	1379	1557	27th	R. Coles 59th	S. Knowles 180th	I. Young 270th	E. Pepper 283rd	I. Wilson 348th	I. Wilson 454th	M. Athawes 385th	K. Pike 566th	T. Soutar 525th
1978-79	Luton	1555	1580	28th	R. Coles 46th	P. Irvine 164th	S. Knowles 306th	I. Young 339th	J. Baldwin 348th	C. Haines 426th	C. Woodcock 426th	G. Spencer 527th	P. Shepheard 650th
1979-80	Leicester	1627	1398	20th	R. Coles 82nd	W. Foster 117th	P. Irvine 190th	I. Wilson 255th	J. Baldwin 322nd	K. Daniel 432nd	A. Frankish 475th	I. Young 619th	T. Soutar 768th
1980-81	Parliament Hill	1546	2040	33rd	R. Coles 66th	I. Young 338th	I. Young 365th	J. Baldwin 388th	K. Daniel 400th	B. Swift 524th	C. Haines 469th	M. Athawes 508th	
1981-82	Leeds	1605	1772	30th	R. Coles 79th	I. Wilson 159th	L. Wilson 252nd	K. Daniel 331st	G. Martin 400th	I. Wilson 556th	G. Martin 591st	K. Pike 611th	B. Swift 788th
1982-83	Luton	1610	2002	39th	R. Coles 93rd	S. Rutherford 366th	M. Jackson 366th	C. Lord 378th	C. Lord 408th	G. Martin 454th	I. Wilson 556th	C. Lord 566th	
1983-84	Newark	1723	3829	76th	R. Coles 251st	P. Betts 518th	K. Pike 518th	G. Martin 796th	R. Cliff 378th	M. Wilkinson 455th	R. Cliff 527th	K. Pike 732nd	
1984-85	Milton Keynes	1806	4147	93rd	R. Coles 36th	G. Martin 451st	K. Pike 145th	M. Colpus 807th	J. Beck 796th	M. Athawes 855th	M. Jackson 942nd	K. Pike 566th	
1985-86	Newcastle	1706	1641	20th	W. Foster 36th	L. Roberts 145th	R. Coles 70th	R. Coe 300th	R. Coe 409th	S. Fitzcosta 880th	R. Coe 1044th	G. Spencer 527th	A. Tilley 818th
1986-87	Luton	2006	1497	24th	J. Barton 34th	W. Foster 70th	W. Foster 41st	M. Colpus 250th	M. Colpus 362nd	K. Pike 669th	P. Ward 616th	K. Pike 671st	
1987-88	Newark	2136	516	3rd	J. Barton 17th	W. Foster 41st	W. Foster 34th	M. Jones 114th	M. Colpus 173rd	M. Colpus 114th	R. Coles 753rd	D. Heath 667th	
1988-89	Ewell	1903	483	7th	J. Barton 32nd	W. Foster 32nd	A. Guilder 71st	A. Guilder 86th	S. Newport 110th	M. Trinca 160th	M. Watling 187th	B. O'Donnell 193rd	R. Coles 197th

Appendix Five
BLACKHEATH HARRIERS ALL-TIME BEST PERFORMANCES
(TRACK & FIELD) AT 31.12.89 Compiled by P.J.G. Baigent

100 yards

9.7	E.L. Page	Hamilton, Ont.	21 Aug. 30

100 metres

10.32	G.L.G. Watson	Birmingham	1 July 83
10.4	P.A. Ashen	Battersea Park	26 June 83
10.47	P.N. Davies	Crystal Palace	21 June 86
10.48	S.M. Green	Crystal Palace	31 July 81
10.6	E.L. Page	Paris, France	9 Sept. 38
10.6	A.D. Coote	Hanover, Germany	14 July 49
10.6	J.R. Evans	Crystal Palace	9 May 84

200 metres

20.62	G.L.G. Watson	Birmingham	5 June 83
21.12	P.N. Davies	Hendon	10 May 86
21.2	P.A. Ashen	Bromley	15 June 83
21.5	S. M. Green	Spalding	2 Aug. 81
21.5	M.R. Williams	Bromley	24 Apr. 88
21.6	E.L. Page	Paris, France	22 Aug. 37

220 yards

21.6†	C.G. Wood	Stamford Bridge	22 July 1887
21.8	I.M. Ross	Eltham	28 May 60

†Straight

400 metres

47.55	J. McCabe	Hendon	18 June 83
47.58	D. Emery	Cwmbran	31 May 82
47.58	J.P. Shaw	Edinburgh	2 July 83
47.9	J.N. Spooner	Richmond, U.S.A.	June 79
48.3	T.R. Foulger	Loughborough	17 June 84
48.36	N. Brooks	Memphis, U.S.A.	19 Apr. 80

440 yards

46.5	E.J. Sampson	Cardiff	22 July 58
48.0	G.C. Thomas	White City	13 Aug. 63
48.2	I.M. Ross	Motspur Park	25 June 60
48.3	B.E. Shurmer	Motspur Park	24 June 67

800 metres

1:46.61	C.A. McGeorge	Lausanne, Switzerland	15 Sept. 87
1:47.01	N. Brooks	Knoxville, U.S.A.	11 Apr. 80
1:47.56	J.N. Spooner	Charlottesville, U.S.A.	24 Apr. 79
1:49.0	D.N. Wright	Rouen, France	24 Sept. 66
1:50.88	A.K. Linford	Glasgow	23 July 88
1:51.0	T.R. Foulgar	Enfield	2 Aug. 87

880 yards

1:48.6	J.V. Baker	Cambridge, U.S.A.	4 May 68
1:49.2	S.C. Wooderson	Motspur Park	20 Aug. 38

1500 metres

3:39.41	C.A. McGeorge	Zurich, Switzerland	13 Aug. 86
3:41.0	D.J. Heath	Loughborough	25 July 89
3:44.9	W.R.G. Foster	Stretford	30 Aug. 86
3:45.1	J.N. Spooner	Piscataway, U.S.A	17 Apr. 81
3:46.8	D.N. Wright	Wimbledon	27 July 68
3:47.2	S. Newport	Loughborough	25 July 89

1 mile

3:56.71	C.A. McGeorge	Cork, Ireland	5 July 88
3:59.36	D.J. Heath	Belfast, N. Ireland	15 July 89
4:00.2	J.V. Baker	Philadelphia, U.S.A.	1 June 68
4:02.39	J.N. Spooner	Philadelphia, U.S.A.	30 Apr. 83
4:02.7	J.B. Herring	Chiswick	25 July 64
4:03.4	J.D. Barton	Tonbridge	26 July 88

3000 metres

7:57.29	J.D. Barton	Gateshead	16 July 88
8:04.07	A.J.A. Guilder	Sandnes, Norway	22 Aug. 87
8:05.57	D.J. Heath	Loughborough	25 June 89
8:06.4	W.R.G. Foster	Loughborough	2 July 87
8:08.51	S. Newport	Loughborough	25 June 89
8:13.0	R.J. Coles	Crystal Palace	11 July 79

2 miles

8:37.6	J.B. Herring	Motspur Park	22 July 65
8:46.4	R. Richardson	Motspur Park	23 July 69
8:48.0	J.R. Baldwin	White City	7 June 65

3 miles

13:27.6	J.B. Herring	White City	14 Aug. 64
13:42.0	J.R. Baldwin	Welwyn	25 June 66
13:49.2	R. Richardson	Edgbaston	7 May 69

5000 metres

13:49.63	A.J.A. Guilder	Crystal Palace	13 Sept. 87
13:51.4	J.B. Herring	White City	14 Aug. 64
13:52.46	J.D. Barton	Derby	4 June 88
13:58.2	R. Richardson	Crystal Palace	31 May 69
13:59.29	W.R.G. Foster	Derby	4 June 88
14:08.6	J.V. Wigley	Crystal Palace'	20 May 84

6 miles

28:39.8	R. Richardson	Crystal Palace	25 Aug 68
29:03.0	J.R. Baldwin	Deptford	16 Apr. 66

10000 metres

28:36.0	R. Richardson	Rennes, France	27 June 69
29:14.2	J.V. Wigley	Bromley	14 June 83
29:17.3	A.J.A. Guilder	Tooting Bec	13 Apr. 88
29:22.3	W.R.G. Foster	Crystal Palace	26 Apr. 89
29:38.87	M.E. Brameld	Crystal Palace	23 July 83
29:40.0	R.J. Coles	Aldershot	30 June 79

Marathon

2:17:51	R. Richardson	Manchester	4 June 72
2:19:06	W.R.G. Foster	New York, U.S.A.	5 Nov. 89
2:20:28	R.J. Coles	London	17 Apr. 83
2:23:28	G. Martin	London	17 Apr. 83
2:23:39	J.A. Clare	Chiswick	13 June 70
2:24:00	M. Willis	Harlow	25 Oct. 69
2:24:00	C.R. Haines	Manchester	4 June 72

3000 metres Steeplechase

8:44.10	S. Newport	Crystal Palace	14 July 89
8:53.97	D. Lee	Crystal Palace	12 Aug. 89
9:04.2	J.R. Baldwin	Crystal Palace	4 June 72
9:05.4	J.A. Farrington	Chiswick	27 July 63
9:08.65	M.A. Jones	Glasgow	23 July 88
9:08.9	D.W. Taylor	Warley	4 July 87

110 metres hurdles

14.1	G.J. Gower	Crystal Palace	15 July 72
14.4	C. Hamplett	Bromley	27 Aug. 89
14.48	K.S. Bunce	Birmingham	18 June 88
14.49	D.L. Wilson	Bristol	13 June 84
15.1	E.J. Sawkins	Aldershot	27 July 57
15.1	A. Fischer	Philadelphia, U.S.A.	12 Apr. 85

400 metres hurdles

52.83	P.R. Austridge	Crystal Palace	26 June 87
53.06	N. Keogh	Crystal Palace	17 June 89
53.82	D.L. Wilson	Crystal Palace	23 June 85
54.2	M.W. McFarnell	Crystal Palace	17 Aug. 68
54.3*	C.C. Higgins	Motspur Park	24 July 68
54.5	M.J. Carroll	West London	10 July 76

*440y −0.3

High Jump

2.20	T. Llewelyn	Crystal Palace	15 July 83
2.18	T.R. Foulger	Crystal Palace	23 Sept. 79
2.16	W.R. Caswell	Aldershot	1 July 87
2.08	M.S.G. Cannon	Aldershot	5 June 82
2.06	A.J. Hodge	Stoke-on-Trent	7 May 88
2.05	N. Terry	Newham	17 Aug. 85

Pole Vault

4.70	S.J. Gascoigne	Aldershot	5 Sept. 88
4.50	J.P. Aubrey	Crystal Palace	15 May 82
4.50	J.D. Andrews	Woking	16 Apr. 88
4.40	A.P. Williams	Crystal Palace	8 May 82
4.30	B.S. McStravick	Edinburgh	20 June 87
4.26	J. Faircloth	Connahs Quay	20 July 68

Long Jump

7.52	J.E.C. Whall	Erith	30 Apr. 60
7.41	P.N. Davies	Crystal Palace	19 May 84
7.38	P.J. Hudson	Loughborough	5 June 68
7.38	D. Heard	Cwmbran	23 July 89
7.37	G.E. Pullen	Birmingham	7 July 84
7.30	J. Lissaman	Erith	14 Aug. 60

Triple Jump

16.60	M.R. Malkin	Birmingham	7 Aug. 88
16.18	A.E. Wadhams	Brno, Czechoslovakia	6 July 69
15.82	G.L. Hamlyn	White City	13 July 68
15.47	D. Heard	Cwmbran	23 July 89
15.25	J.E.C. Whall	Helsinki, Finland	12 Sept. 59
14.77	M.A. Seeley	Birmingham	19 July 87

Shot

19.27	M.A. Winch	Crystal Palace	29 Aug. 77
18.05	J.T. Watts	Edinburgh	19 Aug. 72
17.95	G.C. Savory	Derby	4 June 88
15.47	T.J. Walhen	Portsmouth	21 June 78
14.71	P.D. Yates	Southall	30 Apr. 83
14.43	D. Morris	Grangemouth	27 Aug. 89

Indoors
| 19.53 | M.A. Winch | Cosford | 13 Mar. 82 |

Discus

60.92	G.C. Savory	Birmingham	10 May 86
59.70	J.T. Watts	Crystal Palace	14 July 72
56.80	M.A. Winch	Bristol	11 July 81
55.02	D. Morris	Pitreavie	30 Aug. 89
49.86	K. Horne	Birmingham	14 Aug. 82
49.30	C.S. Ellis	Crystal Palace	17 May 82

Hammer

58.12	N.J. Spivey	Cambridge	May 89
52.74	N.A. Haffenden	Bromley	29 May 88
52.60	M.A. Winch	Crystal Palace	11 July 82
52.14	J.T. Watts	Singapore	17 July 69
47.76	T.J. Walhen	Plymouth	31 May 75
45.66	A.J. Paffett	Birmingham	21 May 88

Javelin

(Old Model discontinued after 1986)

86.28	D.J. Brand	Hendon	15 June 86
85.92	P.D. Yates	Wolverhampton	12 May 84
73.42	M.J. Turner	Southampton	19 June 71
62.74	C. Hodder	Crystal Palace	5 Oct. 80
61.98	C.M. Brand	Chiswick	13 June 70
61.95	B.E.C. Harland	Crystal Palace	31 May 69

Javelin

(New Model)

77.84	P.D. Yates	Los Angeles, U.S.A	21 Feb. 87
74.90	D.J. Brand	Gateshead	27 June 86
61.92	J. Kitching	Derby	1 May 89
59.74	G.L.G. Watson	Newham	25 July 87
51.46	B.S. McStravick	Edinburgh	2 July 88
51.06	H. Bauer	Newham	6 May 89

Decathlon

7563pts	B.S. McStravick	Edinburgh	27/28 July 86
6663pts	T.J. Walhen	Vittel, France	19/20 Aug. 72
6237pts	G.E. Pullen	Parliament Hill	29/30 Aug. 87
6174pts	A.J. Hodge	Hoo	23/24 Sept. 89
6091pts	J.H. Wright	Welwyn	1/2 July 66
5883pts	D.K. Knight	Leicester	29/30 June 65

4 x 100 metres relay

41.1	P.A. Ashen, G.L.G. Watson, J.R. Evans, P.N. Davies	Wolverhampton	12 May 84
41.12	P.N. Davies, G. Proctor, M.R. Williams, N. Thompson	Stoke-on-Trent	19 Aug. 89
41.24	P.N. Davies, G. Proctor, M.R. Williams, D. Heard	Enfield	5 Aug. 89
41.39	S.M. Green, G.L.G. Watson, P.A. Ashen, G. Garland	Hendon	18 Sept 82
41.45	K. Bunce, M.R. Williams, R.V. Bates, P.N. Davies	West London	13 Aug. 88
41.64	G.L.G. Watson, P.N. Davies, B.S. McStravick, S.M. Green	Wigan	5 July 86

4 x 400 metres relay

3 : 13.74	B.S. McStravick, G.L.G. Watson, N. Keogh, D. Emery	Birmingham	10 May 86
3 : 15.47	T.R. Foulger, B.S. McStravick, D.J. Galvin, D. Emery	Haringey	10 Aug. 86
3 : 15.76	————, ————, ————, ————	Birmingham	7 July 84
3 : 15.96	T.R. Foulger, D. Emery, N. Keogh, T. Llewelyn	Newham	25 July 87
3 : 16.4	J.P. Shaw, D. Emery, N. Brooks, J.N. Spooner	West London	13 Aug. 83
3 : 16.5	D.J. Galvin, P.M. Crossan, N. Keogh, N. Thompson	Portsmouth	31 July 88

4 x 440 yards relay

| 3 : 18.4 | I.M. Ross, R.E.D. Taylor, R.A. Donnelly, E.J. Sampson | Chiswick | 9 May 59 |

Appendix Six

Compiled by P.J.G. Baigent

BLACKHEATH HARRIERS A.A.A. CHAMPIONS

100 Yards
1931	E.L. Page	10.0

440 Yards
1886	C.G. Wood	49.8
1887	C.G. Wood	51.0
1912	C.N. Seedhouse	49.8
1914	C.N. Seedhouse	50.0
1921	R.A. Lindsay	50.4

880 Yards
1903	B.J. Blunden	1:58.8
1905	B.J. Blunden	2:02.0

Mile
1935	S.C. Wooderson	4:17.2
1936	S.C. Wooderson	4:15.0
1937	S.C. Wooderson	4:12.2
1938	S.C. Wooderson	4:13.4
1939	S.C. Wooderson	4:11.4

3 Miles
1946	S.C. Wooderson	13:53.2

4 Miles
1881	G.M. Nehan	20:26.2

120 Yards Hurdles
1909	A.H. Healey	15.8

Long Jump
1884	E. Horwood	21'9"

Triple Jump
1959	J.E.C. Whall	49'2¾"
1969	A.E. Wadhams	51'4½"
1971	A.E. Wadhams	49'9"

Shot
1981	M.A. Winch	18.36m
1982	M.A. Winch	18.90m
1984	M.A. Winch	18.39m

4x100 Yards Relay
1932	E.L. Page L.G. Parkes		
	C.A. Wiard L.W. Ellis		43.6
1937	L.G. Parkes N.D. Cullen		
	C.A. Wiard E.L. Page		42.9
1939	T.W. Cotton V.S. Ransom		
	K.M. Torr C.A. Wiard		43.4

Mile Medley Relay
1911	J.T. Soutter C.N. Seedhouse		
	W.D. Lancefield F.T. Browne		3:33.4
1966	D.N. Wright B.E. Shurmer		
	M.W. McFarnall R. Porter		3:27.2

BLACKHEATH HARRIERS A.A.A. INDOOR CHAMPIONS

60 Metres Hurdles
1972	G.J Gower	7.9

Triple Jump
1971	A.E. Wadhams	15.43m

Shot
1979	M.A. Winch	18.60m
1980	M.A. Winch	18.74m
1981	M.A. Winch	18.38m
1982	M.A. Winch	18.82m
1983	M.A. Winch	18.84m
1984	M.A. Winch	18.52m
1987	G.C. Savory	17.52m

BLACKHEATH HARRIERS U.K. NATIONAL CHAMPIONS

100 Metres
1983	G.L.G. Watson	10.43

200 Metres
1983	G.L.G. Watson	20.88

High Jump
1982	T. Llewelyn	2.16m

Shot
1980	M.A. Winch	18.96m
1988	G.C. Savory	17.95m

Discus
1986	G.C. Savory	58.10m

Javelin
1983	P.D. Yates	80.84m
1984	P.D. Yates	82.54m

Appendix Seven

NAMES OF CLUB GROUPS

Page 55 Club Group 1887

Back Row	No names known
Third Row	Third from right (with beard) J. Rampley
Second Row	Fifth from left Cordwell, Centre F.H. Reed
Front Row	Second from left H.J. Barclay, second from right T. Crafter

Page 56 Club Group 1893

Back Row	No names known
Third Row	From the left: 4th F.H. Reed, 11th T.M. Gale, 12th C. Val Hunter, 13th J.H.A. Reay
Second Row	8th from the left (in front of Val Hunter) H.W.E. Sercombe
Front Row	Reclining (left) E.W. Stafford (right) T. Crafter

Page 85 Club Group 1908-9

Back Row	T.W.B. Purchase, G.D. Gray, H.A. Butler, C.A. Langford, H.F. Kitto, W.D. Lancefield, W.A. Dewsnap, P.H. Blackwell, A.H.L. Knapp, E.J.D. Ratcliff, T.K. Grant, W.C. Pinhey, J.M. Robins, E.V. Hollingsworth, H.J.L. Cavenaugh, A.P. Humpleby
Third Row	C. Smith, E.R. Harvey, H.E.J. Southwell, S.J. Wickham, E.J. Denney, P.H.C. Cavenaugh, W.F. Paulton, W.W. Neville, E.H. Neville, L. Latreille, T.E. Hammond, R.H. Openshaw, J.C. Johnson, I.W. Nicholson, E.P. Turner, F. Cannon, E.W. Stafford, S.C.A. Schofield, C.W. Starnes, T.M. Gale, G. Rowell
Second Row	J.H. Williams, C.H. Baxter, T. Crafter, J.J.C. Esson, W. Robinson, Dr. H.A. Munro, H.W.G. Haslegrave, H.J. Barclay, W. Rowland, J.H.A. Reay, H.D. Thomas, J.F. Ponsford, F.H. Blackford, W.D. Whiter
Front Row	W.L. Greenwood, A.H. Woodhouse, F.S. Dixon, E.V. Norman, J.E. Viney, H.C. Cooper, W.D. Smith, H.S. Openshaw, P.H. Small, T.C. Davis, A.R. Small, E.R. Small, Captain H.I. Greig, R.W. Davis

Page 102 Club Group 1919-20

Back Row	J.H. Williams, –––––, H.W.E. Sercombe, W.W. Davis, W. Rowland, H.D. Thomas, J.H. Rampley, J.H.A. Reay, C. Morgan, H. Melliar-Smith, –––––, H.C.F. Cordrey, S.D. Taylor, S.J. Wickham, L.C. Taylor, F.L. Gilbert, C.H. Sercombe, A.H. Atkins
Middle Row	G.J. Basson, J.C. Stevens, N.H. Prior, L.W. Cross, A.R. Pearson, T.C. Davis, E.J.D. Ratcliff, T. Crafter, H.R. Hopper, T.M. Gale, T.K. Grant, H.K. Grant, W.R.J. Clarke, W.S. Smith, T.W.B. Purchase
Front Row	B.H. Lymbery, F. Denman, A.E. Culver, H.A. Wilkinson, E.V. Norman, H. Bellman, A.C. Edwards, A.C. Telfer, L.A. Liddon, E.E. Snelling, –. Slatter, –. Horton, R.A. Wallis, A.D. Thwaites

Page 109 Club Group 1930 – Summer

Back Row	N.L. Burt, P.W. Glover, G.S. Fulton, H.S. Smith, C.A. Wiard
Middle Row	V.V.W. Beardon, C.J.R. Woods, E.L. Page, R.F. Cross
Front Row	W. Holmes, L.G. Parkes

Page 109 Club Group 1930 – Winter

Back Row	––––, C.H.R. Williams, K.N. Willcockson, ––––, ––––, P.J. Bagi, ––––, G.Q. Pollard
Middle Row	J. Thomas, C. Pollard, J. Morrison, J.D. Rogers, R.F. Barclay
Front Row	W.H.M. Vercoe, G.E. Turner, E.J.J. Reed

Page 115 Club Group 1924-25

Back Row T.J.G. Haynes, F.B. Mallinson, J.M. Morrison, J.D. Rogers, E.R. Baldry, —————, L.A. Liddon, R.W. Pattison, G.D. Basan, S.D. Taylor, H.J. Dyball, H.A. Wilkinson, R.H. Gollan, W.S.A. Winter, —————, N.L. Davis, E.M. Mote, A. Anderson, H.D.P. Thompson

Third Row W.J. Parrish, E.J.J. Reed, R. Bailey, H. Bellman, H.W. Lloyd-Mostyn, W.S. Smith, A.G.V. Allen, A.T.H. Pritchard, D.M. Smart, S.G. Beer, W.E. Skeet, H.C.R. Holden, —————, D.J. Mobbs, F.L. Gilbert, W.R.J. Clarke, S.J. Wickham, T.C. Davis, W.D. Whiter, A.D. Thwaites, —————, R.C. Stileman, R.A. Wallis

Second Row D.K. Saunders, A.R. Pearson, E. Allanson, W. Ramsey Moir, S.C.A. Schofield, W. Robinson, H.W.E. Sercombe, E.F. Nicholls. J.F. Ponsford, J.H.A. Reay, W.W. Davis, H.D. Thomas, J. Rampley, —————, H.F. Pash, R. Woods

Front Row C.L. Westley, E.G. Bradshaw, A.E. Bagi, L.C.W. Ratcliff, E. Preston, G.J. Symonds, C.E. Clowser, J.H. Kitton, N.H. Prior

Page 138 World Mile Record Group

Front Row D.E. Reynolds (no.7), R.A. Lindsay, B.C Eeles (in white), S.J. Wooderson, C.J.R. Woods, Sydney Wooderson, A.T. Wooderson, A.G. Hill, A. Metcalf, E.J.N. Hengle (No.5)

Between Lindsay and Eeles L.D. Butler, and on his left J.D. Rogers. Between Hill and Metcalf: C.L. Mobbs and between Metcalf and Hengle: A.G. Chappell

Page 148 Club Group 1938

Back Row P.M. Palmer, L.C. Westacott, F.A. Horn, —————, —————, L.J. Webber, C. Kidd, A.G. Mills, —————, C.O. Davies, S.N. Stockwell, —————, L.R. Clowser, E. Lester, L.E. Hammill, —————, C.B.E. Harden, H.S. Hargreaves, —————, L.G. Towers, —————, J.W. Cockburn, V.G. Trump, —————, B.G. Parrott, —————, —————, —————, E.J.J. Reed, —————, —————, J.P. Clark, W.J.A. Vercruyssen, L.G. Toms, C.H.R. Williams, —————, M.J. Mansell, R.W. Seager, —————.

4th Row, Standing S.A. Bliss, W.H.M. Vercoe, A. Roberts, —————, C.L. Mobbs, D.J. Mobbs, G.H. Wilkinson, S.C. Wooderson, H.S. Smith, R.E. Walker, A.C.J. Poole, L.G. King, W. Hefford, W.F. Dew, —————, D.E. Reynolds, —————, A.G.V. Allen, K.N. Wilcockson, T.C. Allen, —————, —————.

3rd Row, Standing N.W. Page, W. Spray (attendant), W. Parrish (attendant), C. Pollard, A. Fox, W.L. Pollard, G. Tye, —————, A.H. Woodhouse, J.F. Dyball, J.D. Rogers, H.K. Grant, W.R.J. Clarke, A.D. Thwaites, J.M. Scott, R.W. Pattison, H.A. Wilkinson, F.G.W. Paige, —————, H. Aitchison, —————, W.C. Colegate, S.J. Wooderson, —————, —————, A.E. Seager, S.A. Field, C.J.R. Woods.

Seated —————, J.H. Williams, S.D. Wickham, H.J. Staines, W.D. Whiter, G.F. McIvor, J. Morrison, T.C. Davis, R.F. Cross, T. Crafter, H.A. Munro, T.K. Grant, H.F. Pash, A.D. Metcalf, A. Anderson, H.E. King, H.W.E. Sercombe, W.S. Smith, —————, C. Waller, W.H. Pinhey.

Front, Squatting —————, B.N. Jefferies, N.L. Burt, —————, L.D. Butler, R.A.E. Galley, H.D. Charleson, J.L. Bray, L.D. Lee, H.E. Starns, J.D. Woodrow, S.G Beer, G.F. Brooks, —————, F.D. Holt, J.R.D. Cockburn, G.Owlett, —————, B.H. Lymbery, S.D. Taylor, F.W. Parker, —————, —————

Page 171 Club Group 1951

Back Row C.D. Purves, D.J. Stride, P.J.G. Baigent, M.J. Maslen, J.K. Grant, P.D. Hayes, P.A. Upson, G.L. Gosling, T.D. Hammill, L.F. Sargeant, L.J. New, D.W. Taylor, P.W. Eldridge, J.C. Taylor, A.J. Humber, M.G. Ball, A.S. Ross, A.E. Ball, M.D. Jenkins, T. Cavanagh, H.V. Lambshire, R.H. Thompson, R.R. Choat, M.J. Carlile, W.F. Lake, I.A.L. Little, J.P. Clark, R.H. Apps, N.G.R. Sanders, C.S. Wilson, P. Alder, E.L. Collett.

Fourth Row J.H. Scott-Wilson, J.G. Wilkinson, A.E. Beedle, S. Meades, D.P.R. Smith, R.A.A. Gross, R.A. Kirk, A.F. Nash, G. Williams, F.A. Thompson, A.J. Woodrow, A.A. Oldfield, J. Butler, E.J.J. Reed, J.C. Hancock, A.V. Hayday, J.J. Holland, D.G. Child, L.E. Hammill, C.H.R. Williams, P.A.R. Wright, A.E. Grove, I.E.A. Russell, P.G. Watkins, G.F. Sargeant, H.W. Coldwell, J. Cowmeadow (guest).

Third Row J.G. Lymbery, P.E. Sims, L.G. Toms, W.J. Traer, L.G. King, W.H.M. Vercoe, C.A. Standivan, P.G. Stenning, N.F. Everard, P.D. Cronin, V.G. Trump, B.G. Parrott, K.N. Wilcockson, V.W.W. Beardon, E.R. Allen, L. Norris, R.E. Walker, C. Pollard, G. Waller, J.R. Lowes, W.H. Hefford, A.A. Tweedy, J.A. Clear, M.A. Walker, R.H. Pain, H.J. Bishop.

Second Row D.J. Mobbs, A.J. Johnson, H.R. Howard, N.L. Davis, H.K. Grant, E.J. Denney, N. Beyfus, C.W. Starnes, R.W. Pattison, S.J. Wickham, S.D. Taylor, F.W. Parker (President), R.F. Cross, A.D. Thwaites, W.R.J. Clarke, C. Waller, H.A. Wilkinson, N.W. Page, L. Pendered, L.R. Clowser, D.E. Reynolds, J.R.D. Cockburn, H. Johnson, R.J. Webb.

Front Row L.E. Piper, G.O.J. Grier, C. Busby, G.J. Gosling, A.C. Dashwood, G.E. Monshall, A.J. Brent, A.C. Brill, J.E. Withers, A.J. Weeks-Pearson, G.R. Russell, J.M. Parr, M. Raoux, K.J. Johnson, J. Sims, J.E. Lindblom.

Page 194 Club Tour Switzerland 1958

Standing L.F. Fletcher, R. Whitlock, Mrs. Morris (guest), Mrs. R. Whitlock, D.B.O. Davies (obscured), P.J.G. Baigent, I.M. Ross, Mrs. A.J. Brent A.J. Brent, J.M. Toobey, N.W. Page, R.J. Webber, P.G. Bond, J.R.D. Cockburn, N.M. Lachau, A.Nye.

Seated Mrs. L.F. Fletcher, David Fletcher (aged 2), T. Sullivan, G. Hickey, J.R. Baldwin, R.E.D. Taylor, E.J. Sawkins, J. Lissaman, E.J. Jackson.

Page 195 Club Group 1967

Back Row P. Critchley, G.E. Geere, M.F. Fotherby, D.L. Gregory, G.O. Grier, D.G. Tingey, W.F. Lake, B.F. Pearce, A.D. Witherick, G.L. Demar, R.L. Kingsbury, N. Dudley, G.J. Jex, E.M. Pepper, M.A. Taylor, D.L. Jeffrey, G. Pinkney, R.M. Lounton, M.J. Willis, D.G. Chandler, G.B. Botley, M. Weller, D.W. Amner, J.V.F. Bennett, D.B.O. Davies P.I. Tuckett, W.P. Whiting.

Fourth Row T. Cavanagh, P.G. Stenning, D.H. Hopgood, F.G.W. Dudman, W.S.E. Hill, E.L. Collett, L. Norris, C.C. Harding, E. Doorbar, R. Hicks, G.L. Hamlyn, M.W. McFarnell, P.E. Shepheard, A.M. Davis, R.G. Barker, P.G. Horwood, C.R. Haines, B.W. Heaver, E.J. Sawkins, I.F. Smith.

Third Row F.A. Reeve (attendant), C.S. Wilson, J.A. Clear, J.E. White, P.J.G. Baigent, L.G. Toms, K.J. Johnson, A.A. Oldfield, R.A. Morley, A.J. Weeks Pearson, A.V. Hayday, E.J.J. Reed, A.E. Ball, M.A. Walker, B.G. Stone, I.C. Wilson, R. Richardson, J.R. Baldwin, G.R. Last, R.J. Edmonds, F.G. Anckorn.

Second Row A. Nye, G.H. Smith, W.S. Norton, L.G. King, C. Pollard, D.K. Saunders, W.R.J. Clarke, N.W. Page, K.N. Wilcockson, R.H. Thompson, A.J. Brent, J. Sims, J.R.D. Cockburn, L.E. Pendered, G.F. Brooks, J.W. Orr, W.H.M. Vercoe, G.D. Basan, W.J. Traer, P.J. Hudson, J.W.M. Norman.

Front Row P.J. Hart, K. Rogers, M.J. Athawes, R.C. Collins, A.G. Child K.W. Tonkin, K.W. Brown, R.I. Hawtin, S. Clowes N.J. Bailey, J.E. Law, N.A. Morley, C.P. Cook, P.R. Smith.

Page 204 Club Group – October 1988

Back Row Simon Capey, Peter Hamilton, Brian Todd, Roy Savery, Mike Lodwig, Andrew Paffett, Mike Laws, Chris Lord, Derek Larcombe, Ray Wood, Jim Phelan, Brian Hartley, Mike Martineau, Peter Rickell, Steve Freemantle, Rod Turney, Jonathan Brown

Eighth Row Mike Cronin, Peter Barlow, Martin Athawes, Bob Hilton, John Kelly, Bill Graham, Robin Graf, Tony Pontifex, Craig Daly, Simon Michell, Philip Metcalf, VP Peter Hannell (1980), John Taylor, Richard Coe, Stephen Povey, Dave Hassell, Barry O'Gorman

Seventh Row Mick Hamlin, Dale Smith, Neal Newport, Neil Thompson, Phil Davies, Nigel Keogh, Chris Huntley, Jim Hobbs, Graham Canfield, Michael Trinca, Ian Cayzer, Jim Tateson, Tony Bounds, Simon Parsons, Brian Boulton, Michael H Allen, Neil Ebbutt

Sixth Row Jim Bailey, Duncan Fagg, Paul Austridge, Eric Sullivan, Alan Mann, Roy Smith, Andrew Grace, Ian Gold, Peter Rissen, VP Dave White (1988), John Nash, Roger Counter, John Copley, Mark Russell, Brian Swift, Geoff Geere, Peter Lester, Ken Daniel, Mark Jackson

Fifth Row Tony Michell, Tony Calton, David Brookes, Tony Nana, Chris Kelly, Mark Watling, Gary White, Graham Patterson, David Wilcox, VP Jim Bennett (1981), VP Doug Tingey (1956), Gary Clark, Pat Churcher, Adrian Musson, Chris Hall, Bernard Wilson, Peter Lovell, Colin St Aubyn

Fourth Row Alan Davies, VP Dickie Green (1982), Jim Raine, Dave Johnson, Roger Michell, Ken McSweeny, Gary Plank, Andy Kilgour, Sony Nairn, Bill Baxter, Paul Davies, Mike Reynolds, Lawrence Chester, Joe Clare, VP Graham Botley (1976), Lars Hickey

Third Row Ken Pike, Brian Fincham, Ron Chambers, Bill Clapham, VP Tony Weeks-Pearson (1967), Leslie Blight, Peter Long, Jack Groves, Duncan Marsden, Mark Steinle, David Marsden, Roy Green, Phil Saxon, Danny Harvey, George Pearce, Colin Rowe, Bob Cuthbert, Bob Soutar, VP Gordon Hickey (1975), VP Barry Shapcott (1973)

Second Row John Hill, VP Geoff Crowder (1983), VP Jack Clear (1980), VP Jack Parrott (1982), VP John Powell (1985), VP Mike Mahoney (1979), VP Richard Coles (1981), VP Roger Ebbutt (1986), VP Fred Dudman (1978), VP Ian Young (1982), VP David Dunn (1987), VP Steve Cluney (1982), VP Mike Peel (1978), VP Jack Braughton (1980), VP Peter Shepheard (1979), VP Don Hopgood (1970), President Elect Ken Johnson (1988/89), VP Bill Norton (1967), VP Reg Kirk (1988), PP Ian Wilson (1981/82)

Front Row VP Len King (1962), PP Brian Stone (1979/80), PP Johnny Walker (1983/84), PP Colin Brand (1978/79), PP Alan Ball (1974/75), PP George Brooks (1970/71), PP John Baldwin (1975/76), PP Derek Gregory (1986/87), President Peter Stenning (1987/88), PP Laurie Hammill (1962/63), PP Peter Baigent (1971/72), PP Harold Thompson (1965/66), PP Tony Oldfield (1973/74), PP Ian Smith (1980/81), PP Alan Brent (1966/67), PP Will Vercoe (1956/57), PP Bill Lake (1985/86)

Page 222 Club Group 1983 – Over 60s

Back Row A.J. Brent, D.R. Gillate, P.H. Saxon, J.V.F. Bennett, G.W.F. Downs, A.A. Good, W.F. Lake

Front Row G.V. Rhodes, R.A. Kirk, J. Braughton, J.F. Parrott, M.A. Walker

257

Appendix Eight

CLUB RECORDS, WRITTEN AND PICTORIAL: A SELECTION

IN MANUSCRIPT
Early minute books and journals:
No. 1. Contains only a note dated 11 January 1924 by A.R. Pearson
(Hon. Treasurer) recording (a) report in **Bell's Life** for
27 October 1869 of first cross-country run by Peckham
Hare and Hounds on 23 October 1869; (b) extract from
The Sportsman of 15 April 1873 referring to the
formation of the Peckham Amateur Athletic Club in the
Spring of 1870; (c) extract from a letter in the
Camberwell and Peckham Times of 11 May 1872 from
F.H. Reed (Hon. Sec. Peckham A.A.C.) referring to the
formation in October 1869 of the Peckham Hare and
Hounds ''by the gentlemen who were the originators of
the present Peckham Amateur Athletic Club''.
No. 2. 20 June 1870 – 28 October 1871
No. 3. 29 October 1871 – 29 September 1876
Note: Volumes 2 and 3, unlike later ones, include
reports of athletic events as well as of
committee and general meetings.
No. 4. 30 September 1876 – 26 June 1882
No. 6. 4 May 1888 – 3 May 1893
No. 7. 4 May 1893 – 19 November 1897
No. 8. 20 November 1897 – 26 March 1904
No. 9. 26 March 1904 – 12 October 1907
Notebook:
The Peckham Notebook by D.K. Saunders
Letters:
Collection of letters from D.K. Saunders to A.J. Weeks-Pearson

IN PRINT
Scrapbooks of press cuttings, etc.
No. 1. November 1870 – January 1873 Reports mainly from
Bell's Life and **The Sportsman**
No. 2. September 1873 – June 1874
No. 3. June 1874 – April 1875
No. 4. September 1875 – Summer 1876 mainly from **Bell's Life**
and the **Sporting Gazette**
No. 5. 1884 (chiefly old programmes)
No. 6. September 1904 – March 1909
No. 7. 1908 – 1913 cuttings and whole newspapers

The Blackheath Harriers' Gazette and Club Record
Volume 1 (1898) – Volume 91 (1989)

Sydney Wooderson – Forgotten Champion (photographs and text of career)
by David Thurlow published by the British Sports Association for
the Disabled, 1989

PICTORIAL
Representative Club group photographs
1881, 1883, 1885, 1887, 1893, 1897, 1907, 1908, 1911, 1912,
1919, 1921, 1928. Subsequently photographs have been taken
at about four-yearly intervals.

Film (8mm)
A selection of events in Centenary Year.

INDEX

Abbott, H.A., 174

Achilles Athletic Club, 113, 134, 135

Ager, F.L., 123

Aitchison, H.T., 143

Albert Athletic Club, 19, 27

Alexander of Tunis, The Right Honourable Earl, 93, 152

Allanson, H.E., 152

Allanson, K.E., 152

Allen, A.G.V., 117, 124, 144

Allen, J.A., 94, 97, 98

Alverstone, Lord, 76

Amateur Athletic Association, 23, 60, 72, 76, 130, 153, first General Committee Meeting, 42

Amateur Athletic Association Championships, Americans at, 73

Amateur Athletic Club, The, 11

Amateur Athletics, origins of, 10-12, 22-3, see also Gentleman Amateur; growth of modern, 72; in the 1930's 129; future of competitive, 199

Anderson, A, 66

Andersson, Arne, 139, 158

Anerley Bicycling Club, 83

Applegarth, W.R. 51

Argyle Cricket Club, 9

Arlott, John. 46

Artists' Rifles, 97

Ashburnham Hall, 11

'Ashes', taken to Australia, 44

Askey, Arthur, 126

Athletic Clubs, origin of, 9-10

Athletic Meetings, 11

Atkinson, L.J., 161

Aylesford Paper Mills Sporting Club, 144, 160, 188

Aylett, W.A., 176-7

Badminton Library, 'Athletics and Football', 12, 37, 63

Baigent P.J.G., 172

Bailey, E. McDonald, 168

Baker, J., 183

Baldry, F., 89

Baldwin, J.R., 178, 185, 187-9

Baldwin, Stanley. 134

Ball, Phil The Fluter's, 43, 114

Ballington. Hardy, 164, 167

Bandeville, M., 69, 131

Bannister, R.G., 168

Barclay, Sir Harry, 63, 72, 108

Barclay-Esson Cup, 60, 69, 141

Barham, R.H., 33

Basan, D., 84, 97, 108

Basan, G.D., 112,

Baxter, C.H., 93

Bayswater Road, Old Lady in, 149

Beardon, V.W.W., 132, 151, 152, 155, 157, 168-70

Beer, S.G., 98

Belgrave Harriers, 113, 134

Bell, D.R., 174

Bell, R.D., 112, 117

'Bell's Life in London', 7, 23, 38, 41, 44; analysis of Peckham Hare and Hounds list in, 15-16

Bellman, H. 104,

Benetfink, 69

Bennett Cup, 155

Bennett, S.A., 4, 22, 108

Benton, F., 94

Betteridge, T.J., 161, 174

Beveridge, R., 66

Bevington, S., 9, 29

Beyfus, N., 78, 95, 127

B.H.H.Q., Ltd., 123, 128, 144, 150, 153, 165

Bignell, V.A.T., 134

Binks, J., 139

Birchfield Harriers, 41, 134-5

Birkett, G.H., 51

Birkett, W., 3, 51

Birmingham Athletic Club, 11

Beveridge, R., 66

Bisley, 194

Black, C., 7, 15

Blackheath, the place, first mention of in club records 29, Peckham A.A.C's decision to move there 29, historical and sporting associations 33, 35; moves to and from 200

Blackheath Athletic Club, 11, 35

Blackheath Concert Hall, 44, 126

Blackheath Hare and Hounds, 29, 35

Blackheath Harriers, collection of archives 15; badge 22, 52-3; name adopted 29; changes to Club by this move 29; family character of 30; importance of move to Blackheath 35; former name retained for a time 35; early members' attitude to club business 35; early growth of numbers 36; sources of membership 36; first 'Round the Heath' handicap race 37; country for running in early days 38; administrative participation in early days of amateur athletics 42 - 3; 'Blackheath Day' 44, 59; open Steeplechases 46; newly formed entertainments committee 50; establishment and growth at Blackheath 52; club uniform 53; assessment of Club's state in 1890's 58; continuing role in administration of athletics 59; water-polo prowess 65; centre of many sports 66; hedonistic aspect of Club life 66; attitude to running 67; attitude to Club's early history 67; oldest combined cross-country and athletic club 67; tradition of Opening Run 69; volunteers for Boer War 71; new dynamic 71; junior division formed 71; financial crisis 74; the presidency 75; walking race promotions 77; first 'all to score' cross-country race 88; Club 'Cry' 89 effect of First World War on 94;

war emergency fund 96; move to West Wickham
104-5; effect of different country on teams
105; membership following First World War
107; historical review in 'Gazette' 108;
stagnation following War 108; revival under
Dyball 110-13; move to Hayes 119; the new
headquarters 119-24; Diamond Jubilee 128;
strength of medium runners 129; growth of track
and field 131; cross-country in 1930's 143;
effects of Second World War upon 157;
formation of coaching body 170; Centenary
185, 199; turnover of membership 193; use
of Headquarters 193; Club tours 193; Club
spirit 196; Character of 196-7; future of
199-200
Blackheath Harriers Headquarters Ltd., 123, see also
B.H.H.Q., Ltd.
Blackheath Hill Station, 1
Blackheath Hockey Club, 99
Blackheath Lacrosse Club, 84
Blackness 106
Blackstaff, H., 64
Blanch, W.H., author of 'Ye Parish of Camberwell',
9, 27
Bliss, S.A., 152
Blunden B.J., 72
Boer War, 70-1
Bohemian Concerts, 21, 83, 107, 126, 159
Boning, E., 66
Boreham, Mr., 154
Boundary Wood, 106
Bourne Valley, 106
Boutcher, Emanuel, F.R.G.S., 20
Bow Churchyard Athletic Club Sports, 23
Brand, C.M., 174
Braughton, J., 161, 168, 176, 184
Braun, H., 73
Braund, B.P., 117, 152
Brent, A.J., 159-63, 184-5, 188, 190
British Amateur Athletic Board, 130
Brockman, H.G., 60
Bromley 194
Brooks, G.F., 144, 151, 158, 163
Broome, P.A.V., 176
Browne, F.T., 73
Bull, G.H., 84
Bunbury, 88
Bunker's Nob, 106
Burt, N.L., 82
Busby, C., 164, 165
Butler, G., 112, 135, 139
Butler, H.A., 108
Butler, L.D., 134

Camberwell, Ye Parish of, 10
Camberwell and Peckham Times, 10
Cambridge University Hare and Hounds, 46, 49, 63, 88,
89, 107, 151, 188

Camden Cup, 143, 160
Cameron, A.A., 124
Cardus, Neville, 141
Carr, F.D., 87
Castello, E.J., 117, 196
Catford Bridge, 59, 151
Cattlin, C., 37, 47, 58, 84
Caxton Hall, 126
'Centurions', 78, 165, 167
Challenge Cup, 5 Miles Club, 46; 2 Miles Club
('Morgan') 51; 69
Chappell, A.G., 168
Charlton House, 66
Chataway, C.J., 168
Chelmsford, 87
Chelsham, 146
Child, D.G., 123, 155, 160
Chingford, 188
Chislehurst Common, 29
Choat R.R., 144, 160
Churchill, Sir Winston S., 157
Civil Service Sports Club, 11
Clapton Orient Football Club, 72
Clarke, W.R.J., 38, 98, 123, 150, 154, 155, 157
Closing 5 Miles Handicap, 84, 127,
Clowser, C.E., 117, 143, 146
Clowser L.R., 146
Club Olympique d'Aubervilliers, 131
Coates, Sir E.D.C.Bart., 69
Coburn, Charles, 128
Cockburn, J.R.D., 151, 155, 158
Cockburn, J.W.B., 152
Coldstream Guards, 60
Coldwell, H., 155
Cole-Powney, J.H.M., 170
Collins, S., 7, 16
Colombes Stadium, 139
Colson, W.M., 23
Combined Clubs, The 151, 152, 168
Comrades Marathon, 184
Coney Hall, 106, 146
Conner, G.F., 134
Conway, R.R., 46
Cook, A., 59, 82, 88
Cooper, H.C., 86, 93
Coote, A.D., 168, 174
Cornell, 7, 15
Cornish, L.V., 133
Cotton, T.W., 133
Coubertin, Baron de, 76
Cowie, J.M., 51
Cox, S., 168
Crafter, J., 96
Crafter, R., 96, 154
Crafter, Tom, 2, 5, 37, 38, 43, 46, 58, 65, 66, 69,
72, 89, 95-9, 107, 112, 117, 126, 139, 141, 150,
196, 199, 200
Crafter, T. jun., 96

Cremorne, pleasure gardens, 1
Cresswell, J., 154
Cricket Clubs, influence on athletics, 11
Cross, R.F., 143-4, 152, 164
Cross, R.G., 152
Cross-country racing, development of, 38;
    objection to new courses, 42; handicap races in
    1880's 46; first team races 53
Crowe, Mrs., 154
Croydon Athletic Club, 9, 11
Crump, D.P., 152
Crump, J., 139
Crystal Palace, 1, 78, 87, 163, 194
Crystal Palace Recreation Centre, 163, 194
Cullen, N.D., 133
Culver, A.E., 38, 82, 95, 126
Cummings, W., 47
Curlew Rowing Club, 65, 84, 126
Cygnet Rowing Club, 65

Dadd, E.H., 94
Dadd, J., 94, 98
Dadd, S.G., 94
Dadd, S.T., 94
Dale, A., 71
Dale, Albert 151
Daniel, Rev., A.N., 155
Darnell, A., 7, 17, 18
Darnell, W., 16
Dartmouth, Earl of, 2
Dashwood, A.C., 165
Davies, A.H., 42, 49
Davis, A.M., 187
Davis Cup, 141
Davis, R.W., 93
Davis, T.C., 50, 84, 98 117, 143, 146
Davis, W.W., 37, 96, 126, 131
Day, J.E., 179, 183
Denman, F., 69
Denney, E.J., 94
Dennis L., 167
Denyer, H.J., 117
Devereux Hotel, 151
Dewdney, S.H., 152
Dewsnap, W.A., 69
Dicker, C.J., 35
Dodson, Mrs., 150, 157
Dog Farm, 106, 154
Doorbar, E., 193
Dorking Town Football Club, 110
Dover College, 197
Dredge, L., 120
Dryden, J., 7
Dudley, N., 167
Duffy, P., 176
Dyball, H.J., 110-112, 117, 123, 127-29, 131, 142, 200
Dyson, G.F., 168

Eames, H.M., 71
Easterling, see Walter Rye
Easthie (Eastty),J.H., 9, 16
Ecroyd, Henry, 36
Edmonds R.J., 193
Edward the Seventh, King, 89
Edwards, A.C., 96, 117
Elgar, Edward, 89
Ellis, L.W., 132
English Cross-country Championship, 39; growing
popularity of 50
English Cross-country Union, 42, 108, 153
Entertainments Committee, 107
Evelyn, John, 33
Everard, A.A., 178, 188
Everard, N.F., 164
Fancy Dress Carnival, 107
Farmers' Night, 154
Farmers' Walk, 154
Farrell, S.A.C., 69
Farrington, J., 189
Farthing Down, 144
Featherbed Lane, 146
Felsted School, 117
Fentiman, A.G., 69
Field, S.A., 143
Finlay, D.O., 133
Flanders, 93, 97
Fletcher, L.F., 178, 185, 244
Fletcher, R.D., 161
Flying Squadron Race, 73
(Foot) Artillery, 1st Surrey, 12
Football Association, 11
Ford, first car of, 59
Foster, B.J., 165
Four Clubs Match, 168
Fournel, D.J., 176
Fowler-Dixon, J.E., 21, 42, 108, 166
Fox Hill 106, 196
Francis, P.H., 46, 117, 160
Frankeiss Cup, 64
Furniss, J.E., 129, 139, 169

Gale, D.G., 178
Gale, T., 38, 95, 99, 126
Galley, R.A.E., 143. 146
Gallipoli, 93
Gazette and Club Record, The Blackheath Harriers,
    38, 44, 53, 58, 59, 64, 68-70, 71, 72, 73, 78,
    83, 84, 93, 94, 97, 104, 105, 107, 108, 110, 119,
    121, 128, 129, 131, 134, 135, 139, 141, 142,
    146, 149, 151, 152, 153, 155, 157, 163, 167,
    170, 172, 179, 196, 200
Gaul, L.J.L., 94
Gay Nineties Dance, 193
Gedge, A.H., 176

Gentleman Amateur, concept of, 19; 22; unsatis-
 factoriness and injustice of, 23
George, W.G., 2, 47-49, 51, 58, 63
German Gymnastic Society, 9
Gifford, H.W., 93
Gilbert, F.L., 108, 117, 123
Gittings, S.D., 155
Glaeser, C.A., 86
Glaisher, E.C., 134
Glanville, F.R.A., 96, 98
Glass, F.G., 93
Godbold, A.B., 69
Golder, S., 47
Gordon-Smith, R.A., 164
Gosling, G.F., 144, 164, 166, 184
Grace, W.G., 70, 94
Grant, H.K., 38, 96
Grant, T.K., 66, 95, 104, 119
Graves, Robert, 98
Gray, G.D., 94
Green Man, Blackheath, The, 2, 29, 30, 33, 35, 37,
 42, 44, 50, 65, 66, 82, 83, 88, 89, 95, 97, 104,
 119, 124, 150, 196, 200
Green Man, Muswell Hill, The, 82
Green Man, Southend Village, 14
Greer, E.B., 93
Gregory, D.L., 190
Grier, G.O.J., 165
Griffin, H. Hewitt, 11: quoted 33
Gulley, The, 106

Haegg, Gundar, 139
Hahn, D.J., 176
Hamlyn, G.L., 183
Hammill, L.E., 144, 151, 155, 165, 194
Hammond, T.E., 77, 78, 82, 98, 108, 146, 157,
 167, 194
Hampstead Heath, 66
Hampton Court Hare and Hounds, 37
Hanover Arms, Peckham, 12
Hanover Park Rifles, 12
Harding, B.C., 178
Hare and Hounds, the sport of, 9
Hargreaves, H.S.R., 155
Harker, D.J., 178
Harlequins Rugby Football Club, 133
Harper, E., 117
Harriers' Gallop, The, 44
Harris, G.M., 50
Harrison, M.C.C., 94
Harvey, E.R., 66
Haslegrave, H.W.G., 15, 61, 69, 76-77, 78, 88
Hassett, Dickie, 126
Hawes Down School, 163
Hawke, W.H., 9, 16
Hawtin, R.I., 190
Hayday, A.V., 161
Hayes, 104, 119, 146

Hayes Common, 201
Hayward, W., 167, 184
Healey, A.H., 72
Heaver, B.W., 187, 189
Henley, 64
Henman, W., 9, 16
Herne Hill Harriers, 134
Herring, J.B., 112, 176, 179-80, 184, 185
Hickey, G., 178, 179
Hickman, C.T.W., 42,
High Gate, 106
Highgate Harriers, 42
Hill, Albert G., 112, 139
History, writing the Centenary, 200
Hitchings, E.H.C. 69
Hogg, D.F.E., 188, 193
Holland, M.W., 71
Holmes, C.B., 132
Holmes, W., 144
Holt, F.D., 82
Honor Oak, 26, 27
Honourable Artillery Company, The, 97
Hope Rowing Club, 7
Hopgood, D.H., 185
Hopkins, G.L., 84
Hopkins, O.J., 84
Hopper, H.R., 68, 84, 94, 99, 117
Horn, K.M., 169
Hornidge, S.N., 21
Horwood, D.F.G., 133
Horwood, E.H., 51
Hotel Cecil, F.H. Reed architect of, 30
House of Commons, 194
Hudson, P.J., 183
Hunter, C. Val, 23, 42, 83, 92

Ibis Club, 50
Ilex Club, 43
Imperial Arms, Chislehurst, The, 29, 82
Indian Army, 98
Innes, G., 60
International Amateur Athletic Federation, 130
International Cross-country Championship, 69,
 76
Inter-Schools Race, 154
'Irrepressibles', The, See South London Harriers

Jackson, P.R.R., 178
Jackson, Paul, 185
Jarrett, C., 93
Jenkins, M.W., 144, 152
Jenkins, W.D., 176
Jex, G.J., 187
Jobson, K.L., 172
Johnson, A., 7, 15
Johnson Bowl, 78, 82, 167

Johnson, H.G., 82
Johnson, P.W., 185
Jones, Cyril, 151
Jones, L.L., 176
Jubilee, Queen Victoria's Diamond, 68
Judson, E.F., 87, 88, 98, 117

Keer, L'Argent O., 63
Kennington Oval, 21
Kent, Filth and scum of, 33
Kent County Athletic Association, 71, 96
Kent Krawlers, 96
Keston, 89, 106
King, H.E., 66, 95, 144
King's Arms, Peckham Rye, 7, 24, 26
King's Royal Rifles, The, 94
Kinnaird, Lord, 134
Kinnaird Trophy, 134, 179
Kipling, J.H., 71
Kleeblatt, H., 69

Ladies' Nights, 193
Lalande Trophy, 184
Lambeth Baths, 65
Lancefield W.D., 73
Larette, C.H., 24
Last, G.R., 190
Law, A.J., 35
Layhams Farm, 106, 139, 154
Layhams Hill, 106
Lea Harriers, 89
Leafy Grove, 106
Legge, P.H.B., 154
Leidig, G. Capt 128
Leighton, Frederick, R.A., 20
Lennard, family, the, 119
Lennard, Sir Henry, 124
Lennox Rugby Football Club, 50
Levitt, Farmer, 154
Lewisham Churchyard, F.H. Reed collapsing
    with stitch in, 30
Lewisham Hare and Hounds, 65
Lewisham Swimming Club, 65, 84, 93, 96
Lewisham, Viscount, 44
Lindsay, R.A., 73, 108, 112
Lindsay Salver, 112
Lintott, J.H., 88
List, -, 124
Lissaman, J., 179
Liverpool Athletic Club, 11
Liverpool Harriers, 41
Livett, D.R., 176
Lloyd Edgar, 166
Locomotive Highways Act 1893, 59
Lodge Lane, 146
Lombard Restaurant, The, 36
London Athletic Club, 10, 21, 43, 134, 135, 151
London Athletic League, 73

London Chatham and Dover Railway, 1
London County Council constituted, 27
London Hospital, The, 60
London Scottish, 71, 124, 143, 194
London to Brighton Walk, 78
Lorimer, G., 71
Louis, Joe, 139
Lovelock, J., 137
Low, J.H., 146
Lymbery, B.E., 152
Lymbery, B.H., 86, 117
Lymbery, E.G., 151
Lymbery, J.G., 152
Lyon, P.G.R., 176

Mabinogion, The, 93
Macmillan, Rt. Hon. Harold, 194
Mais, S.P.B., 89
Major, J.R., 112
Malden Harriers, 84
Malone, F.J., 169
Manchester Harriers, 41
Marlborough College, code of paperchasing, 13
Married v. Single Race, 69, 126
Marshall, S.J., 93
Maryon-Wilson Cup, 66
Maryon-Wilson, Sir Spencer, 66
Maryon-Wilson, Sir Thomas, 35, 66
Masurier, J. Le, 174
Matthews, St. John Cup, 64
Matthews, St. John, R., 64, 69
Mayson, D.T., 37; part in forming S.C.C.A. &
    E.C.C.U., 42; importance to the Club,
    42, 58
McArthur, C., 65
McIvor, G.F., 131, 141, 152
McLachlan, C., 72
McLean, J., 72
McPhail, J.C., 159
Mekler, J., 184
Merryweather Fire Brigade, 84
Metcalf, Adrian, 22, 76, 99
Metcalf, John, Sen. 14, 21, 22, 76, 157
Metcalf, John, Jun., 22
Metropolitan Board of Works, 33
Metropolitan Commons Act., 33
Midden, 106
Middlesex Rifles, The 2nd, 60
Milligan, J.C., 37, 42, 47, 58, 84
Milocarian Athletic Club, 134
Mobbs, C.L., 131, 142, 144
Moir, W. Ramsey, 112, 124, 128
Monk, F.W., 3, 42, 84
Monshall, G.E., 161, 169, 190
Monte Carlo, The Man who broke the Bank
    at, 128
Morden College, 3, 38, 84
Morley, R.A, 176-77, 184, 187, 188

'Morning Post', The, 48, 139
Morrison, J.M., 144
Morton, A.D., 93
Morton, G.A.C., 134
Moseley Harriers, 41, 49, 51
Motspur Park, 48, 137, 166
Mullins, E.W., 146
Munro, H.A., 63, 84
Music Hall, Victorian, 44

Nash Farm, 106, 201
Nash, J.B., 3, 50
National Cross-country Championship, 188
National Provincial Bank Rowing Club, The, 65
Nehan, G.M., 3, 41, 47, 58, 84
Neville, E.H., 78, 99, 108, 158, 164, 166, 167
New Addington, 106
Newby-Smith, Dr. R., 84
Newgate Prison, record of imprisonment qualifi-
    cation for competition, 23
New Inn, Hayes, 142
New Members' Night, 159, 196
News Chronicle, 139
News of The World, 139
Nicholls Cup, 19, 63, 69, 113, 114, 119, 142,
    144, 188, 189, 190, 197
Nicholls, E.F., 60, 63, 88, 93, 97, 201
Nicholson, I.W., 96
Norman, E.V., 87
Norris, L., 38
Northampton Cricket and Athletic Club, 11
Northern Cross-country Association, 59
Northern Division, the Club's 63, 71, 82
North of the Thames Cross-country Union, 42
Norwood Rugby Football Club, 76
Norwood, South, Cricket Club, 11, 22
Novices Pewter, 66, 196
Nunhead, 19
Nunhead Cemetery, 25
Nunns, H.N., 160, 167
Nye, A., 172

Oastler, Jonah C., 20, 24, 44
Oldfield, A.A., 196
Oliver, Alfred, 22
Oliver, Charlotte ('Toppy'), 22
Oliver, Ernest, 21, 22
One Tree Hill, 25, 27
O'Reilly, T.M., 174
Origin of Species, The, 10
Orion Harriers, The, 88, 113, 143, 149, 151,
    159, 164, 190, 197
Otway Cup, 160
Ovid, 129
Oxford University Athletic Club, 46, 88, 139,
    188
Oxland, J.C., 133

Pack system of training, 39, 50, 169-70, 193
Page, E.L., 112, 132, 135, 141, 168
Page, N.W., 131, 172, 174, 178, 179
Palmerston Restaurant, 126
Paperchasing, (see also Hare and Hounds),
    origins and rules of, 13; development into
    cross-country racing, 38
Paragon, The 3
Parker, F.W., 126
Parkes, L.G., 132, 134
Park House Rugby Football Club, 84, 126
Parrish Cup, 163
Parrish, W.W.J., 124, 163
Pascall, C.T., 144
Pash H.F. 60, 72, 108 157
Pattison, R.V.L., 152
Pattison, R.W., 96, 117
Peace, Charles, criminal, 33
Peachey, C.A., 117
Pearce, B.F., 164, 185
Pearson, A.R., 98, 99, 123-4, 196
Peckham, 2; topography, 25; urban growth,
    26-27; 59, 183, 200, 201
Peckham Amateur Athletic Club, (see Peckham
    Hare and Hounds also) 7 - 9, 14
    reasons for survival 17; early morning
    competitions 17-18; athletic promotions 18;
    growth and extension of 20; written records
    abandoned in favour of press reports 20;
    increased number of open meetings and
    steeplechases promoted by 20, 23-24;
    increased membership 22; club's con-
    ception of amateurism 23; Peckham
    Club spirit 24; choice of country
    limited by presence of other clubs 27;
    summer runs 29; assessment of its
    achievement up to 1878 29-30, 36, 76
Peckham Hare and Hounds 7; formation of 7;
    change of name 9
Peckham Social Club, 11
Pelling, E.H., 88
Pelling-Ratcliff Cup, 88, 126, 190
Pembury, 69
Pendered, L., 50, 196
Peniston, S.A., 22
Pepper, E.M., 187
Peters, J., 168
Pewter, Novice's, 66, 196
Philo, R.J., 146
Pied Bull Inn, Streatham, 29
Pile's, athletic outfitters, 3
Pinckard, D.A., 176
Pinhey, W.C., 121
Piper, L.E., 164-66
Pirie, D.A.G., 168, 169
Points Handicap Competition, 107
Polytechnic Harriers, 113, 134
Ponsford, J.F., 50, 107

Poole, A.C.J., 134, 177
Pooley, D.G., 174
Preedy, A., 86
Pridmore, Felix T., 18, 21
Prior, N.H., 38
Prisoners of War Fund, Blackheath, 152
Private Banks Cricket and Athletic Club, link,
    with, 22, 59, 63, 87, 105, 134
Professional, the modern sporting, Victorian
    advent of, 44
Pugh, S.T., 66, 71
'Punch' 151
Punchbowl Night, 69, 83, 99, 107, 197
Purchase ('Henery The Eighth') W.A.W.B., 86,126
Purton, B.C., 146
Purves, C.D., 174
Pylon Field, 106

Queensberry Rules, 11
Queen's Westminster and Civil Service Rifles, 124
Quigley, C.S.M., 133

'Rags' Trophy, 164
Railway Hotel, West Wickham, 106, 107, 124,
    126, 153
Rampley Cup, 60
Rampley, Josiah, 60, 114
Ranelagh Harriers, 64, 73, 77, 88, 97, 113,
    149, 151, 159, 164, 190
Ransom, V.S., 133
Rapley, E.R., 89
Ratcliff E.J.D., 60, 84, 89, 97, 98, 107,
Ratcliff, L.C., 117
Ravensbourne, 27, 135
'Reading Gazette' Trophy, 134
Reay Cup, 141
Reay, G.M., 83
Reay, J.H.A., 2, 43-4, 71, 99, 114
Reed, E.J.J., 124, 172, 187
Reed Frederick Henty, 2, 3, 4, 9, 15-18, 21,
    24, 25, 29, 30
    his importance in holding Peckham A.A.C.
    together 30; his character and offices
    held, 30; handling of business meetings 36,
    42, 107; becomes President 44, 46, 52,
    53, 58, 67, 74-75, 89, 92, 200
Reed Hayter, 16
Reed, Thornton Hayter, 16
Reiff, Gaston, 140
Repton School, 164
Rex Cinema, Hayes, The, 146
'Rex Cross' Salver, 185
Reynolds, D.E., 133, 160, 162, 164-66, 196,
    197
Rhodes, G.V., 82, 167
Rhodes, H., 82
Rhodes, H.B.S., 82, 142
Richardson, R., 187, 189, 190

Richardson, R.G., 155
Richmond Cricket Club 11
Richmond, G.J., 144
Riverboat Dances, 193
Roache, H.L., 134
Road Runners Club, 144, 164, 167
Road Walking Association, 167
Roath Harriers, 84
Roberts, A.A., 152
Roberts, The Rev. H.B., 99
Robin Hood, Penge, The, 29
Rosemary Branch, The, 17, 20, 24, 26, 183
Ross, I.M., 176, 179
Rouse Farm, 106, 154
Rowing, 64-65
Rowland Cup, 47, 60, 69, 117, 137, 143,
    144, 190
Rowland, W., 3, 4, 21, 24, 25, 29, 37, 67,
    77, 83, 88, 92, 99, 108, 201
Royal Engineers, The, 144
Royal Hotel, Eltham, 29
Royal Military Academy, Woolwich, 11
Royal Military College, Sandhurst, 11, 134
Rugby School, code of paperchasing, 13
Rugby Union, 11
Rushforth, W.J., 89
Rye House, (Hotel)), Peckham, The, 14, 24,
    26, 37
Rye, Walter, 15, 16; 'Easterling' pseudonym 16;
    rebukes Peckham A.A.C. 23; praises
    Peckham A.A.C. faintly 29; 37, 44, 58, 63,
    66, 128

Saddlers' Company, The, 30
Sage, E.E.Le, 174
Salford Harriers, 41
Sampson, E.J., 178, 179
Sampson, J., 179
Sando, F.D., 188
Sassoon, Siegfried, 93
Saunders, D.K., Foreword 128
Saunders, 'Darky', 154
Saunders, Mrs. 'Darky', 154
Sawkins, E.J., 174
Schofield, C.V.A., 78, 98, 167
Scholes, F., 152
Scott , 66
Scott, J.M., 94, 113
Scotting, G.L., 161, 184
Scott-Wilson, J.H., 155, 161
Seaforth Highlanders, The 93
Seedhouse, C.N., 73, 98
Sercombe, H.W.E., 63, 126, 141
Sewell, J.H., 152
Shanghai Harriers, 84
Shapcott, B.M., 178
Shearman, Sir Montague, 12, 48
Shurmer, B.E., 183

Silhouette H. Dauban de, 112
Sims, J., 119, 170, 193
Slykhuis, W., 140
Small, E.R., 86-87, 93
Smith, A.S., 174
Smith, C. Aubrey, 84
Smith, Ernest, 18-19
Smith, H.S., 131-32, 152
Smith, I.R., 176
Smith, P.B., 168
Smith, W.S., 38, 66, 124
Smoking Concerts, 69, 83, 124
Southern Counties Cross-country Association,
   creation of 42, 59, 108
Southern Cross-country Championship, first
   held, 42; debate as to Club's withdrawal
   from 63
Southern Track and Field League, 132, 134
South London Athletic and Bicycling Club,
   37, 65, 126
South London Harriers, 9, 14; origin of 18;
   proximity to Peckham A.A.C. 19; the
   link with Peckham A.A.C. and Blackheath
   Harriers 20; headquarters 27; press
   description of 36; amalgamated run
   with Blackheath, 37, 41, 42, 63
   Nicholls Cup competition, 63-64, 69
   82, 88, 107, 113, 130, 142, 143, 144, 149
   151, 159, 164, 188, 190
South of the Thames Cross-country
   Association, 188
Southwark Park, 7, 17
Southwell, H.E.J., 87
Spartan Harriers, 37, 41, 42
Spence, J.B., 174
Spencer, W.F., 161
Sporting Gazette, The, 16, 199
Sporting Life, The, 87, 88, 92
Sportsman, The, 66
Stade Francais, 63
Stadium, The, 78
Stafford, E.W., 66
Stallard, H.B., 112
Stamford Bridge, 59-60
Stampfl, F., 174
St. James's Athletic Club, 84
Starnes, C.W., 59, 66, 69, 159, 167, 194
Steeplechasing, origin of, 14-15
Steer, A.I., 119-21
Still, W.H., 154
Stocks Tree, The, (West Wickham), 63, 119
Stone, B.G., 176, 190
Streatham Common, 29
Sturgeon, G.N., 71
Suffield, W.G., 88
Sullivan, Sir Arthur, 60
Sullivan, T.T., 172, 176
Sunday Express, 139

Surrey Athletic Club, 113, 134
Surrey Walking Club, 76, 77, 82, 96, 167
Sutton Valence School, 135, 151
'Swan', The, West Wickham, 63, 89, 96, 97,
   99, 106, 119
Sydenham Cricket Club, 76

Taylor, A.J.P., 93
Taylor, R.E., 172, 183
Taylor, S.D., 38, 94, 112, 117, 151, 152-53
   155, 157
Telfer, Rev. A.C., 35, 44, 86, 97, 117, 126
Telfer, Rev. W., 97, 98, 155
Territorial Army, the Club's connection with, 12
Thames Hare and Hounds, 10, 15, 21, 35,
   41, 88, 128
Thames Rowing Club, 9, 15, 65,
Thomas, A.W. Clay, 108, 117, 126, 167
Thomas, G.C., 183
Thomas, H.D., 21, 23, 37, 41, 49, 51, 58, 89
Thompson, R.H., 70, 141, 151
Thurlow Park Harriers, 37
Thwaites, A.D., 59, 96, 142, 146, 149, 150,
   152-54, 155, 157, 159
Times, The, 139
Tingey, D.J., 155, 158, 163
Toal, J.F., 174
Tom Brown's Schooldays, 13
Toms, L.G., 144
Torr, K.M., 133
Towers, L.G., 155
Town Dances, 107
Traer, W.J., 167, 194
Trafalgar Cricket Club, 7
Trail-layer, office of, 38; Club's debt to, 38; 151
Travers-Stubbs Trophy, 134
Trocadero Restaurant, 71
Trodd, H.G., 134
Trumble, D.H., 152
'Two Chairmen, The', 194
Tye, G.W., 152

Ulysses Athletic Club, 29
Union St. Gilloise, 190
United Hospitals Hare and Hounds, 89

Van Putten, H., 35
Vauxhall, pleasure gardens, 1
Vercoe, W.H.M., 152
Vesta Rowing Club, 65
Veterans Athletic Club, 164, 190
Veterans Races, against South London Harriers
   86; increase in 164
Vice-Presidents' Supper 194
Volunteers, City Imperial, 71
Volunteer Movement, 12

Waddilove Trophy, 134, 174, 176
Wade, E., 87
Wade, H., 63
Wadhams, A.E., 183
Waldorf Hotel, 128, 141
Walford, E., author of 'Old and New London',
    27, 33, 36
Walker, R.A., 146
Walker, R.E., 143, 152
Walter, L.T., 132
Walter Steeplechase Cup, 60, 69, 131, 174
Wardle, J.P., 72
Warland, T.H., 65
Warren's Directory of Croydon, 16
Waters, Elsie and Doris, 126
Watts, J., 183
Wayne, Naunton, 126
Webb, A.W.O., 174
Webber, R.J., 185
Weeks-Pearson, A.J., Foreword
Weissmuller, 'Johnny; 139
Weller, M., 185, 190
Well Wood, 106
West, C.E., ('Shrimp'), 88, 201
West London Rowing Club, 11
Westoby, G.B. 112
West Wickham, 29, 63, 89, 99, 104-105, 107, 153, 200
Whall, J.E.C., 179
White, J.E., 172, 183
White, M.P.S., 72
Whitlock, H.H., 142
Whittingham, F.S., 132, 134
Wiard, C.A., 132, 134, 168, 172
Wickham Court, 119
Wickham Court Farm, 154

Wickham, S.J., 127
Wilcockson, K.N., 38, 151, 154
Wilkinson, G.F.N., 94
Wilkinson, G.H., 143, 152, 157, 160
Wilkinson, H.A., 70, 157
Williams, J.H., 69, 84, 88
Williams, Percy, 132
Williamson, A.J.N., 93
Williamson, W.H., 7, 15-18 , 22
Wilson, I.C., 187 190
Windmill Inn, Chislehurst, 29
Windmill Theatre, 150
Wine Committee, 150
Wint, A., 168, 176
Winter, W.S.A., 126, 128
Winterflood, J.S., 154
Withers, J.E., 184
Wood, A.W., 188
Wood, C.G., 47, 51, 72
Wooderson, A.T., 135, 137, 151
Wooderson, S.C., 48, 112, 117, 129, 134, 135-
    141, 143, 144, 146, 151, 152, 158 161, 164,
    168, 179, 184
Wooderson, S.J., 137, 144
Woods, C.J.R., 132
World War, First, 93-99, 152
World War, Second, 149-56, 184
Worms, Baron de, 44
Wrenn, J.H., 12
Wright, D.N., 183
Wright, J.H.P., 183

Zatopek, Emil, 140, 168, 169